Writing Left
The radical journalism of Ruth First
© Mayibuye

hidden histories series

Now available

The making of an African Communist: Edwin Mofutsanyana and the Communist Party of South Africa 1927–1939
Robert Edgar

Forthcoming books

50 Years of the Freedom Charter
Jeremy Cronin and Raymond Suttner

Marabi Nights (with new introduction and CD)
Christopher Ballantine

The secret thread: Personal journeys beyond apartheid
Deborah Ewing

'Beyond our wildest dreams': The United Democratic Front and the transformation of South Africa (South African edition with new introduction)
Ineke van Kessel

ANC: A view from Moscow (second edition)
Vladimir Shubin

Rebellion and uproar: Makhanda and the great escape from Robben Island
Julia C. Wells

Dispatches from the battlefield: A history of South Africa's legendary anti-apartheid newspaper, *The Guardian*, 1937–1963
James Zug

Writing Left

The radical journalism of Ruth First

Donald Pinnock

hidden histories series

Series editor: Raymond Suttner

University of South Africa
Pretoria

First edition, first impression

ISBN 978186888365-3

Published by Unisa Press
PO Box 392, Muckleneuk Pretoria
South Africa

Cover, layout and typesetting: Dawid Kahts

Printed by Jakaranda Printers

Contents

Credits

Extracts from this work were published as *They Fought for Freedom: Ruth First* (Maskew Miller Longman 1995) and a brief introduction by the author was published in *Voices of Liberation: Ruth First* (HSRC Publications, 1997).

I am grateful to the Mayibuye Centre, University of the Western Cape, for many of the photographs in this book.

Series foreword

This series has been conceived as an outlet for research that might otherwise not have been published. Very important studies may have been rejected for reasons that do not affect the considerations that guide our programme.

While the 'Hidden Histories' series aims at producing marketable books that reach a wide audience, the existing market does not govern it. Our primary concern is to add to the knowledge available to scholars and the reading public, and to expand this public and its interests. Consequently, we seek out works that break new ground or cover old ground in new ways.

The South African reading and book-purchasing public is small and most books that are sold in bookstores here were published overseas. This is not because of a lack of material that ought to be available as books, published and marketed in bookstores, but also through other outlets that can be revived or created in order to reach people who do not patronise the plush malls.

While the words 'hidden histories' may have a slightly clichéd ring, they seem best able to convey what we are looking for: writing that we think is worthy of publication but has not yet found an outlet. There has been a shift in writing and scholarship away from certain themes that used to preoccupy scholars in the early years of the twentieth century, in particular monographs on rural areas. We want to encourage writing about places and people who live outside the main city centres. Also, there is now an opportunity to write about people, issues and events, that was not possible in the past.

One of the reasons is the emergence of a democratic South Africa out of a protracted liberation struggle, many of whose participants and activities are little known because they worked secretly. Sometimes these 'unknown' figures performed heroic acts. Sometimes individuals who are publicly known as traitors, who 'worked for the system', were assisting the liberation struggle. There is complexity, then, that has not yet been adequately captured in current literatures. We would like to provide a forum for such works.

There is a sense of urgency in capturing this oral and invisible history because many whose stories have not been told and need to be told, are old. Many are no longer with us, gone with their story unheard, or at best sketchily remembered by others.

At the same time, our view of 'history' is neither narrow nor sectarian. We do not conceive of it as referring exclusively to the past, but also to the present, regarded as part of history.

We encourage publication of works that deal with contemporary problems or with past issues representing causes of great public concern.

This is intended to be an 'engaged' series in the sense that it is intended to raise and investigate problematic, controversial and difficult questions that arise in the context of the ongoing processes of South African history. Such questions may include issues of morality, problems relating to gender relations, questions of identity and the imprint of distinct experiences and belief systems within specific organisations prior to joining.

The form in which such works may be presented seeks to capture the variety of modes that artists, novelists, poets, historians and other scholars have chosen to convey what they consider to be important.

The publication of Don Pinnock's study of Ruth First's political journalism, *Writing Left: the radical journalism of Ruth First*, is an important addition to the series. While doing research amongst veterans of the struggle I have constantly heard that too little is known about Ruth First and her contribution. Described as an intellectual giant, she was able to stand her ground in a male-dominated liberation movement. First was a very independent thinker, differing from both the ANC and SACP over policy towards the Zimbabwean liberation movements, when the ANC backed ZAPU alone, and the Soviet Union.

Beautiful, elegant and fond of fine clothes, First breaks stale stereotypes of what a revolutionary is supposed to look like. None of this taste for the good things of life detracted from her iron will and determination. It was because of this that her life was tragically ended by an apartheid assassin in 1982.

Ruth First was the journalist who exposed the treatment of workers on the potato farms in Bethal, revealing conditions so horrific that they led to a national boycott amongst black people. This was a young white woman, in her twenties, going into dangerous conditions in order to investigate what was happening on these farms. Unfortunately, we do not find enough of that type of journalism anymore. Aspirant journalists need to study this work to see a model of how someone lived out the best traditions of her profession.

Apart from her political journalism, First published on a wide range of issues, including one of the first systematic works on the military coup d'etat in Africa, *The Barrel of the Gun*, co-authoring a work on Oliver Schreiner and many other books and articles. It is hoped that publishing of Pinnock's meticulous study will be a prelude to a proliferation of works on First as well as republication of her various studies.

Raymond Suttner

Acknowledgements

Many people have assisted me in this study, not the least being those who, with good grace, agreed to being interviewed. However, I need to make special mention of a number of people without whom I would not have completed this work:

- Miriam Hepner who, in an act of bravery for which I am ever grateful, opened up for me the world of the Communist Party in Johannesburg at the height of a State of Emergency.

- Joe Slovo, who consented with good grace and humour to being pursued around the world for interviews, Gillian Slovo who commented at length on my early drafts, Robyn Slovo who, more than anyone else, communicated the feeling of the period, Tilly First who terrified, charmed and helped me, and Ronnie First who shared his time to get things right.

- Dr John Daniels, my supervisor, whose manner made criticism feel like a challenge, bad writing like a mere oversight and whose eye for wrong politics and poor syntax made the final manuscript far better than it began.

- The librarians of the Church of Province of South Africa (CPSA) library at Witwatersrand University, the Institute for Commonwealth Studies (ICS) library at London University, the archives at University of Cape Town and Cory library at Rhodes University. All research librarians are the angels of historical research, but special mention needs to be made of Leonie Twentyman-Jones, Anna Cunningham and, especially, Sandy Rowold, all people without whom historical research would probably never happen.

- My wife, Patricia, who taught me about women, words and keeping sane when all seemed to be lost. And my children Gaelen and Romaney-Rose who had to share me with an obsession.

- Prof. Shula Marks, who gave me an academic home at the ICS for six months, access to the Ruth First Trust Collection, and showed me in her own work and in ICS seminars a standard of historical research which, if I could not emulate, I could certainly appreciate.

- Prof. Gavin Williams whose warmth gave me confidence when I was daunted by the size of the task at hand, and whose contacts at Oxford opened doors for me in Britain.

- Dr André Odendaal, whose enthusiasm and supply of useful letters and documents was invaluable.

- Dr Baruch Hirson, who taught me to take nothing on trust and disbelieve all political icons.

- Prof. Colin Bundy, who helped when he could, wrote letters of introduction and demolished my chapters on the Communist Party and assisted in their reconstruction.

- I must also mention the help received by Rhodes University in the form of research grants, the Journalism Department for putting up with my tunnel vision of the 1950s and, particularly, Prof. Gavin Stewart, who understood, allowed me time off, and ignored any lapses of departmental duty while I was writing.

All helped, none can be held responsible for the result.

Introduction

In the 1950s the commercial press in South Africa largely ignored the writings of radical journalists and their newspapers. Their worlds were so different that it is, today, hard to believe they were writing about the same country. In the eyes of mainstream journalists, the political press was marginal, biased and plain wrong, carrying out its propaganda in the fringes of society for a small fanatical audience of communists or 'fellow-travellers'. And by the 1960s history seemed to have proved them right. The radical press had been smashed and the big newspaper monopolies were going from strength to strength.

The eclipse of the radical press was intimately linked to the virtual defeat, by 1963, of the Congress Alliance, that broad front which had united to challenge apartheid. Both the Alliance and its press had been hit by Prime Minister Hendrik Verwoerd's 'granite wall' of determination to preserve racism in the face of a continent rapidly shaking off the yoke of colonialism.

This defeat was to have dramatic personal consequences for the political left. As a result of literally hundreds of 'communist' trials, Congress leaders and members were to be imprisoned and a number were executed. Thousands fled the country. And in a prison cell in Johannesburg one of South Africa's finest investigative journalists, after months of solitary confinement, attempted suicide.

In a sense, information for this book has been gathered around the question of why that journalist, Ruth First – widely published, highly respected, sparklingly intelligent and beautiful – felt her life had reached a point where she wished it extinguished. The answer is not an easy one. It involves who she was, what she believed in and her perception at that moment of the magnitude of the defeat of all she had worked for. But this question has broader implications – it has been asked because its answer throws light not only on the particular journalist, but on the radical press of the period in which she was involved and on the political movements which gave it both life and readers. To answer the question it is necessary to look at the development of a radical ideology in opposition to apartheid, and its manifestation in a newspaper tradition and in a single individual. It is also important to understand the effect of this ideology in the political arena: its triumphs and its defeats.

The relationship between a political tradition, its press and a single individual is a complex and perhaps novel focus for enquiry. Each area struggles for a full study on its own. But separately each would lose something of the movement of the period, something of the relationship between history and the sensitivities of one of its protagonists. In its telling, this book attempts to look at the relationship between Ruth First and the maturing liberation movement, and to understand the complex way in which this relationship was mediated through her journalism and her political involvement. In the end, though, this is about a journalist and her work, and about some of the more important influences that made both what they were.

There is little doubt that First set new standards of excellence in political and investigative journalism. But hers was the product of a tradition – often marginalised in South Africa – which began when John Tengo Jabavu broke from the missionaries to produce *Imvo Zabantsunduin* the late 19th century. This tradition of independent, critical writing was to run through the work of journalists like Sol Plaatjie, Walter Rubusana, James la Guma, Pixley Seme, Jordan Ngubane, Eddy Roux, the *Drum* journalists, Govan Mbeki and Brian Bunting.[1] All worked in what was essentially a colonial context without a democratic press tradition and in which political leaders did not brook challenge, where secrecy was seen as the necessary auxiliary to government and where journalists unsupportive of apartheid or at least neutral were viewed as agents of treason. All used their pens to expose the growing cruelty of apartheid and class oppression.

But among these First has a special place. She was white and could have taken her place among the comfortable colonial elite, but did not. She was also well educated and based in Johannesburg at a particularly volatile period of South Africa's history. She had access to media outlets and, being white, was less easily ignored by either a complacent white population or an increasingly authoritarian white regime. All these factors were to make her effective, controversial and the focus of official disapproval.

This book is the product of a process of information gathering which began in South Africa in 1986 at a time when discussing communism exposed one to the possibility of imprisonment without trial. Looking back, it is clear that in turning to the 1950s I was trying to find the historical precedents of the radical newspapers I had become involved with during the 1980s. Were we a new phenomenon, or had this all happened before, and if so, to what effect?

It also began shortly after Ruth's assassination in Maputo in 1982 and at a time when every written and nearly every human resource necessary for its continuation was under a state ban. But against the wishes of the authorities and with the valuable co-operation of the research librarians in Cory Library at Rhodes University, I started building up documentation on the radical traditions of the 1950s and interviewing people in South Africa, Zimbabwe, Zambia, Mozambique, Britain, Holland and the Soviet Union.

The unbanning of political organisations in 1990 and the return of exiles eased the difficulties of data collection. With the exiles came documentary sources: the large IDAF collection of film and documents returned home to the University of the Western Cape and into the Mayibuye Centre under Dr Andre Odendaal, who was also working on the papers of Lionel Forman. His labours, together with Lionel's wife Sadie, produced the book *A Trumpet from the Housetops* just when I needed it. These added to other collections – the invaluable documents in the Church of the Province library at Witwatersrand University, the *New Age* files which I discovered, unrecognized, in the archives of the University of Cape Town, and the Christopher Gell papers which I unearthed from a garage near Paris. Soon, hopefully, these will be supplemented by the Ruth First Trust collection (presently in the Institute for Commonwealth Studies in London) and the Communist Party papers from the Comintern archives in Moscow. The jury is still out on how much valuable history in the voluminous records of the South African Special Branch in Pretoria and elsewhere was shredded.

Unlike the situation at the beginning of this book, at the time of its completion the radical tradition had returned from exile to its place of origin. This book joins a growing number of works – produced in the free air of a liberated South Africa – which seek greater understanding of the dark decades which preceded the collapse of apartheid. A book written after mine and which I can recommend to anyone interested in the stresses imposed on the Slovo daughters by their parents' political activism is *Every Secret Thing* by Gillian Slovo.

The task of writing this book has been a daunting one, not the least because of the political mythology which has grown around Ruth First since her assassination. And there were her colleagues, friends and family, many of whom helped enormously but each of whom, out of love and respect for her, also communicated a need for any study of her work to come out in the way they remembered it. Their goodwill and understanding were invaluable, but their expectations were there all the same, perhaps because expectations of Ruth herself were high. Fulfilling those aspirations, alas, may not be possible.[2] Finally, I would like to add the point that this book was born not only out of interest and unanswered questions, but also out of a sense of outrage. The very first words written in its execution are still worth quoting:

> 'I write these words in anger. The date is July 9 1986 in South Africa's third State of Emergency. Many of my comrades and friends have been imprisoned by the Security Police. I am on the run. Not a mile from where I sit is Pollsmoor Prison where Nelson Mandela wastes his precious years in confinement.
>
> 'But my anger arises from elsewhere. I have just finished reading Ruth First's book *117 Days*, begged from the library and needing permission from the Director of Publications to be seen. It is a searingly relevant book for these times and I am left shaken and close to tears. The utter awfulness is the knowledge that Ruth, unbroken by her interrogators, was to die by their hand in Maputo on April 20 1982.
>
> 'I begin this work out of a deep respect for a heroic woman, a fine journalist and a fighter for truth and justice in this tortured land. *Hamba kakuhle!* Your struggle will not go unrecorded'.

Notes

1 Plaatjie is best known for his monumental work *Native Life in South Africa* which was written in response to the depredations of the 1913 Land Act. He was editor of *Koranta ea Becoana* and also wrote a book on the siege of Mafeking and a Baralong love story based on Shakespeare's *Romeo and Juliet* called *Mhudi*. Rubusana founded *Izwi Labantu* in 1897 in response to the swing to the right by Jabavu and was noted for his polemical journalism in defence of African rights. La Guma edited *The Liberator,* a socialist paper started by the National Liberation League of South Africa in 1937. Seme founded *Abantu-Batho* in 1912 as the official organ of the African National Congress. It lasted until 1931 and was to coin and popularise many black slogans, including the famous *Mayibuy'i Afrika.* Ngubane took over *Inkundla yaBantu* from Mbeki and under his editorship its circulation reached 7 000 in 1946. Ngubane originally championed the ANC Youth League, but he later joined the Liberal Party and became a critic of the ANC. Many of the *Drum* journalists were later to write books which were to form the basis of a black writing tradition in the 1970s. These writers included Can Themba, Henry Nxumalo, Casey Motsisi, Eskia Mphahlele, Alex la Guma, Arthur Maimane, Bloke Modisane and Nat Nakasa.

2 For more intimate perspectives into the impact of Ruth's political involvement on her family, see the insightful books of her daughter, Gillian Slovo and the film *Worlds Apart*, directed by her sister, Shaun Slovo.

1

Growing up Left

In tracing the patterns of her thought and work we have not tried to cut her away from the tension of her life, for she could do no more than live the contradictions that emerged – Ruth First & Ann Scott on Olive Schreiner

A journalist, her writing and the context within which she wrote cannot be understood in isolation from each other. Heliose Ruth First was to become one of the finest investigative journalists of the 1950s, but she arrived there by a route which was to weave together threads of a political subculture altogether exceptional for a white South African. In the end she was to be declared an enemy of the state and not a word she wrote could be legally read within the borders of the land of her birth.

Ruth was born in Johannesburg on May 4 1925. This much we know from school reports and obituaries. But the context of her early life is much more elusive. Those of her family who were alive when research for this book took place remembered little, and her childhood friends were scattered or are dead. The hot summer days and crisp Transvaal dawns of the intelligent young Jewish girl can now be glimpsed only through the imperfect memories of those few who remain. But what is clear is that the commitments and traditions of Ruth's family gave her a world view which was set her apart from her peers. These traditions were to be the foundation of her journalism and her politics. It would be difficult to point to a moment in Ruth's life and say just here can be seen the influence of these traditions. Rather they were family views and acceptances which were to fire her intense interest in radical social transformation. However, like her grandparents and her parents, the price of this difference for Ruth was to be persecution and exile.

Her parents carried in their memories the poverty, squalor and violence in the area of Russia known as the Pale of Settlement and the pain and hope of one of the greatest migrations in human history. The movement of her grandparents from the western areas of the Tsarist Empire after 1880 was part of a general trend of emigration from almost every part of Europe, an exodus which reached its peak shortly before the First World War when about one and a half million people left Europe every year to find new homes overseas. But the percentage of Jewish emigrants from Eastern Europe was much higher than that of any other group, undoubtedly because of the severe conditions which existed in the Pale of Settlement.

The Pale was situated in territories belonging to subjugated minority populations – Poles, Byelo-Russians, Lithuanians, Latvians and others – and the Russian government showed scant concern for these people. However, by a decree dating back to 1791, Jews were only permitted to live within this area which constituted four percent of Russia's territory.[1] In an article on migrations from Lithuania, C. Gershater notes that between 1800 and 1880 the Jewish population of Tsarist Russia grew from 800 000 to four million. And by 1880 about 94 percent of the entire Jewish population of Russia were restricted to the Pale.[2]

Within the Pale, Jews suffered particular hardships. Added to grave overcrowding were constant calamities: droughts, floods, cholera, famine, deportation and fires. In the hot summer months fires sometimes consumed entire villages of thatched-roof and timber-walled cottages, and their inhabitants would wander to neighbouring settlements seeking shelter. Jews were also debarred from living in various villages and new edicts were constantly issued ordering Jews of an entire village to leave. A report of the expulsion of 400 families from a small village in the early 1880s states that the deportees arrived in the nearby village of Ponevez, and ends with the lament: 'How could the Ponevez Jews accommodate them when as a result of the two fires (there) seven families live in one house'.[3] An account of life in a Lithuanian village in 1858 noted that the Jews live

> in great congestion, very often several families in one small room. Lack of cleanliness ... is a marked sign of their dwellings. The expenses of the Jew are small. His breakfast consists of radishes, onion, garlic, herring or bread. The more comfortable people take tea and soup, fish or meat for their midday meal. There are tradesmen whose families fast the whole day until the breadwinner comes home in the evenings and brings his earnings.[4]

Then, in the spring of 1881, a wave of pogroms spread through the south of Russia. These were the consequence of a general reactionary and repressive policy adopted by the Russian government after the assassination of Tsar Alexander 11 and the accession to the throne of Alexander 111. The government's efforts to eradicate the revolutionary movement which sprang up in response to this repression was accompanied by agitation against Jews who were seen to have been party to the discontent and to the assassination. Anti-Jewish agitation was also seen as a way of diverting the attention of the masses from the depredations of the regime.[5]

The pogroms began in Yelisavetgrad in April 1881 and soon spread to Kiev, Odessa and the provinces of Volhynia and Podolia, as well as to many villages. In one attack, a family of Jews were murdered after being accused of killing a Christian in order to use his blood for ritual purposes.[6] The wave of racial violence created panic among the Jewish population in the south of Russia and thousands began to flee to the western borders. The province of Lithuania was free from pogroms, but the attacks on Jews in the south sent shock waves through the Eastern community. This was compounded by 'legislative pogroms' in 1882 which restricted the further settlement of Jews in villages and granted wide administrative powers to provincial officials.[7]

By 1884 a massive migration was under way. Most emigres from the Baltic states set their sights on England and the United States. But these countries were more interested in production workers than peasants and traders and tended to favour immigrants from more industrialised Poland. So by way of family connections - and particularly because of stories circulating in the Pale about the success in South Africa of mining magnate Sammy Marks who came from Neustadt-Sugind in Lithuania – Jewish migrants soon began heading south. The precise numbers of those leaving the region are not known. Thousands slipped over the border secretly.

But in the three decades following 1880, Gustav Saron in his work on Jewish migrations estimates that more than 16 million immigrants from Europe entered the United States alone.[8] Between November 1901 and October 1902, more than 800 people passed through the Jewish Shelter in London en route to South Africa. In October 1902, 200 people left on a ship for the south. In November and December of that year the monthly migrations were 657 and 870. During 1903, when emigration to South Africa peaked, 71 000 immigrants entered Cape ports.[9] Ruth First's grandfather sailed to South Africa in that year. He was a tailor named Moses Ruben Furst from Bauske Courland in Latvia (his name was written as "First" by a customs official when he landed in Cape Town). His son, Julius, arrived in Johannesburg three years later at the age of ten with his mother and brother. Ruth's mother, Matilda (Tilly) Leveton, was born in Lithuania and came to South Africa in 1901 at the age of four. Tilly remembers that her father bought a house in Fordsburg. He was, she said, a tailor who had spent a year in London before bringing the family to South Africa. No records could be found which documented the experiences of these two families, nor of the memories Julius or Tilly had of Russia. But the wrench of the departure was remembered by a friend of theirs, Bernard Sachs, an immigrant who left the 'old country' at about the same time and whose experiences would have been similar:

> I looked sadly for the last time at the village I knew so well ... Here had for a time flourished my childhood hopes, ambitions, dreams. All in all it was no mean world with its squalor and poverty. For it spoke of Man's capacity for wonder and the sense of mystery enveloping his life ... It was a world of total commitment, such as I have never regained in the Western world with its ampler opportunities. Taking leave of it was indeed a little death.[10]

Despite the solidarity of traditional Jewish life in the stetls,[11] there was not much to commend the material conditions against which the immigrants were turning their backs, and the West beckoned like a jewel: 'We were leaving behind the village with its squalor,' wrote Sachs, 'for the land where, we were told, the streets were paved with gold and we would dwell in marble halls.'[12]

As with almost all Jews bound for South Africa, Ruth's grandparents would have gone first to Immigrants Shelter in London, maintained by the Anglo-Jewish community there. Sachs remembers the disembarkation:

> We were like a procession of the damned in our motley assortment of clothes and colours, as we tramped flat-footedly across one of the busiest of the Thames bridges. My clothes were compounded by my mother of the colourful fragments left over from the materials out of which my sister had made her dress ... Someone guffawed loudly. But my mother kept her course, steadfast and unruffled. They are strong, these Jewish women – stronger than the girders of the London bridges and the bonds holding the Empire together.[13]

Inside the shelter the immigrants settled down to wait for their ships to the New World. According to Sachs 'they sat on their packages, souvenirs gathered from the wreckage of a life and a world of mutilated hopes. On top of their loads they carried two thousand years of bitterness. Birds of refuge, they were rebuilding with the debris of twigs and branches. Their fledglings, with sad eyes, were staring into space'[14]

For most migrants the boat passage was a relief after the waiting, but the long, slow train journey through the semi-desert Karroo was frightful, offset only by the thought that they were approaching the end of their long odyssey. It soon became clear to Sachs, as it would have to most weary travellers, that the streets of Johannesburg were not paved with gold. 'When I looked out of the train window ... mineshafts and pyramids of slime and sand appeared on the horizon. Johannesburg was smoking vaguely.... Our home consisted of three undersized rooms. There was a kitchen, but no bathroom, and no electric light'.[15]

According to Gideon Shimoni in his work on Jews and Zionism, most of the Jewish immigrants in early Johannesburg lived in Fordsburg, Ferreirastown, Mayfair and Doornfontein. Here they set up penny drinkshops, kosher eateries, small shops and offered a variety of services. Others became peddlers, smousing goods to outlying farmers, or set up 'kafereetas' near the mine compounds which encircled Johannesburg.[16]

This was the world in which both Julius and Tilly grew up. They both attended the Jewish Government School in Doornfontein. Tilly recalls that Julius 'sat behind me but I never paid him any attention. There were only three boys in the class. They used to kick a ball about in the girls' part of the playground and they would cover us with dust. That was my first impression of Julius'.[17]

Johannesburg

For both Julius First and Tilly Leveton, politics was to become absolutely central to their lives. There is only fragmentary evidence of their path from the Russian stetl to the Communist Party of South Africa. No mention of Julius can be found in documents up to April 28 1923 when, at the age of 27, he was elected chairman of the Communist Party of South Africa at its second congress.[18] But one can speculate. After leaving school Julius did a bookkeeping course and joined a firm of accountants, doing trustee work. At some time during this period, according to what Tilly could remember, he started a small business 'repairing old beadsteads and iron stoves'. By then he was already politically left and was 'a socialist when I met him – he had been influenced by David Ivon Jones'. He applied to join the International Socialist League but, according to Tilly, 'they refused him on the grounds that he was an employer of labour. He had one African who assisted him! It upset Julius terribly'.[19]

In 1923 he and his brother Louis started a manufactory called Union Mattress, with Julius as the junior partner.[20] Tilly, after completing school, worked in the office of Louis Goldberg, a furniture retail firm. She remembers being 'in charge of two collectors, young men, who had to go out in order to get the instalments'. According to her grand-daughter, Gillian, Tilly's job of re-possessing furniture from miners during the 1922 strike led her to question her previous beliefs.[21] Her son, Ronald, says she would talk about 'the money-grabbing aspects of these people who used to re-possess furniture and confiscate payments that people had made'.[22]

Although Julius and Tilly were born in Russia they would rapidly have become first-generation South Africans, looking forward into the new world for their identity rather than back to the Pale and the pogroms. Neither paid any heed to Jewish custom. Their wedding in 1924 was a no-nonsense affair. According to Tilly they were married in a registry office 'which upset my mother so much – we just went in and got married. But she had to get over that, we didn't pay her any attention. I wasn't religious. I didn't feel religion was any use to anybody'.[23] However, they had grown up within a Jewish sub-culture which was saturated with the affairs and traditions of Lithuania.[24] Within white South African society Litvak culture was noticeably different. Many immigrants could not initially speak English and their religion also served to set them apart from the Boers and the English. But with the troubled life of the Pale behind them, most probably felt the need to integrate into their new country with as little controversy as possible, to make a living and be left alone to pursue their lives in peace. However, the immigrants brought with them two political traditions which were to have a major impact on South Africa: Zionism and socialism. The first Chovevei Zion society in South Africa was formed in 1896 with the aim of restoring Zion as the homeland of the Jews.[25] By 1898, according to Shimoni, there were 5 000 members in the Transvaal and a congress was held at which it was resolved to establish a South African Zionist Federation. With the establishment of the Jewish Board of Deputies some years later the traditions of Zionism became a major force within the Jewish community.

However Lithuania was also the centre of Jewish socialism in Russia and adherents of this tradition often had to put up a spirited resistance to Zionism. In the first two decades of the century several Yiddish-speaking socialist groups were formed, including the Marxist Yiddisher Arbeter Bund, an offshoot of the powerful East European workers' movement, and a 'Yiddish-Speaking Group' affiliated to the International Socialist League (ISL). The Bund, formed in 1900, had branches in Johannesburg, Durban and Cape Town. It created a Society of Friends of Russian Liberty which was short-lived but succeeded in reducing the inaugural public meeting of the Zionist Club to chaos.[26] In 1915 the Cape Industrial Socialist League was formed to oppose the pro-war policy of the South African Labour Party and, according to Evangelos Mantzaris, 'the most militant and dynamic element within the organisation was predominantly Jewish'.[27] In Johannesburg the International Socialist League was founded by English-speakers such as Bill Andrews, Sidney Bunting, David Ivon Jones and Colin Wade, but large numbers of its supporters were Russian Jews.[28]

The successive Russian revolutions of February and October 1917 gave a sudden boost to left-wing politics and from then on the ISL was increasingly sustained by events in Europe. Its Russian-speaking members, most with family in Eastern Europe and some who had participated in the revolution of 1905, kept the organisation firmly focussed on Moscow. When the Bolsheviks assumed power, the ISL endorsed the takeover and attempted to establish direct links with the new government.[29] It has not been possible to establish whether Julius and Tilly First ever succeeded in becoming members of the ISL, but they probably did. Whatever their political opinions, however, their past would have ensured that they were caught up in the momentous 1917 revolution which Michael Harmel, in the official history of the Communist Party, was to term the 'dawn of the world'.[30] When the Communist Party was formed in July 1921, Julius would probably have been at the meeting, and he would have been swept up into the turmoil of the Rand revolt the following year.

The formation of the Communist Party of South Africa (CPSA) marked the culmination of a two-year debate, in which more than 10 organisations, representing about 500 members, argued over the proper form and programme for a revolutionary socialist organisation. In all these debates, relationships with Soviet Russia and the Communist International were central. Much of the discussion was around 21 conditions set for acceptance to the International. The final form of the Party seems to have raised less debate than might have been expected, considering that the result was a highly centralised organisation and the selection of delegates was weighted in favour of the larger Johannesburg membership. Africans had no representation on the executive.

School years

By 1925, with Julius as CPSA chairman, the Firsts were in the forefront of revolutionary politics in South Africa and Ruth, their first child, was born into a family markedly unlike most others in the country. Nonetheless, their politics did not seem to interfere with household arrangements commonly associated with white privilege. The Firsts hired a white nursemaid from London to look after the new baby. According to Tilly, the children 'always had a white nurse ... we didn't have coloured people in the house – whites were better educated.[31] Their house in Kensington was comfortable, well-furnished with the 'servants quarters in the yard as always'.[32]

By the age of three Ruth was 'a restless child – always needing to be amused'. She was also becoming aware of some of the implications of different skin colours. Shortly before her brother Ronald was born, Tilly decided to tell Ruth about it. 'I explained to her that I was going to have another baby. She was very interested and said: "Oh, will it be a black baby?" And when I looked at her she said: "I don't think we ought to have a black baby because no matter how much we washed him he would never get white."'[33]

At four Ruth was sent to a nearby kindergarten school and took to it with delight. She came from a family which regarded books very seriously and in her first year of school she started a library for her classmates. According to Tilly, 'she said the children never read any books and we must really get them books. She used to pressurise them, but I don't think it came to much – the children didn't want to read. She said if they didn't they wouldn't ever know anything'.[34]

An indication of her later tough-mindedness happened the same year. She was supposed to be picked up after school, but her parents were slightly late. 'When we arrived we found she had gone on her own. We rushed down to the tram stop near our house and Ruth just stepped out of the tram. She was only four! We were astounded. She was all alone in the city and she knew where to get off'.[35]

The family moved house a number of times. According to Ronald First 'we must have had five or six houses and apartments in my youth.'[36] One of the apartments was in a building in Yeoville belonging to the parents of Harold Wolpe with whom Ruth was to remain friendly throughout her life. The Firsts never sold the Kensington house, but would move to smaller accommodation when times were financially tight. In 1936 Louis and Julius changed the name of their mattress factory to Anglo Union and converted it to manufacture furniture. About that time Ruth began attending the Jewish Government

School in Doornfontein. A classmate, Adele Bernstein, clearly remembered Ruth's arrival in the school. She was "a skinny girl in a navy gym and white shirt who wore her fuzzy hair short. She was always neat, impeccably dressed and a bit of a class above us."[37] According to Bernstein, 'she put my nose out of joint. I was always very good at English and top of the class in that subject. Then Ruth arrived and she took over. Her parents had a very good library – they even inscribed her books in proper library fashion with the frontpiece and all. She used to lend me books. She was very articulate.'[38]

Doornfontein would have been full of interests for the bright new ten-year-old. It had formerly been a suburb for mining magnates but had become crowded and run down. Small, cheap semi-detached houses clustered between the older mansions and people without yards played and socialised out on the streets. A tram ran down the centre of the suburb and in the early 1930s horse-drawn landaus still clattered up the streets. The area was mainly occupied by Jewish immigrants and the area boasted a number of synagogues. Beit Street bustled with tailors, small grocers and kosher butchers. The two biggest shops were a baker and a delicatessen, but a magnet for the children was the Alhambra Bioscope, where on Saturday afternoons they could watch early Al Jolsen and other heroes for sixpence.[39]

The school was a red-brick structure near the station with a turret on the top. It held classes – mainly for Jewish children – from Grade 1 to Standard Six. Older immigrant children, some up to eigtheen years old, would pass through the lower grades four at a time to pick up English. Bernstein remembers them in her class as 'bigger, older and they smelt musty'. Outside the school gates 'German refugees would sell sweets to children for one penny a packet'.[40]

Ruth spent two years at school in Doornfontein and then, probably because her parents had moved house again, she left for Barnato Park school. Here she became friends with Myrtle Berman who remembered their first meeting:

> Our history teacher was talking about the Soviet Union and I was the only other person in the class who knew what the Soviet Union was. Ruth approached me afterwards and said: 'How do you know? You were the only one!' I can't remember how I did know, but I was a voracious reader, and I said: 'What *does* go on there?' And she said to me: Oh, I can't really explain it all, you should come and meet my mother. She'll explain it to you.'[41]

The result of that meeting probably changed Berman's life, and her memory of it captures something of the atmosphere in which Ruth grew up:

> One day after school I went home with Ruth. Got there about three o' clock and emerged at six o' clock with my head reeling, having had a three-hour lecture from Tilly on the history of socialism, the Russian Revolution, the origins of religion ... without me saying a word! And I remember wandering home and telling my mother, who nearly had a fit at this seditious stuff. But Tilly educated me. She gave me stuff to read. She was the main person who formed my early views.'[42]

At home the children were never excluded from the political domain. According to Tilly:

> When we used to go to the Town Hall steps (to hear communist speakers) we took the children with us. We made them conscious. We wanted them to have an understanding of what was going on. The only people who came to our house were people interested in politics, nobody else. We didn't have ordinary friends. I didn't ever want anybody around who didn't understand what we were talking about.[43]

At the age of fourteen Ruth joined the Junior Left Book club with Berman, reading extensively and taking part in public debates. Ruth devoured books about South Africa and the Soviet Union. In the First household there was, according to Berman, 'constant analysis of what was going on in the Soviet Union and it was absolutely plus, plus, plus all the way. It was very uncritical.'[44] At the Book Club she remembered Ruth as being 'much better equipped in debates than I was, like being able to stand up and talk about red, white and blue and what does it mean to you. Pulling things out of a hat and having to talk about it. I think she was much more steeped. She had a good general knowledge.'[45] Of course, life was also normal in a suburban way. As a teenager Ruth was interested in clothes and boys. According to Berman 'she fancied Arnold Levenburg for years, the boy next door. As a 13-year-old he was extremely good-looking, he was about a year older than Ruth.'[46]

However, Ruth's relationship with her mother was complex and a source of conflict. Julius was the 'traditional father'. He was away during the day and 'he would come in at night and be tired and be much more quiet (than Tilly).'[47] He was, according to Rica Hodgson, 'sweet and soft and not very – you wouldn't call him an intellectual giant. Far from it.'[48] Yet he exuded a warmth which Tilly didn't. In the house, therefore, it was Tilly who was the force, who 'ran the roost.'[49] Ronald First remembers Tilly as being 'very hard politically' and this 'obviously had a stronger influence on Ruth than it did on me.'[50] A neighbour, Harold Wolpe, described Tilly as an abrasive character, 'very impatient' who couldn't brook stupidity. 'As a kid, if Ruth made a child-like statement it didn't get a very good reception.'[51] According to Berman, Tilly would fall over herself to do things for Ruth. 'I was quite aware that Tilly absolutely adored Ruth ... Ronnie was much more an also-ran. But Tilly was a woman who was totally incapable of showing any demonstrative affection. She was not a toucher. I remember when Ruth was staying with us – we were a very affectionate family, always hugging each other – and Ruth said to me: "You know, my mother doesn't love me any less because she doesn't hug me."'[52]

In one of Ruth's final works, the beautifully-crafted biography of Olive Schreiner which she wrote with Ann Scott, one is tempted to see some of Ruth's own predicament in their description of Schreiner: 'She felt herself to be a motherless child: her mother had been superior, distant and severe; her father tender but ineffectual, and a foreigner, ever uncomfortable in Africa.'[53]

Ruth also had to come to terms with another powerful influence in life: an over-active thyroid complaint. In her later years daily medication reduced this problem to a minimum.[54] But in the late 1920s and early 1930s such medication was not available and Ruth was required to deal with it herself from an early age.[55] From very young, Ruth would have had to fight bouts of exhaustion and she would have had to break through this mentally to keep up with her peers. This energy drop stayed with her in later years, and she developed her own way of coping with it. Rica Hodgson remembers that

> she would get terribly flat by eight o'clock – it may have been part of this thyroid thing. She always had this quite badly. And she would go to sleep. You couldn't see that she was sleeping and she was a very quiet sleeper. She would just sit there and sleep. But as soon as there was anything that was contentious she woke up like a bullet![56]

In dealing with a dominant Tilly, an absent Julius, non-stop politics and a physical problem, Ruth's character developed a mixture of toughness and vulnerability which was to confuse people and endear her to them in her adult life. But by the time she matriculated from Jeppe Girls High, her final school, in 1941 she had all the makings of a 'blue stocking':[57]

> She was brilliant ... she always had it up there and she knew she had it up there. But she didn't care very much about how she looked. She didn't have a very good image of herself as a woman in those days. Her hair was very curly, she didn't use make-up. I was terrified of her. But I learned early that she had great vulnerability ... she was very shy, private, she hid herself behind those dark glasses she always wore. That was a kind of hiding-behind.[58]

In trying to develop an identity separate from Tilly, Ruth and her mother would often have rows, 'fighting like two people who are very close.'[59] During her high school years 'you could see the signs in Ruth of trying to seperate from Tilly, getting out from under her.'[60]

Her father presented other problems. According to Hilary Kuny, a psychologist who knew Ruth well, 'we both had dominating mothers and more passive fathers ... The effect hasn't been the same, but there may be a sense of insecurity about intimate personal relationships, some lack of trust in the man ... a sense of weariness at having to be the strong one, being your own father. '[61] This problem is touched on in Ruth's biography of Schreiner and it is, again, tempting to make the connection. 'How could a free woman validate herself?' ask Ruth and Scott. 'Perhaps by experiencing herself as a man.'[62] And elsewhere: 'We see Olive as someone struggling to come to terms with her identity as a whole, trying to fulfil both parts of her nature, to work and live like a man, but like a woman as well.'[63]

This emotional ambivalence was almost to be her undoing in a gloomy prison cell many years later, and her well-hidden insecurity could be seen in her often aggressive treatment of political and intellectual opponents. It seems to be from a special insight that Ruth and Ann Scott said of Schreiner that 'she cut a lonely, isolated figure, issuing prophetic warnings about the future of the country and retreating into a shy personal life.'[64] Only close friends saw Ruth's self-doubt, but in finding it they also came across her warm, sensitive self. Ronald Segal was to observe that 'she was not amongst those people whose private characters are virtually the same as their public ones.'[65] Years later she was to write:

> My introspection gets more and more involved as I go into my favourite pastime of undermining me and my character and seeing my faults ... Pity I never had any talent for philosophy. Then my conflicts wouldn't have to be on a personal plane.... Trouble really is I would like to prove to myself I can produce something worthwhile.... But I'm too directionless and I know at heart that if direction, application and talent aren't there, it's all my own undoing and no one can overcome that.... It's a form of masochism I suffer from; one of my afflictions, like heavy eyebrows and a mole on my nose.[66]

In 1941 Ruth passed her matric with an unexceptional second class, but she knew what she wanted to do next. According to Tilly, 'she wanted to go to university very much. I left her choices to her'. So the following year she registered to do a degree in social science at the University of the Witwatersrand. She was about to discover the comradeship and politics which were to set her course for the rest of her life.

Notes

1 Gershater, 1955 p62.
2 Ibid, p61.
3 Ibid, p63.
4 Opisanie Kovenskoy Guberni, St Petersburg, 1861 p582. Quoted by Jacob Leschinsky in the *Rakishok Memorial Book*, Johannesburg, 1952.
5 Gershater, op cit. p65.
6 Ibid, p72.
7 Ibid, p66.
8 Saron, G: Jewish Immigration, 1880-1913 in Saron & Hotz, 1955 p86.
9 Ibid, p90. The 1904 census gave the Jewish population in the country as 38 101.
10 Bernard Sachs: The Fordsburg-Mayfair Hebrew congregation, 1893-1964, p20. Bernard's brother, Solly, was to become one of the foremost trade union organisers in South Africa.
11 Villages.
12 Ibid, p19.
13 Ibid, p36.
14 Ibid, 37.
15 Ibid, p38.
16 Shimoni, G: *Jews and Zionism: The South African Experience, 1910-1960*. OUP, Cape Town, 1980.
17 Interview with Tilly First, 1988.
18 Report of the second congress of the CPSA published in *The International*, May 4 1923.
19 Interview with Tilly First, op cit.
20 Interview with Ronald First, 1992. According to Tilly, Louis 'married a great socialite who was always looking for important people to invite onto her lawn'.
21 Private correspondence with Gillian Slovo, 1992.
22 Ibid.
23 Interview with Tilly, op cit.
24 In 1924 Lithuanians in South Africa contributed a clear 70 percent of the Jewish immigrants from Eastern Europe, compared to 10 percent from Poland, 8 percent from Latvia and 12 percent from Russia. In 1918 the Jewish population was 58 714, about four percent of the white population in South Africa. Shimoni, Ibid. p7.
25 Ibid, p19.
26 Ibid, p53.
27 Mantzaris: 'The promise of the impossible revolution: The Cape Town Industrial Socialist League, 1918-1921'. In *Studies in the history of Cape Town*, Vol.4, UCT, 1981.
28 Sheridan Johns: 'The birth of the CPSA'. In the *International Journal of African Historical Studies*, Vol.9, No.3, 1976 p375.
29 *The International* January 11, 1918, and Johns, ibid, p374.

30 Harmel: *Fifty Fighting Years*, 1980 p35.

31 Interview with Tilly First.

32 Ibid.

33 Ibid.

34 Ibid.

35 Ibid. There is a possibility that Tilly may have forgotten Ruth's age at the time, but not that she was at kindergarten when the event occurred.

36 Interview with Ronald First, op cit.

37 Interview with Adele Bernstein, 1991.

38 Ibid.

39 Ibid.

40 Ibid.

41 Myrtle was to join the Communist Party and was editor of *Viewpoints and Perspectives* which documented the crucial debates by Party members in 1952/3. She was later to drift away from the Party and, with her husband Monty, was a founder member of the African Resistence Movement (ARM) in the 1960s.

42 Myrtle Berman interview, 1988.

43 Tilly, op cit.

44 Berman, op cit.

45 Berman, Ibid.

46 Berman, Ibid.

47 Ibid.

48 Rica Hodgson interview, 1988.

49 Berman, op cit.

50 Ronald First, op cit.

51 Interview with Harold Wolpe, 1992.

52 Ibid.

53 First & Scott: *Olive Schreiner*, 1980, p334. Scott was a considerably younger than Ruth at the time of writing the book, but their association was a creative experience for both of them and the book received excellent reviews.

54 First: 117 days, 1988 ed. p17.

55 The thyroid is a large gland near the larynx which regulates the rate at which nutrients are taken up into the body. An over-active thyroid condition would have increased Ruth's metabolic and pulse rate, breaking down tissue faster than her body could replace it, causing skinnyness, restlessness and lethargy. Early medication for this condition tended to cause opposite effects: slow pulse rate and overweight, which some of Ruth's friends remember as being her problem in the 1950s.

56 Hodgson, op cit.

57 Before going to Jeppe, Ruth was sent to an Afrikaans school for six months to improve her grasp of the language. But she never did well in Afrikaans and refused to read its literature. See Berman, op cit.

58 Hodgson op cit.

59 Berman, op cit.

60 Ibid.

61 Interview with Hilary Kuny, 1988.

62 First & Scott, op cit. p335.

63 Ibid, p23.

64 Ibid, p17. Scott had a background in feminist studies.

65 R Segal in *Index on Censorship*, 6, 1982, p30.

66 Letter to Joe Slovo, reproduced in the 1988 edition of *117 Days*, p5.

2

University, politics and the Party

On a South African campus, the student matters that matter are national issues – Ruth First

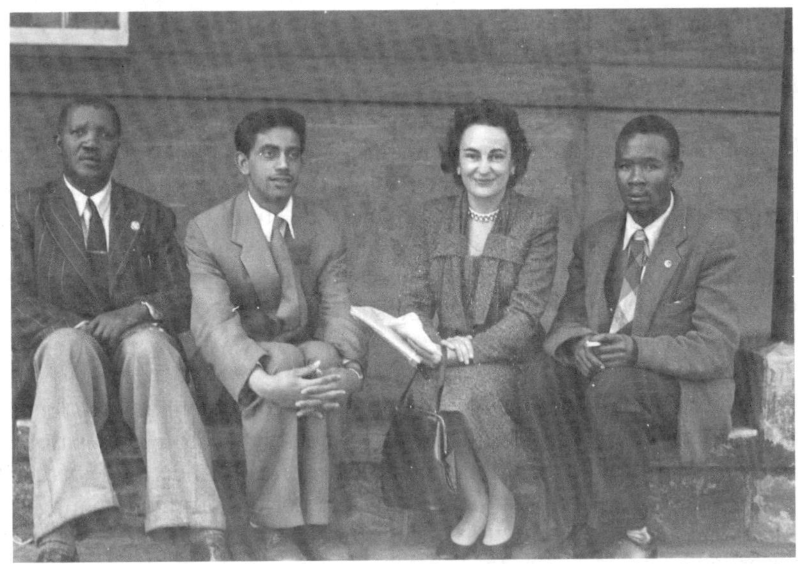

© Mayibuye

Ruth with comrades

Ruth has written very little about her university life. In *117 Days* she was to say that her university years were cluttered with student societies, debates, mock trials, general meetings and 'the hundred and one issues of war-time and post-war Johannesburg that returning ex-servicemen made so alive.'[1]

She has written nothing about her academic achievements. But her records from the University of the Witwatersrand indicate a serious and intelligent student with a wide range of interests. She decided to do a social science degree and, many years later, attempted to add a diploma in librarianship. In all, she was to study no less than 25 courses, of which six were terminated by her arrest in 1963 and another two, during 1945, were not examined. Her records show an exceptional ability in English and African History and little interest in languages (she scored 49% for Zulu and 32% for French). Six of her examinations were passed with firsts.[2]

However, while Ruth applied herself to her studies in her usual focused way, the campus was to offer her direct emotional involvement in wider political struggles. There she found her own measure in a way she could never have done at an all-white girls school, and the campus put her in contact with people of her own age who didn't regard her views as outlandish. One of these was a handsome, effervescent young Indian law student called Ismael Meer.

Meer had completed his schooling at Sastri College in Durban and had gone on to Natal University to do a Bachelor of Arts which included a number of law subjects. However, in the early 1940s the Natal Law Society discontinued law lectures to all 'non-whites'. According to Meer, 'the Society had made representation that we were penetrating into a white profession, with the result that we had to go and get our legal training elsewhere.'[3] Witwatersrand University placed no such restrictions on black students and Meer left for the Reef to complete his studies.

The Meer family had a history of political involvement as long Ruth's own. It owned a newspaper, *Indian Views*, which was founded in 1913 in opposition to Gandhi's *Indian Opinion*. While at Sastri, Meer and a few friends formed the Liberal Study Group which 'trained many young Indian leaders of that period – trained people to think in terms of a non-racial future.'[4] While studying at Natal University, Meer wrote articles for both Indian papers and was a reporter for the left-wing national weekly newspaper, *The Guardian*.

At Witwatersrand University Meer met Nelson Mandela whom he found to be 'the best dresser in the Faculty.' He rented a flat at 27 Market Street which soon became the meeting place for radical students. Mandela, who had rooms in Orlando, found it difficult to get home every night and would often sleep over in the flat.[5] Ruth was attracted by these self-confident, politically-aware students – particularly to Meer. The two were soon close friends. Myrtle Berman remembers Meer as 'very charismatic, very bright, very able. He was a leader who stood out. He and Ruth were so involved with each other.'[6] Meer and First both helped found the Federation of Progressive Students, but their main political activities were in the broader political field. Meer was a leading figure in the Transvaal

Indian Congress and Ruth soon became a central member of the Young Communist League. According to Harold Wolpe, Ruth 'wasn't a campus political person ... she was more involved in, so to speak, adult politics.'[7] Meer and First were both later to join the Johannesburg West branch of the Communist Party.

Meer's flat became the focus of Ruth's social world and her expanding political education. According to Berman the flat was 'dreary ... badly furnished, bloody depressing, looking back on it ... just a place to be.' But it was 'awash with activity, always, it was a hive.'[8]

Political writer Mary Benson saw the social activity in the flat as the welding together of friendships among young people who were later to form the intelligentsia of the Congress Alliance: 'great days – and in Meer's flat over endless cups of tea and curry meals at any time of the day and night. They discussed and argued and planned, they studied and they listened to the gramophone.'[9] According to Benson, they were young, optimistic, and planning for a better world:

> despite the obtuseness of the Government and its continual resort to restrictive legislation, they realised they were part of the world at large, and had the assurance of knowing they were in step with what was happening in Asia and with what was likely to happen in the rest of Africa.[10]

Just down the road from Meer's flat were the offices of Pixley Seme, one of the founders of the African National Congress. His articled clerk at the time was Anton Lembede who, together with other law students of the time including Nelson Mandela and Oliver Tambo, were to found the ANC Youth League. These young lawyers, together with Indian activists, white radical students and, at times, the outspoken priest Michael Scott, would 'read the same kind of books' and plan for a new South Africa. According to Meer 'we were living in an euphoric age where we thought that all man's problems would just disappear once we got rid of imperialism.'[11]

One of the activities planned out of 27 Market Street was a socio-economic survey of Fordsburg which coincided with *Guardian* sales in the area. Following this survey, women from the area were helped to form buying collectives. Ismael, Ruth and other activists staged food raids on shops suspected of hoarding goods during war rationing.[12]

Ruth was becoming increasingly more politically mature and involved. In 1945 the war ended and the university was caught up in the turmoil of what seemed to be new beginnings. She enrolled for four university subjects but did not write her final examinations. Ruth was by then a leading figure in the Young Communist League and was remembered as being 'very quick mentally ... holding her ground ... and somewhat intimidating.'[13] In her own terms her life must have seemed more balanced. She was described as being 'not a blue stocking or a gay socialite but a mixture of both these characteristics.'[14] She was clearly coming out of her shell.

War and the Party

Through her involvement on the CPSA Youth League, Ruth began to add reflection and study to the communist traditions with which she had grown up. She was also becoming

Ismael Meer (Guardian)

actively involved at a time when the Party was in a process of transition from a small group of doctrinaire Stalinists to people with dreams of mass-based socialist organisation. This transformation was intimately connected to the changing profile of the Soviet Union on the international stage.

In 1943, the year Ruth joined the Communist Youth League, the Third Communist International was disbanded, the Internationale was abolished as the official anthem of the Soviet state and the last link with Lenin's dream of a single world communist party was broken. Communist parties throughout the world, which had been under Moscow's orders in one way or another since the formation of the Comintern in 1919, were cut loose from the Communist Party of the Soviet Union (CPSU) in a resolution signed by 30 national parties including the CPSA. This resolution, in dissolving the Comintern, made no allusion to the possibility of international links being made in the future. From being parts of a single world Communist Party, directed by an executive committee whose decisions were binding on all sections of the International 'and which had to be promptly carried out', the communist parties became, overnight, national parties that were wholly independent and (on paper at least) without links between them.

The collapse of the Comintern marked the end of a period in South Africa. Starting in the late 1920s, the CPSA was reduced from a relatively open and growing party to a handful of hardened party apparachiks because of expulsions, internal intrigue and doctrainnaire practices. This political atmosphere had surrounded Ruth 's family during her school years. Her parents, both Party members, remained faithful to the Stalinist line and survived the expulsions. Many others had not.

In the First 's house the children had never been shielded from political discussion. There were many times when Ruth found her parents in intense discussions about the purges. Visitors were involved in debates over complicated issues, often behind closed doors, and her parents emerged looking tired and strained. Lazar Bach was a constant visitor. Others were Mollie and Douglas Wolton, Moses Kotane and Edward Roux. Sydney Bunting may have visited often before his expulsion – his warm nature would have attracted Julius First – but the expulsions must have erected barriers to their relationship.[15]

To these early memories Ruth would have added information about the Soviet Union and world politics in study groups and meetings of the Young Communist League. But one can only speculate about whether she connected these far-off events in the USSR and Europe with processes which had taken place nearer home – or whether the virtual bureaucratic destruction of the CPSA had even been a topic of conversation. But the outcome of the relationship between Moscow and the CPSA was to lay the foundations of her future political orientation.

In the 1930s the Party headquarters had been moved from Cape Town to Johannesburg. Shortly after returning from the Sixth Congress of the Central Communist Party (CCP) in Moscow, Douglas Wolton had told Eddy Roux that the popular Party newspaper, *Umsebenzi*, was not being run on correct bolshevik lines and he also demanded its transfer from Cape Town to Johannesburg. In the Transvaal during the early 1930s the Party was controlled by Douglas and Molly Walton and Lazar Bach, all of whom, according to Roux, 'could quote Marx, Engels, Lenin and Stalin, chapter and verse, on any conceivable aspect of policy'. All three insisted that their 'long and well nigh incomprehensible essays' should appear in full in *Umsebenzi*. The paper became virtually unreadable and circulation slumped.

Moses Kotane, who was both a communist and a nationalist, had tried to remedy the situation by calling for the formation of a United Front of all African radicals. This had provoked from Bach and his supporters the accusation that Kotane wanted to surrender the leadership of the masses to African bourgeois nationalists. Kotane was removed from both the Politburo and from *Umsebenzi*.

The terrible personal strains of the period have never been recorded. They are glossed over in official Party histories, downplayed in biographies and ignored by non-Party writers.[16] The cost to Ruth 's parents for staying faithful to the Political Bureau must have been considerable, and one can only guess at its effects on the family. They left their mark on the children – arousing Ruth 's interest and repelling her brother Ronald. Between 1931 and 1933 the Party had been going through a period of recovery, but by the mid 1930s it was in a 'crisis of right opportunism' and by 1937 it had virtually committed suicide. In an attempted recovery, its headquarters were moved to the less traumatized Party office in Cape Town.

The coming of war was to change the situation dramatically. In an attempt to rally forces to defend the Soviet Union, Moscow amplified its call for a United Front of all socialists against the danger of fascism and war.[17] This was later extended to a call for a Popular Front of all people – socialist or not – against the rising threat of Hitler's Germany. In South Africa this had the effect of supporting Kotane's line against the Woltons and Bach. Bach visited Moscow in the mid-1930s and never returned to South Africa. He was later to die in Soviet detention camps.[18] The Waltons left South Africa for good at about the same time and Kotane was reinstated on the Politbureau and became political editor of *Umsebenzi*. The Party began the slow, painful process of reconstruction.

But its problems were by no means over. On September 4 1939, the South African parliament decided for war by 80 votes to 67. Two days later the ANC issued a circular approving the decision and this was followed by support from the All African Convention. But the outbreak of war threw South African communists into a crisis. Since the mid-1930s, CPSA members had been participating in anti-fascist organisations. However for reasons which are still under dispute, Stalin signed a non-aggression pact with Hitler. The local Party, ever loyal to the Comintern, opposed the war effort. For 22 months Party stalwarts like Ruth's parents, many of them Jewish, had to watch the persecution of Jews and communists by Hitler while publicly justifying their anti-war stance. What made it more difficult was the presence of various pro-Nazi 'shirt' movements whose neutral stance on the war made their position seem perilously close to that of the Party. Militant trade unionists were arrested and interned together with Afrikaner Nazis and Party members were branded as 'Communazis'.[19] Durban Party leader Yusuf Dadoo was fined £25 for distributing a leaflet: 'Don't support this war: where the rich get richer and the poor get killed.' The President of the South African Trades and Labour Council, Archie Moor, launched a tirade against the Party, claiming it had 'established a new religion called Communism, and a new god called Stalin, for whom they would perjure their eternal souls.'[20] Such criticism was particularly painful for Party members who were being labeled 'quislings' for support of fascism which until that moment they had considered to be their mortal enemy. They attempted, by complicated arguments, to justify their position. In a paper delivered at a CPSA conference in March 1940, 'J Morkel' told delegates that, after the Soviet-German Pact was signed,

> the Party was asked to be cautious in its attitude to the war that was ahead, and not to rush in with support ... The Party, therefore, while declaring opposition to the war, stated that at that moment the struggle was in South Africa against the Nazis. This undoubtedly weakened the line of struggle against the war, since it meant passive acceptance of the Smuts Government and its war policy. But the dilemma – support Smuts and the war or oppose the war and support the pro-Nazi, anti-Trade Union, anti-colour Nationalists – could not be avoided by other means than the policy adopted: oppose the war and resist the Nationalists.[21]

About the time Ruth was entering standard nine her household would, therefore, have been the scene of another round of urgent discussions as tensions rose within the Party. But as the family watched the war roll across Europe they kept their personal turmoil to a small inner circle and they held the Party line. Dilemmas within the South African left reflected the rift in the international socialist movement over Moscow's war stance as members broke ranks to sign up. In 1940 Party membership was down to 280, more than half of whom were in Johannesburg.[22] In September of that year *Inkululeko* defended the Party's position in an article entitled 'A year of imperialist war':'What the war has meant to us: higher prices for food, candles, tobacco ... hundreds of people out of work, men who are helping Africans to build trade unions interned ... Dadoo on trial for opposing the war ... Now everyone can see that the Communist Party was right.'[23]

By mid-1941 communists and other left supporters of an anti-war policy were finding themselves increasingly alienated from a wider population caught up in the war effort and castigated by a hostile commercial Press. Then, on June 22 1941, German forces attacked the Soviet Union. Four days later the Party's Central Committee issued a statement calling on 'all democratic and freedom-loving people to give their unqualified and wholehearted support to the Soviet Union in its struggle against the Nazi aggressors.'[24] The sudden swing to a pro-war position may have been a relief for members watching the growth of fascism, but for many it seemed the height of hypocrisy. By 1943 the Party was urging mass mobilisation, all-out production of the war industry and a curb on strike action. In a Party pamphlet entitled 'More Money', workers were told that strikes 'hold up supplies of weapons, of arms, of uniforms, to our army fighting for our (sic) freedom. Strikes today can help our fascist enemies destroy our armies ... and enslave us. Wherever workers can win demands without strikes which stop the flow of goods from our factories, they should

*Ruth with Albie Sachs (left) and the Spanish revolutionary Lopez Raimundo at the World Federation of Democratic Youth in Peking, August 16, 1954 (*Advance*, October 14 1954)*

do so.'[25] Many communists, including Ruth's future husband Joe Slovo, signed up and headed for the battlefields of the north under a flag symbolising colonial domination and in quest of world freedom. Some of these men would, years later, be facing charges of sedition in the courts of the land they were fighting to defend.

The Party's new position on the war caused confusion among African supporters. According to Brian Bunting, 'the Johannesburg district and the Natal district had opposition from audiences who didn't understand why they should support today the butcher Smuts, whom they had condemned yesterday as the apostle of segregation.'[26]

But the turn about attracted a growing number of petty-bourgeois supporters to organisations like Friends of the Soviet Union, Medical Aid for Russia and the Left Book Clubs. Indeed Ruth's political involvement with the Party began when its white public profile was reaching unprecedented heights. In 1942, when Ruth entered university, the Smuts government formally decided to receive a consular representative from the Soviet Union. The following year Mrs Smuts, in a letter to the Medical Aid for Russia Fund, wrote 'we owe Russia so much for all she is doing for us, for all she has done and for all she has sacrificed and suffered for our cause ... .What a magnificent stand she is making. God bless her!'[27] The South African Broadcasting Corporation invited veteran trade unionist and and communist Bill Andrews to address the nation on air.

The dissolution of the Comintern in 1943 was seen as a signal that the Soviet Union had ceased its efforts to export world revolution and was welcomed in the *Inkululeko.*[28] Party membership increased rapidly, as did the circulation of *The Guardian.*[29] The Party put its weight behind a 'Defend South Africa' campaign, it arranged rallies in town halls up and down the country, its newspaper columns gave prominence to war news and the editor of *Inkululeko* 'donned an air-raid warden's uniform and conscientiously patrolled the lanes of Orlando.'[30] Communists were elected to city councils in Cape Town, Johannesburg Durban and East London. Nine white communists entered the field in the parliamentary elections of 1943 and, although all were defeated they used the campaign platform to raise Party issues.'[31] In a report at the end of that year, the Party's Central Committee said it has 'achieved the impossible':

> We have brought together in our organisation men and women of all racial groups in South Africa, working together in comradeship for common ends on a basis of complete equality. We have done this in the teeth of bitter opposition and in the face of the dominant prejudices of society.[32]

Inevitably, the drive to bring 'notable' people on board the campaign for aid to the Soviet Union required a blunting of calls to fight capitalism at home. The sacrifice of radicalism was seen by many as a necessary by-product of the united front ... a part of the patriotism and heroism that the war engendered.[33]

The government found Party support of the war effort useful: it was anxious to secure the loyalty and support of Africans. The CPSA, under attack from the Nationalist Party and the 'shirt' movements, allied itself ever more closely to the Smuts government and attempted to portray Nationalist propaganda as destructive to the safety of South Africa. It demanded that the government 'smash the fascists' and 'arm the people.'[34]

When the war ended, Stalin was the hero of the day. The defence of Stalingrad was commonly acknowledged to be the turning point in the struggle for peace. Large numbers of soldiers returned to South Africa as members of the Springbok Legion, an organisation run by members of the CPSA, and meetings of Friends of the Soviet Union were being well attended. The war had raised the profile of the Party to unprecedented heights.

There was of course another – perhaps more important – side to the Communist Party, one which was to be the deep keel of Ruth 's political life and journalism. At a time when African people were considered by most whites as little more that cheap labour or dangerous savages, the Party was calling for recognition of their political and economic rights. In a society in which even liberals often kept special cups for black visitors to prevent 'contamination', the sheer audacity of this approach was to put whites who held these views beyond the pale of official and even white social tolerance.

Ruth was to do far more than merely hold these views, which were to be at the root of the Congress Alliance – she was to be one of their key propagandists. Her family may have contributed towards her condemnation of racism – although in many ways it was a typical white family with a gardener and a live-in maid – but at university these ideas were to mature into political conviction. Her friendship with Ismael Meer and his circle of friends was to open up a world which prejudice had closed to most of her fellow white students. In this process two events stand out in significance, both of which took place before she became a journalist.

On May 20 1944, a year after Ruth had joined the Communist Youth League, she attended an anti-pass conference in the Gandhi Hall. She was among the 540 delegates who passed resolutions condemning the pass laws and voted to set up a National Anti-Pass Council which would organise to collect a million signatures to an anti-pass petition.[35] After the conference, all delegates marched to the market square in Newtown where a huge crowd awaited them. After two brief addresses by ANC leader Alfred Xuma and Yusuf Dadoo of the Natal Indian Congress a great march of over 15 000 workers, with Moses Kotane as chief marshal, stamped through the centre of Johannesburg.[36] The crowds were headed by a big ANC float bearing hundreds of banners demanding the repeal of the pass laws. This was followed by two brass bands singing national songs.

There is no firm evidence that this meeting alone influenced Ruth 's journalism. Indeed the campaign eventually flopped. But it seems likely. When Ruth entered the political arena after university she was to throw herself into an attack on the pass laws and the migrant labour system. Until her exile in 1963 this cruel system, in all its forms and effects, was to be a central preoccupation of her professional life.

The second formative political event was in August 1946 when 100 000 African miners went on strike. Ruth was completing courses at the university but had taken a job in the Research Division of the Johannesburg City Council:

> I spent my days writing and editing the section headed 'Social Welfare' in a commemorative album of the city's fiftieth jubilee: checking the figures for the number of play supervisors for white children in white parks; the number of beggars still on the streets despite vigorous public relations work by the department to stop the public giving them alms; the number of work centres for the disabled and the handicapped (all white) ... work which bored and disgusted me.[37]

The mine strike was to cause Ruth to resign from her first job in order to become a full-time activist:

> When the African miners' strike of 1946 broke out and was dealt with by the Smuts Government as though it was a red insurrection and not a claim by poverty-stricken migrant workers for a minimum wage of ten shillings a day, I asked for an interview with the (Council) director and told him that I wanted to leave the department....Then he asked: 'Have you another job?'...'A political job,' I said.

It was a tense and exciting time for the young university graduate and it was an early indication of the direction her activism would take:

> The strikers were enclosed in compounds under rule by the army, the mine and state police ... all officials and organisers of the African Mine Workers Union were being hunted by the police. A great squad of volunteers appeared in the most unlikely places, and from lodging rooms like the one I shared with a girl-friend, the handles of duplicating machines were turned through the night, while in the early hours before dawn white volunteers drove cars to the vicinity of the mine compounds and African organizers, hiding their city suits and their bundles of strike leaflets under colourful tribal blankets, wormed their way into the compounds...When the mine strike was over I became a journalist.[38]

The year, however, was to be a traumatic one for Ruth. At the end of 1946 she passed her finals with a first in Native Administration and Ismael Meer graduated in law. In terms of the Group Areas Act, Meer was not allowed to stay in the Transvaal after the completion of his degree and prepared to leave for Natal. Ruth's relationship with Meer had never been easy. According to Berman, 'the four of us (Meer, First, J.N. Singh and herself) used to go around together. We used to walk down Market Street to Ismael's flat and get taunted by the bus conductors on the way because we were walking with two Indians ... it was quite dicey, actually, walking around with them'.[39]

Rumblings about the relationship had also been coming from the political movement. Meer was 'becoming too important in the movement' and it was felt that his relationship with a white woman would work against him.[40] According to Berman, Tilly was also unhappy about the relationship. 'With Tilly's beliefs she could not actually fault it (on racial grounds). But what she felt about it, I don't know. She put it all on the political. But I can't say whether Tilly was only motivated by that ... . After all, it was not a very acceptable thing to do, to have your daughter running around with an Indian.'[41]

As Meer left for Natal they agreed to separate. According to Berman, Ruth was 'absolutely heartbroken'. She was to turn for emotional support to a soldier recently returned from the war – Joe Slovo. He had been born in Lithuania and had emigrated to South Africa with his parents when he was nine. His father had worked as a van driver in Johannesburg and his mother, at times, had hawked goods from house to house. Joe was forced to leave school early in order to earn money and had worked as a shop clerk. When war broke out he joined the army and while he was up north he became an active member of the Springbok Legion, a radical serviceman's organisation. After demobilisation he joined the Communist Youth League. Back in Johannesburg, Joe began studying law at Witwatersrand University. He and Ruth soon became political comrades, trading heated debates and sharing political platforms. They often argued – she was the intellectual, he was to say, and he was the working class man – but the attraction grew. They shared a flat, and in 1949 they married.

Cold War and the fall from grace

Just seven years after the South African Prime Minister's wife had blessed Russia for its magnificent stand and had given her support to Medical Aid for the Soviet Union, an organisation almost wholly run by communists, the Communist Party was to disband in the face of the Suppression of Communism Act. The reason for its fall from grace has commonly been ascribed to the election victory of the pro-Nazi Nationalist Party in 1948. But the truth was more complicated than that, and had as much to do with the international climate as with events in South Africa. As a young member of the Party, Ruth was not to play a central role in these developments, but they were to have a significant effect on her life just the same. The Cold War and its communist witch-hunts in the West and the East were to form a bewildering backdrop to events in the Melville East branch of the CPSA where Ruth had made her political home. These events need some consideration, because they were the fabric from which Ruth was to weave her political understandings.

The Soviet victory in the Second World War had provided new ideological and political justifications for the primacy of the USSR in the world communist movement, but the war and Stalin's own policy also gave rise to attitudes and processes which worked against this. The Comintern was dissolved, quite suddenly, in the Spring of 1943, to facilitate negotiations between Churchill and Roosevelt, whose aims included the partition of the world among the 'Big Three' powers. Two weeks later the CPSA issued a statement which acknowledged the reasons for the dissolution: 'The decision of the Governing Council of the Communist International to recommend its dissolution is in the first place inspired by a desire to bring about the maximum degree of unity between the United Nations in the struggle against Hitler and his allies.'[42]

The demise of the Comintern was closely connected with the need to establish a Second Front in the war against Germany. This was required for a quick, decisive victory – but was being blocked by pressure groups in the West fearful of the Soviet Union's support for world revolution. According to historian William Foster, 'the favourable impression all over the bourgeois world made by the dissolution of the Comintern helped very decisively to break this deadly log-jam.'[43] The dissolution was seen by many communists and reactionaries in the West as a *ruse de guerre*, but in truth it was not – and the death of the Comintern marked at that point the end of Soviet support for the revolutionary aspirations of communist parties in the West.

The leaders of the West needed to know in what direction Moscow's influence would be exercised after the war. Would the communist parties use the economic and political crisis produced by the war to rouse the masses and thereby hasten the downfall of capitalist rule? At its moment of departure, the Comintern recommended the formation of an anti-fascist alliance – the People's Front. In South Africa the Front policy was to lead to a strengthening of alliances between the CPSA and the ANC. But its application internationally, it could be argued, was to have dire consequences for communist parties in the West. Front politics had links to earlier positions adopted by Lenin at the Second Comintern Congress in which he envisaged deepening the struggle through a broadening of alliances. However, the 1943 resolution of the Comintern was clearly intended to keep the anti-fascist struggle within the bounds of bourgeois democracy. The sacred duty of communists, it said, 'consists in aiding by every means the military efforts of the governments of those countries'. The prospect of transformation of the anti-fascist struggle into the socialist revolution was tacitly dropped.[44] In South Africa the CPSA pointed out that 'fascists are the sworn enemies of human freedom.... The People's Alliance, led by the Soviet Union, Britain, China and the USA includes all the forces that stand on the side of freedom.'[45] It called for 'all-out production for victory'. The signal given by the Comintern was thus to subordinate socialist struggle to the preservation of the nucleus of imperialist capitalism, clearing the way to 'the future organisation of a companionship of nations based upon their equality.'[46] The illusion given was that these states, by virtue of being at war with their capitalist rivals alongside the Soviet Union, really intended to build an ideal post-war world. But, according to Claudin,

> The leaders of capitalism were to show themselves able to profit by this additional allowance of moral credit granted them by the leaders of Communism, just as they were to profit skillfully from the margin of manoeuvre that was allowed them by the restriction of the aims of the Communist parties to the framework of bourgeois democracy.[47]

In exchange for the crushing of their capitalist rivals and for guarantees against revolution in the industrially developed West, the United States and Britain 'accepted' the strengthening of the Soviet state and the abolition of capitalism in the most backward part of Europe. The fundamental aim of the Soviet leaders – the division of the world into 'spheres of influence' and the consolidation of the division through compromise with the Washington government – required something more than concealing from the

NAME SLOVO (MRS.) ~~FIRST~~, H.R. GRADUATE
ADDRESS ~~17 Latona St., Kensington.~~
CHRISTIAN NAMES Heloise Ruth
NAME OF FATHER OR GUARDIAN J. First
DATE AND PLACE OF BIRTH 4.5.25 Johannesburg.
ADDRESS ~~17 Latona Street, Kensington,~~ Johannesburg. 8 Congo Rd.
LAST SCHOOL Jeppe Girls' High

MATRICULATION	CLASS	MONTH	YEAR	EXEMPTION CERTIFICATE	EXEMPTIONS	COURSE PERSUED
S.S.C.	II	Dec.	1941	Stud. 16,764		B.A. MODIFICATIONS Soc. STUDIES. Dip. Lib. (1963)

SUBJECTS FIRST YEAR 1942	RESULT	SUBJECTS SECOND YEAR 1943	RESULT	SUBJECTS THIRD YEAR 1944	RESULT
English	70	SOCIOLOGY. I.	70	SOC. ANTHROP. II. 4th	66
History	60	SOCIAL ECONOMICS. I.	59	DEMOG. & SOC. BIOLOGY. 3rd	60
Afrikaans	43	ELEMENTS OF STATISTICS	59	PROBLEMS. OF PHYSIOLOGY. 2nd	53
Bantu Zulu I.	49	SOC. ANTHROPOLOGY. I.	70	SOCIAL PSYCHOLOGY. II 3rd	52
French	32	SOCIAL LEGISLATION	61	ECON. HIST. OF S.A. 2nd	71
				TH. & PRAC. OF SOC. WORK. I. 3rd	56

FOURTH YEAR 1945		FIFTH YEAR 1946		1959 (Occasional)
Sociology II 4th		Native Administration	72	Native Admin. II
Preventive Medicine 3rd	abs	4th Practice of Soc. Work.	61	Cancelled 27-6-59
Native Law I 2nd.	ab.	Elements of Prev. Med	60	
Social CaseWork II 4th		Sociology II	56	
		FLAT 3-51A COMPAYNE GARDENS, LONDON N.W.6		[illegible] 46-1688

NAME First, H.R. (MRS. SLOVO) ADDRESS ~~17 Latona St. Kensington. JHB.~~

Ruth's BA report card from Witwatersrand University, 1941.

peoples the true aims pursued by imperialist powers. It required endorsing the credibility of the West's apparent aims, since this was the only way in which the apparent aims of the USSR in Eastern Europe could be made more credible.[48] Communist gains were made in China, Vietnam and Yugoslavia. But in France and Italy, as a result of compromises, the revolution did not develop beyond the stage of potentiality. It was crushed in Greece and was unable to re-emerge in Spain. The 'independent' revolution in Yugoslavia was also attacked by Stalin and the Communist Party in the United States was disbanded. In Indonesia, Burma, Malaya and the Phillipines communist parties embarked on armed struggle without sufficient preparation and, weakened by earlier subservience to the national bourgeoisie, were isolated or crushed. The Communist Party of India was shaken by fierce internal struggles and was weakened, as was the Japanese Party for similar reasons. In South Africa the good fortunes of the CPSA went into reverse after the war. The government lost no time in turning Western anti-communist rhetoric to its own aims. While Western parties concentrated on links with social democrats, their counterparts in the Third World focused on local nationalist movements to the detriment of worker and popular struggles.

So by 1947 the post-Nazi world was divided into two rapidly militarising blocs. The Allies, whom five years of Soviet propaganda had presented as collaborators in building a new, just, democratic and peaceful world were now cast as rapacious imperialists. The reasons for this need some consideration. The period of alliances among the anti-Nazi powers was, as previously indicated, reflected in a limitation of the action of the popular masses. This was reinforced by the depiction of Western capitalist allies as defenders of democracy and the enemies of fascism. Given the endorsement of this image by Stalin, for national parties to use the war to consolidate their bases by aggressive attacks on imperialism would have demanded a break from Moscow. Tito attempted to do just this and was demonised by Stalin.

However, the defeat of fascism was followed, inevitably, by a new surge of revolutionary consciousness and struggle in both capitalist metropolitan countries and their colonies. What, after all, had the war been fought for if not for freedom? Even under the restraint of Stalin's policy – which most communist parties followed – this new movement had enough momentum to alarm the bourgeoisie everywhere and to drive them to unite across national and colonial contradictions in order to bar the way to revolutionary threat. But while Soviet restraint was insufficient to prevent the rising spirit of democratic forces in the Third World, it was enough to dampen this spirit to the extent that it was powerless in the face of the anti-Soviet agitation which swept the West shortly after the war. In general, it could be said that the Soviet leaders were incapable of giving the war against Germany a revolutionary or socialist character. The establishment of the Cominform in 1947 marked the end of East-West détente.[49] A year later the Soviet Union blockaded access to Berlin and the Cold War began to dominate world politics.

In South Africa, the CPSA continued to be involved in popular action. In April in 1943 the Party organised an anti-pass meeting which, led by Moses Kotane, brought out between 15 000 and 20 000 protesters in the streets of Johannesburg. The gathering was to be the precursor to a national campaign to obtain a million signatures which would be presented to the government on a 'National Anti-Pass Demonstration Day'. But the campaign collapsed. The working committee could not muster a quorum, far fewer than a million signatures were collected, and when demonstrators gathered outside Parliament in June 1945, the leaders were arrested and charged with leading an unlawful procession. Attempts to revive the campaign in 1946 failed.[50]

Also in 1943, the Party gave support to a bus boycott in Alexandra which followed an increase in fares. The banning of a mass march to the city centre simply hardened the residents resolve to walk to work and the boycott finally ended in a victory for residents. A year later, however, when the leader of the burgeoning Orlando squatter movements, James Sofasonke Mpanza, sought allies in the establishment of a civic body, the Party refused and actively discouraged the setting up of camps.[51] The CPSA was later to reverse its policy on squatting and Party members were involved in the establishment of 'Tobruk' camp and also organised the squat of an Alexandra sub-group. It was also instrumental in the establishment of a Joint Shanty Towns Coordinating Committee but this came too late, and within six months most squatter settlements had been moved. Although the Party was involved in popular action in the townships in the immediate post-war period and had some notable successes, it found itself rapidly becoming isolated from 'official' politics.[52] When the Indian Passive Resistance campaign of June 1946 was followed by a strike of 100 000 miners in August, the Smuts government decided to break the Party. Neither confrontation was organised by the CPSA but both had Party support.

The strike was smashed by brutal police action and the African Mine Workers Union was nearly destroyed by the arrests and prosecutions which followed. At least nine people were reported to have died and more than a thousand injured. It was generally conceded that the strike had failed.[53] 'The strike', said Smuts, 'was not caused by legitimate grievances but by agitators' who were 'trying to lead the natives and the country to destruction.'[54] In Johannesburg 52 people, including the entire Johannesburg District Party Committee, were accused in a mass conspiracy trial under the Riotous Assemblies Act. 'In taking this action', said a CPSA statement, 'the Authorities are seeking to put the Communist Party and its policy on trial.'[55]

The charge of sedition was later dropped and the accused were fined after pleading guilty to assisting the strike. However the government was not content to let matters rest there. After further country-wide police raids the Central Executive Committee of the Party was arrested on charges of sedition.[56] The charges were flimsy, the evidence even more so. The indictment was quashed and the accused were re-arrested in court while a new charge and indictment were framed.[57] The proceedings dragged on for more than two years, and the charge was finally dropped after the Nationalist Party came to power in 1948.

However the trial set the climate within which the Suppression of Communism Act of 1950 was framed. In addition, the strike and its aftermath weakened and demoralised workers and their organisations, leading them to play a subordinate role in the struggle against the state in the 1950s. The strike had been badly conceived, hastily put together and brutally repressed. The defeat of the mineworkers was unconditional and no concessions were made by the government or the mines. Speaking about the demoralisation which followed, miner Mpotsongo Mde said 'they never struck again. They were still waiting for that money. They never spoke about it among themselves in later years – nobody ever talked about it. They had been defeated.'[58] The strike coincided with post-war worker redundancies and a tightening of pass and liquor laws. Frustration around these issues was expressed in a series of unorganised protests and riots around the country in the late 1940s. The people lacked strong organisation, there were few indications that the working-class movement had learned to coordinate workplace action with township solidarity. The slogans of the activists were couched in the language of national liberation and not worker solidarity.[59]

By the late 1940s the Party was fighting on all fronts. In the last three years of the decade it had faced an emergency following the mineworkers' strike, raids by police on its offices and those of *The Guardian*, the trial of leading members after the strike, the arraignment of eight members of the Central Committee on a charge of sedition, an election in which it was cast as the root of all evil and a Bill to outlaw communism. At its national conference in January 1950 its predictions couldn't have been more wrong. The world picture, said national chairman Ike Horvitch, 'was one of socialism on the ascent, capitalism on the decline.'[60] The Nationalists were 'inherently weak' and the Party was sounding a 'clear, confident call to democratic South Africans to march Forward to Freedom'. The following week *The Guardian* reported that the government was drafting an anti-communist Bill in line with those being contemplated in Canada, Australia, France, Belgium, Hindustan, Pakistan and Southern Rhodesia. 'It is evident', commented the paper, 'that under the guidance of British MIS, anti-communist measures are being coordinated throughout the Commonwealth.'[61] In the United States, under pressure from the Un-American Affairs Committee, eleven leaders of the American Communist Party had been imprisoned a few months earlier.

'Unable to succeed in any legal charge against our Party,' said a CPSA statement on the Bill, 'the Government is now attempting to suppress our demand for democracy not only by illegalising our Party, but ultimately any organisation which preaches for equality against apartheid.'[62] The Nationalist government, claiming it had details of an imminent communist coup, pushed the Bill through its committee stages with little opposition. Communism, it said 'was a war against Western civilization and against Christianity itself.'[63] *The Star* newspaper, in reporting the allegation, published extracts from Party documents supporting the government's claim and added its own anti-communist comments under the guise of news. However, despite mass protests, it became clear that the Bill would become law, and at a hastily convened meeting of the Central Committee on June 20 the Party voted to disband.[64] Only two members, Michael Harmel and Bill Andrews, voted against the motion.

In most studies covering the period, the dissolution has been presented as a consensual act necessitated by the impending Suppression of Communism Act.[65] The emergence of the South African Communist Party three years later has been portrayed as the reconstitution of the old party with a new name. However interviews with activists have suggested otherwise, and general Party membership was left confused and without direction at the moment the newly-invigorated ANC and Indian Congress were mobilising for the Defiance Campaign. One Party member remembers that 'when the Party was declared illegal, none of us knew what it meant – whether we were going to be picked up and put in concentration camps, we had visions of Nazi Germany.'[66]

Before and shortly after the meeting, the General Secretary, Moses Kotane, visited branches in Port Elizabeth, East London, Durban, East Rand, Johannesburg and Pretoria where the decision was 'unanimously endorsed.'[67] There seem to have been two reasons for the ready acceptance. The first was that many communists thought it was a ruse and that the Party had plans to go underground. Transvaal Party member Hilda Watts recalled that 'we thought ... what they intended was officially above-ground to say the Party had been dissolved, whereas actually it would continue.'[68] According to Party district secretary Rusty Bernstein:

> I think the majority of the rank and file, certainly in the Transvaal, didn't believe that the thing was serious. That's why at a general meeting in Johannesburg where the decision was explained to us by Kotane, we hardly discussed it. Nobody opposed it.... People thought, this is a con-job. We're going to con the government into thinking we're doing something which we're not doing.[69]

So the overwhelming feeling among Party members was that dissolution was a deception, and would be followed by the immediate appearance of the Party underground.[70] Its failure to appear immediately led to anger and confusion, especially in the Transvaal where the SACP was to emerge three years later. According to Rusty Bernstein, 'more than half of the Central Committee were Capetonians ... and the Cape Central Committee dissolved the Party.'[71] His wife, Hilda, remembered that 'the ones who took the decision on the Central Committee intended that it should be disbanded. We waited to be contacted to be told "you're appointed to such-and-such a group," and "you're going to work with so-and-so" ... we were sort of innocent or naive or stupid members of the Party.'[72] A second reason for the unquestioned dissolution of the Party was, according to Joe Slovo, that

> when it came to the push, (members) were not as deeply prepared for the sacrifice as the committed revolutionaries of the early days. The result was that, when it came to the crunch and we were faced with illegality, a great portion just fell away because they weren't ready for that. They weren't the old kind of Bolsheviks, you know.[73]

To operate under illegal conditions, a completely new approach was required and many existing members were not considered capable of operating under the new restrictions:

> I thought: there are a number of people around here who I wouldn't like to have around my feet when I'm starting to get the Party organised on an illegal basis with all the risks that entailed. To have to sort of fool around with this business ... it wasn't going to work. You couldn't take the apparatus we had at that stage and take it underground.[74]

Announcing the dissolution in parliament, communist MP Sam Kahn was at his rhetorical best:

> After this Bill will come the concentration camps; after this Bill will come Belsen and Buchenwald ... (Interruptions) ... and all the sadistic bestialities for which their Nazi soulmates were responsible in Germany. In the name of this Bill will come the extermination of people on the vast scale that horrified, shocked and revolted the whole civilized world.
> The Minister of Transport: Are you talking about Siberia?
> Mr Kahn: I am talking about your black Nazi heart![75]

Three weeks later the Bill became The Suppression of Communism Act, and the witch-hunt of Party members began. Communists 'named' by the government included Ruth First, Joe Slovo and Ruth's parents. Trials for contravention of the Act began the following year. Gradually Party members had to accept that the CPSA had ceased to exist.

Re-orientation

Politically, Ruth's parents were transfixed by events in the Soviet Union and were to remain so for their entire lives. Ruth, however, was to shift her attention from Moscow to Africa and was to develop an extreme distaste for Stalinist practices. Her scepticism of the Moscow line may have developed over the years, but two events were to harden its edge – the anti-Tito show trials and Kruschev's denunciation of Stalin during the 20th Congress of the CCP in 1956. At the same time she was being increasingly influenced by members of the ANC Youth League, a number of whom had been fellow students at university.

At the end of 1946, right after her final examinations, Ruth had left with Harold Wolpe to attend the founding conference of the World Federation of Democratic Youth in London. From there they traveled on to Prague for the conference of the International Union of Students. This was followed by a tour of France, Italy, Hungary and Yugoslavia.[76] In Yugoslavia they 'travelled around and addressed meetings and met partisan leaders who gave us detailed accounts of the partisan struggles. It was just after the war and very dramatic!'[77]

Yugoslavia was the only country within the Cominform which Ruth had found to have successfully combined the war against fascism with a revolution against capitalism. As Yugoslav partisans under Tito began to roll back the Axis forces, liberated zones were carved out and peasants were assisted to re-establish themselves. The Popular Front in Yugoslavia, unlike the Fronts in other countries, was not a coalition of parties, but had become a mass movement with a revolutionary programme created during the war of liberation. To the young communist student from South Africa, Tito must have been a great inspiration. The events which followed on the heels of her visit would have given her considerable reasons for disquiet.

The Yugoslavs initially received Soviet assistance, but Tito had aims of his own in the Balkans which did not coincide with those of Stalin. Moreover Stalin's plans for his European outposts clashed with the Yugoslav desire to maintain national independence. The crux of the problem, however, seems to have been Tito's objection to the extensive spy network set up within all levels of Yugoslav society by the Soviet Union. Similar penetration was going on in Eastern Europe but there the communist parties offered no resistance. In Belgrade, however, the party objected strongly to the spies, and further provoked Stalin by 'illegally' giving assistance to Greek communists fighting American troops, thereby risking a dispute between Moscow and Washington.

Stalin's first attempt to bring Belgrade into line was to block the renewal of a trade agreement between the two countries. He withdrew all Soviet military advisers and demanded the right of Soviet 'experts' to obtain 'information' freely.[78] In April 1948 the Yugoslav Central Committee ordered the removal of Soviet intelligence personnel from the country and began arresting Soviet agents. A war of words followed in which Stalin became increasingly insulting. But Tito, a survivor of the terrible Stalinist purges of the 1930s, held his ground and made public all correspondence on the matter. By June the war of insults had escalated, with Yugoslavia was being labeled as 'nationalist, Bukharinist, Menshevik, Trotskyist and anti-Soviet.'[79] Stalin then tried to engineer a *coup d'etat* against Tito but failed. The plotters were captured and tried.

The Yugoslavian affair was Stalin's first historic defeat. It was the first time that one of the main communist parties had defied his threats and orders. In retaliation, Moscow began a series of anti-Titoist show trials in Eastern Europe which were a mixture of high farce and pure terror. They began with the public trial of Laszlo Rajk, a stalwart member of the Hungarian Communist Party, which opened in Budapest on June 15 1949. The trial, which was widely reported in *The Guardian*, unfolded without a hitch. The accused 'admitted' his crimes, which included being a pro-American Nazi agent. He claimed that the Gestapo had been behind the Yugoslav revolution. Rajk was sentenced to death and hanged with three of his fellow defendants.[80] *The Guardian* concluded that, without doubt, Tito and his 'gang' were working for the Americans and that 'the Yugoslav government never wanted socialism, even immediately after liberation.'[81] Tito was lampooned in cartoons and articles. Beside a cartoon of Tito in uniform 'with 33 medals on it, including a large pearl-studded affair inscribed Proletarian (Dis)Order of the Tito Double Cross, writer 'Nat Low' informed *Guardian* readers that Tito

> awakes rather grumpily, trying hard to remember details of the dream that had kept him tossing uneasily all night. Presses button at bedside, high ranking cabinet member comes in carrying bedroom slippers.
> Cabinet Member (fervently): Heil Tito!
> Tito (feeling better already): Heil!
> Cabinet member kneels, kisses Tito's feet. Tito strokes cabinet member's head gently.[82]

After the 1949 Cominform report, the great purge spread throughout the communist parties of the People's Democracies, sucking in hundreds of well-known leaders and a huge mass of ordinary cadre. Knowledge of the extent of the purges is still fragmentary, but it has been estimated that between 1948 and 1952 the number of people purged was around two and a half million. Of these, between 125 000 and 250 000 were imprisoned. The number of those executed is unknown.[83] Indeed, the confessions recited by the 'Tito-possessed' communists before mounting the scaffolds or descending to the dungeons bore a remarkable resemblance to the witch trials of the Middle Ages, with their double function of explaining and conjuring away natural calamities and social evils.

Yugoslavia, however, survived and doubts began to form in the minds of many communists. Most kept silent rather than fall into the category of spies and Titoists. But the doubts remained and were reinforced by the first reports of concentration camps in the USSR. As if by way of defence, the cult of Stalin took on the tone of mystical love, with the Leader being an earthly guide to the new Jerusalem. None the less, the first breach in the Stalinist monolith made by the Yugoslav revolution began to widen.

In March 1953, Joseph Stalin died. Under the headline: Death of Stalin tragedy for world's peoples, *Advance* (the successor to *The Guardian*) said his death 'removed from world politics a statesman who devoted the last years of his life above all to the defence of peace.'[84] Then came the 20th Congress of the Communist Party in Moscow in 1956. In a secret report, Nikita Khruschev denounced Stalin and the personality cult which had been built around him. *New Age* political columnist Spectator simply couldn't believe it: 'It has been very widely suggested in the anti-Soviet press that the whole of Soviet policy has been changed.'[85] Two weeks later Spectator slammed 'imperialist' critics:

> So frightened do the reactionaries appear to have been by the atmosphere of strength and self-assurance shown at the 20th Congress of the Soviet Communist Party ... that they have now set up an almost unprecedented smoke-screen to hide what actually happened. They are putting out phantasies which are capable of belief only by a public brought up on a diet of American horror comics ....
>
> It is an insult to the intelligence of the readers of the capitalist Press ... to foist on them the absurd speech Kruschov (sic) is alleged to have made in secret.[86]

It was, however, true. At a closed session of the 20th Congress, Khruschev had delivered a stinging attack on Stalin:

> After Stalin's death the Central Committee of the party began to implement a policy of explaining concisely and consistently that it is impermissible and foreign to the spirit of Marxism-Leninism to elevate one person, to transform him into a superhuman possessing supernatural characteristics, akin to those of a god.[87]

Suddenly communists were confronted with the possibility that Moscow had been able to impose dogmas and models on the world movement and to subordinate local parties to its national policy. It had been able to do this because, in the eyes of revolutionaries throughout the world, it was the first embodiment of socialism and the highest point of Marxist thought. The denunciation of Stalin as a dictator sent shock waves through communists in South Africa and many, like Spectator, refused to believe the authenticity of the secret report.[88] Many waited for confirmation from *Pravda*, which came in *New Age* on April 12. This admitted that Stalin's 'lack of personal modesty ... did serious harm to our cause'. However, the article suggested that, in part, Stalin had been misled by the head of the secret police, 'that inveterate agent of imperialism ... Beria'. Later, however, Spectator was to observe that 'there have been terrible errors and terrible barbarities in the building of (the) new world.'[89] Joe Slovo remembered that 'a lot of people, even up until 1980, didn't believe it. But I think this was the crunch point. Both Ruth and I, Ruth perhaps more than me, felt we'd been had.[90] In a pamphlet called *Has Socialism Failed*, Slovo was to say that, looking back, it was 'not enough merely to engage in the self-pitying cry, "we were misled;" we should rather ask why so many communists allowed themselves to become so blinded for so long ... . We cannot disclaim our share of the responsibility for the spread of the personality cult and a mechanical embrace of Soviet domestic and foreign policies, some of which discredited the cause of socialism. We kept silent for too long after the 1956 Khruschev revelations ... . Suffice it to say that the strength of this conformism lay, partly, in an ideological conviction that those whom history had appointed as custodians of humankind's communist future seemed to be building on the foundations prepared by the founding fathers of Marxism. And there was not enough classical Marxist theory about the nature of the transition period to provide a detailed guide to the future'.[91]

But in 1956 more was to follow. It had been possible to see the Secret Report as an imperfect self-criticism which could perhaps open a way for a regeneration of the movement. Perhaps it had left untouched the 'socialist essence' of the regime and the scientific essence of its 'Marxism'. But in October 1956 Soviet troops were called in to put down a popular uprising in Hungary. In Poland three months earlier, between 500 and 600 people, mainly students, had been arrested following a popular demonstration. In Budapest revelations in the Secret Report had coincided with the Nagy government's attempts to democratise Hungarian political life. After a brief withdrawal from the city, the troops in tanks re-entered Budapest in November and the 'Hungarian spring' was over. Despite claims from Moscow that its troops were putting down a 'fascist putsch by counter-revolutionary forces'[92] even Spectator in *New Age* was uneasy: 'Making the maximum allowance for lies and hysteria, the hard facts must remain hard for progressives to take. There has been a large-scale revolt against a people's democratic government ... the sacrifices called for (from the people) were too great, the limitations on freedom out of all proportions to the need.'[93]

These multiple shock-waves from the north were not lost on more sensitive communists in South Africa. They were to loosen the bonds to Moscow and cause Party theorists to return to Lenin in an attempt to deal with their illegality and with the growing strength of the African nationalist movement. It was in this direction that the younger communists like Ruth and Joe were to devote their energies. Their efforts, in combination with African, Coloured and Indian activists, were to lead to the formation of the Congress Alliance.

Notes

1 First 1988, p116.

2 Information derived from University of Witwatersrand student records.

3 Interview with Ismael Meer, 1988.

4 Meer, ibid.

5 On the way to the flat one night Meer and Mandela jumped onto a bus. Although Indians were allowed on the busses, African were not unless accompanied by a white. Meer was charged with 'illegally transporting a Native on a public bus.' He was defended in court by Bram Fischer. Meer interview, ibid.

6 Berman interview, op cit.

7 Interview with Harold Wolpe, 1992.

8 Berman, op cit.

9 Benson: *The struggle for a birthright*,1985 ed, p96.

10 Ibid.

11 Meer, op cit.

12 Meer was arrested for this, and was again defended in court by Bram Fischer who had also been involved in the raids. Fischer offered to recuse himself after a shopkeeper told the court he saw the lawyer 'walking around with two boxes of shorts from my shop'. The magistrate refused and Meer was found not guilty. Meer interview, op cit.

13 Wolpe, op cit.

14 Ibid.

15 The power of the Comintern exercised over the CPSA remains to be fully documented, but it is not appropriate to do so here. Just as the Bolshevik party had been the single party of the revolutionaries of every nationality in the Russian empire, so the Comintern was organised as the 'one world party' of revolutionaries of all lands. Its permanent leading organ, the Executive Committee (ECCI), was endowed with extraordinary powers. Its directives had immediate 'force of law' for all national sections. It could expel members of groups belonging to any country, or entire national sections. It could change the

leadership of a national section, even against the will of the majority of its members. From top to bottom, an iron discipline and a most rigorous centralisation were established. From a far-away centre installed in the beleaguered fortress of 'socialism in a single country', decisions were promulgated on all the details of the political situation in every country, the tactics to be followed were laid down, and party leaders confirmed or replaced in accordance with their willingness to apply the policy prescribed by the ECCI. The effect, according to Spanish Marxist Fernando Claudin, was to 'shut the doors of the Comintern to ... many of the best cadres of the movement, inspired by sincere revolutionary feeling.' At the same time, numerous elements who had no connection with the masses, and for whom it was therefore easier to declare war on the traditional organisations, were able to stand forth as 'good Communists' by the mere fact of showing neophytes' zeal in relation to the new catechism. See Claudin, 1975 p108.

16 Roux 's biography of SP Bunting is an exception.

17 Claudin, op cit, p73.

18 Interview with Apollon Davidson, 1991.

19 Cope 1943, p332.

20 Ibid, p332.

21 J Morkel: The war in South Africa, March 23 1940. This is probably a pseudonym.

22 Alan Brooks 1967, *From class struggle to national liberation: the CPSA, 1940 to 1950.*

23 *Inkululeko* September 1940.

24 *The Guardian*, June 26 1941.

25 Hirson, op cit p88.

26 Bunting: *Moses Kotane*, p107.

27 Bunting, 1975, p113.

28 June 5 1943.

29 Between April 1941 and December 1943 Party membership increased from 400 to 1 500. Between 1940 and 1943 *The Guardian's* circulation rose from 12 000 to 42 000. Simons & Simons, op cit pp538.

30 Lodge, 1983 p2.

31 Party candidates polled 6 800 votes between them. Simons & Simons, op cit, p538 and Harmel, op cit, p72.

32 CPSA 1944: Report of the Central Committee. *Freedom* Vol. 2, No.5, January, pp6-13.

33 Burns, 1987, p41.

34 A pamphlet: *South Africans awake! Our country is in danger*. (Author's collection). It is probable that Ruth, by then secretary of the YCL, was elected onto this Council but no documentary evidence of this can be found.

35 The Guardian, 23.5.44.

36 First, 1965, p117.

37 Ibid. p116.

38 Ibid, p117/8.

39 Berman, op cit.

40 Berman, ibid.

41 Ibid.

42 Dissolution of the Comintern – Statement by the Central Committee of the Communist Party of South Africa', June 3 1943, in *SA Communists Speak*, 1981 p180.

43 W Z Foster: *A history of the Three Internationals*, International Publishers, New York, 1955 p439.

44 Claudin, op cit p29.

45 'Arm the people'. CPSA pamphlet (Johannesburg) 1943. In Harmel, op cit, p119.

46 Claudin, op cit, p30.

47 Ibid, p30.

48 Ibid, p30.

49 The 'red peril' also was an excellent ideological excuse for uniting the West under American control.

50 Hirson 1990, p90.

51 Ibid. p150.

52 Ibid. p161 and Sapire: 'Political mobilisation in Brakpan in the 1950s.'

53 Simons & Simons, 1983, p576.

54 Ibid, p577.

55 *The Guardian*, 28.11.46.

56 A curtain-raiser to the 1956 Treason Trial.

57 Harmel, 1971, p78.

58 Dunbar Moodie: 'The black miners' strike of 1946', in Hirson 1990 p187.

59 See Hirson, op cit p194.

60 *The Guardian* 12.1.50.

61 Ibid, 19.1.50.

62 Ibid,1.6.50.

63 *The Star* 14.6.50.

64 At the time there were about 2 500 members, according to Edwin S Munger in *African Field Reports* 1952-61. Munger was an American academic and was accused by *The Guardian* of being a member of the CIA. He produced an extremely subjective report on the Communist Party in June 1958 for the American Universities Field Staff.

65 An exception is David Everatt's doctoral thesis *Politics of nonracialism: white opposition to apartheid 1945-60* upon which I have relied in this section.

66 Rowley Arenstein in Everatt, 1990, p90.

67 Letter signed by Kotane dated June 24, 1950. Treason Trial Document MK35 Ec 09.

68 Watts interview, 1988.

69 Bernstein interview, 1988.

70 Interviews with Watts, Bernstein, Kodesh, Arenstein, Heymann, Turok, Berman, Sisulu, Forman.

71 Bernstein interview, op cit.

72 Watts interview, op cit.

73 Joe Slovo interview, September 1991.

74 Fred Carneson, interview 1988.

75 The Guardian 22.6.50.

76 *The Guardian*, January 1947 and Wolpe interview, op cit.

77 Wolpe, Ibid.

78 Claudin, op cit, p496.

79 Ibid, p503.

80 In 1956, after Stalin's death, the Hungarian authorities admitted that the trial had been a farce and Rajk was 'rehabilitated'. After this confession by the authorities in Hungary, 300 000 workers, students and intellectuals marched through the streets of Budapest in a national tribute and demanded the removal of a system which allowed the staging of such criminal farces. Soon afterwards, Russian tanks went into action to prop up Hungary's crumbling communist government.

81 *The Guardian* 22.10.49.

82 *The Guardian* 22.12.49.

83 Figures are from F Fetjo: *Histoire des democraties popularies*, quoted in Claudin p527.

84 *Advance* 12.3.53.

85 *New Age*, 8.3.56. Spectator was probably Brian Bunting.

86 *New Age* 22.3.56.

87 Secret report to the 20th Party Congress of the CPSU. In Tariq Ali: *The Stalinist Legacy*, Penguin, Middlesex, 1984 p221. What was particularly galling for communist parties throughout the world was that the report was first published in the *New York Times*, before they had access to it.

88 A good few do still not believe the extent of Stalin's complicity in the excesses, and remain faithful to him to this day. Until his death in the late 1980s, for example, Party stalwart Issy Heymann remained convinced that Stalin had his hand forced by 'others': 'The people who would stand behind a man like Stalin were those people who drove him to extremes. It was enough for him to say alright, do what's got to be done, and they did what they thought had got to be done'. Interview 1988.

89 *New Age* 1.11.56.

90 Interview 1991.

91 Slovo: Has Socialism Failed? *Umsebenzi* discussion pamphlet, January 1990.

92 *New Age*, 3.1.57.

93 *New Age*, 1.11.56.

3

The Congress Alliance

We whites who embarked on protest politics side by side with the Africans, Indians and Coloureds, led a vigorously provocative life. Our consciences were healthy in a society riddled with guilts – Ruth First

The Clarion

THURSDAY, JUNE 12, 1952 — PRICE 2d.

Heroic Stand Begins Against Unjust Laws

JAIL RATHER THAN TYRANNY

JOHANNESBURG.

"WE CAN NEVER GIVE IN TO FASCISM AND WE SHALL NEVER GIVE UP THE STRUGGLE FOR FREEDOM."

With these words on their lips, four of the best-known Non-European leaders of the people — DR. YUSUF DADOO, MR. J. B. MARKS, MR. MOSES KOTANE and MR. DAVID BOPAPE — last week deliberately defied Minister Swart's Nazi ban and spoke from public platforms. Each was immediately arrested.

Refusing bail, they have spent over a week in jail.

Court proceedings under the Suppression of Communism Act started against them on Monday. Unprecedented scenes of public support and loyalty took place when they entered the dock, crowds giving the African National Congress freedom salute with calls of Africa! Africa! Africa!

Also defying the ban, Mr. MICHAEL HARMEL of the Transvaal Peace Council, was arrested last week. His case has been remanded to June 25. With Mr. E. S. (Solly) Sachs, he is the second European to resist Swart's gagging orders.

Their leaders' resistance has set the stage for the people's defiance of unjust laws campaign, beginning on June 26, barely a fortnight from now.

There has been a fresh spurt of volunteers over the past 10 days and African and Indian leaders are confident that the target of 10,000 volunteers will be more than fulfilled by June 26.

Full accounts of the arrests, together with the leaders' defy-the-ban speeches, appear on pages 4 and 5.

MR. MOSES KOTANE, former general secretary of the Communist Party of South Africa, was the first people's leader to defy Swart's ban.

Lift The Ban On The Guardian

Freedom of the Press as one of the great foundation principles of democracy was destroyed by the Nationalist Government's unjust and tyrannical ban on the 15 year-old workers' paper. But The Guardian will reappear when the Malan Government is swept out and Press Freedom re-established.

MR. J. B. MARKS, president of the Transvaal African National Congress. "I am prepared to sacrifice for true democracy."

Dr. Yusuf Dadoo, president of the South African Indian Congress, photographed just prior to his arrest after his stirring speech in the Fordsburg cinema.

"The prohibitions are intolerable," said MR. MICHAEL HARMEL, publicly defying the ban last week.

ON OTHER PAGES

David Bopape, Transvaal Secretary of the African National Congress, speaks at the meeting in the Fordsburg cinema last week, in defiance of Swart's ban. Shortly after this picture was taken, he was arrested for contravening the Suppression of Communism Act.

The Clarion *announces the beginning of the Defiance Campaign (June 12 1952).*

In 1945, when she was secretary of the Progressive Youth Council, Ruth sent a letter to the ANC Youth League (ANCYL) inviting them to affiliate to the Council.[1] The League's reply was a reflection of the uncompromising Africanist perspective of its inception a year earlier:

> We fear that there is a yawning gulf between your policy or philosophic outlook and ours. We are devoting our energies to the preparation for the greatest national struggle of all time, the struggle for national liberation.[2]

A year later Youth League president Anton Lembede spelled out the policy of the ANCYL:

> The history of modern times is the history of nationalism .... Africa is a blackman's country .... Africans are one.... The leader of the Africans will come out of their own loins .... The divine destiny of the African people is national freedom .... After national freedom, then socialism .... Our motto: Freedom in our lifetime.[3]

These sentiments were to culminate in a Programme of Action adopted by the ANC in 1949 and were to change that organisation completely. The Programme claimed for Africans the right to self determination and committed Congress to a struggle for national liberation. It pledged 'to employ the following weapons: immediate and active boycott, strike, civil disobedience, non-cooperation and such other methods as may bring about the accomplishment and realisation of our aspirations.'[4]

When the ANCYL was formed, it saw its immediate task as the need 'to overhaul the machinery of the ANC from within.'[5] In calling for the development of African nationalism as a mobilising force sufficient to challenge the status quo, the Youth League came to see both liberalism and communism as competing ideologies.[6] On two occasions, in 1945 and 1947, the League sought unsuccessfully to have Party members thrown out of the ANC. This conflict, and its resolution, was to have a profound effect on the Communist Party when it re-formed in 1953. According to historian David Everatt, this conflict operated on two levels. Firstly, the ANCYL opposed the Party's calls for a Popular Front because this position attempted to unite workers of all races in a mass struggle against discrimination. According to the League, co-operation between oppressed groups was only acceptable when the racial groups were organised multi-racially. And secondly, both the ANCYL and the Party sought to influence the development of the ANC at a time of growing black mobilization.[7] There were also points of similarity in both programmes, including Lembede's argument: 'After national freedom, then socialism'. This was essentially the Party's policy of two-stage revolution formulated back in 1928 by the Comintern. Implicit in the 1928 slogan was the notion that black South Africans were colonially oppressed. At the time the idea of 'internal' colonialism was hinted at by CPSA member Eddy Roux:

> Here we have a white bourgeoisie and a white aristocracy of labour living in the same country together with an exploited colonial peasantry. Here the participation of the workers of the ruling class in the exploitation of the colonial workers is very apparent ... the exploitation occurs within the confines of a single country ... .[8]

The Clarion

NORTHERN THURSDAY, JUNE 26, 1952 PRICE 2d.

CAMPAIGN OF DEFIANCE UNDER WAY

THOUSANDS READY TO BREAK UNJUST LAWS

Volunteer's Pledge

JOHANNESBURG.

Each volunteer who takes part in the Defiance of Unjust Laws campaign is required to take the following pledge:

"I, the undersigned Volunteer of the National Volunteer Corps, do hereby solemnly pledge and bind myself to serve my country and my people in accordance with the directives of the National Volunteer Corps and participate fully and without reservations to the best of my ability in the campaign for the Defiance of Unjust Laws.

"I shall obey the orders of my leader under whom I shall be placed and strictly abide by the rules and regulations of the National Volunteer Corps framed from time to time. It shall be my duty to keep myself physically, mentally and morally fit."

IN THIS ISSUE

JOHANNESBURG.

TODAY, Thursday, June 26, is the first day of defiance in the campaign against unjust laws, and thus the opening of the greatest resistance movement against oppression this country has yet seen.

Under the direction of the National Action Committee of the African National Congress, and the South African Indian Congress, disciplined batches of African, Indian and Coloured volunteers are openly to defy apartheid regulations, permit and curfew regulations, and all restrictions against freedom of movement. The hated pass laws, "the chains of the people" in the words of the general secretary of the African National Congress, Mr. W. M. Sisulu, will be among the main laws to come under attack by the people.

Acts of defiance are to be committed by volunteers in Johannesburg and on the Reef, in Cape Town and Worcester, in Port Elizabeth, East London, Uitenhage, and other centres in South Africa.

During the court proceedings against Dadoo, Kotane, Marks and Bopape last week large crowds of their supporters gathered round the Johannesburg Magistrate's Court to demonstrate against their arrest. This group of African supporters from Alexandra Township was forbidden to march in procession in the court vicinity. A force of police ordered them to disperse. Here Mr. A. Kathrada, president of the Transvaal Indian Youth Congress, is seen addressing the crowd, which later re-assembled for a meeting on a vacant plot near the Magistrate's Court.

The volunteers, who are coming forward in their thousands in all centres, include working men and women, well-known clergymen, professional men, among them doctors, lawyers, and teachers, university students, traders, trade unionists and members of youth organisations.

The campaign will be a sustained struggle and will culminate in the final victory of the masses," Dr. J. L. Z. Njongwe, Cape Provincial president of the African National Congress, told The Clarion last week.

Dr. Njongwe said: "We do not expect victory within a week or a month. The people are ready for action, and prepared for the struggle. We will in the first instance use only small numbers of volunteers, but the numbers will increase as the campaign gains momentum, until finally it becomes mass action, when victory is certain."

CALL FOR HELP

Dr. Njongwe called upon all Non-Europeans and progressive Europeans to give their maximum support to the families of the volunteers, and also to help the leaders in their efforts to see that meetings are conducted in an orderly manner.

"All those present at the arrest of volunteers must be

(Continued on page 8)

Ngwevela Defies Swart's Ban

Cape Town's Volunteer No. 1 in the defiance of unjust laws campaign went into action on Monday night. He is Mr. J. N. Ngwevela, president of the Cape Western Region of the African National Congress, who was recently ordered by the Minister of Justice to resign from all political organisations and not to attend political meetings.

On Monday night, at a well-attended meeting in the Salt River Railway Institute, Mr. Ngwevela defied the Minister's ban. Now he is in jail awaiting trial for contravening the Suppression of Communism Act. His case will be heard on July 10.

Moses Kotane appeared in court again last week on a charge, under the Suppression of Communism Act, of defying an order banning him from attending public gatherings. This picture of him in the dock of the court was taken during a brief adjournment.

The Clarion *was a key organising medium and kept track of the Defiance Campaign Against Unjust Laws (June 26 1952).*

Both organisations also called for the radicalisation of the ANC leadership and the development of a mass base as preconditions for a successful national revolution. In many ways the ideas of the Youth League were in harmony with younger members of the Communist Party with whom they were socially connected, and gradually the ANCYL and the CPSA began moving closer together. In 1947 the League endorsed the 'Doctor's Pact' between the ANC and the Transvaal and Natal Indian Congresses. This Pact accepted 'the urgency of co-operation between the non-European peoples and other democratic forces for the attainment of basic human rights.'[9] In 1948 the Transvaal branches of the ANC, CPSA, African People's Organisation and the Transvaal Indian Congress proposed a People's Assembly for Votes for All. Youth League agitation prevented the ANC from taking part, the League's argument being that moves towards non-racialism – stressing class above race – would retard the emergence of a strong ANC.

Clashes over the Assembly and other initiatives led to intense debates in the Transvaal within the ANCYL and the CPSA, while Party members such as Marks, Bopape, Tloome and Dadoo worked within the Congress movement to radicalise the ANC and South African Indian Congress (SAIC). The result was that in Johannesburg, Party members like Ruth First found themselves increasingly debating with people engaged in nationalist rather than class politics, whereas in Cape Town the central issue remained the class struggle.[10] Also, as the influence of the League began to increase and its leaders were voted into top ANC positions, the fortunes of the Party began to wane amid Cold War sabre-rattling and the ascent of the National Party.

After the dissolution of the Party in 1950 and the ascent of Youth Leaguers such as Mandela, Tambo and Sisulu in the ANC, the language of leading members of the ANCYL began to resemble that of the CPSA. When the Party dissolved, individual black communists worked increasingly with the ANC, and across the country former CPSA members began a series of debates which were to resolve the ANCYL/CPSA clash in the League's favour. These debates, in which Ruth was intimately involved, were to re-conceptualise the Party's relationship with the ANC and form the basis of a long and fruitful association.

Internal colonialism

In its final report in 1950, the Central Committee of the CPSA tentatively put forward a notion that South Africa combined 'the characteristic of both an imperialist state and a colony within a single, indivisible, geographical, political and economic entity.'[11] Communists, said the report, 'have always regarded the colonial system as a special form of national oppression'. Whereas in colonies without a large settler population a rise in national demands tended to coincide with the ascent to power of a national bourgeoisie, in South Africa the black bourgeoisie was 'small, pinned down in the poorest areas, forced to use subterfuge and illegalities to evade discriminating laws, starved of capital and exposed to constant insecurity. It is not a class that could provide effective militant leadership.'[12]

Indeed leaders of national organisations, with few exceptions, were 'not a bourgeoisie, but teachers, church ministers and professional men.'[13] The report was critical of ANC leadership but concluded, nonetheless, that communists should work with the national movement.

This debate was stalled by the dissolution of the Party, but was re-started in the wake of the 1952 Defiance Campaign. This Campaign was successful in terms of boosting ANC membership, and the growing strength of the national movement demanded a re-evaluation by the white left. In October 1952 the Campaign's Volunteer-in-Chief, Nelson Mandela, called on whites to support the campaign and not to unite in opposition to it. If they did so, he said, they would be 'digging their own grave' by turning the whole movement 'into a racial front with disastrous consequences for all.'[14]

The following month Ruth attended a meeting in Darragh Hall in Johannesburg which had been organised in response to Mandela's call. About 300 whites attended, mainly liberals and former CPSA members. The meeting was addressed by Oliver Tambo and Yusuf Cachalia, who called for a progressive white grouping to co-operate with the Congress movement.[15] The meeting marked the final parting of ways between liberals and former communists. Margaret Ballinger, acting as liberal spokesperson, rejected the call for a universal franchise as well as for a multiracial alliance. Liberals also refused to co-operate with former Party members who were present.[16] The Darragh Hall gathering was followed by three further meetings which attempted to reach a compromise that would lead to a liberal/left organisation. The failure of these meetings was followed by the formation of the Liberal Party, the Congress of Democrats (COD) and the South African Communist Party (SACP).

The Darragh Hall meeting had national implications and was followed by intense debates among the left. In Johannesburg, Durban, Port Elizabeth and Cape Town discussion forums were set up which were to provide the ideological underpinnings for both the Liberal Party and COD. Ruth was involved in the Johannesburg Discussion Club which published its first collection of papers – *Viewpoints & Perspectives* – in March 1953. The Club hoped to furnish an opportunity for 'frank theoretical discussion' which would make 'a real and lasting contribution to the struggle.'[17] In many ways, the debates were an extension of those around the Black Republic and the Popular Front.[18] However, since its inception in 1947 the Cominform had changed its mind on the forms of colonial struggle and presupposed a strong black bourgeoisie in the lead. This did not apply to South Africa, participants argued, and local communists were forced to develop indigenous theories of change.

Most participants agreed that the South African situation was 'unique'. Whites were permanently settled yet controlled a system of exploitation found in other colonial States. Furthermore, under this system, the growth of the black bourgeoisie had been frustrated. The industrial proletariat, however, exhibited little evidence of class consciousness. As elsewhere, racial discrimination had given rise to a national liberation movement, but in the absence of a black bourgeoisie, some argued, this movement was overwhelmingly working class. These factors led participants in the discussion clubs to conclude that orthodox models of resistance in colonial and semi-colonial countries did not apply to South Africa.[19]

The Clarion

SOUTHERN — THURSDAY, JULY 3, 1952 — PRICE 2d.

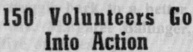

DEFIANCE CAMPAIGN UNITES ALL RACES

Mr. Walter Sisulu, general secretary of the African National Congress, climbs into the police troop carrier after his arrest at Boksburg last Thursday.

DURBAN JULY HANDICAP

Our Cape Town racing correspondent, Damon, tips:

1. MOWGLI
2. RANKLING
3. LORD LOUIS

Our Durban racing correspondent, Owen Tudor, tips:

1. MOWGLI
2. RANKLING
3. DAN

Danger: Montross Star

IN THIS ISSUE

P.E. volunteer Karabo Sello, 17 years old, an executive member of the A.N.C. Youth League, says: "As a youth I realise there is no future for us unless we, the youth, participate fully in the struggle for a better South Africa which will have a uniform law for all its citizens, irrespective of race or colour". Miss Sello went into action with the first Port Elizabeth batch last week.

150 Volunteers Go Into Action

JOHANNESBURG.

MORE THAN 150 MEN AND WOMEN OF ALL RACES TOOK PART IN THE FIRST STAGE OF THE DEFIANCE OF UNJUST LAWS CAMPAIGN LAST WEEK, AND HAVE BEEN ARRESTED.

Acts of defiance were committed in all main centres of the Union. For the first time in South African history, Africans, Indians and Coloureds went into political action side by side, under a common leadership.

IN BOKSBURG 53 Indian and African volunteers went into action under Mr. Nana Sita.

IN JOHANNESBURG 53 African volunteers defied the curfew regulations.

IN PORT ELIZABETH 30 volunteers were arrested for defying railway apartheid regulations.

IN WORCESTER nine Non-Europeans were arrested after they had entered the European queue in the Post Office.

IN DURBAN several Africans and Indians were arrested for selling "Freedom Stamps" at the mass meeting at Nicol Square on June 26.

IN CAPE TOWN Mr. Sam Kahn was arrested when he attended a meeting of the City Council after receiving a "gagging notice from the Minister of Justice.

African and Indian volunteers, led by Mr. Nana Sita, approach the gate of Boksburg location on the afternoon of June 26, to defy the permit regulations.

Among those arrested on the Rand last Thursday were four of the most prominent campaign leaders, Mr. Walter Sisulu, secretary-gener l of the African National Congress, Mr. Yusuf Cachalia, joint secretary of the South African Indi n Congress, Mr. N. R. Mandela, president of the African Congress Youth League, and Mr. H. Seperepere, Volunteer-in-Chief of the Transvaal.

In Johannesburg the charge is one of contravening the Riotous Assemblies Act by conspiring to commit publi violence. In Boksburg all the arrested men face charges under the Riotous Assemblies Act. The prosecutor refused the application of Mr. Seperepere for bail. There would probably be a preparatory examination, he told the court, and police investigations were still being conducted.

The opening of the campaign finds the Government seriously worried at the spirit of the Non-European people, and the police nervous and jittery.

(Continued on page 8)

T. U. Deputation

Govt. Made No Concessions

JOHANNESBURG.

It is clear from the deputation that interviewed the Prime Minister and Ministers Schoeman and Swart last week, that the trade unions will get no concessions from the Government on the application of the Suppression of Communism Act.

Urged to amend the Act to give trade unionists threatened with proscription the right of appeal to the courts, Mr. Schoeman said that if this were done the whole purpose of the Suppression of Communism Act would be defeated.

Both Malan and Swart seem to have left most of the talking to Schoeman, the Nationalists' labour "expert".

The advisory committee of seven trade unionists previously offered by Schoeman to advise him as to trade unionists against whom the Government wishes to take action (nicknamed the Hangman's Committee) was rejected at the recent unity conference by all but five

(Continued on page 7)

For defiers across South Africa, The Clarion *was a source of inspiraton and direction (July 3 1952).*

These debates were to throw up divisions between those who gave primacy to the national struggle, and those who held class struggle to be the sole basis for organisation. David Everatt notes that these differing analyses

> generated different understandings of the best means of pursuing class struggle – through an intimate working alliance with the Congresses, or by building an independent working class organisation which would enjoy limited cooperation with the Congresses but would retain separate structures.[20]

In the discussion which followed a lecture by Daniel Tloome at the Johannesburg Discussion Club in February 1953, Myrtle Berman argued that there were differing views on the nature of the struggle in South Africa:

> The one view holds that, in the course and realisation of the National Liberatory Struggle, an African bourgeoisie will develop, and the classic pattern will follow from then onwards. The proletariat will have gained certain political freedoms but not its economic freedom. Holders of this view claim that only when this political freedom has been achieved will the proletariat become truly aware of the nature of their still present economic disabilities and develop class consciousness.
>
> On the other hand, just because (as in the other view) there is no well developed bourgeoisie it is just as likely that the class conscious elements will assume leadership and that the interests of the bourgeoisie will be pushed aside. In this case the nature of the struggle will broaden to include economic demands ... a fundamental change in economic relationships.[21]

In an attempt to find a middle course between class and national struggle, SACP leaders developed the theory of 'colonialism of a special type'(CST) or 'internal colonialism'.[22] On a theoretical level, CST was an attempt to resolve the differences over race and class, but its political objective was to establish a rapport with former Youth Leaguers who were now in senior ANC positions and looking for a way to understand the struggle ahead. In November 1953 the Youth League signalled that it was listening. In its journal *Afrika!* the League explained that

> The path of liberation for the colonial people in the twentieth century lies in the building of powerful national movements which, united with the progressive forces in the metropolitan countries, will defeat the imperialists. South Africa is both colonial and imperial at the same time, the liberation movement having to be built in close proximity with advanced elements in the oppressor group.[23]

In January 1954, former ANCYL President Joe Matthews outlined CST in a public speech. 'South Africa', he said, 'is a colonial country. But it is not a typical colonial country.'[24] No capitalist class had emerged among the Africans who, he said, suffered 'economic exploitation as workers and labourers and oppression and humiliation as a Nation.'[25]

CST provided an ideological mid-point at which both nationalists and communists could meet. This was the result of a move away from extreme nationalism by the young lions of the ANC and support for national struggle by the new SACP. This alliance was to lead to the formation of the Congress of Democrats, of which Ruth was a key figure.

The Congress of Democrats

In 1950 the Slovo's first daughter, Shaun, was born. Gillian arrived two years later and, in 1953, Ruth found she was pregnant again. At the same time she was a full-time journalist and, before the year was out, would be elected onto the national executives of the South African Congress of Democrats and the South African Peace Council. She would also be plunged into top-secret discussions which were to give rise to the South African Communist Party. It was clearly going to be a difficult year.

On January 22 1953, Ruth was to write a report in *Advance* announcing the formation of 'a new organisation called the South African People's Congress'. In its constitution it rejected 'the preaching and practice of apartheid, segregation, white supremacy and trusteeship' and declared that 'these racialist doctrines are inimical to the future peace and prosperity of South Africa'. Nine months later the new organisation, now called the Congress of Democrats, met with members of the Springbok Legion and the Democratic League of Cape Town to form the South African Congress of Democrats (SACOD).

The new organisation was really a phoenix of the Springbok Legion which was finding organisation under its original charter increasingly difficult. The Legion started life in November 1941 to 'fight against fascism and for democracy' among South African soldiers.[26] Between its official launch in 1944 and 1948 it had a membership of about 60 000 with an annual budget of £20 000 and was a major force within the South African Defence Force both in South Africa and up north. In the year of its launch it thumped its political stamp into print with an exposé on the Broederbond called *Meet Your Enemies*. Four years later the Legion correctly assessed the impending success of the Nationalists and tried, unsuccessfully, to get Prime Minister Smuts to change his tactics in time. In many constituencies the National Party fought harder against the Springbok Legion in the 1948 election than against the ruling United Party.

After the Suppression of Communism Act, and with the unity of soldiers receding into the background, membership of the League fell off. In 1952 the Annual Report of a much-reduced League noted that it could 'look back and point to the 1951 National Conference as marking the lowest ebb of the tide. There was a frank air of defeatism abroad ... an unspoken belief ... that the government would step in and give us the finishing blow. Our membership ... was trailing in the dust.'[27] By then the membership was down to 3 000 with an active core of about 200. Then, early in 1953, the Legion began talks with the ANC and the South African Indian Council which resulted in a combined call on white democrats to form a white organisation to join the Congress Alliance. The chairman's report of the League that year said that 'in assessing the post election situation' the National Executive Commitee (NEC) was strongly moved to bring into being a new national organisation of democrats.'[28] This was echoed in a circular letter from Bram Fischer of the Johannesburg Congress of Democrats who said 'what is urgently needed today is a body of Europeans ... which will not seek to bargain or buy off the non-Europeans, but which will march with them.'[29] In an 'urgent and important' letter in June 1953 the Legion asked its members if they would agree 'not to disband ... but to reform to meet the new and urgent situation.'[30] Discussions were opened with COD and the Democratic League in Cape Town 'with a view to forming such an organisation', and out of these joint efforts a National Conference was called which set up the South African Congress of Democrats.[31] A resolution at the conference recognised 'that in the light of the present policies and scope of the three Congresses, the continuation by the Legion of its political work...is a duplication of effort and a source of diversion rather than unity.'[32] It resolved that the liabilities of the Legion 'be liquidated as soon as possible and that thereafter the National Coordinating Commitee (NCC) be empowered to dispose of any of its surplus assets in the interests of the Springbok Legion or the SA Congress of Democrats.'[33] These assets consisted of £400 and the journal *Fighting Talk*.

At the first meeting of SACOD, the Legion's vice-chairman, Pieter Beyleveld, and its secretary were elected to lead the new organization.[34] Both Ruth First and Joe Slovo were on the executive committee.

SACOD was a child of the debates around internal colonialism, but it was also the product of the shift in political balance which followed the Defiance Campaign. In his report to its first annual conference, Beyleveld said SACOD had come into being because of

> political needs which arose out of the fact that the Non-European peoples of South Africa had, through the Defiance Campaign, unequivocally staked their claim for equal and full democratic rights, thereby creating a situation which made it imperative for democratically-minded Europeans to mobilise themselves in support of a people's movement for freedom and equality.[35]

Its specific task – which was to cause problems for whites used to working in black townships – was 'white work': winning to the Congress Movement 'the militant white anti-nationalists.'[36]

There were to be many critics of the new white Congress. The appearance of whites willing to work within the Congress Movement was a direct threat to the Liberal Party, which ascribed to this the hostile criticism it received from the ANC over the Party's formation. Liberal writers were to claim that SACOD was the Communist Party in a new guise, and presented the split between liberals and radicals following the Darragh Hall meeting as communist manipulation.[37] Karis and Gerhart have described it as a communist-led 'ginger group' whose policy 'was one of adherence to the Universal Declaration of Human Rights rather than to any Marxist programme,' but whose 'emotive language ... was characteristically Communist.'[38] *The Africanist*, a cyclo-styled sheet which anticipated the formation of the Pan Africanist Congress, described 'the firm of C.O.D. (Curse Of Democracy)' as being 'directors of the African National Congress' and the product of 'the Vodka Cocktail parties of Parktown and Lower Houghton.'[39] Liberals also criticised SACOD because of the seemingly racist connotations of its policy of 'multiracialism' – the organisation of the Congresses along separate racial lines.

However, these criticisms ignore differences which emerged in the white discussion clubs which pre-dated SACOD. Former CPSA member Dr Guy Routh argued that the launch of COD should be postponed until common ground existed between liberals and radicals. He and his supporters were out-voted because there was the possibility of 'alienating the eight million non-Europeans for the sake of possibly winning some additional support from Europeans.'[40] In Cape Town the Democratic League had argued against the multiracialism inherent in the formation of SACOD. The League had been built on non-racialism and it brought the Cape arguments around class and colour into

SACOD. However, ANC leaders claimed that the black population was not yet ready for a non-racial organisation, however desirable it may be. Congressmen argued that multiracial structures 'had their roots in the realities of the situation' which placed people in politically and geographically separated ethnic communities.[41] Albie Sachs, eager to work in black areas, was told by Moses Kotane: 'You whites, you all love running to the location. You get big cheers from the people ... Water always follows the path of least resistance. We don't have access to the whites, we can't organise amongst them. That is really where you people have to be, but you always run away from that. Because it is more difficult.'[42]

Non-racialism was clearly tactical, and SACOD held to the position that 'what is good for one Congress is good for all', but this placed the organisation in an awkward position. Many former communists refused to join the organisation because of its racial position, and it was born without the support of both liberals and a 'significant number' of former CPSA members.[43] However it immediately became a full and equal member of the Congress Alliance and threw itself into preparations for the Congress of the People.

According to Tom Lodge, SACOD was to remain small but was to play an important role in the nationalist movement:

> Its members, many of them highly experienced in the fields of political and trade union organisation, with a mobility, level of affluence and education denied to most blacks, helped shape the overall development of the Congress movement. Individuals in SACOD controlled a newspaper (*New Age*) which provided Congress with consistently sympathetic publicity on a scale it had never enjoyed before.[44]

The formal acceptance of the white Congress into the Alliance was to catapult Ruth into the role of a key 'liberation publicist' for the mass movement.[45] She was called on to assist with and write SACOD's publications and particularly its news sheet *Counter Attack*, which lasted for about three years.[46] She was also to take over editorship of *Fighting Talk*, the Springbok Legion journal which was to become firmly Congress-orientated under her guidance. *New Age*, while nominally independent, supported SACOD from its inception and also clearly benefited from its hot line to Congress leaders through the political involvement of journalists like Ruth, Lionel Forman, MP Naicker, Govan Mbeki, Michael Harmel and Brian Bunting.

A second organisation which demanded Ruth's time in the early 1950s was the South African Peace Council. This Council was, in fact, part of an international strategy to halt the retreat of the communist movement in the West. The escalation of the Cold War had demanded a tactical shift in Moscow in an attempt to force the United States to return to the policies of the Yalta conference. This would enable Western communist parties to return to the policy of national unity and the parliamentary road to socialism. In 1949 Ruth attended the first World Congress of the 'Fighters for Peace' in Paris. The main task of the Fighters was to collect signatures calling for the banning of the atomic bomb, for general disarmament and as protest against the Atlantic alliance. One of its central aims was the 'relaxation of the Cold War and the arms race.'[47] By 1950 some 500 million signatures had been collected in 79 countries, among whom were 'the whole adult population' of the USSR and China.[48] For five years from 1948 the national and world peace congresses and conferences, the assemblies, meetings, festivals, appeals, petitions and resolutions for peace, the hundreds of millions of signatures followed without a break under the fighting slogan: 'Peace will not wait, peace must be won!' According to Stalin, the peace movement had the aim of 'drawing the popular masses into the struggle to preserve peace and avert a new world war'. It did not, therefore, seek to overthrow capitalism and establish socialism; it limited itself to democratic aims in the struggle to preserve peace.[49]

In South Africa the launch of the Transvaal Peace Conference in 1950 coincided with attempts by the left to re-tool its radical message in order to gain wider support. The call for peace was seen by many democrats as a way of re-mobilising the war-time support for democracy, and the global theme of peace was linked with local threats to it such as fascism within government policies, racism and colonial domination. The Council had strong links to the Friends of the Soviet Union, the pro-Soviet pressure group founded in the 1930s and headed by the Reverend Douglas Thompson. In an interview, Thompson remembered the origins of the Council:

> The need was felt for a peace committee in South Africa, in the particular circumstances of South Africa, and to fall in line with peace committees elsewhere in the world, that is, the urge for peace against the atomic bomb.... I feared the possibility of nuclear war. A meeting was called in Johannesburg ... probably by Jewish progressive groups. (The Council) was established at a conference sponsored by the Transvaal Indian Congress and the Transvaal ANC.[50]

The South African Peace Council was launched in August 1953 out of a merger between the Cape Provisional Peace Council and its Transvaal equivalent. Its slogan was a reflection of the mood of the Defiance Campaign: Peace is within your grasp: Make your effort now.[51] It first executive included Ruth First, Helen Joseph, Hilda Watts, Yusuf Cachalia and Douglas Thompson.[52]

Membership lists for the Council have not survived, but mailing lists for *Counter Attack* indicate that the news-sheet's audience was mainly black. It also sent copies to 61 trade unions as well as to the middle and upper rungs of Congress leadership. In part, the Council's attraction was linked to a decline in the activities of the various Congresses in the face of increasing repression following the Defiance Campaign. Until moves for a Congress of the People began to emerge in 1954, the collapse of the Defiance Campaign had deflated the Congress movement. But through this period the Peace Council and the Friends of the Soviet Union (FSU) continued their activities and acted as a temporary focus for democrats. Their gatherings continued to be well attended and were 'a way to continue meeting and maintaining contact in a period of quiescence, activity that was not yet regarded as threatening by the authorities, and was thus largely overlooked at the time.'[53] The Peace Movement executive included many SACOD members and the goals of the two organisations were seen as being similar.

As a result of her work in both organisations, Ruth was offered a trip to the Soviet Union and China in 1954. In a booklet she was to edit called *South Africans in the Soviet Union*, she claimed she was 'not one of those who went to the Soviet Union expecting to find paradise on earth' and noted that 'footwear struck me as still below standard ... washing machines, vacuum cleaners and even refrigerators are still in short supply.'[54] The trip to the USSR was hectic. In a letter home she wrote:

> Have seen three ballets in the last three days, including the Swan Lake tonight ... . Have seen exhibitions, libraries, museums and galleries; the new Moscow Canal; the Park of culture and rest; a 3-dimensional film during which birds appeared to be flying through the cinema ... . Caviar for lunch, sturgeon for dinner, meals at crazy hours ... the pace is terrific. But deeper impressions will have to wait until I see you.[55]

Both in China and the USSR she was shown the usual round of electricity projects, dams, canals and housing projects. But her sharp eye noted the effects of hard work on the face of the people and the sadness of some of their songs – 'lingering perhaps from their history in the days of persecution'. China clearly made a great impact on Ruth and she noted that

*Defiers in Johannesburg formed an African Volunteers Army which paraded through the streets, closely monitored by the police (*Rand Daily Mail*, June 1952).*

'any achievement we have ever made in our country pales into utter insignificance in comparison with what has been done here.'[56]

The Party is reborn

Ruth returned to busy planning sessions for the Congress of the People, public meetings for SACOD and the Peace Movement – as well as secret gatherings of the new South African Communist Party. Ever since the dissolution of the CPSU, former members had been thinking about re-starting the Party. According to Fred Carneson

> The Party was banned but the communists were still there! It took us a little time before we sorted things out ... we used to have these informal meetings of former Party leadership and always – invariably – what about restarting the Party? (Finally) we shrugged our shoulders and said those of us who are prepared to get on with the job, let's get on with the bloody job![57]

In the absence of any national initiative, communists at a local level began 'a slow process of feeling out each other's attitudes'.[58] According to Johannesburg activist Hilda Watts:

> After a while when we weren't approached and nothing happened, people tentatively began to speak to others and little groups began forming. It was at that time that some people in

> Johannesburg decided well, it's going to be dangerous. Everybody's going to be forming little Communist Party groups and things, we'd better get together and establish a proper Party.... It must have been '51 or '52.[59]

The initiative was taken by the Transvaal group where 'a sort of leadership group (had) started getting together ... with a view to seeing whether the basis existed for forming a new Party.'[60] Watts confirmed that the new leadership was

> mainly people from the Central Committee in the Transvaal. It was a Transvaal group. It started with them, and later it was canvassed round the country. It came out of the old Party without any doubt. But even before the Party was dissolved in 1950, from about 1946 onwards there had been consistent pressure from the Transvaal for the Central Committee to be returned to the Transvaal where it obviously should have been.... And when the Cape Central Committee dissolved the Party, I think the reconstitution took place from the leadership of the old Party but with its Transvaal base rather than the Cape base.[61]

This group included Ruth and Joe as well as older cadres such as Michael Harmel, Rusty Bernstein, Hilda Watts, Jack Hodgson, Moses Kotane, Yusuf Dadoo, JB Marks and Bram Fischer. They began a tentative process of national consultation which culminated in a national conference in Johannesburg in 1953.

The new Party seems to have cut across other similar initiatives and gave rise to criticism. According to Myrtle Berman, who was to be one of the founders of the African Resistance Movement (ARM), a small group she was involved in had formed its own underground Party: 'We didn't know the existence of the official one ... . And it was at that stage that Michael Harmel in fact tried to absorb our group ... . I had no time for Mike Harmel. I thought he was a twister ... . We found we had been sort of taken over ... . But we were kicked out over Hungary. I was very much a dissident and very unhappy in (the Party).'[62] As a result of the secrecy the whole style of the Party changed. Fred Carneson remembers that

> we evolved rules for recruitment ... .We were very careful who we enrolled into the Party. We put everyone through a real sieve. You've got to think of everything – if you're thinking of a man, you think of his relationship with his wife, or if you're thinking of a woman then you think of her relationship with her husband. Because the thing can become a security risk if you don't get the mixture right.[63]

This system, no doubt necessary under the circumstances, caused problems for former CPSA members used to working in a more open political environment. Rowley Arenstein was to complain that

> It was a new party entirely with a completely different outlook. The Communist Party of South Africa from 1939 to 1950 really had a democratic outlook. Nobody felt compelled to obey the line without first being given the opportunity of arguing about it, and nobody was disciplined or expelled or thrown out because you disagreed with the leadership. Now underground, of course, the excuse (was) that there had to be high discipline, but there was a tendency which grew that you must accept the leadership. The leadership tells you basically what to do, and if you don't listen to the leadership you're an enemy of the people. It didn't come out straight away, but that was the tendency.... People who were sort of lesser people in the Party were quite scared of people like Ruth and others.[64]

The theoretical basis upon which the new Communist Party was based was Colonialism of a Special Type (CST), and the orientation of the Party was the product of the experiences of the Transvaal communists in their contact with ANCYL leadership figures such as Oliver Tambo, Nelson Mandela, Walter Sisulu and Joe Matthews.

The new burst of political activity was to place considerable strains on Ruth. She was now a high-profile activist, a working journalist, an underground revolutionary and the mother of three small children. Soon after the formation of SACOD, the penalties of this form of existence began to make themselves clear .

In 1953 the Nationalist Party won the election with an increased majority. It took this as a mandate to smash the Congress Movement. Organisations were raided by police who insinuated that treason charges were their aim and activists were banned. Given the mounting pressure, it might have come as something of a relief to Ruth in 1955 when she was served with a banning order which prevented her from taking part in any public meetings or appearances. However, although this may have cut back her public appearances, it still allowed her to continue work as a journalist and did not prevent her from involvement in private gatherings. So it was not long before she found herself elected onto the drafting committee of the Freedom Charter.

The People's Charter

The conception of the Charter was not immaculate and had its origins in earlier formulations of principle. In 1943 the ANC had adopted Africans' Claims in South Africa which, in turn, had been influenced by the Atlantic Charter of 1941. Many similar demands were made in the Ten Point Programme of the Non-European Unity Movement adopted in 1943, the 1944 Manifesto of the Congress Youth League, the People's Charter adopted at the Peoples' Assembly for Votes for All and organised by the CPSA in 1948, the Youth League's Programme of Action ratified by the ANC in 1949 and the Women's Charter adopted by the Federation of South African Women in 1954. What made the Freedom Charter different was its method of production.

The idea of a Freedom Charter was raised at a meeting of the Joint Congress Committee meeting near Groutville, Natal, in late-1952.[65] According to Rusty Bernstein

> the issue before us was, well, what are we going to do now? The Defiance Campaign had finished, there had been some talk about an anti-pass campaign – it hadn't got off the ground, and we were clearly at a sort of impasse.... And then ZK (Matthews) came up with a suggestion which, looking back on it, I think was one of the most revolutionary proposals ever put before the South African political movement ... he said why don't we spend a year or two drawing up a voters' roll ... then convene a constituent assembly. (And) a constituent assembly would presumably draw up a new South African constitution. That really was seditious![66]

The idea of the Charter was raised publicly by Matthews shortly afterwards during his presidential address at the Cape Congress of the ANC in Cradock. 'I wonder', he asked, 'whether the time has not come for the African National Congress to consider the question of convening a national convention, a congress of the people, representing all the people of this country irrespective of race or colour, to draw up a Freedom Charter for the democratic South Africa of the future.'[67]

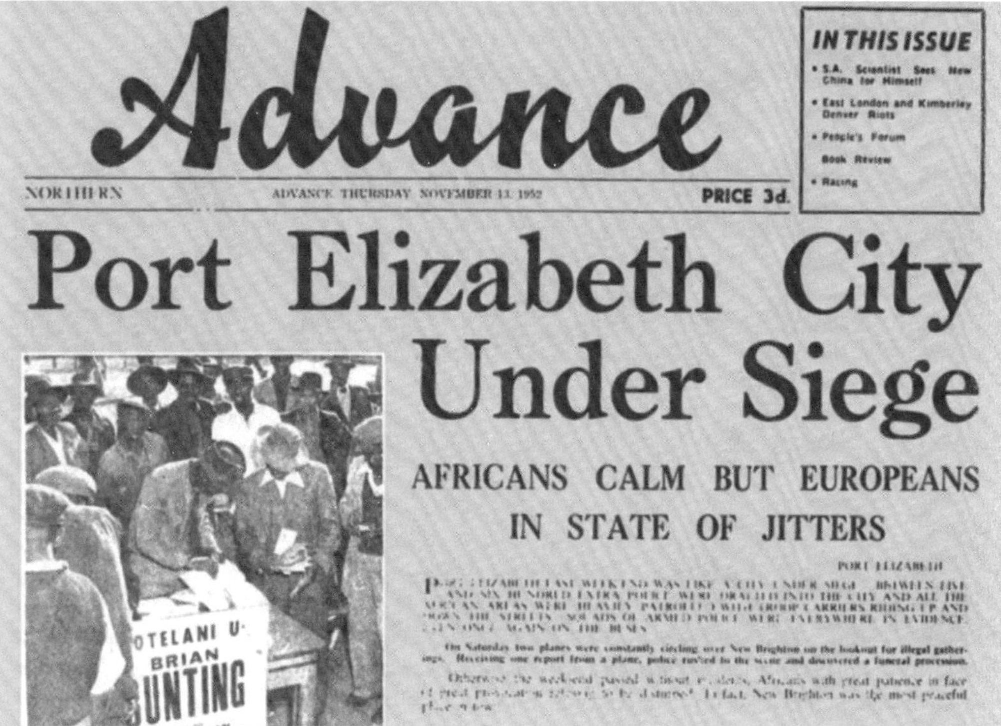

Advance

IN THIS ISSUE

- S.A. Scientist Sees New China for Himself
- East London and Kimberley Denver Riots
- People's Forum

Book Review

- Racing

NORTHERN

ADVANCE THURSDAY NOVEMBER 13, 1952

PRICE 3d.

Port Elizabeth City Under Siege

AFRICANS CALM BUT EUROPEANS IN STATE OF JITTERS

PORT ELIZABETH

*The government, having lost the moral advantage in the peaceful Defiance Campaign, opened fire on defiers in Port Elizabeth, claiming that the campaign had turned violent and should be banned. (*Advance*, November 13 1952)*

Later that year the idea was approved by the ANC's National Executive in Queenstown. A National Action Council was elected with representatives from all members of the Congress Alliance to put the idea into action. This council drew up an elaborate plan of action which included the recruitment of 50 000 'Freedom Volunteers' to 'gather in demands ... from the whole country in writing' and to collect financial contributions from as many people as possible.[68] The plan also envisaged the deployment of 575 political teachers, the production of a fortnightly bulletin and the drafting of the Freedom Charter from demands sent in.'[69] In a post-campaign analysis, the National Action Council admitted that the plan had to be considerably narrowed through a lack of organisation, a spate of government banning orders and a shortage of funds. It had also failed to link the campaign 'with the day to day struggles of the people' and had received little response from miners, factory workers or peasants.[70] Despite these drawbacks – and being virtually ignored by the commercial press – the campaign was to be a huge political success.

The Charter was preceded by *The Call*, a stirring poem written by Rusty Bernstein, and people were urged to elect a 'parliament of the people' in order to gather freedom demands. 'Men and women representing every citizen in this land' were called on to 'demand even the smallest thing which they consider necessary for their happiness'. These were to be written down and sent to 'the Secretary, PO Box 11045 Johannesburg' together with donations of 1d, 3d, 6d or 1/- or £1, any amount whatsoever.'[71] The aim, according to Walter Sisulu, was 'to get the people themselves to express their true aspirations and get

*Defiers across the country filled the jails after being arrested for burning their passes. These are from the Krugersdorp ANC branch. (*Clarion*, July 17 1952)*

them embodied in the Freedom Charter. We want the people to take an active and direct share in the future destiny of South Africa.'[72]

As people responded to the call, an extraordinary range of demands started to pour in to the COP headquarters in Johannesburg. According to *New Age*, writing just before the congress began, 'for months now the demands have been flooding in to COP headquarters, on sheets torn from school exercise books, on little dog-eared scraps of paper, on slips torn from COP leaflets.'[73] In order to cope with this flood and turn it into a single charter, a drafting sub-committee was appointed consisting of Ruth First, Yusuf Cachalia, Rusty Bernstein, Walter Sisulu, Duma Nokwe and Pieter Beyleveld – most of whom were banned at the time. This committee, working 'day after day, week after week, for a very long period during the whole campaign', began sorting out the demands and attempting to draw together the threads.[74] According to Cachalia, the demands would arrive from the COP offices and from organisations 'in batches, on all sorts of paper – scribblers, exercise books, good paper and whatnot' and would be given to Ruth for preliminary sorting and condensing into coherent statements. 'She was the journalist, you see', he explained, 'there were a lot of demands and she could digest them fast and present them to the committee.'[75]

The committee clearly had a free hand in interpreting the demands. They also studied other similar documents, including the United Nations Charter, and were assisted by SACOD which submitted a summary of demands including the nationalisation of 'mines, banks ... large-scale monopoly-owned enterprises and printing plants'. SACOD also called for the confiscation of large-scale landholdings and the distribution of the land among those who worked it.[76] In the end, though, the drafting team was constrained and guided by the mass of popular demands. According to Rusty Bernstein

> There were fewer demands on macro-economic matters than others, because who other than the students or the commercially-oriented puts the capitalism/socialism issue in the forefront of their demands? The formulation of the Charter on these issues derived from 'demands', but from few demands. The issue of the land and its redistribution are vague, representing again the paucity of demands actually collected from the reserves and rural cultivators ... . The formulations (were) the best we could devise.[77]

The conclusion to the document: 'These freedoms we will fight for, side by side, throughout our lives, until we have won our liberty', was written in by Sisulu. 'He said: "I would like this to be in," and we said okay.'[78] Ruth, under a banning order, had to suffer the frustration of being barred from attending the Congress at Kliptown. She had to read the descriptions afterwards:

> Midday Saturday: there are some ten thousand people here, speaking all the tongues and representing all the races, colours and creeds that make up South Africa. Three thousand of the ten have been sent here to speak for groups of men and women scattered through the four provinces. The rest are spectators.... There are some – if anyone asked their affiliation – who would reply Liberal, Labour, Torch Commando, Christian, Muslim, Democrat. There are thousands who would reply: 'Congressman!' This is the most truly national convention in all South African history.[79]

However, Ruth was lucky she did not break her ban – on the second day of the Congress hundreds of police surrounded the gathering, confiscated all papers and took the name of everyone present.

Fraternity of the Left

Reflecting on the 1950s, Ruth was to say that whites who embarked on protest politics side by side with the Africans, Indians and Coloureds, led 'a vigorously provocative life':

> Our consciences were healthy in a society riddled with guilts. Yet as the years went by our small band led a more and more schizophrenic existence. There was the good living that white privilege brought, but simultaneously complete absorption in revolutionary politics and defiance of all the values of our own racial group. As the struggle grew sharper the privileges of membership in the white group were overwhelmed by the penalties of political participation.[80]

The size of this 'small band' was fluid and changed throughout the period. The inner circle for the Slovos was undoubtedly the Communist Party underground. By the late 1950s this consisted of about 100 people nationally, most of whom were in Johannesburg.[81] The intellectual centre of this group was Michael Harmel. According to Party member Ben Turok, Harmel represented 'the core of the Party, the real Party. I had some reservations about him as an individual, on a personal level, because Michael could be a very tough customer, and very awkward, but historically he's a giant. He was a leading opponent of dissolution and was the biggest Leninist South Africa ever had.'[82]

Around this 'core' was a cell-structure consisting of people who were both politically and socially linked – through the Party and their many other activities – into a fraternal sub-culture of the Left. They were people of all races united by their opposition to apartheid and by their dreams of a socialist society. They were, according to Turok, 'a formidable bunch and capable of influencing opinion of the movement as a whole ... they were pretty tough (and) had survived in or taken up leadership positions in the ANC, COD – extremely committed people.'[83]

Within the cells security was intense – even people like Helen Joseph, who worked with many of the communists politically, didn't know of the Party's existence until it emerged in 1960.[84] The cells met regularly, often fortnightly, reviewing the work of each member and discussing issues which affected the Party.[85] People within the cells formed a lobby within the wider political movement through the careful placement of key individuals. According to Ben Turok, they always made it a rule that the Party 'did not try to impose its policies by unanimous action but through the leadership of individuals ... the people we selected were key people and each one had to be a leader in his own right.'[86]

Party influence in SACOD was considerable but by no means absolute, as the State was to suggest. There were few actual Party members in the white Congress, but according to Turok 'we could be sure that COD would follow a good line by virtue of the people we had, so there was no need to steamroller people like Rusty Bernstein, Michael Harmel, Joe Slovo, Ruth First, Bram Fischer'.[87]

Increasingly, though, whites within this political circle became social outcasts from the white society which surrounded them. Initially this was of little consequence – their 'consciences were healthy' and, according to Joe Slovo, they were 'sort of euphoric about prospects and a bit blind as to what would eventually happen'. But the effect of shared interests, secrecy and increasing State and social pressure was to tighten the social circle of the Left. According to SACOD chairman Pieter Beyleveld, the process was inevitable: 'If you share ideals and views, those are the people you choose your friends amongst. That sort of friendship extended beyond the European group ... in a town like Johannesburg you had a group of friends that was really multi-racial.'[88]

But in a society where being white generally meant being relatively wealthy, the anomaly of this situation was apparent. The Slovos, like many other white activists, lived in up-market suburbs and were mixing socially with people who were living in township *pondokkies*. According to Myrtle Berman, 'we were all elite – all whites were the elite, we were cushioned ... . I mean we were living the most comfortable bourgeois life whilst being involved in the political movement.'[89] This group were eventually to sacrifice this lifestyle for their political beliefs, but while it lasted they used it to its fullest extent. Their income and skills helped to keep the political movement alive, and their houses became the neutral venues where 'normality' could exist amid the racism with which they were surrounded. Their parties became legendary.

Ruth loved a good party. Her 21st birthday party, while she was still at university, was a taste of things to come. 'My god it was hectic', remembered Sadie Forman. 'Everybody was drinking like mad and people were dancing. It was enormous, everybody was there, black, white, everyone.'[90] At her wedding, according to Issy Heymann, 'the ANC turned up and there wasn't enough room – and they had an enormous big house ... they were eaten out of house and home![91] Rica Hodgson remembered that the left had 'absolutely wonderful parties, wonderful food and masses of booze, and wonderful music, kwela music, and we danced like hell. They were mixed parties, of course, all of them.'[92]

New Age, *December 2 1954*

In October 1958, when the indictment against the accused in the Treason Trial collapsed, the Slovos invited everyone concerned to their home in Roosevelt Park. According to Issy Heymann, 'Soweto and Alexandra and every township around Johannesburg, they were there!' At about 10 pm a cameraman from the *Die Vaderland* newspaper jumped through a window and began taking photographs. He was immediately followed by policemen from the Liquor Squad and the Special Branch. They searched the house, took all the liquor and left. The *Rand Daily Mail*, reporting the incident the next day, ended its story on a disapproving note: 'After midnight the celebration was still going on – now with soft drinks and chips. And by then the green-overalled servant girl was doing the kwela with a bespectacled European.'[93]

These gatherings had a far wider purpose than entertainment; they were the social cement which held the Congress leadership together. In a society skewed by apartheid this was how like minds met. Hilary Kuny, a Johannesburg psychologist, remembered that Sunday lunches at the Slovos were almost standard affairs: 'That's where I met Winnie Mandela, and God knows who else. They were nice, they were lovely, we'd sit in the garden and drink wine. Her cook made lovely cranberry sauce for the turkey!'[94]

Ruth oiled the social wheels with style. She was an excellent organiser with a passion for 'doing a list' to get things done. According to Hodgson, there were three things Ruth loved – 'good, expensive Italian shoes, expensive luggage and silk shirts. But she also loved a picnic ... she always said food tasted much better in the open air. There was

NATS TERRIFIED BY FREEDOM CHARTER

SOUTHERN EDITION Registered at G.P.O. as a Newspaper

Vol. 2, No. 12 THURSDAY, OCTOBER 27, 1955 PRICE 3d.

INSIDE STORY OF POLICE RAIDS

CAPE TOWN.—THE MAIN OBJECT OF THE SPECIAL BRANCH OF THE POLICE IN THE RECENT RAIDS WAS TO UNEARTH INFORMATION ABOUT THE FREEDOM CHARTER AND THE CONGRESS OF THE PEOPLE, ACCORDING TO INFORMATION WHICH HAS BEEN GIVEN TO NEW AGE.

Among the documents with which the raiders were armed was a roneod document in Afrikaans marked "C." and entitled: "Internal Publications, Books, Pamphlets, etc. Which Must Be Searched For."

The document lists a number of publications, together with the name of the organisation or individual responsible for publishing them, and even indicates the number of copies which must be seized, if found.

The most important document in the list is the Freedom Charter, described as issued by the Congress of the People.

"THIS IS THE MOST IMPORTANT DOCUMENT," SAYS THE POLICE CIRCULAR. "ALL COPIES MUST BE SEIZED." ("DIT IS DIE BELANGRIKSTE DOKUMENTE—LE BESLAG OP ALLE KOPIE.")

Also listed are "petitions with signatures in connection with the Congress of the People." The circular directs that "all petitions, with or without names, must be seized."

THE CALL

The call to the Congress of the People, entitled "Let Us Talk of Freedom," figures prominently on the list, though in this case the police are directed to seize only one copy.

One section in the list, headed "Congress of the People Publications," includes the following items (reproduced exactly as in the original):

"(a) Congressman
(b) Call to the People of
(c) Volunteer forms
(d) Credential forms
(e) C.O.P. Pamflette, ens."

These are described as "published by the organisation or by persons on behalf of the organisation in connection with meetings, announcements, etc." One copy of each is wanted.

Other items on the list are the constitutions of the African National Congress, the S.A. Indian Congress, the Congress of Democrats, SACPO and the Communist Party. The raiders are also instructed to search for the "constitutional programme" of the Communist Party, and a publication entitled "Freedom Summer 1948," said to have been issued by the Communist Party of South Africa.

Here is a list of the remaining items, together with the organisations or individuals held to be responsible for publishing them:

Africanist—Organ of the A.N.C. Youth League.
African Lodestar—Organ of the A.N.C. Youth League.
Counter Attack—Organ of the Congress of Democrats.
Fighting Talk—Congress of Democrats.
Let Us Talk About Russia—Organ of the Friends of the Soviet Union.
Life is More Joyous—B. Bunting.
Land and National Oppression—Dr. G. Goel.
Liberation—Democratic Discussion Club.
New Day—Organ of the National Union of Distributive Workers.
New Life in China—Ruth First.
New Views—Modern Youth Society.
Peace Movement and the Congress of the People—S.A. Peace Council.

BANNED BOOKS

The raiders were also armed with typed lists containing the titles of hundreds of political and other publications whose importation into the country has been prohibited by Dr. Dönges in terms of the Customs Act. The police searched through [illegible] using the list as a guide, and removed all books which were on the black list.

Among the titles on the list are such items as "Culture and Education in New China," the "Chinese Medical Journal," "1954 Diary for Youth," "English Language Periodicals—printed in China," "Seretse Khama and the Bamangwato People," "Social Insurance in the U.S.S.R.," several volumes of the selected works of Lenin, and Stalin's

(Continued on page 3)

Classification Condemned, SACPO Supported, at

HUGE COLOURED MEETING IN P.E.

PORT ELIZABETH.—In one of the biggest meetings ever held by the Coloured community in Port Elizabeth, two thousand people gathered at the Jarman Hall, Schauder Township, last Thursday to voice their protest against the Government's treatment of the Coloured people, and to form a branch of the S.A. Coloured People's Organisation.

Hundreds who came late were unable to gain admission to the hall and had to stand outside craning their necks to see and hear what was going on in the hall. At the end of the meeting the entire available stock of SACPO application forms was used up as hundreds queued to join the organisation.

Explaining the purpose of the meeting, Miss Cissy Jasson stated that the time was long overdue when the Coloured should come together and fight for their rights.

"For years we have been slighted by the White Governments of this country," declared Lilly Diedricks, "for we have looked on while the Africans were struggling to hold the fort. The present reclassification is but one of those weapons which the Nationalists are using to humiliate us as a people. Are we going to sit back and see our rights whittled away one after another?"

Messrs Mkwayi and Fazi, who brought fraternal greetings from the New Brighton and Korsten branches of the ANC, assured the meeting that the ANC stood with them in their struggle against the injustices that the Nationalists were perpetrating against the Coloureds.

"Often the people have been misled into believing that the United Party would do something to redress their wrongs," they said. "In 1936 you witnessed the disfranchisement of the Africans, today the Nationalists are taking away the franchise from you.

"The Nationalists have imposed Verwoerd's Slave Education on the African; tomorrow Slave Education will be imposed on you. The Na-

(Continued on page 5)

Women's Deputation For Pretoria Today

JOHANNESBURG.—At the time of going to press women of all races up and down the Reef were making enthusiastic last-minute preparations for their protest to the Union Buildings in Pretoria, due to take place today (Thursday, October 27).

From the Minister of the Interior no reply had been received by the beginning of the week to the request to him to receive the mass deputation. The Minister of Labour, De Klerk, replied that he will be in Bloemfontein on official duties, and Swart, the Minister of Justice, has replied that he is "unable to receive the deputation."

The Federation of South African Women has written to De Klerk and Swart asking that they appoint deputies to receive the women.

ALL THE SIGNS THIS WEEK ARE THAT EASILY OVER 1,500 WOMEN WILL GO TO PRETORIA. EACH WOMAN WILL CARRY A COPY OF THE PROTEST IN HER HAND.

To Minister Verwoerd, who refused to receive an inter-racial deputation, the Federation has replied that as it cannot accept the principle of a deputation from one racial group only the protest will go on.

REFUSED

The Federation applied to the Pretoria City Council in terms of the bye-laws to be allowed to hold a public meeting in front of the Union Buildings. Last week the Pretoria Town Clerk replied that the application had been refused after representations to the Council from the District Commandant of Police in Pretoria. The women have again made representations to the Council contesting the Council's ruling in terms of the bye-laws.

Hundreds of women desire through the mass deputation, says the Federation, to exercise the fundamental and traditional right to present their case to the Government of their country. The time-honoured procedure of expressing public opinion by a public march has been permitted to other sections of women. It is difficult to escape from the conclusion that permission has been withheld to the Federation on racial grounds, as European women are permitted such protests.

(Continued on page 6)

The South African people's support for and solidarity with the people of Morocco, who are fighting a bitter struggle for their emancipation from French rule, was expressed by a delegation which visited the French Consulate in Cape Town on Friday of last week. The delegation wished to hand the Consul a letter from the Cape Western Region of the African National Congress which reads: "Our African people desire to register their strongest protest against the massacre of their brothers and sisters in Morocco by your Government and through you, we on behalf of our people would like to express our indignation to your Government that continues this wanton waste of human lives. We demand the immediate cessation of hostilities and the establishment of peaceful negotiations with representatives of the people with a view to granting their national demand for self government and independence which is their rightful inheritance."

Although the French Consul read the letter, he refused to accept it. Political protests must go to the French Embassy in Pretoria, he said. He even refused to talk to the whole deputation, giving a hearing only to Mr. Len Lee-Warden, M.P., chairman of the Congress of Democrats, and to Mr. John Mtini, Cape Western president of the A.N.C., who handed him the letter. The picture shows part of the delegation—from the left: Mr. Lee-Warden, Mr. J. Ngulube, Mr. Mtini and Mr. J. Morolong. Mr. A. Sibeko represented the South African Congress of Trade Unions.

***New Age*, October 1955**

New Age, *October 27 1955*

Ruth with Albertina Sisulu at a mass meeting on Human Rights Day, 1952 (UCT memorial pamphlet, 1983).

always very elegant food and wine. She had goat's cheese and one had it with pears. That was Ruth ... always very elegant.'[95] But this was a world destined not to last. It was surrounded, in the words of Wolfie Kodesh, by 'the morality of a wicked society which increasingly impacted itself on all of us.'[96] And although the adults could create their own world, their children were daily involved with another. For reasons of security, and perhaps in the hope of shielding them from the consequences of the political actions of their parents, children of the new generation of left-wing whites seem to have been excluded from political discussion. According to Joe, 'we just kept our kids in ignorance and, therefore, they were bewildered and isolated from their own society. They had no support. A black kid whose parents got arrested becomes a hero in the school. A white kid whose parents got arrested was a subject of derision ... communist scum.'[97] By the time the State of Emergency was declared in 1960 the tensions were intolerably high. The fraternity of the Left had become a clandestine affair – and would soon be deemed a conspiracy by the State.

Notes

1 Some members of the League were her fellow students.

2 Document 52, Karis & Carter Vol 2: Letter from the ANCYL (Transvaal) to the Secretary of the Progressive Youth Council, March 16 1945 p316.

3 Karis & Carter, Vol 2: Policy of the Congress Youth League. Article by AM Lembede, in *Inkundla ya Bantu*, May 1946.

4 Karis & Carter, Vol 2: *Programme of Action.* Statement of policy adopted at the ANC Annual Conference, December 17, 1949.

5 Karis & Carter, op cit: Letter on the Youth League from AP Mda to GM Pitje, September 10, 1948.

6 Everatt, op cit, p59.

7 Ibid, p61.

8 Bunting: Kotane, op cit, p37.

9 Joint declaration on cooperation, 1947. In Everatt, op cit, p63. The CPSA had endorsed a similar position in 1943, calling for separate organisations representing Africans, Indians and Coloureds coordinated at a regional and national level.

10 Everatt, Ibid, p73.

11 Freedom, December 15 1949.

12 Ibid.

13 Ibid.

14 *People's World*, 2.10.52.

15 Everatt, op cit, p48.

16 Liberals were later to claim that white communists 'packed' the meeting and controlled the proceedings. See Everatt, Ibid, p48.

17 *Viewpoints & Perspectives*, 1/1 March 1953, Introduction by Myrtle Berman (editor).

18 In 1928, to the consternation of many white communists – especially Sydney Bunting, the Comintern provided a new campaign slogan for the CPSA. It was to campaign for 'an independent native South African republic as a stage towards a workers' and peasants' republic, with full and equal rights for all races, black, coloured and white'. Amid much acrimony it was accepted by the local Party and laid the theoretical foundations of the CPSA for many decades. However, it was buried. in the turmoil of the expulsions during the mid-1930s.

19 Everatt, op cit, p48.

20 Ibid, p100. These debates were to re-emerge in 1990 with the unbanning of the ANC and SACP.

21 V&P1/1 p25.

22 By defining the South African situation as a colonial one, Internal Colonialism (IC) and CST brought it within the scope of the struggle for a 'national democratic revolution'. The issue, as we have seen, can be traced back to the Lenin/Roy debates in the early 1920s. But it can be traced back much further: to a fundamental dilemma of Marxist theory. Marx and Engels developed a historical schema according to which the completion of the bourgeois democratic revolution and the development of capitalism preceded and creates the conditions for the transition to socialism. However, in 1848 the bourgeoisie of Germany and Austria failed to fulfil their responsibilities, and at the end of the century the Russian bourgeoisie showed few signs of preparedness to overthrow Tsarism. Lenin sought to resolve the dilemma by redefining the 'democratic' revolution as one against feudalism led by an alliance of workers and peasants. This revolution, he said, could proceed directly to the socialist revolution, given support by socialist revolutions in industrial Europe. In 1920 Lenin transferred the theory of bourgeois democratic revolution to colonial countries in the form of the national democratic revolution. Surprisingly he accorded the 'national bourgeoisie' a progressive role in this, in opposition to the Indian communist MN Roy. This approach about national and 'comprador' elements varied over the years but the national democratic revolution remained. This theory provided implicit support for arguments which linked together national liberation and socialism as part of a single process. Without it, the divergence between nationalists and socialists could emerge and be recognised as antithetical to one another. So CST was an attempt to think through processes which went far beyond the relationship between the CPSA and the ANCYL. See Gavin Williams: Review essay. *Social Dynamics* 14(1)57-66 1988; Transformation: Critical perspectives on South Africa Nos. 1-4 1986-87 and Maria van Diepen: *The National Question in South Africa* (Zed Press, London, 1988).

23 Afrika! quoted in *Advance* 17.12.53.

24 J Matthews: African nationalism today, January 1954. CAMP Reel 12A:2:XM65:81. Quoted in Everatt, op cit, p109.

25 Ibid.

26 The Springbok Legion: *History and Policy*, Treason Trial defence document probably written by Jack Hodgson, p1.

27 Chairman's report of the 9th annual national conference of the Springbok Legion, April 1952. p7.

28 *History & Policy*, op cit, p13.

29 Letter from COD, author's collection.

30 Letter from the Legion dated June 15, 1953, Treason Trial exhibit AP21.

31 *History and Policy*, op cit, p13.

32 Ibid, p14.

33 Ibid, p14.

34 The League chairman, Jack Hodgson, would probably have been elected but he had received a banning order.

35 Chairman's report to the first annual conference of SACOD, Johannesburg, June 24, 1955. Author's collection.

36 Resolutions submitted by the National Executive Committee to the 1956 national SACOD conference in Johannesburg, 1956. Treason Trial Collection, Wits University, Doc. G967.

37 Karis & Gerhart, 1977, p13.

38 Ibid.

39 *The Africanist*, Vol.4, No.2, June/July 1958. Author's collection.

40 Ivan Schermbrucker in Everatt, op cit, p132.

41 Interview with Yusuf Cachalia, in Everatt, Ibid, p147.

42 Albie Sachs in Frederikse: Non-racialism, 1990, p58.

43 Everatt, op cit, pp146-153.

44 Lodge, 1983, p69.

45 She was described as this by Joe Slovo in the introduction to the 1988 edition of *117 Days*.

46 Most of SACOD's expenses in its first few years of existence were for printing. In 1956 printing was 55% of its running costs. SACOD statement of expenses. Author's collection.

47 Hilda Watts, in Report of the First National South African Peace Congress. 22.8.53.

48 Claudin, op cit, p578.

49 Stalin: 'Derniers Ecrits', 1950-53. *Editions Sociales*, Paris, 1953, p125. In Claudin, op cit, p580.

50 Interview with D Thompson by SA Institute of Race Relations. (A1906 I Douglas Thompson Collection, University of the Witwatersrand).

51 *Advance* 20.8.53.

52 Minutes of meeting November 26 1953. Treason Trial document D39, Wits University.

53 Burns, op cit, p94.

54 *South Africans in the Soviet Union*. Published by Ruth First. Ruth arrived in Moscow on June 14 and visited Leningrad and Armenia. On July 3 she was in Peking. Her daughters at the time would have been four, two and just under one year old. Some people interviewed for this book note that she was criticised for leaving her young children at home during this time and prioritising a trip to the USSR and China. In

the light of her history, however, it was unlikely that anything would have deterred her from such a trip.

55 Reprinted in *Fighting Talk*, August 1954.

56 Ibid.

57 Interview with Carneson, 1988.

58 Ben Turok in Everatt, op cit, p94.

59 Interview with Watts, 1988.

60 Interview with Bernstein, 1988.

61 Interview with Watts, 1988.

62 Interview with Myrtle Berman, 1988.

63 Carneson, op cit.

64 Interview with Rowley Arenstein.

65 Meetings were often held there in order to include Chief Lutuli, who was banned and restricted to his home area.

66 Interview with Rusty Bernstein, 1988.

67 ZK Matthews: Freedom for my people. 1981, p174. The speech was made in 1954.

68 The Congress of the People: Draft plan of campaign. Author's collection.

69 Ibid.

70 Report of the National Action of the Congress of the People to the joint executives of the ANC, SAIC, SACPO and SACOD. Author's collection.

71 Draft for flyer: *What is the role of our people there?* n.d. Author's collection.

72 *Advance* 8.4.54.

73 *New Age* 23.6.55.

74 Interview with Yusuf Cachalia, 1988.

75 There have been many claims about the authorship of the Charter, but none have been based on interviews with members of the drafting committee. Everatt is an exception.

76 *Demands of the People.* Author's collection. There has been much subsequent debate about the socialist content of the Charter. It is possible that the more radical demands came from the SACOD document, but this is not to say that similar demands were not gathered from many people. Unfortunately the original demands were seized by the police or lost.

77 Interview with Rusty Bernstein.

78 Cachalia, op cit.

79 *We are many.* SACOD pamphlet 1955.

80 First: *117 Days,* p116.

81 Turok interview, 1988.

82 Ibid.

83 Ibid.

84 Helen was invited to join SACOD by Ruth. Joseph interview, 1988.

85 The denunciation of Stalin was intensely discussed within the cells. According to Turok 'it shook us terribly and we discussed that at length'.

86 Ibid.

87 Ibid.

88 Beyleveld interview, 1988.

89 Berman interview, 1988.

90 Forman interview, 1988.

91 Heymann interview, 1988.

92 Hodgson interview, 1988.

93 *Rand Daily Mail* 14.10.58. Following the raid, Ruth claimed £5 000 damages from *Die Vaderland* for alleged injuria. There is no record of the outcome of her action.

94 Kuny interview, 1988.

95 Hodgson, op cit.

96 Kodesh interview, 1988.

97 Slovo interview, 1991.

4

A Press with a mission

A free press was never a terror to the people – it was their hope. It was the governing classes who were under alarm. – George Holyoake, 1840

"Volkswil"

The Guardian, *May 15 1952, shortly before it was banned.*

Ruth First was an activist who acted mainly through her journalism. For this reason her writing was essentially political. But was it simply propaganda? If this term suggests manipulation of information in the service of a political end, then it becomes necessary to ask another question: did she manipulate information in order to promote the ideas of the Communist Party and the Congress Alliance? The answer is not as easy as it might at first seem – she was no mere Party hack. Her meticulous attention to detail and her tendency, at times, to run ahead of Congress ideas do not allow her writing to be easily categorised as propaganda in the more common sense of the word. Moreover, propaganda is a politically loaded term – each side thinks the other side does it.

The chapters which follow attempt to answer some of these questions, but it is necessary to begin at a point which pre-dates Ruth's journalism and to briefly sketch some of the traditions from which it emerged – and which it opposed. Probably because of the predominance of studies on mass media, the radical origins of the press have been buried in the measurement and criticism of that which succeeded it in the West. But the traditions of the radical press pre-dated those of the commercial dailies, and it is worth remembering that the first-born newspaper began life not as an instrument of government or commerce but as a rebel. These issues had direct bearing on the development of the press in South Africa but have been largely ignored by historians. In them were embedded understandings which were to divide the press traditions of the 20th century into worlds apart.

Trumpeters of freedom

The origin of the press in South Africa was closely tied to the combination of two traditions – one political, the other commercial – which came out of the struggle for a free press in Britain during the 19th century. In his assessment of British press practices in that century, Stanley Harrison was to observe that 'neither at the beginning nor at the end is the newspaper press placed neutrally apart from society – though at the end it endeavours by all means to wear that appearance. Politics is about power and the press is about politics'.[1]

The invention of movable type was itself a political act, and it was immediately put to the service of interests within the Church. Its emergence into secular service, for the reasons given by Harrison, was an event watched nervously by the ruling classes. Indeed, the first newspaper ever officially licensed in Britain in 1622 had its license revoked for offending the Spanish Ambassador. Printing presses and dangerous ideas were to remain close companions ever afterwards. In England, early notions of communism were noted by an alarmed observer to be causing 'mischief' among soldiers in Cromwell's army by way of 'pamphlets which they abundantly dispersed'.[2] During the reign of George 111 (1760-1820) an early journalist, George Holyoake, complained that 'the printer was treated as an enemy of the State' and in times when corruption among the gentry ensured that 'the price of a seat in the House of Commons was better known than the price of a horse', cheap news-sheets and sedition were constant bed-fellows.[3] The high point of the British radical press began with journalist John Wilkes (*The North Britain*) in 1762 and ended with the closure of the London penny quarto, *The Red Republican*, in the 1850s. For decades, and at immense cost to themselves, these journalists and their newspapers tackled what one of their number, William Cobbett, was to call simply 'The Thing': all the accumulated evils of a corrupt system of government. In his colourful style, Cobbett set his paper, the *Political Register*, against 'despotism at home, supported by a bought press, in the interests of a mob of court-sycophants, parasites, pensioners, bribed senators, directors, contractors, jobbers, hireling lords and ministers of state'.[4]

These papers, and the ideas they contained, were read by the literate to those who could not read in coffee shops and taverns throughout Britain. They were a key factor in bringing the country, in 1918, the closest it had ever come to a socialist revolution. In that year the submerged class of farmers ruined by the Enclosures and impoverished factory workers began breaking the surface in a rolling wave of mass meetings which were only put down by considerable state force. At Peterloo fields in Manchester the Yeomanry attacked a crowd with drawn sabers, leaving eleven people dead and 400 injured. In the wake of Peterloo a crop of new radical journals emerged, representing the views of 'journeymen and labourers'. These began to debate the problems facing workers as a class and the possibility that this class was capable of shaping the future. Out of these ideas was to come the great Chartist movement of the 1840s. And out of them, too, was to come the Communist Manifesto which was first published in English by the *Red Republican* in 1850. The radical publishers and editors of the Chartist press – Feargus O'Conner, Bronterre O'Brien, George Harney, Henry Vincent and dozens more – were also the movement's charismatic leaders and orators. They campaigned for the abolition of repressive laws, for universal manhood suffrage, a 'cheap and honest press' and a check on the 'Rotten House of Commons.'[5]

The challenge of Chartism failed, and the traditions of the radical press lay half-buried in the middle-class triumph which succeeded its defeat. These traditions took root elsewhere: in Europe, the United States, Russia and South Africa. But in Britain of the 1850s another form of press ethic had gained predominance, one based squarely on the growing prosperity of the industrial classes. This is best represented by the growth of *The Times*.

This newspaper, first called the *Daily Universal Register*, was founded in 1785 by John Walter 1, a bankrupt coal merchant who had taken up printing to repay his creditors.[6] It began life as a government-subsidised sheet, receiving 300 pounds sterling a year from the Treasury. Under Walter's son, who became sole manager of the journal in 1803, it embarked on a course which was to give it the first image of independence from control by government. In 1852 the paper, using steam presses and with an excellent reputation for its foreign dispatches, signaled the new ethic. In two articles written by Robert Lowe on instructions from *Times* editor Thomas Delane, the paper spelled out its political independence: 'The duty of the journalist is the same as that of the historian – to seek out the truth above all things, and to present to his readers not such things as statecraft would wish them to know but the truth as near as he can attain it'.[7]

This conceptual founding document of the capitalist free press had two important aspects. On the one hand it broke with the oligarchy's idea of the newspaper press as a basically venal activity to be used at will by government or political faction. On the other hand it bound the press to a Free Trade doctrine in which it owed allegiance to nobody but its advertisers. The new teaching of *The Times* was based on the fact that by the 1850s it held a near-monopoly of newspaper sales (50 000 copies a day compared to the 5 000 of its nearest rival) and was the mouthpiece of the new capitalist class which demanded a voice of its own and paid for it through advertising patronage. Indeed, the very first elaborations of the new notion of freedom declared dependence on commercial advertisements to be the foundation of this freedom.

The Times, and the many newspapers which were to follow its lead, began to see itself as the consensus voice of basic ruling class interests – 'ever strong on the stronger side' as it was described in the *Edinburgh Review* of the time.[8] The question, asks Harrison, is freedom for whom?

> The dependence on advertisers ... attached the press to ... a class rather than to any one capitalist interest or state administration. It permitted the emergence of ... journalism as a respected and apparently free and self-sustaining liberal profession following its own laws and devices. From this seed of Free Trade, however, not noble champions but the dragon of today's monopoly situation in the press eventually grew.[9]

The dragon showed its teeth very early. When stamp duty on newspapers was abolished in 1855 after a long fight by the radical press *The Times* objected. It would lead, it said, to 'the multiplication of other, jumped-up newspapers of a cheap class' which would 'purloin and reproduce the news which we believe to be our principal attraction, and to obtain which we spend immense sums of money.'[10] In his book on the printed word, Christopher Small, observes that for *The Times*'s news was a commodity which it had, in commercial terms, cornered such that it was a luxury article, the high price of which helped it to maintain the monopoly ... ownership of news was something to be protected not only by getting it fresh, but also by keeping it expensive.'[11]

NEW AGE, THURSDAY, NOVEMBER 20, 1958 5

DON'T BE MISLED BY THE PAPERS YOU READ

The so-called Non-European newspapers are like wolves in sheep's clothing. They speak for big business, not the people, says BRIAN BUNTING in this detailed study of the Non-White Press.

SOUTH AFRICA is a country in which the Press is dominated by Big Business to a greater extent than in most other capitalist countries. A handful of rich men control almost all the big daily newspapers, which faithfully reflect the interests of the bosses. The majority of the

among their readers hundreds of thousands of Non-Whites in all

Daily News, etc.) in all the main centres of South Africa and the

at least formally, the more vicious aspects of the Government's apartheid policy.

It is only when you consider the big business interests which dominate the *World* that you understand why:

● it opposes every A.N.C. campaign and supports the "opposition" in Congress, whether they are called Africanists, Nationalists

An attack on the commercial black press by Brian Bunting published in New Age, *November 20 1958.*

The *Iskra* tradition

After its defeat in Britain, the radical newspaper tradition was to take root elsewhere. In St Petersburg in 1895 Lenin published *Rabochi Dyelo* (Workers' Cause). It was seized by the police before leaving the press, but shortly afterwards he started a group around the production of a newspaper called *Iskra* (The Spark). This paper became not only a theoretical guide, but an organisational centre and was to form the basis of the All-Russian Party of the proletariat.

The close relationship between the political Left and the press emerged from notions of socialism and its relationship to propaganda. In a speech to the Society of Russian Workers in 1887, Pierre Lavroff told his audience:

> Socialism represents a moral ideal of life in society; it realises the highest possible form that relations based on justice can currently aspire. Thus, it requires a propaganda capable of struggling ... to lead the fraction of humanity tending to put its conviction into practice, or even, simply, to be awakened into moral life.[12]

In a statement remarkable for its clarity, he said socialism was faced with its 'co-religionists who want, and must, increase the force of their thinking and activity', its possible allies who had to be won over, and its enemies who had to be weakened. What was important was to develop ideas in peoples' minds which undermined belief in the morality of the existing social order and pointed out the means to struggling against it.[13]

Out of his work with *Iskra*, Lenin developed the idea of a newspaper as a collective organiser, the tool of a group of 'professional revolutionaries'.[14] A year after starting *Iskra*, Lenin issued his epoch-making brochure *What is to be done?* The document, which laid down the principles of Party organisation, became a veritable storm-centre of debate in Russia and elsewhere. In it Lenin developed the idea of a vanguard of revolutionaries who were the 'liquidators of outworn historical periods.'[15] On the basis of his *Iskra* experience, he rejected the notion that a people's newspaper should be edited directly by the people, and characterised it as a direct tool of the communist vanguard. Newspapers had to become the organs of the various party organisations, and their writers 'must by all means become members of these organisations'. Freedom of the press was 'a bourgeois or an anarchist phrase ... the freedom of the bourgeois writer ... is simply masked dependence on the moneybag, on corruption, on prostitution.'[16]

These ideas about the role of the press were later to be developed by other theorists and were taken up in resolutions of the Comintern. In 1921 the Comintern issued direct guidelines for the communist press which it said had to be developed by the Party with 'indefatigable energy'. No paper, it said, may be recognised as a Communist organ if it did not submit to the directions of the Party.[17] The Party had to pay more attention to having good papers than to having many of them and these were to stay out of the clutches of capitalists: 'Our paper must be independent of all capitalist credit institutions. A skilful organisation of the advertisements, which render possible the existence of our paper for lawful mass parties, must never lead to its being dependent on the large advertisers.... It must be our best agitator and the leading propagator of the proletarian revolution.'[18]

The Communist paper, it said, had to strive to become a communist undertaking – it should be a proletarian fighting organisation, 'a working community of the revolutionary workers, of all the writers whom regularly contribute to the paper, editors, type-setters, printers and distributors'. The chief duty of these workers was to carry on revolutionary propaganda and agitation, the principal forms of which were:

> (i) Participation in the industrial and political labour movement,
> (ii) Propaganda through the Party Press and distribution of literature.
> Every member of a legal and illegal Party is to participate regularly in one or the other of these forms of propaganda.[19]

According to the report, the proper element for the militant Communist Press was direct participation in the campaigns conducted by the Party: 'If the activity of the Party at a given time happens to be concentrated upon a definite campaign, it is the duty of the organ to place all its departments, not the editorial pages alone, at the service of this particular campaign. The editorial board must draw material and sources to feed this campaign, which must be incorporated throughout the paper both in substance and form'. Writing in *Kommunismus* the same year, Adalbert Fogarasi drew a sharp distinction between the capitalist and communist press:

> The capitalist press is an ideological weapon in the class struggle, employed by the ruling class in oppressing the proletariat ... it achieves the systematic advancement of ignorance in the form of communicating an abundance of knowledge and information. (It) seeks to satisfy fully the reader's hunger for knowledge not only in order to perpetuate his ignorance as a lack of knowledge, information and ability to orient himself, but to mold the whole mentality of the reader into this form of ignorance.[20]

The communist press, on the other hand, was the 'historical agent of truth'. In the transmission of facts themselves and 'historically-critically true evaluations of the facts,' truth was the condition of the liberation of consciousness from the ideology diffused by the capitalist press.[21] The criteria of truth, according to Fogarasi, did not lie in individual facts but in the totality of communist theory and praxis: 'To develop consciousness of this totality, to present information, insights and news in a coherent context in which every aspect relates to all others, so that the most trivial news preserves its meaning through its links to the basic truths of communism and serves the continuous rejuvenation of these truths – that is the task!'[22]

The Scottish transplant

Both radical and commercial press traditions were to influence the development of newspapers in South Africa but, long before Lenin, it was the ideas of the British radical press which were to launch the newspaper industry. In 1820, two years after Peterloo, Thomas Pringle arrived in the Eastern Cape with a British settler party. He had been the editor of a small campaigning paper called *The Star*, described as 'the only true liberal newspaper in Scotland' and had been influenced by the independent radicalism of Wilkes and Cobbett.[23] Cape Governor Lord Charles Somerset described Pringle as 'an arrant dissenter who had scribbled' for a Scottish journal.[24] Within two years Pringle had sent for a fellow journalist, John Fairbairn, and had gained the permission of Somerset to start

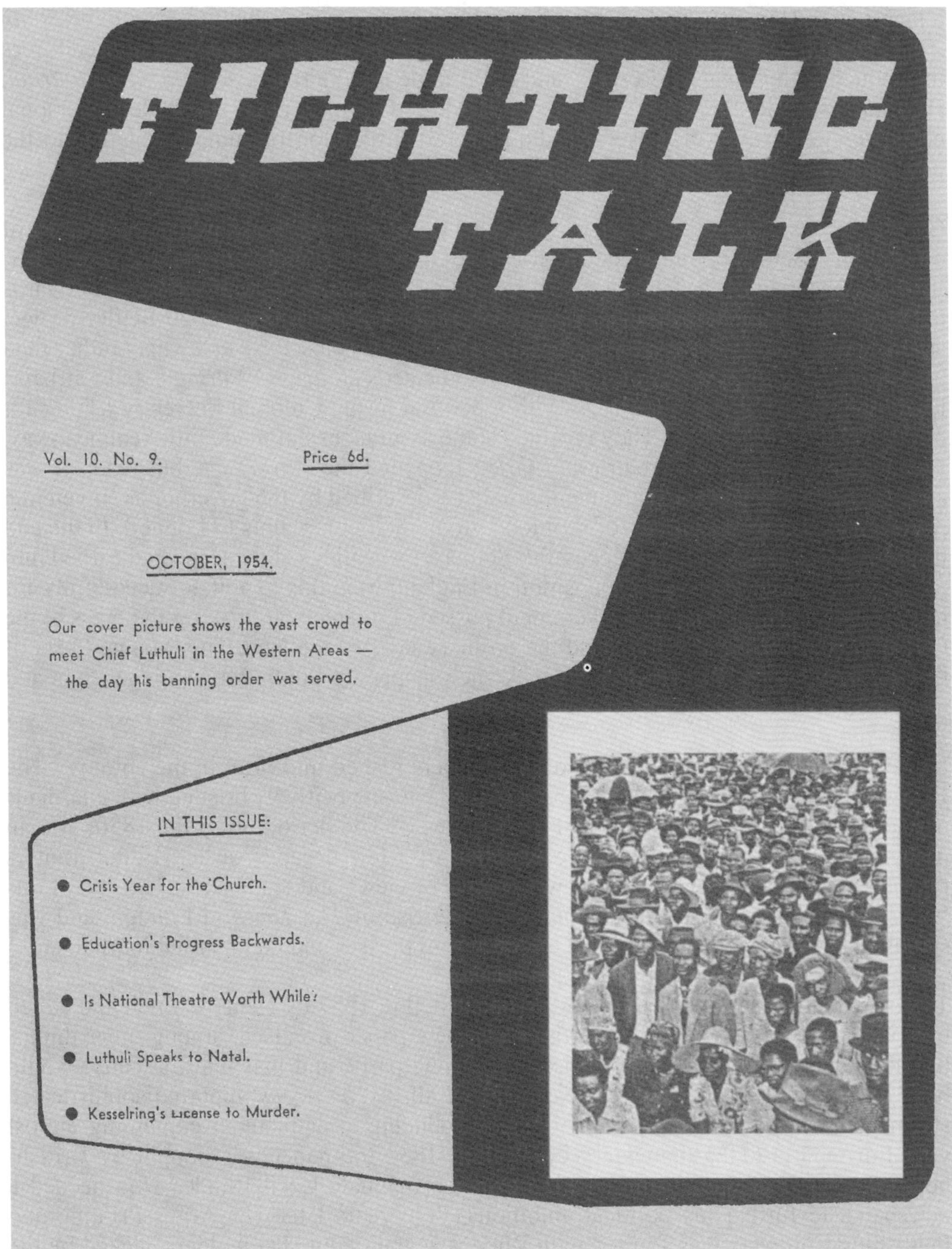
FIGHTING TALK

Vol. 10. No. 9. Price 6d.

OCTOBER, 1954.

Our cover picture shows the vast crowd to meet Chief Luthuli in the Western Areas — the day his banning order was served.

IN THIS ISSUE:

- Crisis Year for the Church.
- Education's Progress Backwards.
- Is National Theatre Worth While?
- Luthuli Speaks to Natal.
- Kesselring's License to Murder.

Ruth's editorial in this edition of Fighting Talk *(October 1954) begins: "The slow motion re-creation of South Africa in the image of Hitler proceeds."*

a newspaper. However, an English printer, George Grieg, beat them to it with the *South African Commercial Advertiser*, but after the first two editions the three men joined forces to produce both Grieg's *Advertiser* and the Pringle and Fairbairn's *Cape Town Journal*. Both papers, under Somerset's orders, were required 'to most rigidly exclude all personal controversy, however disguised, or the remotest discussion of subjects relating to the policy or administration of the Colonial Government.'[25]

Grieg soon exceeded this brief in reporting a court case dealing with allegations of corruption in Somerset's administration and the Governor demanded to see all proof sheets. In true Cobbetian style, Grieg refused to do this and was deported. Shortly afterwards the *Journal* fell foul of Somerset's displeasure for describing the 1820 Settler project as an 'ill-planned and ill-conducted enterprise' and was closed by its owners rather than being 'subject to the state of Lord Charles Somerset's stomach.'[26] Pringle and Fairbairn left for London in December 1824 with a petition to the Colonial Secretary asking for press freedom at the Cape. They received some assurances but made little real headway. A year later, however, Fairbairn and Grieg reopened the *Advertiser*, but when it was again threatened, the printer and the journalist – described by the governor as 'inveterate radicals' running an 'academy of sedition' – took their complaints to London. In the end their tactic was spectacularly successful. Somerset's dealings at the Cape had earned him many enemies, and the Whig opposition in England used this to agitate successfully for his recall. In 1829 the British government passed Ordinance 60, making the press at the Cape subject only to the courts and the ordinary laws of the land. This Magna Carta of the press fulfilled Pringle's dream to make newspapers in South Africa a legal right and not a favour.

In the wake of this success, a crop of newspapers rushed into print in the colony.[27] The Eastern province had more than its share, and 'the bush positively bristled with guardians of the rights, liberties and morals of the citizens.'[28] The period up to the 1850s was in many ways a re-run of the British experience of a few decades earlier: Editor/printers running on a pittance and voicing a wide range of views and tendencies. The end of this 'messy individualism' was to coincide with the rise of *The Times* in London, and was signalled by the introduction at the Cape of steam presses and commercial journalism.

The new trend was embodied in *The Argus*, started in 1857 by Henry Darnell and edited by Richard Murray. A leaflet advertising the new paper promised, among other things, that the paper would not be beholden to any one party, and that 'its first cause would be to secure free expression for the opinion of all.'[29] *The Argus* imported sophisticated steam presses and made a name for itself producing a supplement containing almost verbatim reports of Parliamentary debates. In 1881 the paper was bought by British-born Francis Dormer with money from mining magnate Cecil Rhodes who needed a newspaper to further his political ambitions. Five years later The Argus Printing and Publishing Company was formed with Rhodes as the major shareholder. Backed by the mining industry, the Argus Company began taking over existing newspapers until, by the 1930s, it had acquired newspapers in almost every city or town except Port Elizabeth.

Shortly after the Boer War a new paper, *The Rand Daily Mail*, was started and was soon acquired by mining magnate Sir Abe Bailey. In 1906 Bailey funded a weekly called *The Sunday Times*. Both professed to be 'loyal to the fingertips, and Imperialist to the backbone.'[30]

These early newspapers were heavily influenced by British journalistic tradition, and most of their top posts were staffed by graduates from Fleet Street and British universities. A journalist who worked under these men was to note that 'the newspapers they produced gave few hints that there were grevious wrongs to be righted in a land where, many of them felt instinctively, their most important mission was the perpetuation of British influence in a most conservative form.'[31] And their allegiance to mining capital was never in doubt. A former *Argus* editor, HL Smith, was to comment in 1945 that 'it has been the policy of the daily press ... that ipso facto whatever is best for the gold mines is best for South Africa as a whole, and that end is kept ever foremost in mind.'[32]

More than 10 years later the editor of *New Age*, Brian Bunting, was to complain that it took 'a great upheaval among the non-white population before the daily press will take notice of what is going on'. The views they printed were 'not the views of the non-european people or their organisations, but in the last resort the views which Big Business would like to foist upon the non-european people and their organizations.'[33]

The Afrikaans press was no less blind to African affairs, but it was not part of the 'objective' British tradition and was openly partisan from its inception. The first Boer-supporting paper was *De Zuid Afrikaansche Tydschrift*, started by Rev. A Faure with the help of Pringle in 1822. *De Zuid Afrikaan*, which appeared in 1828, found itself obliged to fight 'the radicalism of the negrophilist philanthropists.'[34] Throughout the 19th century small Dutch newspapers campaigned for church, language, land and schooling for the volk, and when Harm Oost started *Het Volk* in 1914 the issues remained the same. *Het Volk* rallied support for a 'pure South African nationalism' and argued against the integration of different cultural and racial backgrounds, asserting that 'God's purpose was to have different nationalities develop in their own separate ways.'[35] *Die Burger*, started in 1915, was edited by a man who was to become a Nationalist prime minister, Dr DF Malan, and ever afterwards the route to top political posts in the National Party was often by way of newspaper editorship. *Die Transvaler's* first editor was Dr HF Verwoerd, who made little distinction between his roles as theologian, politician and journalist. During the Second World War he was to be found guilty of publishing Nazi propaganda.

The African press had a slightly later start. The first recorded vernacular publication was a set of religious tracts in Tswana produced by the London Missionary Society in 1836, and the first newspaper, *Umshumayeli Wendaba* was published in Xhosa from July 1837. The first newspapers for vernacular-speakers all came out of the missions, the high point of this phase being *Isigidimi Sama Xosa* which had an African editor and came out in 1876.[36] The first paper to be owned and controlled by an African was *Imvo Zabantsundu*, edited by John Tengo Jabavu, and this heralded a period of independent black journals airing grievances against colonial administration. Notable among these were *Abantu-Batho, Ilangalase Natal, Izwi Labantu, APO, Indian Opinion, Worker's Herald*, *Umsebenzi* and *The Torch* which, together with *Imvo*, formed a new perspective on the depredations of colonialism.

As more Africans learned to read, it became clear to white financiers that an economically viable black newspaper was a possibility. In 1920 the Chamber of Mines started *Umteteli wa Bantu* which soon employed some of the most talented black journalists of the day. Then in 1932 Bertram Paver launched *Bantu World* which, when it ran into financial

FIGHTING TALK

Registered at the G.P.O. as a Newspaper

Vol. 11, No. 5. Price 6d.

JUNE, 1957

African Women against Passes

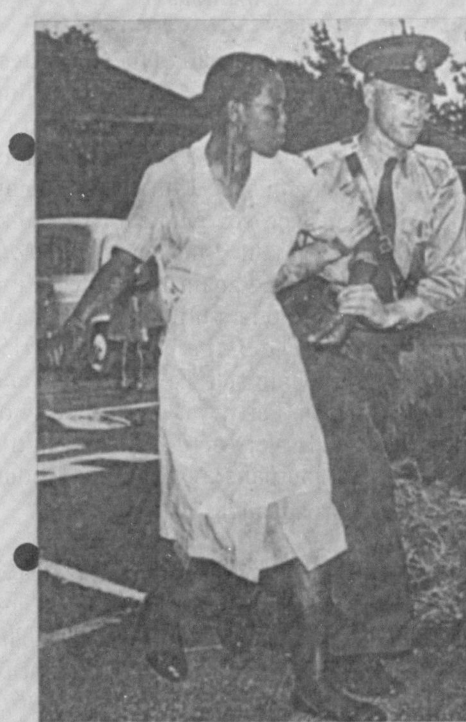

"THE BITTER HARVEST"

By Alfred Hutchinson

SOUTH AFRICA'S SECRET POLICE

THE H-BOMB

THE COLOURED SEATS: Should They Be Boycotted? *By Alex Hepple M.P.*

THE £1 A DAY CAMPAIGN

The Group Areas Act

A MONTHLY JOURNAL FOR DEMOCRATS

Fighting Talk, *June 1957.*

trouble, was taken over by the Argus Company. Bantu Press, formed by the Argus, began taking over black publications and by 1945 it owned ten weekly newspapers. The newspapers of this group were generally conservative in tone. According to Bunting, *The World* 'opposes every ANC campaign; never advocates the formation of an independent mineworkers' union; opposes unity of the oppressed peoples of South Africa in the Congress movement; never criticises the mining industry ... (and) when the Congresses launched their campaign for £1-a-day, *The World* opposed it and started its own campaign for 10s a day.'[37] In 1951 Jim Bailey, millionaire son of Sir Abe Bailey, started *Drum* and later a newspaper for the black market called *Golden City Post*. These publications catered for a new class of upwardly-mobile black readers. *New Age* noted that

> Tribute must be paid to these journals for having made a valuable contribution towards the training of non-white journalists and the opening up of careers for them. But the editors, managers and directors of policy on both journals are white, and the papers themselves, like *The World*, reflect the interests of the financial groups which back them.[38]

When *Post* attacked the ANC for being too greatly influenced by left-wing organisations and demanded that it put its house in order, *New Age* wrote a sniffy comment that the paper's only qualification to open its mouth was that it had big money behind it: 'They can issue ultimatums to the prostitutes, thieves, murderers, pimps and adulterers who provide them with such a great proportion of their copy. But they have no right at all to expect, and they have done nothing to deserve, the confidence of any of the people's liberatory organizations.'[39]

In the face of rising printing costs and the commercial assault on the black press, newspapers which had earned this confidence – independent African publications – rapidly lost ground. By 1950 they had disappeared. Writing in 1958, Bunting was to say that 'when we survey the field ... it comes as something of a shock to realise that in South Africa today there is not a single daily or weekly newspaper wholly owned and produced by Africans and which can claim to voice the national aspirations of the African people.'[40] By the 1950s the only newspaper which published in the radical tradition of Cobbett, Pringle and Lenin was *New Age* and one of its most prolific journalists was Ruth First.

The party press

The Guardian, the newspaper Ruth was to join as Johannesburg editor in 1947, was therefore the inheritor of an old tradition of press radicalism. The early communists in South Africa were strongly influenced by the *Iskra* group and considered newspapers to be essential collective organisers. British immigrants such as David Ivon Jones, Bill Andrews and Sydney Bunting also brought with them memories of Peterloo, Chartism and the English radical press. Newspapers soon became central to the development of socialist ideas in South Africa. In 1915 members of the International Socialist League started the *International* and later *Inkululeko* (1915) and the *Bolshevik* (1919). In 1930 the Communist Party of South Africa launched *Umsebenzi* and in February 1937 Party members founded the *Cape Guardian*. This paper was soon renamed *The Guardian*, then, following the bannings of *The Clarion, People's World, Advance, New Age* and finally

WARM WELCOME TO THE CLARION

CAPE TOWN.

"I WELCOME The Clarion and the contribution that it will make to the struggle back to a better way of life than we now enjoy," Mrs. Margaret Ballinger, M.P. told The Clarion representative on Tuesday.

She went on:

"The banning of The Guardian is the natural action of a Government which is determined to stamp out its own views on the community and to resist by all the

and hope that it will enjoy full freedom of expression. Whilst assaults are made on still more of our valued freedoms, it is good to see that the freedom of

When The Guardian *was banned in mid-1952 it was replaced immediately by* The Clarion.

Spark. As it was a vehicle for much of Ruth's finest journalism – and because it was itself a particular set of social and technical processes which were to influence her writing – the life of this extraordinary newspaper needs some consideration.

The *Cape Guardian* began after a sub-committee connected to the Left Book Club was formed to explore the logistics of starting a paper in Cape Town.[41] This committee began raising finances and mobilising people around the project, and they appointed *Cape Times* womens' editor, Betty Radford, as editor.[42] She was to recall that 'the editorial office was a desk at the printers on the floor on which the paper was stored ... we had neither typist nor office boy, and for some months not even a telephone.'[43] The focus of the newspaper was indicated in a letter from the secretary of the S.A. Typographical Union in the first edition:

> From what I can gather it will be a purely trades union paper, free from all prejudices such as race and colour, and will stand for democracy in the true sense of the word ... I wish The *Cape Guardian* every success and I hope and trust it will do its best to uplift and enlighten not only the trades unionists, but those outside the ranks....

According to its future editor, Brian Bunting, *The Guardian* started off as a trade union-oriented, liberal journal. 'It didn't have any specific political colour that you could identify ... but it gradually came to reflect the view of the Communist Party'. The committee sold the newspaper from house to house in working-class areas, outside factories and to trade

A studio photo of two Guardian *street sellers in Cape Town published in the newspaper in 1940.*

union members. Under the Party's internationalist perspective, the newspaper began to keep watch on events beyond the country's borders. Its reputation was established in its early years by its 'brilliant exposure of the appeasement politics leading up to the betrayal of Czechoslovakia by the Munich Agreement.'[44] After a couple of years, the weekly feature, Behind the News, by Vigilator (Harold Baldry) was advertised by the paper as 'famous'.

As war loomed in Europe, *The Guardian*'s overseas news began to pick up the paper's circulation. According to Michael Harmel, the paper's 'broad anti-racist and anti-fascist position in exposing the events of the 1930s came at a time when the English-language press, controlled by big mining and finance houses under pressure from the Hertzog government were virtually silent about Nazi crimes, and the Afrikaans press under editors like Verwoerd, increasingly sympathetic.'[45] In a year-by-year resumé of its activities printed in 1945, the paper was to define its activities in terms of its international coverage:

> 1938. Its first birthday found it at war with the Chamberlain gang, then busy putting Spain to death. Later that year came Munich. *The Guardian* was growing up in a tough school.
>
> 1939. The year that brought the war made inevitable by Chamberlain. But the hoary Tories of England weren't keen to fight Hitler, only itching to go at Russia. In the Finnish war, the youthful *Guardian* was the only South African paper to keep its head.[46]

The Guardian also printed a pamphlet called *The Munich Swindle* which sold 25 000 copies and was to start a long tradition of Guardian pamphlets.[47] In 1938 the paper was selling 4 000 copies a week, and by 1940 this was up to 12 000. But after Hitler turned against Russia (and the Communist Party swung around to support the war effort) *The Guardian*'s circulation shot upwards in step with the rising visibility of both the Soviet Union and the Party. The paper's editorial policy on the War wavered with the Party, then settled down to cautious support for the Allies:

> At present Chamberlain's line of action can be used for progressive ends, and the obvious duty of progressive people is to support the war for as long as that position lasts – that is, until Hitlerism is destroyed. The important thing is that their support must be critical. Those who have betrayed us so often must not be blindly trusted, but watched at every stage.[48]

Guardian street sellers, though, found the new line very useful on the streets: 'We used to go out collecting ... the political climate was so favourable to the Left, especially after the Soviet Union was attacked by the Nazis, there was a feeling of good will. We used to go from door to door and we used to say: 'Look, this is the only paper that is anti-Hitler, anti-Nazism. And we must fight it. This is the only voice' and so on. We collected money that way'.[49] Sales of *The Guardian* also began to increase on the Rand. According to a seller:

> I went to Johannesburg ... and nobody there would sell *The Guardian*. (There was) the People's Bookshop. It used to lie there and people used to buy it there. And I said: 'What the hell! We always take *The Guardian* to meetings'. And all of a sudden I became *The Guardian* seller and I used to take *The Guardian* to meetings.[50]

By 1941, weekly sales were 22 000 and a year later they were nearly 50 000. While other newspapers had their supply of newsprint drastically reduced during the War, both *The Guardian* and the Communist Party's *Inkululeko* received increases in their allocation. In the favourable war climate *The Guardian* opened offices in Johannesburg, and Port Elizabeth. By the time the Nationalist Party came to power in 1948, it was an established player in the Liberation Movement.

Keeping the red flags flying

By the 1950s all that was to change. *The Guardian* was despised by the new Nationalist Party government and – whichever way you measure it, financial or political – it was a newspaper which had little hope of survival in the postwar climate of intolerance. From week to week, month to month, it teetered on the brink of closure, with pennies in the bank and policemen at the door. It was written and edited by a small group of people who worked on several publications simultaneously and shared a common dream. But the costs were high. *The Guardian* in its many forms was banned outright five times, sued, fire bombed, spied on and had its presses sealed. It was banned from news stands and constantly raided by the police. Several Commissions of Enquiry investigated its activities. Its editors received personal banning orders, most of its staff were arrested and charged at one time or another, its street sellers were harassed and beaten up, and many went on trial for high treason. Yet, except for the State of Emergency in 1960, *The Guardian* (by then named *New Age)* came out every week for 25 years, one of the longest runs of any left-wing paper in South Africa. Its survival is a tale of enterprise, bravery, tenacity and luck. It was to be central to Ruth's journalism during this period.

NEW AGE, THURSDAY, SEPTEMBER

WHY WAS NEW AGE BANNED?

WHILE the last issue of New Age, dated April 7, was still being printed, a Government Gazette Extraordinary was issued by the Minister of Justice banning the newspapers New Age and Torch under the Emergency Regulations.

Guinea, and such news of the situation in South Africa as the editorial staff felt would not fall under the definition of "subversive."

It was hard to decide what was subversive and what was not. The Emergency Regulations defined a subversive statement as any statement calculated or likely to have the effect

gency Regulations were promulgated.

In other words, not a single issue of New Age was prepared, printed and published after the Emergency Regulations were promulgated. Yet the Minister could make the claim that he had examined New Age and was satisfied that there was "a systematic publishing of matter . . of a subversive character."

The end of New Age, *September 8 1960.*

Though *The Guardian* had good international news at a time when the world was at war and was critical of the government at home, against apartheid and without peer in its political coverage, these factors cannot explain its centrality on the left in the 1950s. Its longevity had more to do with the difficulty the African National Congress found in producing a newspaper, and with the poor performance of the commercial press.

When asked about *The Guardian*, journalists who worked on *The Star* and the *Rand Daily Mail* during the 1950s claimed it was 'politically untrustworthy and often factually incorrect.'[51] But they admitted they read it to find out what was happening on 'that' side of the political spectrum. *Guardian* journalists were even less complimentary about the mainstream press and deemed it shallow, willfully inaccurate and politically naive. In an editorial about the National Protest Week in April 1958, *The Guardian* claimed that:

> the line of the English-language press, dailies and weeklies, is, as usual, to trade on the white reader's abysmal ignorance of most things African ... . The basic delusion of this press seems to be that if you ignore a ticklish problem for long enough it may dissolve itself. Either these papers print no news at all, or play down the news and hope that if they, ostrich-like, keep their heads buried in the sand long enough, others will take up the same position ... . Has it struck no one on the big newspapers that withholding a true assessment of a situation from one's readers is an open invitation to panic and hysteria if what you prophesy won't happen does come off after all?[52]

Two years earlier the white-owned African-oriented newspaper, *The World*, had its reporter barred from the ANC's national congress for inaccurate reporting and anti-congress bias. *The Guardian* was particularly offended by *The World's* mindless brew of sex, sin and soccer written in the name of the toiling masses. '*The World*', wrote the *Guardian* editor, 'parrots (Prime Minister) Strydom.'[53] Brian Bunting was to reflect that the *Rand Daily Mail* only began to notice township life and politics after *Spark* (the final form of *The Guardian*) was banned and it was required to find its own township news.[54]

Unlike the commercial press, *The Guardian* did not act as if its only readers where white. Week after week it wrote about events which affected the lives of millions of South Africans yet which seldom even made fillers in the mainstream newspapers. For this it was much appreciated by its readers. 'I have always regarded *Advance* as *The Guardian* of the people', wrote the Reverend Douglas Thompson in 1954. 'It gives facts and information about the lives of the people of South Africa that I have been unable to find anywhere else.'[55] Less literate readers said it their way: 'I am an old man and there's no work in town for me. And I am just got out of hospital. I am glad you remind me of the paper, because all other papers they can stop but my paper I don't want to stop till I die.'[56]

Apart from its popular coverage, another factor which increased its importance of *The Guardian* was the absence of other voices on the left. Despite several short-run papers put out by the ANC Youth League, the ANC itself never managed to sustain a newspaper voice of its own and undoubtedly suffered because of this.[57] A sampling of 30 black newspapers which supported the ANC from its founding to its banning in 1960 shows an average life expectancy of 27 months.[58] Congress never had a truly national paper, and the quality of *Abantu-Batho*, its first and only official paper during that period, cannot be assessed because virtually no copies have survived.[59]

During its 'constitutional' phase, before the days of mass action, the ANC's largely petty-bourgeois membership was able to make do without an official organ because it could rely on its influence on the fledgling black commercial press. Many of the ANC's 'old guard' were journalists from an older, independent phase of the black press. They were able to influence the content of *Bantu World* and other papers through personal relationships. A more strident voice was that of *Inkundla ya Bantu*. From 1943 it was edited by Jordan Ngubane, who replaced Govan Mbeki. Ngubane was a prominent member of the ANC Youth League who was bitterly opposed to the Communist Party and, according to Mbeki, was 'viciously critical of the ANC'. It was also an intermittent publication and collapsed when it failed to make a profit.

The ANC continued to be aware of the need for its own media. At its 1949 Congress, the newly-adopted Programme of Action called for 'regular issue of propaganda material through the usual press, newsletter or other means of disseminating our ideas ... and the establishment of a national press'. In 1957 Congress was still calling on its executive to investigate the possibilities of bringing out its own newspaper.[60] But, as *The Guardian's* printer, Len Lee-Warden, observed, 'the ANC weren't great pamphleteers ... if they did have (some printing) done, they'd have a leaflet saying there's a meeting and then what they've got to say they'd say it at a meeting.'[61] There seems to be two reasons for the scarcity of ANC media. The first was structural:

> It should be borne in mind ... that great difficulties face the African people with regard to the establishment of an independent press. The greatest difficulty is the lack of capital. In addition ... the establishment of a press requires the right to own freehold property and to carry out business undertakings with the maximum security, all rights which are denied to the African people. Any paper which openly voiced the policies of the liberation movement would also find it extremely hard to attract advertising (and) even a printer willing to handle the job. It would (also) be extremely difficult for an African paper to keep its staff together. An African journalist who incurred the wrath of the authorities would always be liable to arrest and deportation without trial.[62]

The second reason concerned the nature of the ANC. The organisation was essentially four regional bodies linked by an annual national congress and with an executive forever short of cash for travel. To hold such a disparate organisation together required regular contact and information, and to accomplish this it relied increasingly on the skills, finances and media of the Communist Party (and after it disbanded, on former members of the Party). For this reason *The Guardian* came to be an important organisational force in the transformation of the ANC from a collection of protest meetings into a single fighting force. The organisation 'did have an occasional conference and the occasional meeting,' according to Bunting,

> but if you think of the period before 1950, the organisation that did the running around and day-to-day agitation was the Party, it wasn't the ANC. We had the meetings, we ran around with the paper ... we ran around with pamphlets, we held the meetings on the Parade. The task of mobilising, propagandising, organising the people was a Party task much more than the ANC. I think that was one reason why the ANC didn't have a paper ... there's no question about it, the ANC people regarded *Guardian/New Age* as their paper, especially after 1950.[63]

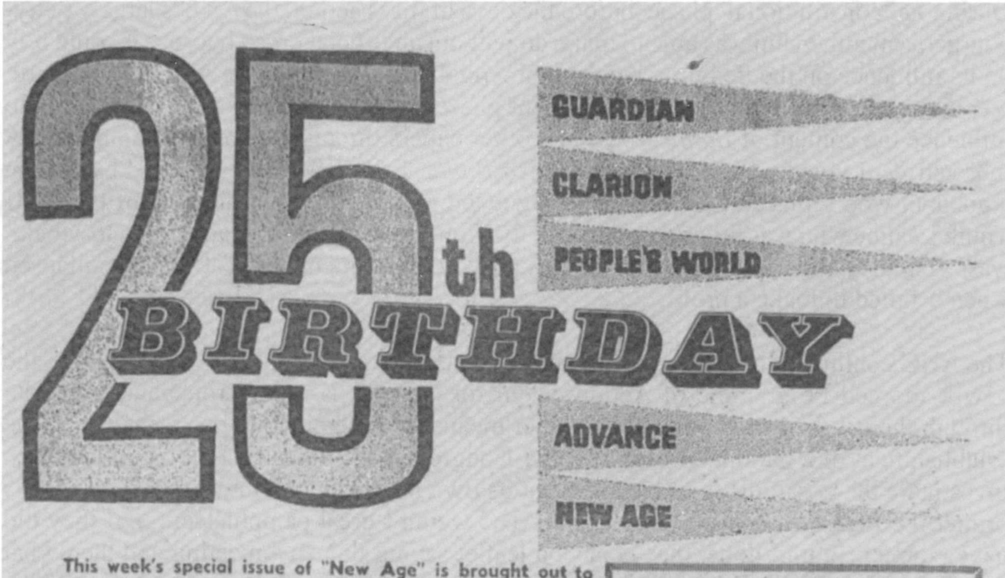

This week's special issue of "New Age" is brought out to mark the 25th anniversary of the progressive press—the "Guardian" newspaper was born in Cape Town on Feb. 19, 1937.

In honour of the occasion, "New Age" has received messages of greeting and congratulation from leading figures and organisations both in South Africa and abroad.

Here is the message from CHIEF A. J. LUTULI, Nobel Peace Prizewinner and former President-General of the banned African National Congress:

NEW AGE

Vol. 8, No. 23. Registered at the G.P.O. as a Newspaper 6d. 5c.

SOUTHERN EDITION Thursday, March 22, 1962

Chief A. J. Lutuli

CONGRATULATIONS to New Age and its predecessors. Twenty-five years of uninterrupted production is an achievement that is remarkable for the progressive press of any country. It is even more so in the case of New Age and its predecessors which have had to face all the hardships imposed against them by successive Governments.

Despite arrests of members of its staff and bannings, New Age and its predecessors have regularly come out, not giving in on any basic question affecting the civil and political rights of any person, black or white, in this country.

Since my advent into active politics I have found New Age to be forthright and brave.

I have not always agreed with everything it says, but on questions affecting the non-white peoples in S.A., New Age has been and continues to be, the fighting mouthpiece of African aspirations.

I sincerely trust that in the future, too, New Age will play its part in exposing the rottenness of the society in which we live and to this end, I want to add my best wishes to the paper and all members of its staff, from the Editor downwards.

More power to your pens, gentlemen, the people need you as much as they need their organisations.

The struggle to which you have dedicated yourselves must triumph. Forward to a non-racial democratic South Africa in which colour bars and discrimination between man and man will be a thing of the past.

Amandhla! Awethu!

MORE MESSAGES ON PAGES 8 AND 9

A message From London

From Oliver R. Tambo, Nelson R. Mandela, Mzwandile M. Piliso, Robert M. Resha, London:

WE congratulate New Age on the 25th anniversary of the progressive press.

New Age has a record which few newspapers in South Africa can equal or even remotely approach. No other newspaper in the country has been subjected by the Government to such systematic persecution or faced such formidable difficulties.

Yet this is one newspaper which has consistently exposed and condemned white domination in all its manifestations, and continues to serve as a reliable source of news and an effective medium of expression for all who have ceaselessly fought for genuine democracy in South Africa.

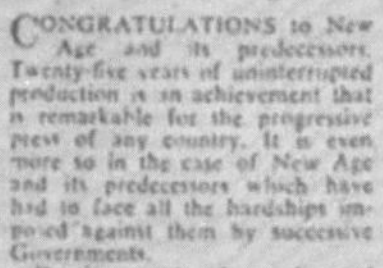

Mr. Nelson Mandela

"GOVT'S INVASION PLOT IS A FRAUD"

Warning By Chief Lutuli and Dr. Naicker

DURBAN.

"THE Minister of Defence, Mr. Fouche is using high pressure tactics in order to create panic among the white electorate so as to enable his Government, through the Minister of Justice, to introduce legislation during the present session of Parliament further restricting the freedom of the individual in South Africa;" says a statement issued jointly by Chief A. J. Lutuli, former President-General of the b… African National Co… and Dr. G. M. N… President of the Sou… can Indian Congre…

The statement add… after the announcement… Minister of Justice that he intends introducing a Bill for the more 'efficient maintenance of law and order' in the country, the Minister of Defence told Parliament that certain Afro-Asian countries were plotting an armed invasion of the Republic.

"This scare of an 'invasion plot' is nothing more than a move to make the white electorate and a feeble Parliamentary opposition submit to further Nationalist onslaughts against the legitimate opposition by the people to its apartheid policies."

Calling on all democrats to oppose these Nationalist tactics, the statement warns the white voters of the country not to allow themselves to be stampeded into making enemies of four-fifths of the South African population as well as all the independent countries in Africa.

"The new danger we face in this political climate created by the ruling Party must clearly be seen as a move to further restrict the freedom of the individual—both White and Non-White," ends the statement.

In Johannesburg Adv. Duma Nokwe, former Secretary-General of the banned ANC, said:

"Mr. Fouche may feel that it would be national suicide to accede to the demands of the people for the vote, the right to work and to live decently and freely, but in fact it is these war statements of his that will lead to his undoing.

"Do the whites here, like the 'ultras' in Algeria, think that they can rule against the express will of the people for ever?"

By 1962 the radical newspapers which began with The Guardian *in 1937 had, despite frequent bannings, an unbroken publishing record of a quarter of a century. (*New Age, *March 22 1962.)*

When the Communist Party was disbanded, members focused their attention increasingly on the ANC. Here they were initially to come into conflict with the Youth League in its attempts to transform the ANC into a liberation movement. This struggle was to have a detrimental effect on *The Guardian's* circulation, coming as it did amid Cold War hysteria. However, the confrontation was finally resolved and *The Guardian* remained the principal newspaper of the movement. Since the 1940s, the paper had used the ANC's membership for newsgathering and distribution. For the Congress to have started a newspaper of its own in the 1950s, according to Bunting, would have meant 'really doing something in competition with *The Guardian*, for no good reason.... Considering the costs and the distribution problems and all the rest of it, it was simpler just to say and do whatever you had to do through *The Guardian.*'[64]

So, increasingly through the 1950s, *The Guardian* and its successors became the weekly heartbeat of a liberation movement constrained by money and physical distance. This was reflected in 1957 when a range of political figures referred to the political significance of the radical press during an appeal for funds in support of *New Age*:

- Walter Sisulu (Secretary General of the ANC): *New Age* is an organiser of the oppressed and exploited people of our country.

- Lilian Ngoyi (Federation of South African Women): *New Age* is the only newspaper which fearlessly presents to the world the truth about the conditions of the oppressed people in South Africa.

- Dr W Conco (ANC): *New Age* is the only paper in the country which breathes the spirit of liberation.

- Piet Beyleveld (Congress of Democrats): *New Age* is our source of information and means of contact with our fellows in the struggle for freedom in the various parts of South Africa. It is our voice ... without which the struggle would have been much more difficult.

However, this situation placed a burden of political responsibility upon *New Age* journalists. In 1957 Bunting was to reflect that '*New Age* is a battlefield ... in its pages you can read the people's struggles and victories. Its headlines and stories pass the people's verdict on the history of our times. Never have so many left so much to so few.'[65] *New Age* journalists, particularly members of the Party underground like Bunting, Govan Mbeki, Lionel Forman Fred Carneson and Ruth First, were thus to play a role which far exceeded that of their counterparts on the commercial press. Their journalism, and the politics which influenced their world view, became the way in which the liberation movement came to see itself.

Process and pennies

Given the paper's centrality and importance, it is interesting to note how precarious its position remained throughout its existence. In 1945 a non-profit company, Guardian Newspapers (Pty.) Ltd., was formed with a paid-up share capital of £71. The board of directors was Radford, WH Andrews (the CPSA chairman), Donald Molteno (a Native

Representative in Parliament) Dr Yusuf Dadoo (a Party activist and president of the Transvaal Indian Congress), MP Naicker (a Party member and trade unionist) and the Reverend Douglas Thompson (a founder member of Medical Aid for the Soviet Union). Molteno resigned soon afterwards on the grounds that *The Guardian* had given 'special and strong support to the Communist Party.'[66] Over the years, the holding company was to change its name and directors in a series of transformations which were to prove rather profitable. Its functions, however, remained the same, as did its problems: money, printers and the police. As Radford was to reflect, 'left newspapers do not usually have an easy passage, and *The Guardian* is no exception. Sometimes ... it very nearly succumbed to malnutrition.'[67]

Printing was a headache which took years to solve. Initially the paper had been run off by Stewart Printers. After the war, however, Charles Stewart bought a rotary press and upped his prices. *The Guardian* moved its custom to *Die Suiderstem*, a United Party-controlled printshop. But this company became 'strained financially' and Radford looked around for other alternatives. A former apprentice of Stewart's, Len Lee-Warden, was approached but he did not have the equipment to handle the paper's size and circulation. *The Guardian*'s business manager, Fred Carneson, offered to put up the money for a flat-bed press and Lee-Warden agreed to take the paper. The source of the money for the press is something of a mystery. According to Lee-Warden, 'a very high up man in the Catholic Order' who was 'connected with the Catholic paper *Southern Cross*' agreed to put up £3 000 and became a sleeping partner. But this arrangement was to run into trouble:

> One day (this man) came into the business very worried. And he said it had come to his notice that we were printing *New Age*. He hadn't known what we printed. And he said because of what he knew about *New Age*, he couldn't continue as a director in the company, and either we would have to stop printing it or give him his money back. This was an impossibility because we had used the money.[68]

So until the money could be scraped together (nearly a year later) the paper was forced into a curious subterfuge:

> At about 6 o' clock after all the staff had gone, my partner and myself and a couple of people would go into the works and we would set up the paper. We would lock it up in forms.... I had special boxes made that the forms fitted into ... then at half past four in the morning I would go up country to the *Worcester Standard*. They would print it, fold it and dispatch it.

For *Guardian* papers, though, the ever-pressing problem was money. And because of its political standpoint it was, for most of its life, starved of the one source which kept the commercial press alive: advertisements. Briefly, during the war years, the situation was different and *The Guardian*'s pages were 'chock-a-block with advertisements.'[69] But this was not to last, and after the war advertising income dropped to a few hundred pounds a month. Lee-Warden was to reflect that:

> a normal newspaper is carried by the advertisers. What they get from their circulation is small in relation. With us it was the other way round. It was what they got from subscribers that carried them more than what they got from advertising. Not many people liked to advertise in (*The Guardian*) because it carried a certain stigma politically.[70]

Every month the books just didn't seem to balance. In 1958, desperate to convince readers of the seriousness of the situation, *New Age* published its monthly budget (in pounds) which seemed to suggest that it was losing more than £10 000 a year:

Direct printing costs (printing etc)	£865
Distribution (postage, railage etc)	£620
Total production costs (excl. salaries)	£1 485
Editorial costs (salaries etc)	£240
Administration costs (wages, rent etc)	£449
Total admin. and editorial costs	£689
Total monthly costs of *New Age*	£2 174
Income from sales	£1 243
Income from advertising	£32
Loss	£899
Loss per copy	5.25d

'It was always a question,' according to business manager Fred Carneson, 'of not knowing at the beginning of the month whether you were going to be able to pay wages and the printer at the end of the month.'[71] With costs often exceeding sales and advertising, he was forced to find other sources of income. Three other methods were used: funders, fiddles and Christmas clubs. And, in view of the paper's long if precarious existence, they worked passably well. According to their printer, 'their cheque never bounced'.

'Pay up or we're going down'

Ray Alexander was to remember that the *Cape Guardian* was started with money from 'trade unionists, artists, journalists, academics and professionals' and funds continued to

be provided by a number of 'sleeping partners' and 'anonymous friends.'[72] These sources, according to Carneson, included a wide range of supporters:

> A big building firm run by a family. Very generous. They'd fork out thousands and thousands to help us over the difficult period. Mary Butcher came from a wealthy Natal family. She would put down a thousand quid sometimes. Paddy Manning, a retired Irish dentist. He'd put a thousand pounds on the table, or five thousand. This bloke I went to, I got ten thousand quid at one go from him. And others have got even more. This was just a straightforward donation.[73]

Despite dark hints from the government and the mainstream press from time to time, there is no evidence that *The Guardian* was funded by the Soviet Union.[74] When things became tight, *The Guardian* staff would organise fundraising drives. According to Wolfie Kodesh, who handled distribution of the paper in Johannesburg, the biggest one-off funders were 'local Whites and Indians'. Johannesburg was sometimes lucrative, and Party member Margaret Street 'collected a lot of money from the business community.'[75] In Cape Town, according to Bunting, 'Fred Carneson and my wife would go around regularly to business people, particularly Jewish business people'.

But the best supporters were members of the Indian community, particularly if well-liked political figures could be persuaded to come along on fundraising trips. 'If you took Bram (Fischer) there', remembered Carneson, 'you knew you'd get money. For the Indian merchants: Go with Dadoo or Cachalia'. Dadoo, particularly, was good news of funding drives. According to Wolfie Kodesh,

> When Dadoo came along we used to go to Indian merchants, mainly. They used to say: 'There you are, there's the cheque book, you write it out'. We went on trips, but we never collected as much as Dadoo. The merchants used to say: 'Look, you come here, we'll give you some money. But if Dadoo comes we'll give him the cheque book.'[76]

The drive for funds would also become a political roller-coaster. 'It wasn't just going out and collecting money', according to Carneson. 'You'd talk to people and give them your view of things. They'd ask you how do you see things and so on and you'd put across the Party line. It was never a question of going in and somebody saying "here's your cheque" You'd sit down and talk to them.'[77]

The campaign for funds also went on in the pages of *The Guardian* and *New Age*. Week after week, year after year appeals, ranging from aggressive, through imaginative to desperate, could be found in their pages. Readers where exhorted to send donations, collect with tins or lists, organise dances or parties, hold talks, publicise the importance of *The Guardian*, obtain new readers, help get *New Age* agents, sell the paper, or 'appoint a sub-committee or member to pay special attention to *New Age'*. Over the years the newspaper formed support committees, a Guardian League, a Fighting Fund, Guardian Scouts, and a National Campaign to Save *The Guardian*. But after the Suppression of Communism Act, many people began to distance themselves from anything 'Red', often to ensure their own political survival. Funds and circulation dropped. In October 1952 the newspaper gave notice on the front page that 'revenue from functions, dances, lectures etc. has declined because of police intimidation. Many people who normally support us have been driven away by police raids.... If money is not forthcoming we will ... be compelled to close down our Durban office and reduce staff in other centres and reduce the paper to four pages.'[78] In July 1954, *New Age* was

> Fighting the battle for survival. Unless a miracle happens – and that is not very likely – our accumulated deficit at the end of this month will be £1 000. We have never had such a big deficit in the whole of the proud history of our paper ... the plain fact of the matter is that our expenditure has exceeded our revenue almost every month since the beginning of this year. Our creditors are getting a little tired of promises. The outcome of the battle depends on you, our readers. If you want *New Age* to continue its irreplaceable service to democracy, then you must pay for it … .[79]

Two years later, clearly having survived the earlier crisis, *New Age* admonished readers with a warning: 'With just one week to go until the end of the month, we are not even one quarter of the way to our target of £2 000 … . Where there should have been a steady stream, there is only a painfully slow trickle, scarcely strong enough to wet the backs of our postage stamps.'[80]

In March 1956 the newspaper launched a national campaign with the target of raising £10 000 and increasing sales by 20%. By then it had 'reached the stage where we do not know from one month to another whether we shall be able to continue publication the following month'. When response was poor, the editor told readers that the time had come to do some serious talking: 'The response so far to our appeal has been extremely disappointing ... if our readers, and the whole democratic movement, do not make a special effort now, *New Age* will cease to appear as from the end of May, 1956. No, this is not idle talk. We mean every word of it...'[81] Even a drop in the bucket at that stage was clearly welcome:

> Selwyn Hilner ... is not quite eight years old. Last week a family visitor made him a present of ten shillings – a small fortune to a little boy, even in these days of inflated toy and sweet prices. Without any prompting, he decided 7/6d of his ten bob must go to *New Age*, and nothing could make him change his mind. Thank you Selwyn!

By September the paper was still 'hanging by a thread' and the need to order newsprint meant that without money 'we shall be caught short at the end of December and that will mean the finish of *New Age*'. By the middle of the following year the newspaper was still signalling 'a desperate financial situation' and with eight members of staff involved in the Treason Trial it was reduced to four pages for one edition. This obviously had the desired effect, because the following week the editor announced that 'you who have given money in the last two weeks have saved *New Age*'. The largest donation was from 'The Congress of Democrats in Johannesburg.'[82]

The following month the newspaper's cover price was doubled to 6d, but a few weeks later the paper gloomily noted that 'despite the price rise, at the end of this month we can't pay all our bills'. In mid-1958 it was still facing 'a financial crisis of the first magnitude', but after a funding drive backed by leadership figures in the liberation movement, *New Age* was still alive in August, 'but only just'.

SWART'S NEW THREAT TO PRESS FREEDOM

NEW AGE

Vol. 5, No. 19 Registered at the G.P.O. as a Newspaper

NORTHERN EDITION Thursday, February 26, 1959 6d.

Bill Puts Iron Curtain Round Prisons

CAPE TOWN.

DRASTIC amendments of the existing law are brought about by the Prisons Bill to be introduced by Mr. Swart, the Minister of Justice, during the present session of Parliament.

This is mainly a measure to consolidate the laws relating to prisons, but it contains at least one amendment which gravely imperils the rights of prisoners and the freedom of the press.

If this Bill becomes law, it will be an offence to sketch or photograph any prison, portion of a prison, prisoner or group of prisoners, whether inside or outside a prison;

(Continued on page 6)

If Swart's Bill Becomes Law, We Couldn't Publish this

Cry For Help From Bethal Jail

BETHAL.

TWO scribbled sheets of paper, torn from a school exercise book, were smuggled out of a Bethal jail last week, and reached the African National Congress and New Age.

Written in pencil, these letters are a plea from long term convicts in Bethal for the outside world to be told of their conditions.

"We apply for help," say the letters.

Thirteen prisoners have

(Continued on page 4)

Another Spy Uncovered

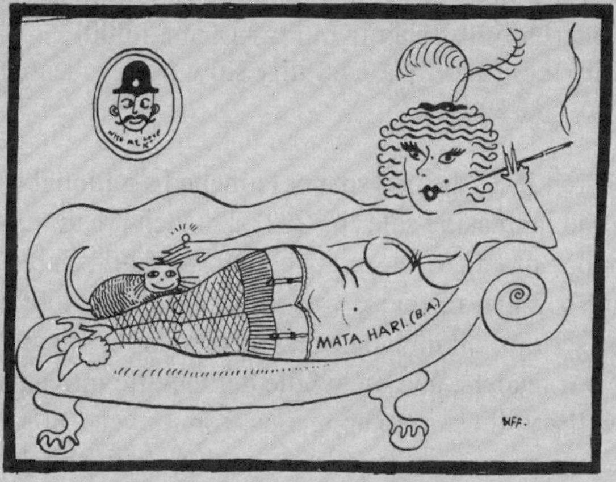

WHAT'S THE LATEST NUSAS, DAHLING?

[Special Branch please note: Any physical resemblance between this woman and your university spy is purely coincidental.]

SPECIAL BRANCH PLANTS AN INFORMER IN NEW AGE OFFICE

JOHANNESBURG.

THE Special Branch of the Police sneak spies and informers in wherever they can, and they have been doing so for years.

They even had a man planted in the Johannesburg offices of New Age for a while.

This same man wriggled his way into the Randfontein branch of the African National Congress and served, as a co-opted member, on the committee of that branch for a short time.

He is Mr. Oliver Mti, now working as a reporter on the staff of the (Bantu) World.

He was sacked from New Age some months ago but has recently taken to making curious phone calls to the office checking up on the movements of some staff members.

GAVE GAME AWAY

He gave the game away himself. Look at the evidence:

An invoice for a suit bought at an outfitters' firm in Randfontein records his name and address:

Oliver Mti,
404 Old Loc(-ation),
c/o Special Branch, C.I.D.

The suit was bought on December 1 last year.

Two weeks later Oliver Mti who gave his address care of the Special

(Continued on page 2)

Invoice made out to Mr. Oliver Mti, c/o Special Branch, C.I.D.

Durban's Mass Protest Against Group Areas Act —page 4

Congress Plans For Economic Boycott

JOHANNESBURG.

THE Congress Movement will this year launch a new phase of the economic boycott and will announce new products and institutions to be boycotted and the date of the boycott.

This was one of the decisions taken last week-end by the conference of the executives of the ANC, SAIC, SACPO, COD and SACTU.

This conference also approved a resolution of the Accra Pan-African conference on the launching of a boycott of South African goods.

AFRICA DAY

All Congress organisations and

(Continued on page 6)

New Age, February 26 1959.

'We had a lovely big loss'

The Guardian's business team were all communists. But their attempts to keep the newspaper alive would be a credit to the most adept capitalist tycoon. The publication was closed down four times and common sense suggests a loss of revenue each time. But instead, each assault by the state was turned to financial profit. Or in the words of the paper's business manager, Carneson, 'losses could be offset against future profits'. Each closure of the paper was never unexpected and, in good time, 'shell' companies were 'lined up' before a banning and the name of the next version of *The Guardian* was registered. When the paper was finally closed, according to Carneson, 'we had a lovely big loss there. And there are people who are interested in buying companies with big losses, because they set it off against profits and they don't pay tax.'[83] When *The Guardian* was banned in 1952 its shares were worth about three shillings in the pound, which provided a convenient financial black hole for a purchaser.

> We did it every time! Do you think we wanted to lose money? Whoever buys the company from you takes over the losses against any profit which he makes from business. If he takes over a ten thousand pound loss, he resumes his business activities under the name of *The Guardian* company trading as whatever ... . He can make ten thousand quid and not pay a penny tax on it.[84]

The Guardian, working through its attorneys, would sell to 'anybody, bloody anybody.[85]

'Johnny's specials, the worker's request'

Perhaps the most ingenious *Guardian* scheme was the Christmas Club. Towards the end of the war John Morley arrived in Cape Town after being discharged from the British Army following a 'problem' over disability payments. He became interested in the government's food rationing system and started organising the women who queued at government trucks selling scarce produce. He also found the women to be willing buyers of *The Guardian*. He soon had food committees going, and when the food van system ended he and the committees turned their attention to rice hoarding by merchants. Rice raids were organised and shopkeepers found themselves forced by angry crowds of women to sell their hidden supplies at the fixed rates. In consultation with the food committees, Morley started Johnny's Christmas Parcels. The scheme was relatively simple. People received a book and each week they bought a stamp to stick into it. A full book at the end of the year entitled them to a Christmas hamper. According to Carneson, 'there were other Christmas clubs around, but they were a rip-off. Johnny would consult with the women's committees on what should be in the parcels. It was good-quality stuff. Merchants would pack the parcels and deliver them door to door just before Christmas'.

And with each subscription to the Club went a 'free' *Guardian*. The scheme was replicated up on the Reef by Arnold Selby, *The Guardian's* circulation manager, and became Arnold's Christmas Club. Club subscriptions sold about 20 000 copies of *The Guardian* every week – nearly half the total circulation in the 1950s – and earned the paper between £10 000 and £20 000 a year 'plus interest on weekly contributions.'[86] According to Carneson, 'the

Clubs were a major contributor to *The Guardian* ... we couldn't have survived without them'.

So, despite decades of financial stringency and many near-disasters, when the newspaper did finally close in 1963 it was by state decree and not through insolvency. Except for the six months of its banning in the 1960 emergency, the paper had never missed a week since its inception in 1937.

The party connection

The Guardian was always at pains to publicly separate itself from the Communist Party. According to Bunting the paper 'was never an official Party organ.'[87] Its business manager claimed there was no direct link between *The Guardian* and the Party 'except that there were a lot of communists and former communists active on the paper.'[88] When *New Age* was banned, the paper opposed the banning in an affidavit which claimed that the paper

> (i) never ... professed to be a publication for propagating the principles or promoting the spread of communism,
> (ii) was never published or distributed by or under the guidance of an organisation declared unlawful,
> (iii) never ... served as a means of expressing the views propagated by such organisation,
> (iv) never at any time or in any manner served as the means for expressing views or conveying information calculated to further the achievements of any of the objects of communism.[89]

However, the newspaper's public stance was clearly tactical. *The Guardian's* founding editor, Radford, was to become a member of the CPSA's central committee as was Bunting, her successor.[90] Shortly before she left the paper (as a result of disillusionment following a trip to the Soviet Union), Radford wrote in an editorial that 'our support for the Communist Party has been more consistent and vigorous for the simple reason that communist policy has been in harmony with our own .... So long as the Communist Party fights against colour-bars and capitalist exploitation, so long will *The Guardian* continue to support it up to the hilt.'[91] Party activist 'Rusty' Bernstein considered that in the Transvaal, *The Guardian* 'was our sort of voice but not our property'. But the distinction was juridical. In the 1950's, according to Lodge, under the editorial control of SACOD members, the paper 'devoted much of its space to descriptions of Soviet achievements, justifications of Russian foreign policy and criticism of Soviet dissenters.'[92] And Bunting was to reflect that

> The central committee would perhaps discuss from time to time what it would like to see in the paper. Later on, for instance, when I was elected to the central committee, whatever would be discussed and debated would be reflected in the columns of the paper.... I suppose that explains quite a lot about the development of the paper, because the connections between the two were very considerable.[93]

Of at least 41 people who worked on *The Guardian* over the years, 15 were listed as communists by the state and quite probably were. This number included all key journalists (most of whom joined the SACP underground in 1953) and most of the administrative staff. So the successes and weaknesses of *The Guardian* cannot be assessed without an understanding of the changing fortunes of the Communist Party itself.

Lowering the flag

Given the political climate of the 1950s, it is not surprising that *Guardian/New Age* and its staff were harassed, detained and banned. What is surprising is that the paper survived

HELP SAVE NEW AGE!

National Campaign For £10,000

Of all the newspapers at present in circulation, New Age is the only one which constantly and consistently exposes the tyranny and injustice of racial oppression, which willingly opens its columns to all those individuals and organisations whose views would otherwise be suppressed or ignored.

Week after week our paper, and ours alone, fearlessly voices the demand of the oppressed people for freedom and equality, for peace, for a better life for themselves and their children. While other sections of the press have allowed themselves to be threatened and brow-beaten into virtual submission to the dictates of the Nationalist Government, New Age alone has refused to be deflected in any way from its own freely chosen course.

There are few democrats in South Africa who do not realise the difficulties involved in producing our paper, or who do not recognise the paramount political importance of New Age. Yet the number of helpers directly involved in the task of keeping our paper going has been growing smaller and smaller. Many who assisted the progressive press in the past have dropped out of activity altogether. Others have, by and large, given their attention to other tasks and, unfortunately, pay but scant and superficial attention to our problems. New Age is taken far too much for granted by many who should know better.

To allow this situation to continue is to court disaster. We have already reached the stage where we do not know from one month to another whether we shall be able to continue publication the following month. This is an impossible state of affairs and it is obvious that something must be done, and done soon, to place New Age out of danger.

Our Target

For these reasons we have decided to launch a four-month NATIONAL CAMPAIGN, with a target of £10,000 and a 20 per cent increase in circulation by the end of JUNE. The achievement of our objective will put our paper on a firm footing, enable us to weather any storms which may lie ahead, and strike an effective blow against fascism in South Africa.

EVERY DEMOCRAT MUST BE PREPARED TO PLAY HIS PART IN THIS IMPORTANT CAMPAIGN. Indeed, without the co-operation of everyone we shall not succeed. Given that co-operation, success is certain!

What You Can Do

- Make the biggest personal donation you can afford.
- Collect money from your friends. (Collection lists are available.)
- Keep a "New Age" collection tin in your home.
- Organise a dance, a party or some other function on our behalf.
- Introduce New Age to new readers, either by selling the paper regularly, getting new subscribers or sending us the names and addresses of those you think may be interested in our paper.
- Talk New Age, think New Age and get your friends and the members of your organisation to do likewise.
- Raise the question of New Age at your meetings—persuade your organisation to make a donation and to undertake to hold a function or organise collections on our behalf.

New Age needs you, just as you need New Age. Call in personally, or write to any one of our offices today. We shall be only too pleased to tell you exactly how to set about things.

THE TASK OF STRENGTHENING NEW AGE, OF EXTENDING ITS INFLUENCE, OF STABILISING ITS FINANCES, IS AN ABSOLUTELY ESSENTIAL PART OF THE STRUGGLE FOR DEMOCRACY!

In the meantime show your solidarity with, and support for, NEW AGE by sending us the biggest personal donation you can afford. Give our campaign a good kick-off. Let us hear from you soon.

SPARK

New Series. Vol. 1 No. 18 PRICE 5c February 28, 1963

VORSTER'S NEW BAN A THREAT TO "SPARK"

Named and Banned May Not Work For Press

CAPE TOWN.

BY means of a notice published in a Government Gazette Extraordinary last week, the Minister of Justice has launched the Government's most serious offensive to date against the democratic press.

The notice applies to three classes of people. They are:
(a) named Communists;
(b) people who were office-bearers, officers or members of any organisation declared unlawful under the Suppression of Communism Act (the Communist Party and the Congress of Democrats);
(c) people who are banned or restricted under the Suppression of Communism Act.

None of these three classes of people may after April 1 1963 become or remain office-bearers, officers or members of an organisation which in any manner prepares, compiles, prints, publishes or disseminates any publication as defined in the Suppression of Communism Act, or which in any manner participates or assists in the preparation, compilation, printing, publication or dissemination of any such publication.

Exemptions may be granted from this new blanket ban by the Minister or "the magistrate concerned."

DEFINITIONS

Publication is defined in the Suppression of Communism Act as "any newspaper, magazine, pamphlet, book, handbill or poster."

Organisation is defined in the Act as "any association of persons, incorporated or unincorporated, and whether or not it has peen established or registered in accordance with any statute."

The ban is clearly directed in the first place against "Spark". Since the Government has failed on so many occasions to silence the democratic press by banning the papers, it is now getting at the personnel themselves.

(*Continued on page* 14)

PASSES FOR WOMEN

Women have had to carry reference books since February 1—and here a young girl has her fingerprints taken prior to becoming subject to the De Wet Nel-Vorster slave laws like all other Africans.

*In February 1963 the government prevented named communists or people banned under the Suppression of Communism Act, from working in the media. It would be the end of Ruth's South African journalism. (*Spark, *February 28 1963.)*

at all. *The Guardian's* legal problems began early in its life. It set a tack into stormy seas during the Second World War by refusing to sign a 'voluntary censorship agreement' by which editors pledged not to publish 'any information ... which might be useful to the enemy.'[94] Nonetheless, it was subject to a pre-publication censorship system operated by a Defence Force brigadier. Between November 1939 and April 1944 the government issued no less that eight proclamations relating to control of news and information, one which included provisions for the registration and control of homing pigeons 'to prevent leakages of military information.'[95] During the 1946 strike the newspaper's offices were raided and a number of its staff, including the editor, were arrested on sedition charges. This was to be a pattern for the future.

The new nationalist government's first intervention in the paper's publication came in 1949 when, on instructions from the Minister of Transport, Paul Sauer, the Railways banned *The Guardian* from bookstalls and private shops on railway concourses. In Parliament, the Minister of Justice, CR Swart, indicated that '*The Guardian* and all other publications which stirred up hatred between Europeans and Non-Europeans could be banned. We are not,' he said, 'going to stand for any nonsense from the communists in South Africa.'[96]

The growing multi-racial alliance was a problem for the new Afrikaner government, and it continued to attack these moves, paradoxically, in the name of preventing race hatred. Some years later this tortured thinking was expressed with no hint of irony by a magistrate in his summation of a case:

> It is common knowledge that one of the aims of communism is to break down race barriers and strive for equal rights for all sections of the people and to do so without and discrimination of race, colour or creed. (Equality) would endanger the survival of Europeans and therefore legislation must be pursued with the objects of suppressing Communism. The object (of the Act) is clear. It is to stop at the earliest possible stage the fermentation of a feeling of hostility between Europeans and Non-Europeans.[97]

After a raid on all the offices of *The Guardian* in Cape Town, Port Elizabeth, Durban and Johannesburg during November 1950 it became clear that the paper was subject to a secret judicial investigation. In October 1951 the findings of a Committee of Enquiry were submitted, and claimed *The Guardian* was a communist newspaper. The paper denied the charges and a 'Save *The Guardian*' campaign was launched. Meetings were held, a mass signature campaign was started and people were urged to send postcards of protest to Swart. But, despite the campaign and representations made by Bunting to the United Nations Commission of Human Rights, the Minister of Justice banned the paper in May 1952 under the Suppression of Communism Act – the first newspaper to be closed for political reasons since Lord Charles Somerset halted the *Commercial Advertiser* in 1824. In the view of the three-man investigating committee, the paper 'had been published under the influence of the Communist Party'. Carneson remembers:

> We got the paper out and they banned us. I got this message at home. I was in the middle of moving from the house where we were staying ... and we forgot to report to the bloody police. We were both banned, and one part of the banning order was that if you moved you had to advise the police. At this moment they ban the paper! I had to rush in to the newspaper office to make all sorts or arrangements, get new things going, start the new company of the new

> paper ... we tried to be as legal as we possibly could. And as we stepped out of the door of the office into the street the bloody police screamed to a halt and arrested my wife and I. Took us off to Caledon Square for not reporting.[98]

The paper's banning followed the Van Riebeeck celebrations and a mass rally of 15 000 people in Johannesburg at which the president of the ANC, James Moroka, pledged to struggle against unjust laws. According to Bunting, the Minister's action 'set alight the fuse which led to the explosion of the Defiance Campaign.'[99] *The Guardian* was replaced immediately by *The Clarion*, produced by the same staff and run off the same presses. Bunting was to reflect that 'much amusement was caused by a press photo of Sam Kahn selling a copy of the first issue to Minister of Justice Swart outside the Houses of Parliament.'[100]

For technical reasons (there was another publication of the same name) *The Clarion* became *People's World* and then *Advance*. The paper's communist staff, together with its twin focus on apartheid and the glories of Russia, remained a thorn in the flesh of the new administration and a problem for the mainstream press. The South African Society of Journalists passed a resolution allowing it to reject 'any application received for membership, irrespective of what the constitution lays down, from people who admit themselves to be communists.'[101] Bunting and *Guardian* reporter Naomi Shapiro were only admitted after threatening to sue the society for libel over remarks by its president in *The Journalist*.

In 1954, shortly after the formation of SACOD, *Advance* was banned and re-appeared as *New Age*. Reviewing the banning, the new publication said it was

> A sad reflection on our democratic instincts that the banning of the newspaper *Advance* has brought scarcely a murmur from the South African public .... The more the public sees of this law and its operation, the more alarmed it ought to become .... The ordinary rights enjoyed by a common thief are denied to politically undesirable persons.[102]

New Age had a particularly long run, although its staff were constantly being banned, arrested and spied upon and its Cape Town offices were gutted by a mysterious fire in March 1957.[103] The paper was closed down for six months during the State of Emergency in 1960, but it re-opened and continued until November 1962. It was banned following the investigations of a government committee, the findings of which still remain secret. Applications to have the ban set aside were refused by the Minister of Justice, BJ Vorster. Its successor, *Spark*, carried a defiant comment on its demise (perhaps with an eye on later historians):

> Paper can be burnt or thrown away,
> But these records shall not perish
> Or be obliterated.
> They'll live forever in the people's memories, the safe Guardian
> Of our heritage, as we advance to a New Age
> Cheering the Spark of liberation
> Struck from the anvil of struggle by pioneers.[104]

With the banning of *New Age*, it became an offense to possess any copies of newspapers banned under the Suppression of Communism Act, and *Spark* advised all readers to 'get rid of your *Guardians, Advances* and *New Ages'*. By this time Bunting, First, Mbeki, Carneson and Kodesh were all under personal banning orders.

The appearance of *Spark* was, politically speaking, pretty cheeky. The publication had been registered more than a year previously and had been putting out ghost editions to fulfil its registration requirements. According to Bunting, editions of *Spark* were

> published and circulated and sent round to libraries, although the circulation was about 10, just so we could have the legal basis for carrying on with the paper if we had to. The whole run of *Spark* was possible because the foundation had been laid – otherwise legally it couldn't have been done. The whole atmosphere we functioned in was (by then) one of persecution and repression.[105]

In February 1963 all national offices of *Spark* were raided by the Special Branch. Reporting the raids, the paper noted that 'the warrant said there was reason to believe an offense had been committed but did not specify the nature of the charge'. Then, early in 1963, the state banned 547 people, including almost everyone associated with *Spark*, and prohibited them from associating in any way with 36 organisations. *Spark* staff were required to resign from virtually any left-wing political organisation from April 1 1963. The ban was the most devastating yet experienced by *The Guardian* stable. *Spark* observed that the ban was 'to knock out the people's press, the most outspoken of the government's opponents, the most vigorous critics of apartheid. The government wants to do its dirty work in silence.'[106] According to Bunting

> We could have carried on publishing if we'd been able to find a printer. But when we were sort of swept aside by the personal prohibitions which were served on us we could only have carried on with completely new people ... everybody who could have come forward from our ranks at that stage was incapacitated. It would mean starting with completely new people from scratch ... politically it would have been a different story. We didn't want to take the chance. We thought about possibilities of carrying on production outside the country – that was one of the reasons I went out. But it was impossible....[107]

On March 28 1963 *Spark* announced it had sold the paper to a new owner, 'Babla Saloojee.[108]

> We hope he will be able to continue the publication in some form or another, but we want to make it clear that the journalists who have worked on all these papers for so many years are no longer able to accept responsibility for the production of a newspaper, and the weekly paper which has been the mouthpiece of the people's movement up to now will no longer appear.[109]

The paper's final banner headline read: 'Vorster murders *Spark*. We say goodbye – but we'll be back'. But it never reappeared.

Fighting talk

Before turning to Ruth's work on *The Guardian*, it is necessary to consider another outlet for her writing and political agenda-setting. In between her work as a weekly journalist, Ruth nurtured another publication which was more exclusively her creation: the monthly 'journal for democrats' *Fighting Talk*. Shortly after the Springbok Legion was absorbed into SACOD in 1953, its monthly journal was 'disposed of by way of a gift to an independent committee of sympathisers and supporters of the Congress Movement.'[110]

The first edition of *Fighting Talk* had been published as a soldier's paper in January 1942 to counter a conspiracy of silence about the newly-formed Springbok Legion in the daily press, which it found 'as impenetrable as a sergeant-major's heart.'[111] When the organisation was formed it did not anticipate the hostility it was to meet from 'influential quarters' which greeted the new militant organisation with accusations of it being controlled by 'Jewish communists': 'We could not foresee that almost every important paper in the country, as though under instructions, would close its columns to us and deprive us of our right to let the country know what we stood for.'[112] The first edition of *Fighting Talk* was a four-page pamphlet which sold out all 3 000 copies in a week. Thereafter, the publication came out monthly throughout the life of the Legion, its direction guided by the organisation's three principles: belief in racial harmony, opposition to fascism and faith in democracy. As the decade progressed, *Fighting Talk* became more strident in its attacks on Nazi tendencies in the Nationalist Party, the Broederbond, the New Order and the rightwing 'shirt' movements. It popularised the Torch Commando after the war and urged all 'lovers of democracy' to spare no effort in blocking a Nationalist victory in 1948.

Soon *Fighting Talk* had established a popularity beyond the Legion's membership, and when SACOD was formed the journal was located in the organisation's offices. In March 1954, the journal told readers that it was no longer the organ of the Springbok Legion but was 'an Independent Monthly Review, edited and managed by an independent committee of supporters of the Congress movement.'[113] The new editors pledged to continue in the tradition of the Legion and to make *Fighting Talk* a voice of the Congress Movement. But they intended to broaden it to include Congress supporters who had until then little chance to express themselves in print and who had been 'fed to choking with the ideas of apartheid: Fine feathers, we know, do not always make fine birds. Our first concern will be with the substance and the content of our magazine. At the same time, we hope that by the changes we are making in its layout and make-up, to render *Fighting Talk* more readable and more effective.'[114]

Editorship initially remained with Rusty Bernstein, who had been producing it under the Springbok Legion. But in November 1954 *Fighting Talk* ceased publication for three months due to 'printing difficulties', and when it reappeared in March 1955 Ruth had become the editor.[115] Under new management it promised to be 'more vigorous and outspoken than ever in the democratic cause'.

The editorship was a challenge to Ruth. The position carried no salary and required hours of hard work writing and soliciting articles as well as dealing with printers and organising circulation. But it allowed her control of its direction and content, and she set to work crafting a journal for 'thinking democrats of all races'.

SPARK

CAPE TOWN, MARCH 28th, 1963

SPECIAL FAREWELL ISSUE

As with *The Guardian*, finances and distribution were ever-present problems, and at around £100 a month, the printers were the major expense. SACOD members were called on to send donations, while others held jumble sales, film shows, socials, play readings and 'recitals of African songs' in order to raise money. In 1954 most copies were being marketed through *New Age* street sellers and organisational contacts. The journal was also sold through bookshops, but at the Johannesburg branch of CNA returns were far higher than sales, and analysis sheets also listed, under distribution, entries like: 'Confiscated by the CID – 378.'[116] As the quality and distribution network improved, the print run was increased, and by mid-1955 it was 2 500.

Bulk sellers were keen to distribute, particularly as they were entitled to keep half the cover price of 6d for every copy sold. Aspirant agent Hanley Kaba's request was typical of the many Ruth received: 'I beg to apply to be an Agent of *Fighting Talk* in the Grahamstown district. I would like to be sent 30 copies to start with and I will later on need more when I have a considerable number of customers.... Thanking you in anticipation.'[117] ANC secretary in Kwa Thema, CL Matime, applied to be an agent because '*Fighting Talk* is one of the few means that can be employed to smoothen the road to our liberty.'[118] Some subscribers were even more enthusiastic. Abel Zwane of St Francis College at Marionhill wrote:

> The fascists and reactionary cliques shall perish like their Nazi brothers and Italian fascists deed (sic) in the past decade. Your paper is the real voice of the masses in South Africa. The capitalists, not of course excluding the Dutch feudalists and fascists, are terrified at such papers as yours … . Enlist me as your subscriber and please include the issue of April. I enclose the sum of 2/6 to cover the cost at present.[119]

Subscribers provided the journal's ensured income, and by late 1955 there were 350 of these in South Africa and many other parts of the world. But with the bulk sellers, magazines went out but, often, no money returned. Even SACOD branches sometimes proved poor payers. In May 1955 Ruth wrote an irritable letter to the Durban branch:

> At the end of 1954 you owed *Fighting Talk* £3.3s. Since then we have continued to send you 36 copies a month. We have never received a payment from you. We will have to stop sending you your monthly order if we do not hear from you ... . There is a good demand for *Fighting Talk* these days but far too little income from sales, so we will be compelled to stop supplies to poor payers.[120]

But *Fighting Talk* continued to come out monthly throughout the 1950s, and in its pages appeared the writings and ideas of most of the Congress leadership and of many creative writers who would have had no other avenue for their work. The list of contributors to the journal was a Who's Who of the political spectrum left of the United Party. They included economists, politicians, statesmen, writers, poets and priests. Within the weekly 16 pages could be found Mandela, Tambo, Kotane, Harmel, Lutuli, ZK Matthews, Mbeki, Dadoo, Kenyatta, Ben Bella, Nkrumah, Sekou Toure, Nyerere and many other leading political figures of Africa – all of whom Ruth coaxed and cajoled into print. It was in *Fighting Talk* that Trevor Huddleston chose to print his farewell article in 1955, where Basil Davidson voiced his controversial theories on African history, where Es'kia Mphahlele reflected on his exile in Ghana and where Nkrumah pondered the problems between a one-party state and democracy. But the stalwarts of the journal, ever willing to respond to Ruth's requests,

A New Age *street seller doing his bit for a boycott of capitalist commodities.*

were Cecil Williams, Duma Nokwe, Lionel Forman, Hilda Watts and, particularly, its former editor Rusty Bernstein.

Bernstein was an irrepressible political debater who could craft elegant prose in defence of international socialism and the Congress Alliance. His rhetorical style complimented Ruth's sharp irony and Forman's impish humour and their writing set the tone of the journal. The Call to the Congress of the People, written by Bernstein in 1955 and printed in *Fighting Talk*, was one of the most stirring political invocations to come out of South Africa. But his ability to see beyond the current situation and asses its implications was something he shared with Ruth. A week before the Congress of the People, for which he had been working so hard, Bernstein stepped back from himself in an article in *Fighting Talk* to reflect on the efforts of the small group of organisers:

> Sometimes, reading history of the days that have gone, one thinks with envy of the men who lived in the great periods of change, when all men's destinies were being determined by their own acts. Perhaps, in some future time, men will look back on our age with such envy; for it is easier to live in the presence of history than to be aware that we are making it. Yet insistently the thought keeps recurring that, whether we are aware of it or not, we are making history in our time with this Congress of the People.[121]

Ruth's letters to Forman, urging him to submit articles and teasing him about his work – preserved by Forman's wife Sadie after his death – provide one of the few glimpses in print of Ruth's correspondence with authors and at the same time of the gentle and funny side of her relationships with her peers: 'Notice that we had to skip an issue. Dearth of articles was one reason!!! Now we're in a flap we haven't got good enough stuff for the November issue and we need it by the 22nd and not a day later. PLEASE. PLEASE. PLEASE.... Write pronto. And in English, not gibberish.'[122] Some time later Ruth was urging Forman again:

> Ha! I've thought of something for you to write for our November issue ... a piece on Soviet African writing ... . Cut the jargon out, though, and don't elaborate too fully on any specific marxist study that will involve long definition and back-to-the-source material on What Is A Nation. Remember we are a popular journal! Yes, the other popular too, our friends and admirers tell us![123]

Forman retaliated to Ruth's prodding with an equally sharp but witty pen. During the boring hours of the Treason Trial he profiled Ruth in two short limericks:

> There was a young liberal called Ruth,
> An absolute stranger to truth,
> Whose temper was bad
> (I know it - By Gad)
> A temper most sadly uncouth.
>
> And of young Miss First
> This was not the wirst
> For she spoke so fast
> She left you aghast
> And when she was puzzled she curst.[124]

Ruth used *Fighting Talk* to attack passes, police brutality, labour conditions and to support bus boycotts, the Freedom Charter and the Congress Movement. But she also used it as a platform from which to challenge readers and stimulate progressive writers. According to Brian Bunting:

> Ruth had the capacity to dig out facts and talent, to harness not only her own energies but also those of others. Nor was she content merely to propagandise or sloganise. She believed the best propaganda was the facts and editors and readers knew they could rely on every word she wrote. Nothing was left to chance, nor was any stone left unturned. She worried and worried at a problem until it was solved.[125]

The journal was a venue for issues of Communist Party concern, such as the debates which followed the fall from grace of Stalin and the Soviet invasion of Hungary. But it also provided space for a range of voices far wider than the Congresses. *Fighting Talk* carried many short stories which were published in its pages for the first time. It also reflected Ruth's interest in the theatre and books. Cecil Williams, writing regularly, was to support and popularize a whole genre of theatre which seldom made the pages of the commercial press, and the many book reviews tantalized readers with publications seldom seen on the shelves of the CNA.

When the State of Emergency was declared early in 1960 *Fighting Talk* ceased publishing for six months: 'In the countrywide swoops in which 2 000 South Africans of all races were rounded up and detained, *Fighting Talk* lost writers, readers, editorial and circulation staff, sales agents and our most staunch supporters.'[126] When it resumed in August 1960 its focus had prudently but tactically altered: The edition focussed on Africa and carried no articles on South Africa. From then on *Fighting Talk* clearly ran at the very edge of State tolerance and in March 1963 it was banned.[127]

Notes

1 Harrison, 1974, p9.

2 Ibid, p11.

3 Ibid, p14-16.

4 Ibid, p38. Cobbett was one of the foremost investigative journalists of his time. His two books, Rural Rides, were a searing expose of the terrible conditions in the British countryside in the early 19th century. He is often considered to be the father of British radical journalism.

5 Ibid, p106.

6 Westmancoat, 1985, p26.

7 Quoted in Harrison, op cit, p154.

8 Quoted in Harrison, ibid, p41.

9 Harrison, ibid, p156.

10 Small, 1982, p86.

11 Ibid, p86.

12 Speech to the conference of the Society of Russian Workers, Paris, January 15 1887. Reprinted in A Mattelart and S Siegelaub, 1983, p118.

13 Ibid, p119.

14 D Ivon Jones: Lenin's first newspaper. The article first appeared in the *International* 1924. This text was taken from *African Communist* No.42, 3rd Quarter, 1970 which reprinted it from *The Communist Review* Vol 5, No.2, June 1924 (London).

15 Ibid, p64.

16 Lenin in *Novaya Zhizn*, November 12 1905. Reprinted in Mattelart & Siegelaub 1983, p125.

17 Text adopted by the Third Congress of the Communist International, Moscow 1921. Reprinted in Mattelart & Siegelaub, 1983, p133.

18 Ibid, p133.

19 Ibid, p128.

20 Adalbert Fogarasi in *Kommunismus* 2, July 15 1921 (Vienna). Reprinted in Mattelart & Siegelaub, 1983, p150.

21 Ibid, p151.

22 Ibid, p151.

23 De Kock, 1982, p29.

24 Papers relating to the *South Africa Commercial Advertiser* and its editor, Mr Grieg. London: January 1827. (Command Paper 470).

25 Ibid, p42.

26 Ibid, p52 and Hachten & Giffard, 1984, p26.

27 Between 1840 and 1950, 11 opened in Cape Town alone.

28 Anthony Delius, quoted in Hachten & Giffard, 1984, p27.

29 Hachten & Giffard, ibid, p30.

30 Ibid, p39.

31 Ibid, p40

32 Smith, 1945, p72.

33 Bunting: The story behind the Non-White press. *New Age* pamphlet nd. p2.

34 J du PScholtz: *Die Afrikaner en sy Taal* (Cape Town, Nasou, nd.) p41.

35 Hachten & Giffard, op cit, p43.

36 Switzer & Switzer, 1979, p2.

37 Bunting: *The story behind the Non-White press*, op cit. p3.

38 *New Age* 27.11.58.

39 Ibid.

40 Bunting, *The story* ... op cit, p6.

41 This consisted of Bill Andrews (Party member and trade unionist), Jimmy Emmerich (secretary of the Cape Town Tram and Omnibus Workers' Union), Dr George Sachs (a surgeon and socialist), Harold Baldry (a lecturer in classics who became 'Vigilator'), Carina Pearson (Baldry's wife), Thomas Ngwenya (of the Cape Town branch of the ANC), John Gomas and Jimmy la Guma (of the National Liberation League), Arthur Trom (a German who had escaped from Nazi Germany and was a typesetter), and Charles Stewart (the owner of Stewart Printing Co. who was to print the *Cape Guardian*). From Ray Alexander, private correspondence.

42 She was not a member of the Party at the time, but she and her husband, George Sachs, joined in 1941.

43 *Guardian* 25.7.46.

44 Bunting in *Moses Kotane*, 1975 p90.

45 A Lerumo (Michael Harmel): *Fifty Fighting Years*, p68.

46 *Guardian* 22.2.45

47 Simons & Simons, 1978 edn. p583.

48 Vigilator in *The Guardian* 22.9.39.

49 Jean Bernadt in Bernstein, 1988 p70.

50 Ibid, p67.

51 Interviews with 'Ossie' Osman and Benjamin Pogrund: (Johannesburg & London, 1988).

52 *New Age* 10.4.58.

53 *New Age* 2.1.58.

54 Interview with Brian Bunting, London, 1988.

55 Letter to *Advance* 9.9.54.

56 In *New Age* 13.4.58.

57 It is interesting to speculate on the effect of a nationalist liberation movement seeing itself reflected weekly through Communist Party eyes.

58 L Switzer & D Switzer, 1979 p24.

59 *Abantu-Batho* was started in 1937 as *The Territorial Magazine* and changed its name in 1939. The paper's first editor was Govan Mbeki, who worked on it until 1943 when its owners felt he was too radical. It was then taken over by Jordan Ngubane, who was later to join the Liberal Party. When the paper got into financial difficulties its owners approached Mbeki for help but he was unable to raise funds and it subsequently collapsed. Private correspondence with Mbeki.

60 *New Age* 12.4.58

61 Interview by Bernstein, 1988.

62 Interview with Bunting, 1988.

63 Ibid.

64 Ibid.

65 *New Age* 14.3.57.

66 Molteno Papers C5.69 and *The Guardian* 11.1.46.

67 *The Guardian* 22.2.45.

68 Interview with Lee-Warden, Cape Town, 1988.

69 Bunting, document M1.1.2, private collection.

70 Lee-Warden in Bernstein, 1988, p124.

71 Interview with Fred Carneson, London,1988.

72 Private correspondence with Alexander.

73 Carneson Interview, 1988.

74 According to Brian Bunting, *The Guardian* once got £5 000 from China. 'I don't know where it came from or why – out of the blue. But that's all.' Interview, 1988.

75 Interview with Bunting, 1988.

76 Interview with Wolfie Kodesh, London,1988.

77 Interview with Carneson, 1988.

78 *Advance* 21.10.52

79 *New Age* 29.7.54.

80 *New Age* 23.9.54.

81 *New Age* 12.4.1956.

82 *New Age* 28.3.57.

83 Interview with Carneson, 1988

84 Ibid.

85 Ibid.

86 Ibid.

87 Kotane, 1975 p96.

88 Interview with Carneson, 1988.

89 Document held by author.

90 Bunting became editor in 1948.

91 *The Guardian* 17.1.46

92 Tom Lodge: *Black politics in South Africa since 1945*, p72.

93 Bunting interview, 1988.

94 *The Guardian* 20.4.44

95 *The Guardian* 20.4.44.

96 Hansard 19.5.49. In 1948 the newly-formed secret police had recommended the establishment of a public commission similar to the Un-American Activities Commission of Senator Joe McCarthy.

97 Quoted in National Action Committee, 1952,1.

98 Interview with Carneson, 1988.

99 In Bunting: *Kotane*, p185.

100 Ibid.

101 Bernstein, op cit, p131.

102 *New Age* 2.12.54.

103 *New Age* 7.3.57.

104 *Spark*, 25.12.62.

105 Interview with Bunting, 1988.

106 *Spark* 28.2.63.

107 Interview with Bunting, 1988.

108 He was later to be detained under the 90-days clause and during interrogation he jumped (or was pushed) to his death from a window of the Security Police building in Johannesburg.

109 *Spark* 28.3.63.

110 *History & Policy of the Springbok Legion*. Treason Trial defence document probably written by Jack Hodgson in the late 1950s. p15.

111 Springbok Legion (promotional pamphlet) n.d. p1.

112 Ibid, p1.

113 *Fighting Talk* March 1954, p1.

114 Ibid.

115 *Fighting Talk* March 1955, p2. The earliest indication I have that Ruth was working on *Fighting Talk* is a letter from Joe Matthews to Ruth as editor in April 1954. Personal collection.

116 Sales analysis figures for *Fighting Talk*. Author's collection.

117 Letter to *Fighting Talk* 18.7.55. Author's collection.

118 Letter 13.6.55. Author's collection.

119 Letter April 13 1955. Author's collection.

120 Letter 20.5.55. Author's collection.

121 *Fighting Talk* June 1955, p2.

122 Letter October 15, 1957. Forman Collection.

123 Forman was never to write that particular article. He died during an open heart operation 17 days after Ruth's letter to him on October 1959.

124 Forman Collection.

125 *Morning Star*, August 24 1982.

126 *Fighting Talk* August 1960.

127 Its activities during this time are discussed in Chapter 12.

5

Building a campaign

'Bethal', said one African, 'is the worst place that God has made on earth'. It is an eloquent commentary – Ruth First

LOCKED IN THE LUGGAGE BOOT

TWO AFRICANS POISONED AND BURNT

(By RUTH FIRST)

JOHANNESBURG.

TWO Africans are lying in a Johannesburg hospital, one of them still dazed and unable to talk after four days in hospital, with carbon monoxide poisoning and body burns.

Most people won't believe their story at first. But this is what I managed to piece together.

Last week a car drew up outside the casualty station of the hospital. Two Europeans got out. They went to the back of the car and opened up the luggage compartment.

INSIDE WERE LYING TWO AFRICANS, CURLED UP IN THE RESTRICTED SPACE, UNCONSCIOUS.

other, in faltering English, could not say much. His mouth was sore, he said.

Both were from Nyasaland. I learnt, as, with an interpreter found in the ward, we began to piece together the story.

One had been in the Union three years, working as a garden boy in Linden. One day, while he was walking in Newlands, he

*Ruth discovered that two white farmers had transported two black workers 60 miles to Johannesburg in the boot of their car. When they opened the boot the men were near death, so they deposited them at the Johannesburg hospital and drove away. (*The Guardian*, March 31 1949)*

The discussion so far has been on the politics, people, media traditions and newspapers which underpinned Ruth's journalism and gave it direction. But though her writing was deeply influenced by her context, it was also essentially her own – words crafted at breakneck speed in a busy office, words agonized over late at night or before the children woke up in the morning, sometimes sarcastic, sometimes damning, nearly always clear. Her output was prodigious – up to 16 stories a week at times, in between longer articles, political reports and pamphlets. Sorting through 15 years of her writing in South Africa, it soon becomes clear that the relationship between a journalist and her context is a problematic one. Unlike the writings of a novelist or a poet, the work of a journalist is more transparent, less individualistic and provides fewer clues to the personality behind the news report. The tools of her trade were the pen, notebook and typewriter. But they were also her political understandings, her values and her interpretations, and these were closely connected to her social and political context. She wrote insightfully and at times brilliantly about what she saw and knew, but she was also, in a sense, written by this context.

Ruth was not an objective reporter and never intended to be. She was a passionate political reporter in the grand tradition, using her skills as a means towards the development of the class awareness of the oppressed, consciously attempting to mobilise them and to bring about tangible political results. This approach was to make her an investigative reporter of an unusual kind. It integrated her into a situation where she was reporting the advance of history through the voice of the protagonists of history – but in the process it transformed her into one of South African history's political protagonists.

Her journalistic frame of reference was South Africa from the mid-1940s to the early 1960s. But it was a picture viewed from the perspective of the Communist Party and the Congress Alliance, from the position of an educated white woman who was both an observer of the life around her and a social participant in what she observed.

But it would be entirely incorrect to say that Ruth was merely a propagandist for the political Left. Hers was a probing, dissident perspective, setting ideas and events against one another, sharpening and clarifying differences and thereby intensifying commitment to certain ideologies and discourses. At times she was to develop ideas which were in advance of and even out of step with the communist, nationalist and liberal thinkers and activists around her.

The Congress Alliance and the Party provided the platform from which she wrote, but they were not a cage for her ideas. An integral relation was to develop between her private and her social destiny and this was to be reflected in her writing. Historian Gavin Williams has identified three underlying ideas which ran through her work and which will be looked at in the following chapters:

> That the proper focus of social explanation should be on capitalism;
> That there are times when the masses are able to seize the political agenda from the hands of

their rulers and shape the political agenda; and
Her commitment to socialism, despite the difficulties of achieving it.[1]

Out of these ideas core themes were to emerge in her journalism. An abiding theme which was to underlie most of her work was the conflict between non-racialism and apartheid. But it was the form in which these two ideological discourses manifested themselves which captured her attention and for which, in the case of apartheid, she reserved her utmost scorn. There was the moral positivism of the Congress Alliance, its commitment to non-violence and its preparedness to rest its case on the intrinsic justice of its cause. It was a justice which, it was felt, no rational being in possession of evidence could deny. This evidence was presented as argument. Thus, as Stephen Clingman was to point out in his work on Nadine Gordimer, 'the Defiance Campaign demonstrated the indignities of apartheid as much as it was an attempt to fill the goals. The gathering of the women in Pretoria and the Congress of the People, both events high in symbolic value, were also presented as a kind of social testimony: of the dedication, dignity and vitality of an alternative South Africa.'[2]

Potato workers in the fields, Fighting Talk

A central theme within Congress policy was to demonstrate the moral superiority of non-racialism over apartheid, to explore to the full the frontiers of the existing reality without ultimately crossing the boundaries. The terms of its challenge did not suggest social revolution, and increasing state attacks on the movement not only entrenched this perspective, but demanded that it be spelled out in great detail in the movement's defence at the Treason Trial. Only the historical developments of the 1960s contradicted this perspective.[3] More clearly than most other writers at the time, Ruth was to perceive that the struggle over apartheid was also a struggle between labour and capital. Apartheid, she concluded, was about the delivery of cheap, docile labour to the door of the capitalist. The 1950s was a period when the Nationalist government (and increasingly capital) attempted to inculcate racial capitalism as the 'natural' order of things. Through Acts of Parliament, by-laws, regulations and a massive ideological onslaught by the government, apartheid began to take on the character of an immutable, eternal and god-given order. For people of all colours it became almost 'common sense' that whites should rule and be wealthy and that blacks should be poor and be workers. For apartheid to be effective as an ideology it depended, to a considerable degree, on being merged with a background of 'rational' bureaucratic discourse – projecting its practices as mechanical necessity or universal common sense.

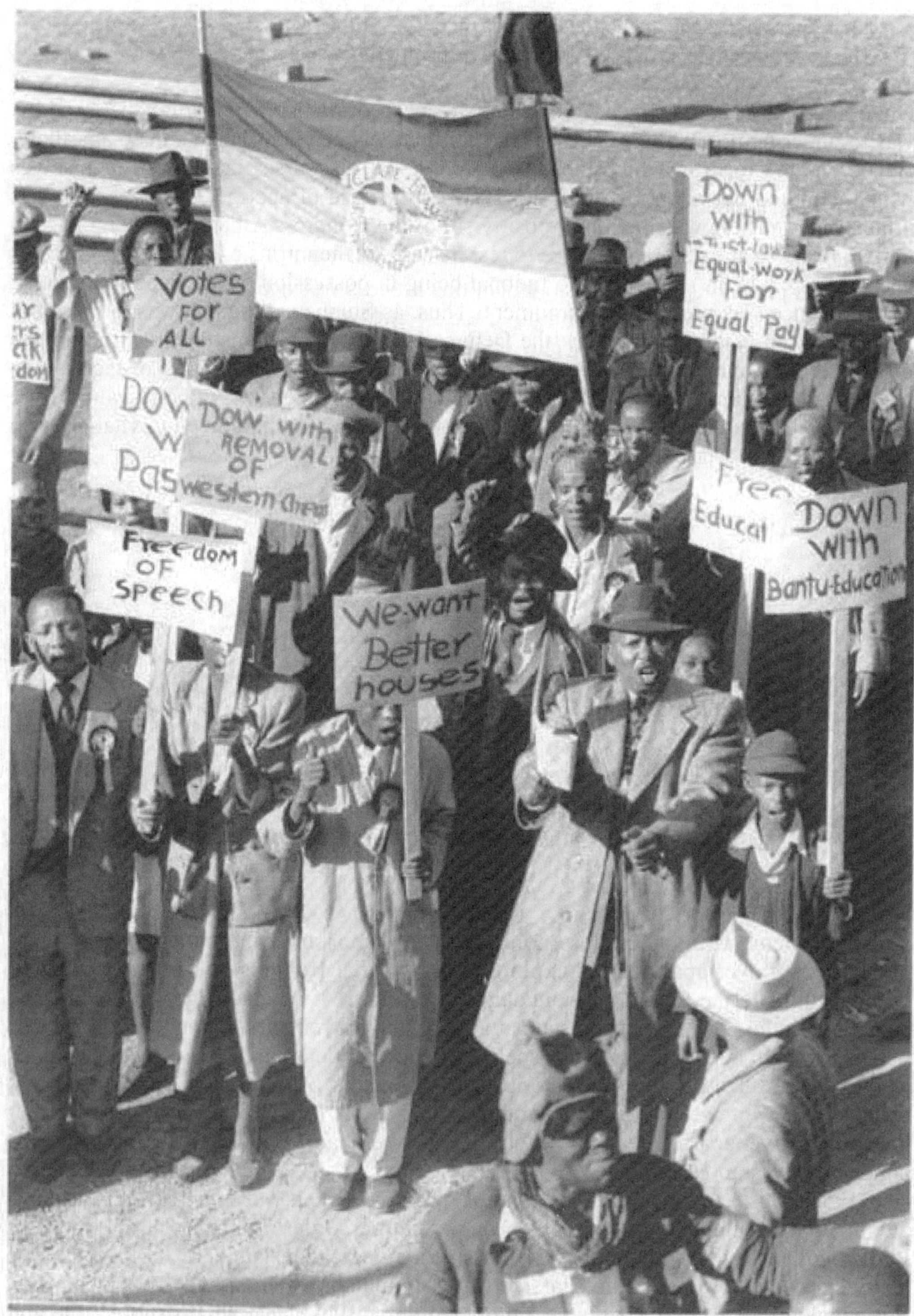

Protesters from Western Areas in Johannesburg campaigning for better conditions

Immediately after its election victory, the new Nationalist government began re-structuring social relations through a mass of parliamentary legislation, burying apartheid in institutional practices which, despite opposition, became increasingly naturalized. While the parliamentary opposition and the commercial press attacked the cruder icebergs of this policy, the vast, bureaucratically submerged re-ordering of the state remained largely unchallenged, either because it was not seen, or because it simply accelerated the 'common sense' practices of racial capitalism already in place before 1948.

The difference between Ruth's journalism and that of her contemporaries on the commercial press was the degree to which this process was accepted as common sense. In its ideological dimension, common sense is itself an effect of power. But power is the outcome of political contest, and if people become aware that a particular aspect of common sense is sustaining power inequalities at their own expense, it ceases to *be* common sense, and may cease to have the capacity to sustain power inequalities. It is not clear whether Ruth understood this by political deduction or intuition, but her attempts to disorganize state legitimacy by focusing on the subterranean processes of apartheid labour organisation – on the daily indignities of passes, grimy court procedures, prison conditions, township squalour and farm conditions – was to strike at the heart of apartheid ideology and leave state officials beside themselves with uncomprehending anger. The effect of such reporting, connecting as it did with the daily lives of ordinary people, fed into the calls by Congress politicians for an end to apartheid and to inequalities of wealth.

Two distinct discourses were, therefore, to emerge from the ideological struggles of the 1950s. One was couched in the language of anti-communist racism and was inculcated by the holders of state power; the second was a mixture of socialism, non-racialism and moral outrage, communicated by the Congress Alliance and in communist and liberal groupings, and which found weekly expression in *The Guardian, New Age, Fighting Talk* and various other smaller publications.

Of course, neither of these discourses sprang into the arena fully armed. The ideas and language were worked up over the years by politicians, bureaucrats, orators, preachers, journalists, pamphleteers and initiators of bold practical action. Both, however, were to develop their own themes and forms of expression, and in 1956 it was these themes and this language which were to find themselves in the dock at the marathon Treason Trial.

It was for this reason that the radical press was so central to the political struggles of the 1950s. Its columns not only reflected the events of the period, but developed a popular 'anti-language' as a conscious alternative to the dominant discourse. The stake was more than 'mere words'. It was an attempt to control the contours of the political world, to de-legitimize state policy, and to shift existing power relations in favour of the Congress Alliance and the working class. To do this, it not only reported the daily indignities of apartheid, Congress activities and the world of international socialism, but by focusing on those issues which were most likely to galvanize its readers into action, it was central in building a tradition of resistance. In this it was spectacularly successful. The next three chapters investigate the links between Ruth's journalism and this action in campaigns around labour conditions, pass laws and township poverty.

The road to Bethal

In June 1947 Ruth, newly appointed as Johannesburg editor of *The Guardian*, was shown a report in a daily newspaper by the controversial priest Michael Scott. The 'rather cryptic little paragraph' indicated that the Boere Arbeid Vereniging in Bethal had decided not to supply labourers to farmers who ill-treated their workers.[4] Ruth followed the report back to the Bethal newspaper, *De Echo*, which cited a court case against farm foreman Johannes Brenkman. He had been tried for setting dogs on farm labourers who were attempting to desert and for having them beaten with sjamboks. After the assaults, according to evidence, the labourers were bound together with donkey chains and taken to the compound where they were forced to sleep naked and chained together. Ruth and Scott decided to investigate.

The trip to Bethal was to mark the beginning of Ruth's investigative labour journalism and would open a window into the subterranean processes of apartheid. They were shocked by what they found. According to Ruth

> The sort of thing that happens on these farms sounds like a story from the history of some ancient slave empire. Labourers are cursed, beaten, locked in their compounds at night, have their clothes taken from them and savage dogs set over them in case they should try to escape.[5]

Farm workers were found 'squatting on heaps of sacks which were also their working clothes'. They had no blankets, no boots and worked from 4 am to 6 pm under the eye of *indunas* with whips. They were served 'a clod of mealie meal and a pumpkin wrapped in a piece of sacking, each man taking a handful at a time.'[6] Ruth was to report that 'it is not every day that the Johannesburg reporter of *The Guardian* meets an African farm labourer who, when asked to describe conditions on the farm on which he works, silently takes of his shirt to show large weals and scars whipped on his back, shoulders and arms.'[7] Ruth and Scott returned to Johannesburg on a Thursday night – too late to make that week's edition of *The Guardian*. Eager to release the story, Scott contacted the *Rand Daily Mail* which published the exposé on Friday, June 27, under the headline: Near Slavery in Bethal District. It caused an uproar.

Both the *Rand Daily Mail* and *The Guardian* called for a full and independent investigation into the matter. It caused a Ministerial flurry. Prime Minister Smuts, concerned 'that South Africa's efforts at the forthcoming General Assembly meeting of the United Nations may be jeopardized by the behaviour of a few farmers', summoned his Minister of Justice, HG Lawrence, to the Union Buildings and insisted that he 'remedy the position once and for all with the most drastic means at his disposal.'[8] Lawrence conferred with the Acting Secretary of Justice, the Attorney General of the Transvaal, the Acting Commissioner of Police and the Minister of Native Affairs. Officials of the Department of Native Affairs 'worked until 2 o'clock (in the) morning preparing a report for the Prime Minister.'[9] In a letter to the *Rand Daily Mail*, the General Manager of Native Labour for the mines vehemently denied any collusion between farmers and the Chamber of Mines in the procurement of labour, and Lawrence announced that the police would 'act at once to clean up the unsatisfactory conditions on some farms in the Bethal district.'[10] Michael Scott was invited back to Bethal to 'place his case before the farmers'. Against advice he agreed, and he and Ruth returned to the town, fully expecting trouble from the angry white farmers. The tensions surrounding their return must have been considerable. First was to recall that the town 'could probably compare well with any small town in the Southern States just before a lynching'. About 1 500 farmers and townspeople packed the hall, and Scott was to confess that confronting them was among 'among the most frightening episodes of (my) life.'[11] The farmers demanded that Scott publicly withdraw his 'unfounded allegations' and when he refused the crowd became threatening, shouting 'Tar and feather him. He is an Uitlander, deport him.'[12]

Scott and Ruth barely escaped with their lives, but on the way out of town they quietly met representatives from a meeting in the Bethal location who had collected £17 to 'send six representatives to Johannesburg to state their case and views to the press.'[13] According to Ruth, they considered 'that Michael Scott, far from exaggerating the bad conditions of farm labourers, (had) not told the worst aspects of the story.'[14]

© Mayibuye

ANC supporters gather in Johannesburg

Despite the initial flurry, the scandal was downplayed by the government which attempted to 'buy off incensed farmers by promising them convict labour – one shilling a day and guaranteed docile.'[15] The affair was soon buried in the run-up to the 1948 election.

The commercial press lost interest, but Ruth refused to let the matter drop and began digging deeper. As far back as 1878, anti-squatting measures in the Cape had attempted to restrict residents on white farms to bona fide employees.[16] In 1891 the Chief Magistrate of Pondoland, Walter Stanford, had written that 'there is no more vacant land for the young swarms to hive off into now. Thus the labour question is bound up with the land question. The man who has no land and no trade must work for someone else who has.'[17]

From the Act of Union in 1910 state land policy had aimed to further deprive Africans of their land and to force them into the labour market. The 1913 Natives' Land Act had restricted African land leasing and purchasing rights to the reserves – a mere 17 per cent of South Africa. In the rest of the country, Africans were there to labour but, preferably, not to live. However, the reality of the situation was that hundreds of thousands of Africans had grown up in cities, towns and on farms and were resident there. Total segregation was virtually impossible and, for white farmers, undesirable. These farmers found themselves fighting against two drains on their labour supply – into towns and into reserves – and, to ensure their vote, government was required to take these problems seriously.

Two sources of rural labour which had developed over time were squatters and labour tenants. Squatter settlements had grown up on farms let out to Africans by absentee landlords. White farmers were anxious that labour from these so-called 'kaffir farms' should come their way. But, increasingly, squatters refused to work for farmers who paid them a pittance and treated them badly.

Labour tenancy was another form of ensuring agricultural labour. Under Hertzog, the Pact government of 1924/1932 passed the Native Service Contract Act which tied all Africans in white rural areas to a period of between three and six months compulsory service to farmers. Tenants on farms were granted ploughing and grazing rights on a farm, but in return were expected to provide labour for the white farmer when he needed it. The great merit of labour tenancy for the farmers was that they could prescribe terms to fit their needs exactly. However tenancy had its problems for both white and black farmers, particularly in the Bethal area. Tenants, unemployed out of season, tended to drift to the mines and towns and never return. And labour tenants could also not be expected to like the one-way interest of the system. According to Marion Lacey, 'the deal was delivered to them, take it or leave it, with ample scope for the farmer to make further demands as time went on. Denied the right to negotiate for themselves, the tenants who were dissatisfied had only one way out – to vote with their feet and leave.'[18]

The type of farming in the Bethal area was intensive agriculture, with an emphasis on maize and, particularly, potatoes. This required a large seasonal labour force and did not lend itself to the provision of space for tenants to farm or to raise stock. Conditions on the farms were so harsh, and the work so poorly paid, that no labour could be attracted to the Bethal farms. Workers were often expected to manure soil and dig out potatoes with their bare hands so as not to damage the vegetables with spades. [19] As far back as 1930, the historian Macmillan could write that 'Highveld maize farmers about Bethal (must) draw supplies of labour from the Cape Reserves, from anywhere except from the neighbouring Lowveld.'[20] Ruth was to discover the full extent of this 'anywhere'. In July 1947 she tumbled on a Government notice stating that from March of that year 'unregistered foreign Native labour' was to be 'rounded up' in the towns and given the alternative of being thrown out of South Africa or working on the farms.[21] The following month she found that 1 853 of these foreigners had been arrested in Johannesburg 'by seven special police sections working by motor-car, motor-cycle and on foot to bring foreign Natives to book.'[22] Others were being recruited for the farms as they stepped over the border at Messina in the Northern Transvaal:

> About 20 000 Nyasaland Africans come to South Africa on their own every year. Many walk all the way, taking as long as two months to walk through the Rhodesias to the Limpopo and over the border into the Union. At Messina, even on the banks of the river, no obstacles are put in their way – as long as they are prepared to work on the farms. This is their alternative to repatriation.[23]

She discovered there were no less that 40 000 foreign contract labourers working in the Bethal area. But, she found, it was not only foreigners who were being recruited. In the reserves, recruitment had been taking place for years, and she was to discover the precise relationship between the collapse of the reserves and capitalist needs:

> Recruitment of labour (here) depends on poverty. In times of drought and poor crops, recruiting figures soar. In better times, fewer men present themselves at the depot of the recruiter.... Labour agencies recruit farm labour (but) recruiting on a really tremendous scale is done on behalf of mining interests in South Africa....[24]

Then, in November 1948, another pool of labour was opened for exploitation. Johannesburg was declared a 'closed area' in terms of an Act passed to fulfil a Nationalist Party election pledge: the Urban Areas Act. Police and pass officials were encouraged to interpret this legislation as a way to force people arrested for pass 'offenses' into farm labour. Urban policemen soon found themselves to be the labour catchers of the farming sector, a task they threw themselves into with enthusiasm. Police vans prowled the cities checking people's passes for 'irregularities' and at Johannesburg Station hundreds of people were arrested as they stepped off their trains coming in to work.[25] By 1949 the pass offices in Johannesburg were 'comparatively deserted' after hundreds of workers queuing to get their passes stamped were deported to the farms.[26] In June that year Ruth made a sensational discovery: court officials were 'selling' pass offenders to farmers:

> Early each morning the pick-up vans drive up (to the Native Commissioner's Court in Fordsburg). They bring the men – and some women – picked up by the police raids the night before.... Lining the streets outside this court can be seen cars and lorries with an assortment of Platteland number plates. From the maize and potato belts come the farmers looking for cheap labour. In a shed near the court, as they wait, Africans are pressed to accept farm work. The prisoners, none of whom have yet appeared before the court, let alone been found guilty, are told ... if they accept work the charges against them will be withdrawn.[27]

The men were told that the alternative to 'voluntary' farm labour was months or even years in a penal colony. They were required to place their thumb prints to contracts which had not been read to them, or to sign away their freedom by touching the pencil in the hands of a white official. The truth of the matter was that most offenders, if they appeared in court, would only have been fined a few pounds for failure to produce their pass. When the exposé appeared the 'police, Bantu Affairs Department officials and farmers denied knowledge and responsibility for it, accused and counter-accused one another, trying to shrug off any part in the operation of its irregularities.'[28] The Deputy Minister of Bantu Administration and Development claimed that 'not a single Native is working as a farm labourer in lieu of prosecution for minor offenses.'[29] A Native Commissioner said it was 'made plain to the men that this is a voluntary scheme' and the police went on record as saying that 'if there was any irregularity in the contract, the Native Commissioner's office is to blame.'[30]

But the practice continued unabated, and into Ruth's office at *The Guardian* poured a steady stream of information as well as groups of brutalized labourers who had escaped from the farms. In 1954 she was to unearth concrete proof of collusion between the police and farmers in procuring labour: a secret circular from the Secretary of Justice and the Commissioner of Police sent to all Native Commissioners and Magistrates. It is common knowledge, read the circular:

> that large numbers of Natives are daily being arrested and prosecuted for contraventions of a purely technical nature. These arrests cost the State large sums of money and serve no useful purpose. The Department of Justice, the South African Police and (Native Affairs) have therefore ... evolved a scheme, the object of which is to induce unemployed Natives now roaming the streets ... to accept employment outside such urban areas.[31]

The circular laid down that Africans held in terms of the Urban Areas Act or the Natives Tax Act would be 'removed under escort to the district labour bureau and handed over to the employment officer.... Priority should be given to farm labour.'[32] To be unemployed, therefore, was a crime, but to obtain a job in an urban area a worker needed to have registered accommodation. Given the massive housing shortage in Johannesburg during the 1950s, at least a third of all Africans were, therefore, liable to be 'canalized' by the state into less-desirable jobs in the economy – notably farming. As her investigations progressed, the alliance between mining, agriculture and the state in the maintenance of poverty and cheap labour became increasingly clear. She was to reflect that 'no other country with a comparable degree of industrialisation exists on a semi-slave labour force in the rural areas, with the state acting as a recruiting force for bad farmers who cannot attract labour by normal means.'[33]

The workers fight back

The flurry of state activity around the exposé did nothing to alleviate the problem. If anything it got worse. But with encouragement from the extraordinarily courageous ANC activist Gert Sibande, the farm workers began to fight back. Sibande, who became known as the Lion of the East, had been a farm labourer in Bethal. But conditions there brought him into open revolt and he began to campaign for better conditions. He would sit in the Bethal court, 'a silent monitor, his very presence a rock ruffling the stream of legal proceedings, discomforting the dispensers of justice, intervening on behalf of (farm) deserters.'[34] It was Sibande who had led Scott and Ruth past watch-dogs onto the Bethal farms and into the smoke-filled compounds. He was driven out of Bethal by the

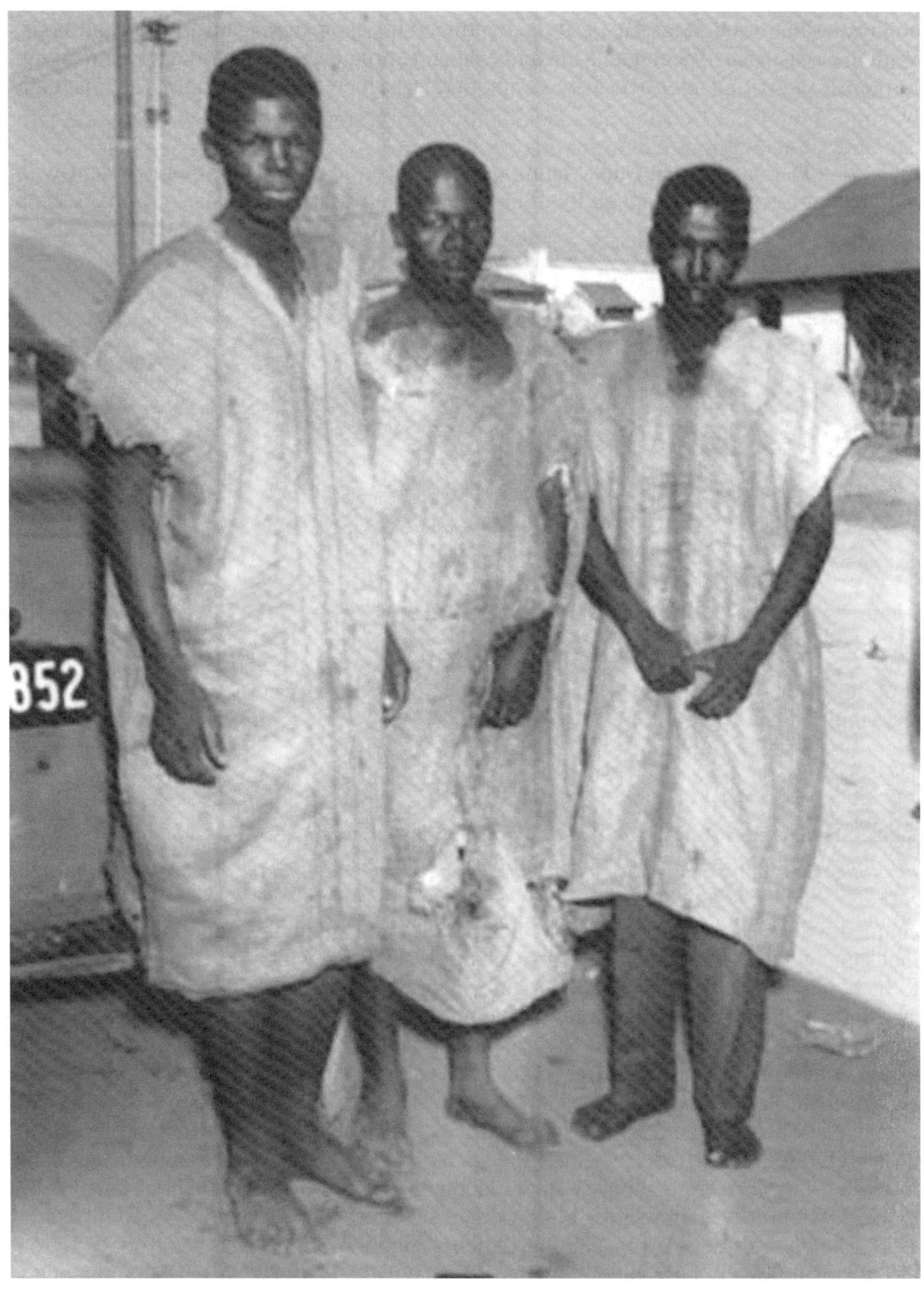

New Age *found these three workers dressed in the sacks the farmer had given them to wear to dig potatoes. (*New Age*, Sept 1 1955)*

authorities but throughout the 1950s he continued his campaign against farm conditions. With the assistance of Sibande, Ruth and *New Age*, brutalised farm workers began taking farmers to court, and interdicts were sought to release men detained on farms against their will.

In 1951 a Delmas farmer, Max Mann, was sentenced to five years imprisonment with hard labour after being found guilty of 39 assaults on his farm. Mann had originally been

© Mayibuye

Pass offenders captured by police in Johannesburg and sent to Bethal farms as convict labour

charged with 87 assaults with whips, pick handles and sjamboks, and evidence was led that some workers had been locked up each night in a room which was too small for them to lie down in. Then, when a *New Age* informant was charged with perjury after signing an affidavit about the death of a farm labourer, the newspaper helped fight the case and won.[35] And following allegations of forced labour by Ruth in *New Age*, the Supreme Court ordered the release of two workers.[36] Beaten, bruised and dazed men an women continued to flow into the newspaper offices.[37] But farmers were feeling the effect of negative publicity on their labour supply and in 1949, 'owing to a shortfall of 60 percent in Native farm labour requirements', the Bethal Farm Labour Bureau announced plans to build a farm prison to supply convict labour.[38] The use of convict labour dated back to 1932, when it was known as the '6d a day scheme.'[39] The scheme was abolished in 1947 following criticism from the Lansdowne Commission, but was reintroduced soon afterwards following a strong lobby from farmers. By 1952 more than 40 000 prisoners were working on farms. Two years later the figure was 100 000 and by 1957 nearly twice that many prisoners were sent to farms from 165 jails throughout the Union.[40] In 1956 *New Age* found that 90 percent of the farmers in the Ladismith area were using convict labour.[41]

Treatment of both convict and farm labourers in the Eastern Transvaal continued to be brutal, and Ruth sought out and exposed the system wherever she could. Then in 1959 *New Age* was asked by a distraught mother to help find her 13-year-old son who had disappeared near Umtata in the Transkei. Ruth traced the boy to a potato farm in the Kinross area to where he had been abducted by a farmer, and her investigations led to the boy's release. She then started to investigate child labour, and found that as the reserves became poorer recruits tended to become younger, some only eleven years old: 'This is where the recruiting bodies cash in, literally, with a price paid for the head of every (youth) *bought* in this trading in human beings.'[42]

New Age then linked the 'sale' of children to the issue of passes for women. The newspaper warned that when women were issued with reference books they would be liable to be picked up on police raids and sent to farms. In the same issue of the paper, Ruth reported the death of a labourer, Bethuel Khosi, who was buried in a shallow grave on a farm in Nigel after being assaulted by the farmer.[43] The following month she uncovered 'hair-raising details of a new scandal in farm semi-slavery, enough to move South Africans hardened even to Bethal.'[44] On a farm owned by PJ Potgieter, two men died after assaults and were buried on the farm. Beatings were found to be the order of the day and workers were deliberately cut on the feet with hoes to prevent them from running away. Ruth assisted in obtaining an urgent court application for the release of one of the workers, a herbalist called Musa Sadika. Following a *habeas corpus* application by his wife, Musa was freed and affidavits on the terrible conditions on the farm were made public. They claimed that about 80 workers had escaped from the farm within a few months but, because Potgieter's son-in-law worked for the local farm labour depot, the farm always had a fresh supply of men. Treatment of workers was severe: 'Whenever Potgieter arrived and hooted in his car the boss boy immediately started moving among the workers, hitting out at anyone within striking distance of their knobkerries. Potgieter would shout: Slaan hulle dood! (beat them to death).'[45]

Using *New Age* as its mouthpiece, the ANC called for a public commission of inquiry into farm labour. This call was supported by the Black Sash and the lawyer in the Potgieter case, Joel Carlson, sent a letter to the Minister of Police demanding action. Gert Sibande, now Transvaal President of the ANC, challenged the government to put him on a commission to investigate farm conditions.[46] In the following edition, Ruth wound the campaign into high gear. She had found a Bantu Affairs Department 'youth camp' in the Eastern Transvaal which was 'selling' 15-year-olds to Bethal farmers for labour. The camp was a 'place of safety' for youths 'picked up off the streets'. Some boys were being sent to the camp without their parents knowing where they were.[47] She found that the previous year the camp's boarding master had been convicted of sodomy.

Three days later the ANC's National Anti-Pass Conference in Johannesburg, responding to the court cases and to reports in *New Age*, called for a national boycott of potatoes.[48] The police had banned ANC President Albert Lutuli from attending the conference – and then banned the mass rally planned to welcome him. The conference retaliated by calling for a total ban on the purchase of any item on the day of June 26, after which the potato boycott would begin. The move was, according to Ruth, 'the first use of the economic boycott weapon in the struggle' and was launched 'as a protest against the horrifying conditions of farm labourers on the big potato farms in the Transvaal.'[49] The report of the conference planning committee noted that Africans were the greatest economic asset in the country:

© Mayibuye

Pass offence prisoners working in a logging company in the Eastern Transvaal

'What is our economic power? It is the power of our LABOUR (and) our PURCHASING POWER. By withdrawing our purchasing power we can punch them in the stomach.'[50] The conference also recommended that a boycott of products of Nationalist-controlled institutions be embarked upon.

New Age, in announcing the boycott, again demanded a judicial inquiry into farm labour. Its call coincided with another appearance in court of the Heidelberg farmer, Potgieter, following an affidavit for the release of two labourers. A number of organisations and individuals, including the Anglican bishop of Johannesburg, Ambrose Reeves, responded to the campaign by setting up a committee to help trace missing farm workers and to establish a legal and medical bureau for victims of the system.[51]

In the following edition of *New Age,* Ruth reported that five more actions for the return of labourers were heard in court that week. The judgment by Mr Justice de Wet was to hit at the roots of the farm labour system. The judge, no doubt influenced by the campaign, echoed what Ruth had been saying for years: 'The court would not countenance a procedure where a man was arrested and told he must either go to a farm or to jail. What authority is there for this? Is it not compounding an offense? It was a breach of the policeman's duty for him to arrest and not charge a man. What right has he to hand him over to someone else?'[52] The lead story in the newspaper following the case was: FARM SLAVE SCHEME CRACKS:

> First sign that the exposure of the evils of the forced labour system is having effect came this week when an Eastern Transvaal farmer who had been taken to court to produce some of his labourers surrendered his entire labour force and drove them back to Johannesburg. By Tuesday his example had been followed by five other farmers...[53]

FARM LABOURER "LIKE A BELSEN CASE" – AND HE'S ONLY A CHILD

From Ruth First

JOHANNESBURG.

IS he 12 years old, or 14? He can't tell you that because he can't count: has never been to school. He is a slip of a youngster, with trusting, innocent eyes. It is not that he isn't willing to talk now—though not so long ago he was terrified out of his wits and spoke only in semi-delirium. But, though he listens carefully to the questions put through the interpreter, he is able to give very little information.

Today he is in the ward of a Reef hospital. When brought there he was in a state of gross emaciation. He could not walk and had to be carried in to the hospital. **"Like a Belsen case!"** exclaimed one of the doctors who examined him. He was markedly underweight, his bones protruded, he was apathetic and listless and when offered food showed no inclination to eat. He was swarming with lice. One of those frightful cases of extreme malnutrition—the polite word for starvation—that had to be

since with other boys, some of whom came from his home dis-

New Age, *May 6 1957*

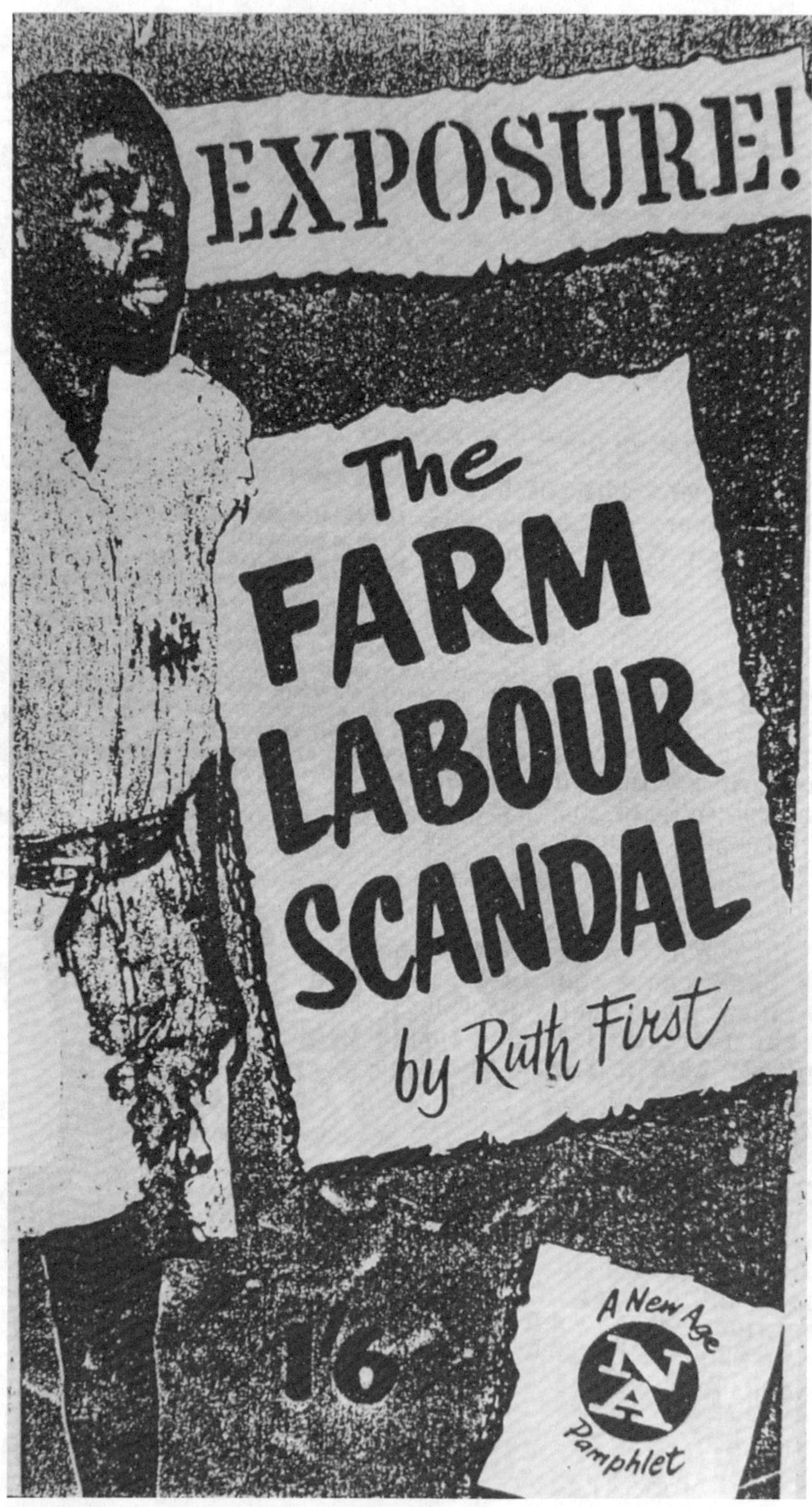

In 1957 Ruth gathered together all her information on farm labour to produce a booklet, published by New Age.

Under the slogan *awadliw ga de jeoe!* (we don't eat them), the potato boycott picked up momentum. Newspapers reported potatoes piling up in markets and shops in Johannesburg, Durban and Port Elizabeth. As the day for the national boycott drew nearer, mass rallies were planned, fake leaflets calling on people to boycott mealies appeared and the Minister of Police warned of mass arrests. The day before the boycott on June 26 *New Age* ran with a headline: 'Potatoes: Supply good, demand poor.' The boycott campaign was remarkably successful and spread from the cities to smaller centres. For the next two months Ruth was tireless in pursuit of farm exposés. In one edition alone – July 23 – she unearthed no less than four 'scandals' about farm conditions. Mostly as front-page leads, she ran stories under the headlines:

> He died at Bethal
> Must these men starve?
> The scandal still continues
> Farm labour: Swart is guilty!
> Swart calls this 'rehabilitation'
> Police, farmers, BAD (Bantu Affairs Department) on Government farm labour commission!
> Native Commissioners sell potatoes
> Brutal beating by farmer alleged
> Farmer said: 'I don't care a damn'
> When will it stop?

The Farmers' Union and the Bantu Affairs Department each appointed independent commissions of inquiry into farm labour. Under pressure, the Government appointed a parliamentary Commission of Inquiry, but as Ruth pointed out, 'the conclusions of the Agricultural Union's commission is that abuses on farms were isolated. The (BAD) commission has also completed its inquiry. The Government commission consists of

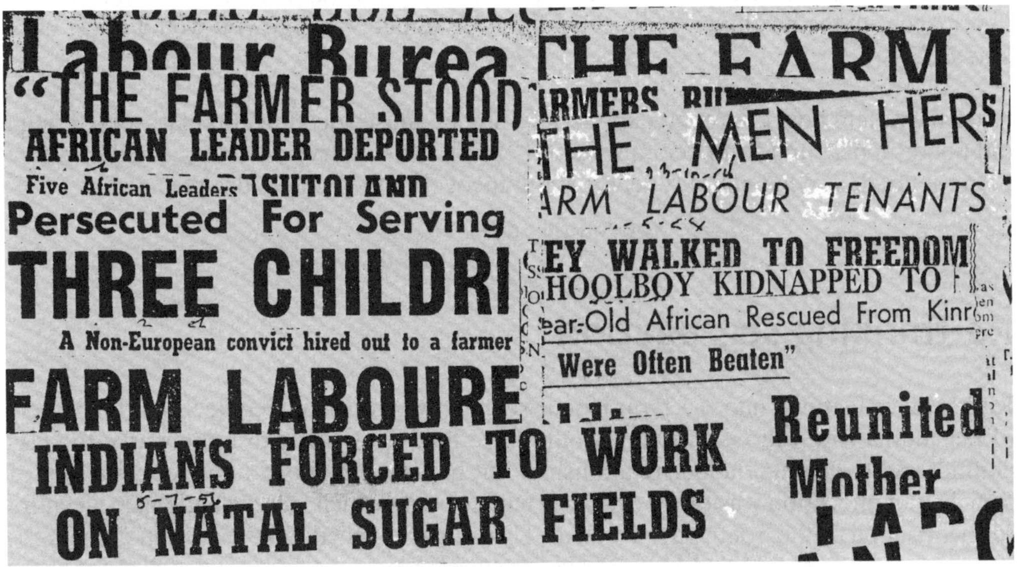

Labour Burea
"THE FARMER STOOD
AFRICAN LEADER DEPORTED
Five African Leaders
Persecuted For Serving
THREE CHILDRI
A Non-European convict hired out to a farmer
FARM LABOURE
INDIANS FORCED TO WORK
ON NATAL SUGAR FIELDS
THE FARM
THE MEN HERS
ARM LABOUR TENANTS
EY WALKED TO FREEDOM
HOOLBOY KIDNAPPED TO
ear-Old African Rescued From Kinr
Were Often Beaten"
Reunited
Mother

FARM SLAVE SCHEME CRACKS

Some Farmers Release All Their Workers

From Ruth First
JOHANNESBURG.

FIRST SIGNS THAT THE EXPOSURE OF THE EVILS OF THE FORCED LABOUR SYSTEM IS HAVING EFFECT CAME THIS WEEK WHEN AN EASTERN TRANSVAAL FARMER WHO HAD BEEN TAKEN TO COURT TO PRODUCE SOME OF HIS LABOURERS SURRENDERED HIS FARM'S ENTIRE LABOUR FORCE AND DROVE THEM BACK TO JOHANNESBURG.

By Tuesday his example had

As a result of the publicity and court cases resulting from Ruth's exposés, some farmers began transporting their workers back to the city.

police, farmers and BAD officials, and it starts its work with these two whitewashing reports already before it.'[54]

Two weeks before the potato boycott ended on August 31, Ruth produced a 24-page booklet entitled *The Farm Labour Scandal*. In it she documented, in her clear, concise style, the farm labour scandal from its inception to the boycott. On June 17, the State suspended the forced labour scheme pending the findings of its inquiry. A government spokesman admitted there had been a 'technical fault' in the allocation of labour.[55] Ruth's newspaper ran the headline: '*New Age* did this! Without *New Age* you would never have known.'

After the potato boycott, reports about farm labour abuses declined dramatically, though did not disappear and Ruth kept a watchful eye on the countryside. But she had proved a point: journalists need not only report about the world, they could also change it.

Re-thinking segregation

Ruth's investigations into the farm labour scandal was to set a deep keel into the waters of her journalism. Marxist training would have predisposed her to be sensitive to class conflict and the capital/labour relationship, but her investigations into the institution of state labour allocation was to provided her with insights which were to anticipate an entire re-theorisation of the South African state. These insights need to be placed in context.

Historian Saul Dubow has argued that from the 1930s liberal writers began rejecting the earlier segregationalist paternalism of English-speaking intellectuals like Edgar Brooks,

Howard Pim and Charles Loram and began attempting to show the incompatibility between segregation and capitalist development.[56] By the late 1920s Dubow noted a marked liberal disillusionment with the whole idea of segregation. In 1927, 'amid profuse breast-beating', Edgar Brookes announced that his previous advocacy of segregation had been misguided.[57] Four years later liberal politician Jan Hofmeyer was still advocating a 'gentle' segregation, attempting to soothe whites by making a distinction between social and economic segregation. But he warned that 'the European ... in his own interest ... cannot allow (the African) to remain an inefficient, jog-trot worker, without any stimulus to his ambition to raise himself in the scale, and by the lowness of his standards depriving the poorer white man of an economic basis of subsistence.'[58] A decade later the historian de Kiewiet was to make explicit the connection between the objections of liberals to segregation and their prosperity as a class:

> Not one but a whole series of commissions have challenged the wisdom of a rigorous Colour Bar....Whatever restricted the power of the native population to earn or to increase its capacity to produce also restricted its power to consume ... the whole of society suffers when any important group within it suffers from excessive poverty, inefficiency, inadequate use of intelligence, wasteful organisation of its labour, or restrictions upon its ability to work or to produce.[59]

By far the most articulate exponent of this position was the leader of the Liberal Party, Margaret Ballinger.[60] In a speech delivered in Parliament in 1943 (and described by a *Rand Daily Mail* reporter as 'one of the most challenging, sincere and able speeches I have heard in the House for many years') she described segregation as 'cutting across the whole economic trend of this country' and as being 'unsound in its foundation.'[61] Gold

NEW AGE

Vol. 5, No. 37 Registered at the G.P.O. as a Newspaper 6d.

NORTHERN EDITION Thursday, July 2, 1959

FARM LABOUR: SWART IS GUILTY!

VREK HOM!
VREK .HOM!
The Farmer Said

TEACHER MADEIRA:
"I nearly lost my life"

HOW JUNE 26 WAS CELEBRATED — see page 5

Former Prime Minister

THE Minister of Justice, Mr. Swart, told the Senate angrily last week that his department had "absolutely nothing" to do with forced farm labour. The scheme, he said, was administered solely by the Department of Bantu Administration.

We declare that Mr. Swart—not for the first time—has given the public wrong information.

Mr. Swart's hands are not as clean as he would have South Africa believe.

The farm labour scandal has a good deal to do with his department and the Minister knows this very well.

The Circular under which the illegal forced labour scheme operates is issued under the authority of the South African Police and the Department of Prisons as well as the Bantu Administration Department.

And apart from this Mr. Swart's prisons are the second big source of forced farm labour.

They Half-Killed This Teacher

If proof were needed it came forward last week in the case of teacher Gabriel Madeira.

Madeira had been a teacher at a Roman Catholic school in Newclare and on April 22 appeared in court charged with being in possession of a stolen watch. The lawyer briefed to defend him was not in court when he was tried and Madeira was sentenced to two months hard labour.

Madeira was taken to the Johannesburg Fort. There, **though he protested that he was sickly and was not willing to go, he found himself being transported to a farm at Trichard in the Eastern Transvaal, where he was to serve his jail term.**

Not long after his arrival on the farm Madeira was involved in an accident with a tractor and, unable to walk, he lay in a heap in a corner of the compound.

Representations to the Fort superintendent resulted in Madeira being fetched by the police and taken to a hospital for an x-ray examination but after that he was taken back to the farm.

On Sunday June 21 Madeira's term of imprisonment was up. Together with another convict, Amos Cebekulu he approached two sons of the farmer and asked for his discharge.

The two Africans were sworn at and told to go to the police station, Madeira told the Supreme Court.

Madeira and Cebekulu walked to the police station about two miles away. The policeman telephoned the farmer and then said that Cebekulu should be released that day but Madeira would be released only the day after.

"The policeman said if he were the Baas he too would keep me on the farm for a further three weeks.'

On their way back to the farm Madeira and Cebekulu were passed

(Continued on page 3)

*The Minister of Justice denied police collusion in catching pass offenders for farm labour. Ruth had evidence to the contrary. (*New Age*, July 2 1959)*

Following Ruth's reporting of conditions on the Bethal farms, the ANC called for a boycott of potatoes. They were soon piling up in grocery shops.

mining, she said, was a wasting industry and in order to maintain 'our standards', the massive development of secondary industries had to take place. Industrial development, however, 'cut at the roots' of segregationist policy by breaking the link between town and country and cutting across the intention to keep the African population in the countryside. Urban Africans, however, had been 'refused all those rights on which a stable population is based'. The result, she said, was morally indefensible and led to low productivity and poverty. It hit at white prosperity: 'Even this enormous (wartime) industrial development we have had has not been enough to absorb the whole of the European population on a level that any of us here would regard as adequate to maintain the European standard of living.'[62] Her solution was to build a strong home market through the expansion of industry and a rapid increase in black spending power:

> I contend ... that the low purchasing power of our native population and the low productivity of our labour forces are both the natural result of the policy that we have pursued with regard to our native population, that while we have been progressively industrialising the country, we have been progressively impoverishing the people on whom, in the last resort, the foundation of our industrial development depends.[63]

She argued that labour regulations required employers to hire expensive white labour in preference to cheap black labour, restricted the supply of skilled workers and interfered with the mobility of labour. Sustained economic growth, she and other liberals argued, would increasingly undermine 'irrational' policies imposed to protect sectional interests and held in place by the atavistic ideology of Afrikaner Calvanism.[64] The 'whole future of the European' therefore depended on unencumbered industrial development, the resulting death of segregation and on giving Africans a claim in the cities. This cry was taken up by Leo Marquard in the early 1950s. Discussing apartheid legislation, he contended that 'while some of the provisions in these Acts may entail economic hardship ... their main purpose is not economic. It is, rather, an attempt to achieve as much social separation as possible, even at the cost of economic efficiency.'[65]

These liberal perspectives on segregation resonated with those of the African National Congress in the post-war years and became received wisdom for political campaigners for African rights. However Ruth's experiences in the 1946 mine strike and the Bethal farm scandal were to lead her to different conclusions about the relationship between apartheid and capitalist development. For her, apartheid structures served employers, delivering labour to their doorsteps and policing strikes and township disturbances which threatened to disrupt production. Nadine Gordimer, embodying the liberal perspective, was to view apartheid as a problem of consciousness. Ruth, on the other hand, had crossed those mental boundaries. Apartheid, for her, was a problem of fascist structures and capitalist greed.[66]

It is commonly held that the challenge to liberal perspectives on apartheid took place in the early 1970s with the work of revisionist writers like Martin Legassick and Harold Wolpe.[67] In 1971 Legassick rejected the liberal notion that segregation represented the imposition of earlier outdated and 'uneconomical' racial attitudes on South Africa's process of industrialisation. He argued that segregation was about the 'alliance of gold and maize' in creating and perpetuating the system of migrant labour which characterised the country's road to industrialization.[68] Wolpe argued that segregation was designed to maintain the productive capacity of pre-capitalist economies in the reserves so as to provide capitalist industry with a cheap supply of migrant labour.[69] As early as 1947, however, Ruth was laying the foundation for this perspective, and throughout the 1950s she was to develop and refine these notions, basing her position on fine-grained studies of the daily processes of apartheid. Her work was well known to both Wolpe and Legassik, and it is from many of her articles that they would have, consciously or unconsciously, developed their re-formulation of the apartheid state.[70] Ruth's involvement with the 1946 mine workers' strike, followed by her Bethal exposé, was to focus her writing on labour issues in a way no other journalists of the period were doing. She was, therefore, best placed to see the capitalist implications in the plethora of legislation and regulations which followed the 1948 election and to understand the baggage of labour legislation which the new government had inherited from the old. For Ruth it was not the individuals or the individual Acts which made history, but the context which made them possible. Her writing did not follow the lead of the English mainstream press which howled in protest at the more visible manifestations of the new apartheid administration. Nor did she spend much time dealing with the 'great social forces' and broad class analyses of contemporary Marxist writers like Michael Harmel, Brian Bunting and Lionel Forman. Ruth was aware that these abstract forces took institutional forms, and that these social institutions and interest groups influenced both the larger social forces and the individual. She wanted to know how institutions worked, who they were composed of, where the power lay, who benefited from them and how they impacted on individuals.[71] She also wanted to break them open to public scrutiny and action. These perspectives were to manifest stylistically in her writing.

SLAVE LABOUR ON THE FARMS

Shocking Disclosures in Delmas District

JOHANNESBURG.

BETHAL has a black and fearful name to Africans as far away as Portuguese East Africa and Nyasaland, and Delmas is fast becoming a second Bethal. One African in the Delmas district said: "I would rather spend all my life in jail than work on a Delmas farm". He knows — he once worked on a farm in the district.

This is the reputation the dreaded potato belt of the Union has, and it does nothing to help solve the problems of South African farming.

*A labourer told Ruth: 'I would rather spend all my life in jail than work on a Delmas farm.' (*The Guardian, *March 15 1951)*

Hers was not the journalism of closure where ideas and facts were a given and intended for the reader simply to consume. It was not pre-determined. Her writing was always peppered with strings of questions, inducing the reader to take an active part in the formulation of ideas. About Bethal she would ask:

- If conditions of farm labourers are not as bad as reports say, why must the men be locked up in the farm compounds at night?
- Why do labourers run away in darkness of the night in desperate efforts to escape from the rich and fertile farms of this area?
- Why do key witnesses in the trial (against a white farmer), bearing on their backs the marks of their assaults, have to be kept at police headquarters under guard for their protection?
- Why were farm labourers dressed in sacks?
- During police detention Mr M– was presented with an ultimatum to accept work on a farm or be sent to prison. To how many other people in this township is the same ultimatum put?
- How many end up in jail?
- Who would voluntarily submit himself to harsh labour conditions, poor pay and (in places like Bethal) the risk of bodily harm or even death were he not compelled to do so by the unjust laws of the country?

In response to a call by ANC president Albert Luthuli, men across the country burned their passes.

- Who took this young boy away from home (to work on a farm)? And why?
- How many recruiting agencies 'take a chance' and sign on youngsters in the reserves well under age?
- Why, under Verwoerd's laws, are mothers torn away from their children, wives from their husbands – all in the name of preserving Western civilisation?
- Why this history of persecution?

According to Gavin Williams, who worked with Ruth on *Review of African Political Economy*,

> She always had more questions than answers and the answers anyway raised more questions. There (was) always more to be known and more to be done. The most important task (was) to ask the right questions, not to provide the correct answers. Consequently, the form of the argument is always open-ended.[72]

The effect of this form of writing was to leave a gap between where the reader was and where he or she would like to be, between goals and the means of accomplishing them. If things were to get done then it was up to the reader to decide. For better or worse, the gaps had to be closed by action – the responsibility rested with the reader. But underlying this form of writing was an intention to disorganise the legitimacy of the existing regime.[73] This was the essence of radical journalism.

Notes

1 Williams, 1984, Contribution ... p4.

2 Clingman, 1986, p62.

3 After Sharpeville it became clear that the state had left no grounds on which to base a moral stand, that reason could not win against apartheid and that races could not be equal when the material conditions of equality did not exist. This marked the end of the efforts of the Congresses to operate within a public discourse and their shift to guerrilla symbolism.

4 First in *The Guardian*, July 3, 1947.

5 Ibid.

6 *Rand Daily Mail*, June 27, 1947.

7 *Guardian*, op cit.

8 *Rand Daily Mail*, July 7, 1947.

9 Ibid.

10 *RDM*, July 2 & 8, 1947.

11 Troup: *In face of fear*, p136.

12 *The Guardian,* July 17, 1947.

13 Ibid.

14 Ibid.

15 *The Guardian*, July 24, 1947.

16 Lacey 1981, p121.

17 Quoted in Lacey, ibid. p121.

18 Lacey, Ibid. p137.

19 Often this had to be done virtually at a jog, bending double, 12 hours a day.

20 WM Macmillan: *Complex South Africa: An economic footnote to history*, (London, Faber, 1930) p249.

21 *The Guardian*, July 3, 1947.

22 Ibid August 7, 1947.

23 Ibid.

24 Ibid December 11, 1947.

25 Ibid, May 26, 1949.

26 Ibid.

27 Ibid June 2, 1949.

28 First: *The Farm Labour Scandal, New Age* Pamphlet, n.d. p6.

29 Ibid, p6.

30 Ibid.

31 Circular 23 of June 14 1954. In Ibid. p9.

32 Ibid, p10.

33 Ibid, p22.

34 Profile by Alfred Hutchinson in *New Age*, September 6 1956.

35 *New Age*, 19.1.59.

36 Ibid, 11.7.59.

37 On October 11 1956 *New Age* published a story about the construction of special compounds for women labourers at Bethal. Some of the workers were 15 years old or less.

38 *The Guardian*, March 3, 1949.

39 First: *The farm labour scandal*, op cit, p16.

40 Ibid, p16.

41 *New Age*, October 4, 1956.

42 Ibid, February 5, 1959.

43 Ibid, 26.3.59.

44 Ibid, 30.4.59.

45 Ibid, May 7, 1959.

46 Ibid, May 21, 1959.

47 Ibid, May 28, 1959.

48 Bunting, 1986 p170.

49 *New Age*, June 4 1959.

50 Ibid, June 4, 1959.

51 Ibid.

52 Ibid, June 11 1959.

53 Ibid.

54 Ibid, July 23 1959.

55 *Rand Daily Mail*, June 17, 1959.

56 Dubow, 1989.

57 Ibid, p47.

58 Hofmeyer: *South Africa*, 1931, p319.

59 De Kiewiet, *A History of South Africa*, 1941, p243. He portrays segregation in terms of the imposition of a retrogressive 'frontier mentality' on the attitudes of the 20th century. In this view he was supported by Eric Walker. See Dubow, 1989 p22.

60 She was elected as a Native Representative in Parliament in 1938 and remained in that seat until 1960. She was president of the Liberal Party from 1953 to 1955, but was out of sympathy with the party's later shift to more radical positions, particularly its endorsement of a universal franchise for Africans.

61 *RDM* 17.3.43 and private transcript of her speech to Parliament, 16.3.43.

62 Speech, ibid.

63 Ibid.

64 Williams: 'Ruth First's contribution to African Studies', 1984, p7.

65 Marquard: *The Peoples and policies...* 1952, p123.

66 Clingman, 1958.

67 Dubow 1989 and Lacey 1981.

68 Legassick: 'South Africa: Forced labour, industrialisation and racial differentiation.' In R Harris, 1975, p250.

69 Wolpe: 'Capitalism and cheap labour power in South Africa: From segregation to apartheid.' In *Economy & Society*, 1.4.1972.

70 They were both her personal friends and political colleagues.

71 This interest was to be followed in her later studies: *Power in Africa, The barrel of a gun, Libya, The South African Connection* and *Black gold.*

72 Williams: 1984, Contribution ... p3.

73 Years later Ruth was to express these views on the role of the radical activist: 'Marxist analysis requires examination of the material conditions which determine the possibilities for and obstacles to revolutionary action by the exploited classes'. In Classes in *African Review of African Political Economy* 3, 1975.

6

Building an identity

The Native Commissioners before whom the women's vigorous anti-pass protests have been staged this year are showing they know all the finer points in the game of Bluff, Bamboozle and Hoodwink – Ruth First

"Hey, you've got the wrong connection, mister!"

Advance, *November 20 1952.*

By the time the bullet-riddled bodies were buried in Vereeniging and Cape Town in 1960, South Africa had given the world's political vocabulary two new terms: passes and Sharpeville. By then passes were an absolutely central issue in South Africa resistance politics. But although they were key documents for most Africans, the process by which they moved from being irritating paper to international symbols of oppression was an exercise in ideological mobilisation by the Congress Movement, the Federation of South African Women and *New Age* against the state's labour laws and practices.[1] At the centre of this campaign, however, was another dynamic which had to do with the re-emergence, after 40 years, of African women into the political arena.

The first clash between African women and the State took place in the Orange Free State in 1913.[2] And it was to become a struggle between, on the one hand, the self esteem and survival of these women and, on the other, attempts by the state to excommunicate them from the cities as 'labour units' and 'undesirables' and import them back as super-exploitable migrants. It was fought out in the streets, on busses, in compounds and in court rooms, but it was also, importantly, fought out in Acts of Parliament, government notices, speeches, articles and studies which attempted to both refine and to reject the ongoing processes of apartheid. In a sense, it was a struggle for the soul of African women who were emerging as a new force in the industry and cities of post-war South Africa. This chapter is not a history of these events, but an assessment of the role of Ruth's journalism in the evolution of an ideological campaign around passes, the smashing of which was to propel the apartheid government into the wastelands of international disapproval. It is also about the role of written language in the process of political mobilisation.

In the 1950s African women found themselves struggling against three very different conceptions of themselves – as labour units (by the state), as 'harmlessly inferior' (by African men), and as the self-imposed passive minors of the traditional social order. These contending discourses were to be central to the anti-pass campaign.

4,000 PRETORIA WOMEN IN BEST-EVER ANTI-PASS DEMONSTRATION

PRETORIA.—To Pretoria women must go the honours of the largest anti-pass protest yet. Last week 4,409 women blocked the traffic in town when they went to see the Native Commissioner to protest against the extension of the reference book system to them. Pretoria locations and townships were represented in force.

In 1956 around 20 000 women gathered in the amphitheatre of the Union Buildings to protest the proposed issuing of passes to women. They sang: 'Strijdom, you have touched the women, you have struck a rock'.

'I am a reference book'

The National Party's conception of African women was connected to its construction of an urban labour policy. This policy lay at the core of apartheid ideology, and was to be the product of intense debates and power struggles within the party structures.[3] One pole of the argument within the ruling group – which Deborah Posel characterizes as that of the 'purists' – pushed for total geographical and cultural separation of races. At root, this position was based on a fear of 'swamping' of whites by Africans migrating into the cities. In its most virulent forms it was embodied by Nazi-influenced right-wing movements like the Ossewa Brandwag. And it was often given a biblical twist by Afrikaner preachers who mixed religious pronouncements and secular politics in the pulpit with fluency:

> The black giant of Africa is eating bread for which he has not sweated, he wants to wear clothes which do not fit him, he wants to pay with what he does not have yet, distribute what he does not possess yet, wants to talk about things he does not yet comprehend, wants to be where he still in not.... David taught us that a Philistine cannot be merely prayed away – he must also be beaten away. We must unite in the face of common danger. The black masses of Africa do not seek the white man's friendship but his destruction. The snakes of unrest and agitation have crept out of their holes.[4]

Cape Town women protesting outside the Native Commissioner's offices in Salt River.

The most articulate form of total segregation was put forward by an Afrikaner think-tank, the South African Bureau of Racial Affairs (SABRA). Bureau academics argued for a disentanglement of African and European economies and a 'humanitarian' separation of races through an upgrading of the reserves. In 1951 it told HF Verwoerd, then Minister of Native Affairs, that economic integration of races not only placed the 'sovereign and separate existence' of whites in 'decided danger', but also implied a 'dark future of uncertainty and strife' for Africans:[5]

> The committee told the Minister that it was convinced that such integration, if allowed to continue unchecked, would have fatal consequences for both Europeans and Natives.... It pleaded for a policy of separate development of the two races with proper opportunities for Natives to develop in their own areas.[6]

Such views were to come into conflict with those at the other pole of the Nationalist labour lobby which was sensitive to the findings of the United Party's Fagan Commission and liberals who held that settled urban labour and the creation of a black middle class was the road to prosperity and peace. This 'practical' faction was led by Afrikaner agricultural, industrial and commercial capitalists who were, predictably, less enthusiastic about 'economic segregation':

> It must be acknowledged that the non-white worker already constitutes an integral part of our economic structure, that he is now so enmeshed in the spheres of our economic life that for

> the first fifty/hundred years (if not even longer), total segregation is pure wishful thinking. Any government which disregards this irrefutable fact will soon discover that it is no longer in a position to govern.[7]

The Sauer Report, often seen as the blueprint of apartheid, wove together these two mutually exclusive conceptions of apartheid but was unable to choose between them. It both endorsed total segregation and opposed some policy measures to limit white access to African labour.

After the 1948 election it was the 'practical' faction which gained predominance within the all-powerful Native Affairs Department under Jansen and then Verwoerd. The NAD accepted growing white dependence on African labour in the urban areas and set itself the task of solving the political pressures this entailed by re-working the ideological conception of the African worker. A key document in this endeavour was the Tomlinson Commission, a mammoth report submitted in 1956. This commission attempted to solve the two Nationalist perspectives on African labour and to come up with a practical solution.[8] The result – and perhaps the essence of the report – was the ideological reconstruction of the 'Bantu' as a migrant and as a member of a distinct Bantu national culture. In order to prevent the disappearance of 'European' culture in South Africa, it said, it would be necessary to reduce 'culture contact', and to do this would mean that 'a reorientation of the economic structure of the country on a more or less comprehensive scale will become inevitable.'[9] The Commission's purpose in this regard was twofold. It had to demonstrate that 'the Bantu Areas could prove adequate to the task of constituting national homes for the Bantu peoples, while showing how the labour requirements of the European economy could be met through a scheme based on migration.'[10] Apartheid's solution, therefore, lay in the control of labour, and to that end it was necessary to conceptualise all Africans as being foreigners in white South Africa, 'temporary sojourners' enjoying the 'privileges' of the white economy but no rights. The Native Question was therefore to consist of 'welfare' in the reserves and control in the cities.

Verwoerd largely ignored the Tomlinson Commission's findings, particularly its insistence that the reserves be upgraded to cope with those endorsed out of the cities. But he agreed that 'the White man can protect his continued existence only if he sees to it that this increased Bantu population is not accommodated in the White urban areas, (otherwise) swamping of the Whites will result.'[11] And if he ignored the recommendations of the report, he accepted its spirit. Commenting on the commission's findings, he said that 'when one does not accept the methods suggested by someone, or does not accept them in every detail, one is not necessarily rejecting what is valuable in his trend of thought, particularly not the direction of his thinking.'[12]

So the Tomlinson Commission served its purpose by default. It established the 'scientific' grounds (coincident with Nationalist sentiments and government ideology) for a defence of the steadily increasing repression and violence necessary to maintain the existing structure of the state.[13] This was to issue in what TC Moll was to describe as a period of growth without development.[14] And the technical details of this process were left to the Native Affairs Department, soon to be appropriately renamed the Bantu Affairs Department (BAD).

By the time the Tomlinson Report was made public, enabling legislation had already been passed which provided the legal framework for the state's social labour engineering.

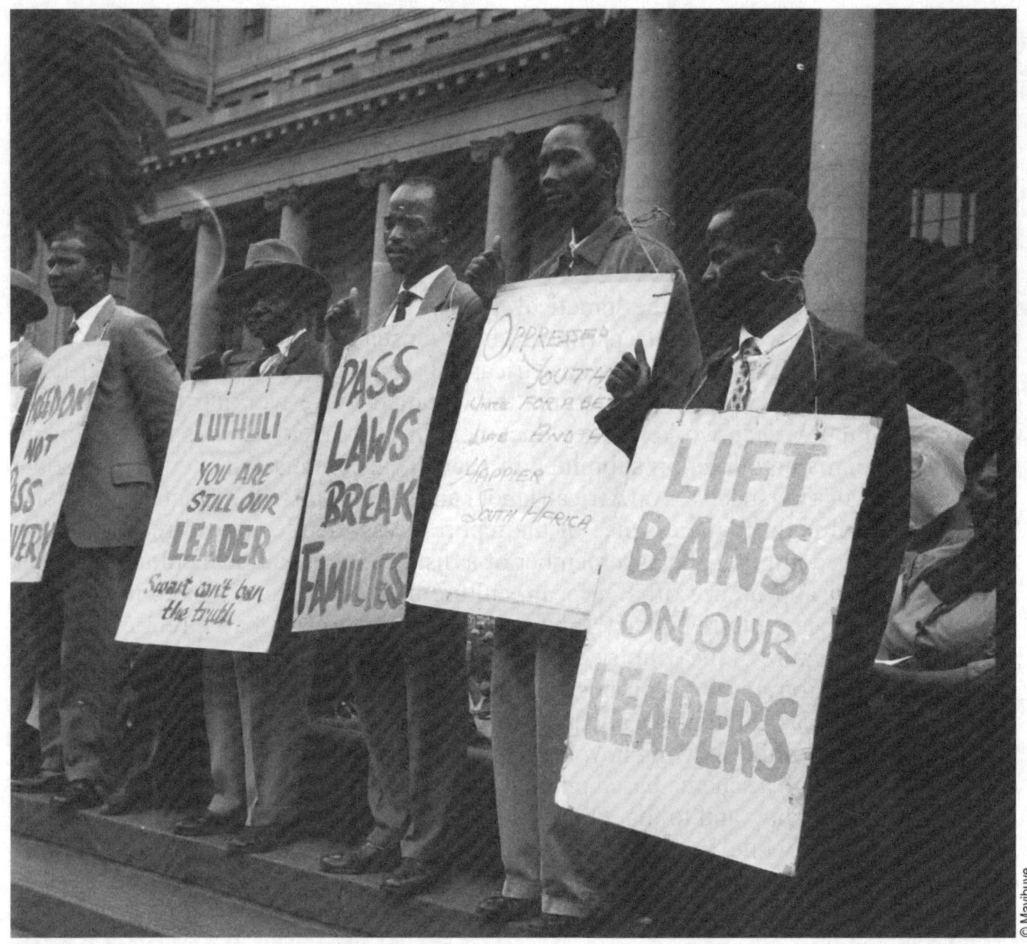

© Mayibuye

Throughout the 1950s oppressed people staged voiciferous campaigns against the increasing brutality of apartheid, resulting in the detention of thousands and lengthy court battles.

In 1952 Section 10 of the Native Laws Amendment Act was passed. Building on older legislation, it divided the African labourers into urban 'insiders' and migrants and provided for the excommunication of 'undesirables'. The Natives (Abolition of Passes and Co-ordination of Documents) Act of the same year did not abolish passes, it renamed them 'reference books' and required that all African males over 16 carry them. Both Acts made provision for the extension of these documents to African women. In October of that year a government notice provided for the establishment of labour bureaux throughout the Union and required that all workseekers register at one.[15] The central aim of these laws was 'influx control', in terms of which the size of the urban African population would be frozen and all additional labour would be supplied by temporary migrants. According to Labour Bureau regulations,

> Unless a Native was born and is permanently resident in an urban area, or is otherwise resident in an urban area, or is otherwise legally entitled to remain permanently in the area (in terms of Section 10), the Native will not be allowed to register for, or take up, employment in the urban area while there are unemployed workseekers in the area who are legally entitled to be there.[16]

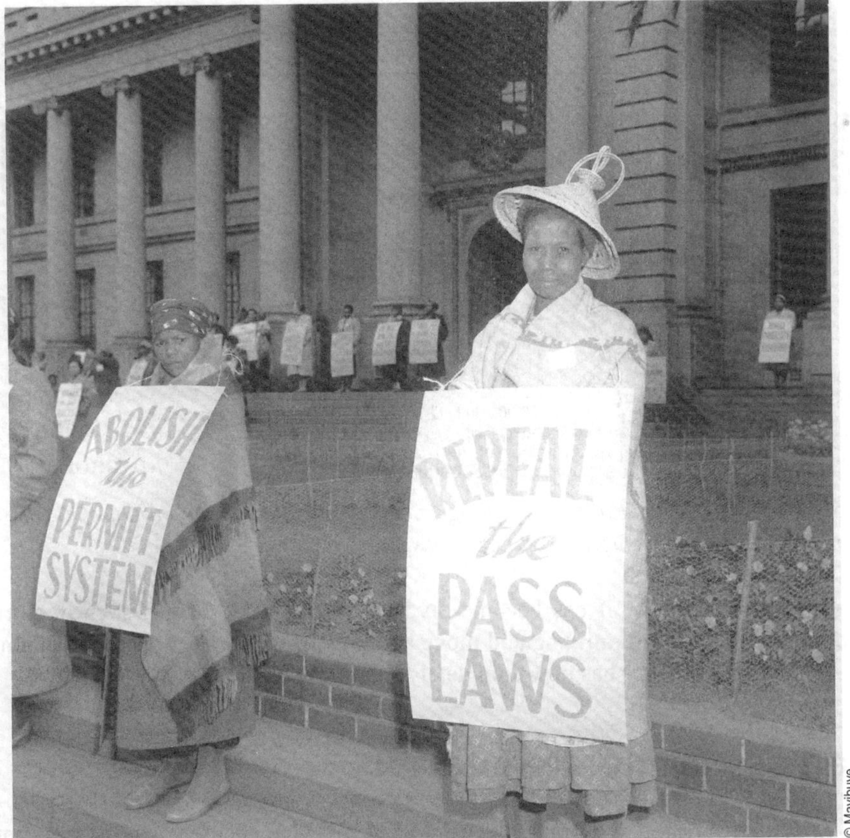

Women protesting against pass laws in Johannesburg.

This clinical language of social engineering concealed a conception of African workers which did not escape the notice of its victims. The word 'native' was used to define a person who was 'generally accepted as a member of the Aboriginal race or tribe of Africa.[17] This definition was further explained by a series of negatives: a native was 'neither white nor a Turk nor an Asian nor a Hottentot, Bushman or Koranna nor an American Negro nor a Griqua or Cape Malay or Coloured.'[18] A 'native workseeker' was someone who fitted the above category and who was not employed nor a pupil but was capable of being employed.[19] Between the class of workseeker and 'idle person' was a very thin line. A native was 'idle' if he was 'habitually unemployed and has no sufficient honest means of livelihood ... is addicted to drink or drugs..., fails to provide for his own support..., begs (or is) undesirable.'[20]

Being unemployed was, quite simply, a crime. A worker 'declared' undesirable under these laws could be 'removed from the urban of proclaimed area and detained until removal or sent to a work colony'. All definitions of race, place and status were embedded in the pass book. And throughout the 1950s the State attempted to get African women to carry this document – and to abide by the social definitions which carrying a pass implied. In 1959, the writer Lewis Nkosi captured the mood of millions when he wrote:

> I do not live apart from my own reference book any more. In fact I have decided I AM THE REFERENCE BOOK! It stands for my personality. It deliniates my character. It defines the

PORTUGUESE EAST AFRICA SUPPLIES

FORCED LABOUR FOR RAND MINES

By Ruth First

JOHANNESBURG.

The tragedy of the deaths of the Portuguese African miners in the Waterval Boven train disaster has shaken South Africa. The tragedy of their lives is less well known.

about £8,000,000 this is an important source of revenue.

The Portuguese African miners work on a deferred pay system,

latter about one-third of the labour is recruited. From Portuguese East Africa all the labour is recruited; none comes voluntarily to the mines.

NO CHOICE

In the 1950s Ruth was alerted to the crippling effect of migrant labour on countries bordering South Africa. It was to be the subject of later books she was to write.

> extent of my freedom.... It has become my face. What began as a system purporting to smooth my efforts to earn a living and move about with sufficient proof of my claim to the citizenship of this country has now completely subordinated me.[21]

Women as harmlessly inferior

The way in which African women were regarded by African men was to be another – perhaps even harder – political barrier to cross. When the Federation of South African Women (FSAW) was launched in April 1954 *Advance* got off to a bad start by failing to report the fact for more than a week, 'indicating that it did not regard it as an event of major importance on the calendar.'[22] Commenting on this, Cherryl Walker has suggested that 'perhaps the men of the Congress Alliance were more apprehensive about a conference to promote women's rights than they were prepared to admit'. When, a month later, *Drum* magazine put the question: 'Should women have equal rights with men?', 101 readers out of the 159 who replied said 'no'. The winner of the prize for the best letter wrote: 'Let us give them courtesy but no rights. They should continue to carry no passes for they are harmlessly inferior; put on their bonnets everywhere, for it is a shame for a woman to go bareheaded.'[23]

When FSAW was formed there were mutterings within Congress about women's role in politics. The ANC Women's League, founded more than 10 years earlier, had been limited to conventional 'women's work' such as fund-raising and catering, and a delegate to the 1954 ANC Congress complained that 'women have been used as tools to raise money without representation in Congress.'[24] At the time of the FSAW launch, the gap between theoretical endorsement of equality between the sexes and daily practice was still a large one within the ANC. When the Federation decided to mount a demonstration outside the Union Buildings the following year, Helen Joseph noted that

> although the African women were emerging rapidly and making their influence felt, the men were not always happy about the idea of a women's demonstration, one from which the men would be excluded. 'What about the children?' they would sometimes ask, and we would

reply: 'That day the men must be in the kitchen ... while the women go to Pretoria! This was a new idea for African men.'[25]

So although most Congress men supported an end to discrimination in general terms, the idea of sexual equality raised disturbing questions. It also placed in jeopardy one of the few areas where African men were assured of a position of relative power and prestige: the patriarchal family. But as the women gathered their political muscle, both state and Congress attitudes towards them began to change. At FSAW's founding conference Lilian Ngoyi was applauded when she complained that if husbands had not kept back their wives there would have been many more delegates present: 'The husbands talked of democracy but did not practice it.'[26] Another speaker told delegates that 'if the men stand in our way, we shall sweep them aside for our rights'. In her report of the conference, Ruth noted that there was something which would always be remembered about the gathering: 'Delegates were served with refreshments and lunch. But not one woman worked in the kitchen.'[27]

RUTH FIRST REPORTS ON

HARRISMITH

Why Trouble Is Brewing There

JOHANNESBURG. — The town was almost deserted. Everybody was at the Harrismith agricultural show. Everybody, that is, except the few important people who could not desert their official duties— and the thousands of Africans who live in the Harrismith location, and are seething and troubled about many things to-day.

Ruth's reporting style was to listen to the problems of ordinary people, an approach that produced gutsy journalism in opposition to apartheid.

"RUSSIAN" LEADER SAYS POLICE BACKED HIS GANG

NEW AGE

Vol. 2. No. 41 Registered at G.P.O. as a Newspaper

SOUTHERN EDITION THURSDAY, AUGUST 9, 1956 PRICE 3d.

Startling Allegations At "Unity" Meeting

JOHANNESBURG.

THE allegation that police were protecting the "Russian" gangsters in the Reef townships was made by one of the "Russian" leaders at a mammoth meeting held by the African National Congress in the "Russian" zone of Newclare last Sunday.

The "Russian" leader, who was the star speaker, revealed that the police had urged them to attack the people in North Newclare.

Speaking in Sesuto, translated into Zulu and English, he told how a certain constable had approached one of his men and expressed misgivings about their presence at a mass area meeting the week before.

(Continued on page 8)

See "Evaton—What Is The Fighting All About?" by Ruth First—page 6.

WOMEN'S MIGHTY PROTEST AGAINST PASSES

THEY SIGNED THE LETTER TO STRIJDOM

Helen Joseph, secretary of the Federation of South African Women (Transvaal), and Elizabeth Motingoe, secretary of the African National Congress Women's League, signed the letter asking Strijdom to meet their deputation.

All Eyes On Pretoria Today

JOHANNESBURG.

ONCE again this has been the week of the women of South Africa, as in every city and township the anti-pass protest to Strijdom in Pretoria got under way.

At the time of going to Press, all signs were that this week's protest would be far larger than last time—provided there was no interference from the police, who last year spared no effort to smash the demonstration but were still outwitted by the women.

Twenty-odd spirited local protests to Native Commissioners, the prosecution of the women of Winburg who burnt their pass books (the first ever issued to women), the daily miseries inflicted by the raids and pass searches—all this has stimulated the militancy of the women and they want to show the country and the world in no uncertain fashion that THEY DO NOT WANT PASSES.

● Women members of the Liberal Party decided they would go to Pretoria with the protest.

● Mr. L. Lee-Warden, M.P., Labour members of Parliament Father Martin Jarrett-Kerr and other prominent figures had agreed to be present as observers.

● A call went out to the Black Sash women to take part, but they replied in so many words that they are too busy! They added that their constitution does not permit them to join with other bodies.

By Monday of this week the first protesters were arriving in Johannesburg.

INTER-RACIAL

More even than last year, this was an inter-racial protest and contingents of protesters composed of the foremost fighters for women's rights among the African, Indian, Coloured and European communities were to take part.

Women from Winburg, the first area to have women's pass books inflicted on it, sent their spokesmen to Pretoria.

Mrs. Luthuli was expected, with her a group of women from Stanger, where her husband has been exiled for over two years.

The Congress colours of green, gold and black this week again dazzled the streets of Pretoria, and interspersed between the national dress were the uniforms of the women's Church movements.

LEADERS

The leaders of the deputation, representing all sections of the community were: Mrs. Lilian Ngoyi, Mrs. Rahima Moosa, Miss Sophie Williams, Mrs. Helen Joseph.

They were joined by: Mrs. Frances Baard of Port Elizabeth, Mrs. Lily Diedricks of Port Elizabeth, Miss Florence Mkize of Durban, Mrs. Anna Moeketsi of Pretoria, Mrs. M Jinotlhakwana of the Free State Mrs. Katie White and Mrs. Louisa Kellerman from Cape Town.

In Pretoria itself the preparations have been perhaps among the mos

(Continued on page 3)

Strijdom Backs Down

JOHANNESBURG.

Three days before the women's protest, Prime Minister Strijdom wrote to the Federation that it was "not possible" for him to meet them. Echoing Verwoerd's voice last year, he said it was not correct to state that the pass system had been extended to Bantu women.

The women would nevertheless be at the Union Buildings, replied the Federation.

Thousands of women were making great personal sacrifices to undertake the journey to Pretoria. The women cannot accept the claim that the pass system has not been extended to them.

(See "The Petition The Women Sent To Strijdom"—page 3.)

"DROP THE WHOLE INQUIRY," NON-EUROPEANS TELL GROUP AREAS COMMITTEE

(From Naomi Shapiro)

CAPE TOWN.

"OUR general position is that we hope to make the Committee realise the whole thing should be dropped and the position left as it is," Mr. A. H. Broeksma, Q.C., told the chairman, Dr. J. F. van Rensburg, last Thursday, at the opening of the Group Areas inquiry into the zoning of the southern suburbs of the Cape Peninsula.

Mr. Broeksma is appearing for the Group Areas Co-Ordinating Committee, which represents 24 organisations, two Malay organisations and the Teachers' Educational and Professional Association.

After Dr. van Rensburg had declared that his Committee would refuse to hear objections to the principle of the Group Areas Act, as they did not consider this relevant to the inquiry, Mr. Broeksma said:

"We are here as citizens of our land to try to put a stop to the fear and insecurity of every Non-European in this area and of the Europeans as well."

"We shall try to show that it is completely impossible on statistical, economic and sociological grounds to implement this legislation," he continued, asking the chairman to place before the public factual information on the number of people living in the areas concerned, the value of properties, etc.

FANTASTIC

"We are entitled to have statistical information and then we shall try to show the fantastic inanity of this type of legislation because it is based on purely ideological and theoretical approaches without any relation to our life in the Peninsula."

Giving a ruling on which organisations and individuals the Board will hear, Dr. van Rensburg said no one could demand as a right to be heard. It was left to the discretion of the Board.

"We received many representations (and this applies to your clients, Mr. Broeksma), roneoed, duplicated, in which people say they are in principle against the Group Areas Act. But this committee is not here to defend the Act or attack it. We are here to apply the Act to the best of our ability. Objections of principle are irrelevant."

(Continued on page 6)

INSIDE

Garment Leaders Join With Nat Opposition

JOHANNESBURG.

Last week saw the formation of an all-white garment workers' union in which the plums of office were shared out between the old union officials and the Nationalist-controlled Germiston branch which for years has tried to capture the union for the Nats.

The new union is to be known as the Garment Trade Union of European Employees (S.A.).

A few months ago the Garment Workers' Union justified the splitting of the union into racial groups on the grounds that if they did not "get in first" to register an all-white union in terms of the new I.C. Act, the Nat. anti-trade union elements would create a split and capture the union.

Now the union has done a deal with these same elements!

Several weeks of closed-door

(Continued on page 3)

New Age, *August 9 1956*.

© Mayibuye

The women protesting passes converged on Pretoria; orderly, dignified and unstoppable.

Fighting Talk devoted half a page to document in detail this unusual event. In it Paul Joseph observed that 'the women were in revolt ... the men were in the kitchen.'[28]

When 2 000 women marched on the Union Buildings in 1955 – and 20 000 the following year – to demand an end to passes, it was clear that a new political identity had been formed. After the 1956 demonstration, Helen Joseph wrote with approval that at the bus ranks after the march the men waiting for transport fell back when they saw the women returning from the Union Buildings and, in an uncustomary gesture, gave the women first choice of seats on the buses.[29] However, as women moved to the front ranks of Congress activity, FSAW continued to be frustrated by the reluctance of the ANC to take up the fight against passes. This manifested as a general ANC passivity to the struggle rather than active opposition. While the Coordinating Committee of the Congress Alliance insisted in taking a lead in the anti-pass campaign, FSAW's attempts to translate this into action after the Pretoria demonstrations met with no success. By 1958 FSAW was still complaining that the men had not made an 'active entry' into the anti-pass campaign and that the women 'awaited this with impatience.'[30] Finally, in late 1959, the ANC decided to launch an anti-pass campaign and started to organise for a 'direct assault' on the hated document. But in March 1960 the PAC jumped in ahead of Congress in the pass-burning campaign that was to end in the massacre by police at Sharpeville.

However, the real gains of the womens' anti-pass campaign were neither the end of sexist attitudes nor the abolition of passes (they were finally made compulsory in 1963) but the building of a new gender identity through its mobilisation of thousands of African women throughout the 1950s. And central to this process was the interplay between anti-pass campaigns and the radical press.

'We woke up and saw the light'

FSAW's style of organising was one of protest – mass marches, petitions and demands to government. This had emotional high points, particularly the march by 20 000 women to the Union Buildings in 1956, which followed the ice-breaking demonstration a year earlier. Other key moments in ideological mobilisation was the FSAW launch and the drafting of a Women's Charter, the wave of campaigns which followed the issue of passes to women in the Free State Town of Winburg in 1956, the rural anti-pass campaign in Zeerust in 1957, a massive demonstration in Johannesburg the following year and the women's uprising in Natal in 1959. Between 1955 and 1959, demonstrations against passes took place at dozens of cities and towns throughout the Union, giving the impression of a rolling demonstration which tended to coincide with the arrival in each area of the state's mobile pass-issuing unit.

GETTING READY FOR AUGUST 9

Mrs. Lilian Ngoyi African women's leader, in characteristic pose during a recent demonstration against passes for women.

*ANC firebrand Lillian Ngoyi at an anti-pass demonstration in Evaton. (*New Age, *July 19 1956)*

At the heart of these campaigns was an ideological re-working of the image of African women, and this can be seen (and was often crafted) through Ruth's reporting in *New Age*. In responding to marches and FSAW statements, Ruth provided readers with the impetus and ground-rules for further demonstrations and built, as she did, new myths, heroes and symbols of struggle. This was done by what can be called articulated reporting – linking together events and issues into a particular world view – and by the language and ideas in individual stories which sharpened the focus on particular associations of events. This is best illustrated by comparing Ruth's reporting of a single event, the 1955 march on Pretoria, with that of a commercial daily, in this case *The Star*.

The march, planned by FSAW and a prelude to the huge gathering at the Union Buildings the following year, was a daring strategy – an assault on the symbolic seat of government by women. The women were told if they undertook the march that October they would be arrested. The City Council refused permission for the march to take place, transport licenses for the women were cancelled and the railways were instructed to refuse the women rail tickets. But still they came. One of the organisers, Helen Joseph, was apprehensive about the outcome of the demonstration, 'but as I drove alongside a railway embankment I saw a train high above me; it was filled with African women leaning out of the windows and singing in triumph. I couldn't hold back my tears of joy and pride. We were on our way to Pretoria.'[31]

New Age had begun reporting the anti-pass initiative in January of that year, covering demonstrations in Cape Town and Durban as well as the run-up to the Pretoria march. Nobody reading the paper could have been in any doubt about the issues at stake. Predictably, the government refused to meet a delegation from the assembled women and afterwards called the affair a 'scandalous incitement'. It vowed to prevent any further 'desecration' of the seat of government.[32] *New Age* and *The Star* reported the march in the following way:

New Age:

Pretoria conquered by the women!

Protest delivered at Union Buildings

The Ministers ran away!

From Ruth First

JOHANNESBURG - IN A MASS MULTI-RACIAL DEMONSTRATION AGAINST UNJUST LAWS, NEARLY 2 000 WOMEN DESCENDED ON PRETORIA LAST WEEK AND MADE THEIR WAY TO THE UNION BUILDINGS TO PRESENT THEIR PROTEST TO FOUR CABINET MINISTERS.

Pretoria had never seen anything like it before. Overcoming every obstacle, major and petty, placed in their path, the women came from all parts of South Africa to take part in the demonstration. For hours they poured up the steps of the Union Buildings and congregated in the concourses while their leaders attempted to deliver their protest.

THE CABINET MINISTERS RAN AWAY FROM THEM - SO THE WOMEN LEFT THE PETITION FORMS ON THEIR DOORSTEP TO MAKE SURE THEY SAW THEM WHEN THEY EVENTUALLY RETURNED TO THEIR OFFICES.

The police resorted to every kind of stratagem to try to stop the demonstration. The Transportation Board at the last minute refused permits for the buses.

The railways refused the request of the Federation of South African Women for special coaches. When the women presented themselves at the ticket offices on the morning, clerks at some stations refused to sell any woman a ticket to Pretoria.

Cars were stopped on the roads leading to Pretoria; taxis ticketed; large contingents of women held up at police stations.

But the women were indomitable. They were determined to get to the Union Buildings. And they did!

ENDLESS STREAM

In all 1 600 of them converged on Pretoria; sitting for hours outside the Pretoria station while a ferry service of taxis and private cars were organised to take them to the Union Buildings. For hours on the morning of Thursday October 26 there was an endless colourful stream of women, many of them carrying their children, winding up through the lovely government gardens and to the amphitheater.

There they filled the great granite semi-circle; triumphant that they had arrived, elated as the hours went by and their numbers swelled, but calm, disciplined and quiet in their unanimous protest against passes for African women, Bantu education, the Population Register, the Group Areas Act, the Suppression of Communism Act, Criminal Laws Amendment Act, Public Safety Act and all oppressive laws.

From the early hours of the morning the women began to assemble at arranged meeting places in their townships. They came with their infants, carrying lunch baskets and suitcases and paper carriers; some with blankets, many with huge sunshades. Many found their way blocked at the last minute. but undeterred they got round the obstacles.

The women of Natalspruit found their buses had been canceled and drivers of hired trucks threatened with prosecution by the police if they conveyed the women. So the women of Natalspruit set out for Germiston station - a distance of eight miles - and there they bought their tickets to Pretoria.

The women of Orlando were told by the ticket clerk that no tickets would be sold to the women. Some found men to buy tickets for them, others persevered and at the end of two hours the clerks resumed selling tickets to all comers.

The women of Germiston travelled on a composite train ticket for 307. The women of Brakpan bought a composite ticket for 202. Benoni refused to sell tickets to Pretoria to women. The people of Alexandra boarded the normal P.U.T.C. bus for Pretoria. Five miles outside Pretoria the bus was stopped, directed back to the police station and held there for two hours. Then the police had to let the bus go. The women of Alexandra arrived at the amphitheater when the protest was already over, in time to see the last women climbing down the steps. But they got there!

A large number of women from Marabastad in Pretoria were kept in custody of the police and released only when the protest was already over.

FROM NEAR AND FAR

From Bloemfontein, the Free State Congress sent a delegation of five women to take part in the protest. Women came from Klerksdorp and Rustenburg.

One Johannesburg clothing factory closed for the day: the workers were in Pretoria.

Indian women were there in their exquisite saris; Coloured women from the Coloured townships and the factories; a band of European women who did sterling work helping with the transport arrangements.

An old African woman, half blind, brought her daughter to lead her. African churchwomen were there in their brilliant blue and white; women dingaka in their beads and skins with all regalia; smartly dresses and emancipated young factory workers; housewives and mothers; domestic servants and washerwomen; and, holding the delegations together and giving the great gathering that impressive discipline, the women Congress workers who started this protest rolling in the locations and townships some eight weeks ago when the Mothers' Congress first resolved on it.

At 10.30 a.m. the first batches of women were at the foot of the Union Buildings, and the walk towards the amphitheater started. For two or three hours there was a steady stream of women winding upwards and as they reached the amphitheater each woman (and there were not many who were not puffing and panting) handed in her signed protest to four women from the four organisations stationed there to receive them.

Then the women took their seats around the amphitheater. Throughout they sat in hushed silence and as the morning went by the crowd grew more enormous. From the windows and balconies of the Union Buildings the civil service looked on in amazement at this impressive demonstration. The pile of protest forms grew until there were 1 600.

From the cupola Mrs Helen Joseph, Mrs Lilian Ngoyi, Miss Sophia Williams and Mrs Rahima Moosa announced that they would deliver the protests to the Ministers. They moved off to a great cry of '*Afrika*' and the raised thumb salute. The women went on sitting quietly.

Tailed by reporters and photographers and with the Special Branch never far off, the four went first to the office of Dr Verwoerd, Minister of Native Affairs, who only a week before had told the women his policies were a subject of 'praise not protest'. The door was locked (it was lunch hour) so a pile of protests was left on the doormat to await the Minister's return. In the office of the Minister of Justice, a '*niksvermoedende meisie*' (unsuspecting girl according to *Die Transvaler*) said with alacrity as the women asked her to hand the protests over to the Minister: 'Certainly!'

When the four returned to the amphitheater and reported that they had delivered the protests, the hush was broken again as the women rose to sing 'Inkosi Sikelele' and the sound and harmony rang out from the tiers of women.

No orders had been given, there was no bustle, no confusion, no panic or any hitches. With their dignity, their discipline and their determination they had carried the day.

The Star:

Women of all races gather in Pretoria

Converge on Union Buildings to protest against laws

By the Political Correspondent

IN SPITE OF MANY OBSTACLES about 1 200 Native women supported by some Coloured, Indian and European women, gathered in Pretoria today from many parts of the Transvaal and converged on the Union Buildings.

As they reached the amphitheater of the Union Buildings they handed to an organiser signed protests demanding the repeal of the Bantu Education Act, the pass laws and Population Registration Act, the Departure from the Union Regulations Act, the Industrial Conciliation act and the Native Labour (Settlement of Disputes) Act, the Criminal Laws Amendment and Public Safety Acts, the Riotous Assemblies Act and the Group Areas Act.

The protests said that these laws discriminated unfairly against the non-Europeans, denied them human rights, and attempted to divide them.

The protests were all headed 'The demands of the women of South Africa, presented by the Transvaal region of the Federation of South African Women'.

The scene was an unusual one.

Streams of non-European women, some clad entirely in beads, others in saris or beautifully cut European costumes, came silently to the cupola, handed in their protests and then sat on the amphitheater steps to await the arrival of yet more of their comrades.

Some carried Native drums, some smart handbags. Some wore leopard-skin headdress, others wore hats.

By 1.30 p.m. all the protests had been handed in and the organisers delivered them to the offices of the four Ministers concerned - Native Affairs, Justice, Interior and Labour.

They found Dr Verwoerd's office locked so they left the documents on his doormat.

The huge gathering then sang 'Inkosi Sikilele Afrika' and, after crying 'Mayibuye Afrika' three times, dispersed as quietly as they had come.

Although a different emphasis in these articles is immediately clear, it is not easy to describe either as misleading or biassed. This is because what is carried away from an article, what is retained in memory, is often not explicit but implied, and lies embedded in assumptions and associations that are located as much with the reader as with the author.[33] This requires reciprocal assumptions between journalists and readers – a knowledge of which is called 'news sense' – and the degree to which these assumptions are congruent is the degree to which news reports are considered to be 'true' or factual.

However, no newspaper report is ideologically neutral. It is a representation of the world for a culture (the world is perceived according to the ideological needs of a culture) and an ideological map, working by segmentation; by partitioning the material continuum of nature and the undifferentiated flux of thought and events into slices which answer to the interests of the reader community.[34] It is in this sense that newspapers can construct readers, building a world view which may be common sense to one segment of society but totally alien to another. For a political journalist like Ruth, this construction was conscious and strategic, while for the Star's reporter these processes would have been subsumed into the ideological ethic of 'objectivity'. In this regard, it is instructive to ask of both articles: What do they say? What do they assume? Who were their perceived audience? And what was their underlying intention? These are not easily answered, but an approach can be made through the language used.

Most journalism does not in so many words define the nature of the world. Rather it takes place against the background of a world which is silently taken for granted by the majority of its readers. Indeed all readers carry around a mental dictionary or lexicon which stores ideas in sets structured around certain formal, logical relationships such as opposites, inclusion, equivalence, taboo.[35] It is, therefore, often illuminating to distill out lexical registers from a text by removing its content. Such a register of the way in which the demonstrating women are described in the two articles about the Pretoria march looks like this:

New Age: Pretoria conquered

MASS ... DEMONSTRATION...DESCENDED ON ... PROTEST … never seen anything like it ... Overcoming every obstacle ... demonstration ... poured up the steps ... deliver their protest ... MINISTERS RAN AWAY ... women presented themselves ... women were indomitable ... determined ... And they did! ... ENDLESS STREAM ... converged on Pretoria .. .endless colourful stream ... winding up ... filled the great granite semi–circle ... triumphant ... elated ... numbers swelled ... calm ... disciplined ... quiet ... unanimous protest ... assemble ... carrying ... huge ... undeterred ... got round the obstacles ... But they got there! ... large number ... released ... FROM NEAR AND FAR ... delegation ... workers ... a band ... sterling work ... brilliant ... smartly dressed...emancipated...factory workers...housewives...mothers... domestic servants ... washerwomen ... holding the delegations together .. great gathering ... impressive discipline ... protest ... resolved ... steady stream ... winding upwards ... hushed silence ... crowd ... amazement ... impressive demonstration ... protest ... a great cry of 'Afrika' ... with alacrity ... rose to sing ... harmony rang out ... No orders ... no bustle ... no confusion ... no panic ... dignity ... discipline ... determination ... carried the day.

Women at the Union Buildings making their discontent known.

> *Star*: Women gather
>
> Converge ... protest ... supported ... gathered ... converged .. .handed to ... protests ... demanding ... denied ... attempted to .. .unusual ... Streams ... clad ... beautifully cut ... came silently ... await ... comrades ... carried ... wore ... delivered them ... sang ... crying ... dispersed ...quietly.

A description of those who opposed the women is also instructive:

> *New Age*: Pretoria conquered
>
> Ministers ran away! ... UNJUST LAWS ... CABINET MINISTERS RAN AWAY ... EVENTUALLY RETURNED TO THEIR OFFICES ... every kind of stratagem ... stop the demonstration ... refused permits ... refused the request ... refused to sell any woman a ticket ... Cars were stopped ... taxis ticketed ... held up at police stations ... Bantu education ... Population Register ... Group Areas Act ... Suppression of Communism Act ... Criminal Laws Amendment Act ... Public Safety Act ... oppressive laws ... blocked ... cancelled ... threatened ... prosecution ... no tickets ... refused to sell .. .bus was stopped ... held ... kept in custody ... Special Branch ... door was locked ... '*niksvermoedende meisie'*.
>
> *Star*: Women gather
>
> Bantu Education Act ... pass laws ... Population Registration Act ... Departure from the Union Regulations Act ... Industrial Conciliation Act ... the Native Labour (Settlement of Disputes) Act ... Criminal Laws Amendment and Public Safety Acts ... Riotous Assemblies Act .. .Group Areas Act ... denied .. .office locked.

It is part of our communicative competence to recognise these registers, and to be unconsciously aware that they mark off distinct value systems – they have a categorising function. This categorisation by vocabulary is an integral part of the reproduction of ideology in newspapers, and can be the basis for subliminal approval or discrimination. According to Roger Fowler, 'these associations and dissociations are the surface-structure

WOMEN'S CAMPAIGN

AUGUST 9 IN

IST THE

'WE'D

MEN TO BLAME FOR NATAL

TROUBLES

Women Charged With

Pass Book Robberies

"WE WANT

Waar's Jou Reference

ANTI-PASS CAM

THURSDAY, SEPTEMBER 24, 1959

Africans Want More

EDITORIAL

Cassocks No Protection

Natal Women's Peaceful Prot

Women's Leader Given Spare

WILD SCENES

Reference Book Issue Starts This Week

CAPE WOMEN PICKET PASS

ISSUING DEPOTS

Natal Women Hold

CAPE WOMEN

FIGHT PASSES

outcrops of underlying abstract paradigms of the discourse, the values and relationships that underpin this particular newspaper's theory of the way the world is organised and the way it should be.'[36]

In the *New Age* article the women conquer, they are indomitable, determined, undeterred, brilliant, orderly and dignified. They carry the day. They are triumphant and strong. The report had been contextualised in the weeks before the march, and its effect would be documented in the year that followed. In Ruth's article, the vocabulary dichotomizes the demonstration into a struggle between the women and the 'system' and predicates a struggle between them. The government and its officials refuse requests, refuse permits, stop cars, threaten, cancel, prosecute, block and make oppressive laws. When confronted by the women, they run away.

In *The Star* article the women converge, demand, sing, cry and disperse. They do not conquer, they merely gather, present their protests and leave 'as quietly as they had come' – lightly rippling the tranquil waters of the newspaper's white readers, posing no threat and raising few questions. There were no earlier reports about plans for the march in *The Star* and few follow-ups. Government officials merely pass laws, deny and lock offices. For *Die Transvaler* which carried the story, the women were simply agitators, nannies and led by white communists. If the effect of *Die Transvaler* article was to stigmatise, *The Star* article tended to neutralise and Ruth's article to politicize the gathering.

Of course, the African women were not necessarily undeterred, indomitable, determined and strong. For decades, perhaps even centuries, they had been socially weak and subservient to authority. In attributing to them heroic qualities, Ruth was encouraging the women to embody them, and to do so against and in contradistinction to an oppressive apartheid state. This was the essence of her political journalism – not distorting information

Pass resisters making their way from the Port Elizabeth jail after having been released.

O.P.-S.12987—1951-2—5,000-200. S.

N.A. 375.
(old ou Revenue/Inkomste 401.)

UNION OF SOUTH AFRICA.—UNIE VAN SUID AFRIKA.

Department of Native Affairs.—Departement van Naturellesake.

Tax Identity No.
Belastingaanwysingsnommer
Last Tax Receipt No. and Year
Laaste Belastingskwitansie no. en Jaar.
Tax Liability —
Belastingaanspreeklikheid :—
General Tax £ Year
Algemene Belasting Jaar
Local Tax £ Year
Plaaslike Belasting Jaar
Quitrent £ Year
Rekonie Jaar
Crown Rent £ Year
Kroongrondhuur Jaar
Squatters Rent £ Year
Plakkershuur Jaar

P113370

Date Stamp.—Datumstempel.

NATIVE ADMINISTRATION ACT, No. 38 of 1927.
NATURELLE-ADMINISTRASIE WET, No. 38 van 1927.

DEPARTEMENT VAN NATURELLESAKE
Posbus 1199 P.O. Box
29-4-1953
JOHANNESBURG
DEPARTMENT OF NATIVE AFFAIRS

PASS.—PAS.

(Proclamation No. 150 of 1934.—Proklamasie No. 150 van 1934.)

Granted to :—
Uitgereik aan :—
Name (native name)
Naam (naturellenaam)
Name known by
Naam waaronder bekend
Tax registration No. and district
Belastingregistrasie no. en distrik
Location or place of residence
Lokasie of woonplek
Tribe or nationality
Stam of nasionaliteit
Travelling to
Reisende na
By way of — Rail or Road.
Langs (Route.—Roete.)
For the purpose of — To be out of Johannesburg
Vir die doel om — Urban Area by

Valid for 30 days (not to exceed 30 days).
Geldig vir dae (nie meer as 30 dae nie).

Has in his possession
In besit van (Stock or property.—Vee of eiendom.)

District/Distrik

Authorised Officer.—Gemagtigde Amptenaar.

NOT TO BE EMPLOYED IN THE URBAN AREA OF JOHANNESBURG

Designation.—Ampstitel.

N.B.—This pass confers no authority to move stock.
N.B.—Hierdie pas verleen geen reg om vee saam te neem nie.
This pass is to be retained by the Employer until the expiration of the contract in terms of section 18 (1) of Proclamation 150 of 1934—*See endorsement at back of form.
Hierdie pas moet deur die werkgewer gehou word totdat die kontrak ingevolge artikel 18 (1) van Proklamasie 150 van 1934 beëindig is—*Sien endossement op keersy van vorm.
PASS AREAS.—The Province of the Transvaal and the Province of the Orange Free State, excluding the native areas scheduled under Act No. 27 of 1913, or any amendment thereof.
PASGEBIEDE.—Die Provinsie Transvaal en die Provinsie Oranje-Vrystaat, behalwe die ingelyste naturellegebiede ingevolge van Wet No. 27 van 1913, of enige wysiging daarvan.

All Africans out of their designated areas or in white areas at night were required to carry a pass.

'STRIJDOM, YOU HAVE STRUCK A ROCK"

20,000 WOMEN SAY "NO" TO PASSES

New Age, *August 16 1956.*

to serve a Marxist world view, but highlighting and contextualising specific qualities and facts and mobilising readers against a future view of themselves and the state which Ruth held to be possible.

The effect of her journalism in the anti-pass campaign – in step with FSAW leadership – was the ideological mobilisation of African women. By seeking out, reporting and supporting every militant action by the women, embedding within each story tacit approval and a heroic dimension, she began to build with FSAW a new self-image for the urban township woman.

This type of journalism was, therefore, not only involved in the business of informing its readers, but in their discursive construction. Embedded in the texts were instructions about who, what and how to be with regard to passes, the government and the Congress Alliance. Readers of all newspapers are positioned according to the presumptions of journalists, but they need not comply with the demands of the 'reading position' constructed for them. Options range from not being a reader at all, through being a critical, distanced reader to refusing to enter into a reading position and reconstructing the text completely.[37] The most effective journalism, therefore, is not necessarily the 'shock, horror', variety but that which seems plausible, natural and uncontentious – from the reader's point of view – and obvious. This is true for both mainstream and political journalists. But for the latter there was also an attempt to dislodge readers from the dominant ideological position – to subvert that position – and to use news stories to construct or buttress an alternative world view.

This can be illustrated by an example from the last major demonstration by African women against passes and, again, by contrasting the reports of *New Age* and *The Star*. By mid-1958 government pass-units began operations in the larger towns – a sign of increased confidence on their part – and in October they approached Johannesburg. Their strategy was to start with the huge army of domestic workers in the white suburbs and a circular was sent to employers instructing them to send their 'Native female servants' to the Native Commissioner's offices in order to be issued with reference books.[38] On October 21 Sophiatown women marched to the Commissioner's offices to stop the domestic workers taking out passes. Police intercepted them and arrested 249 women. The demonstrations continued and by the end of the week nearly 2 000 women had been arrested.

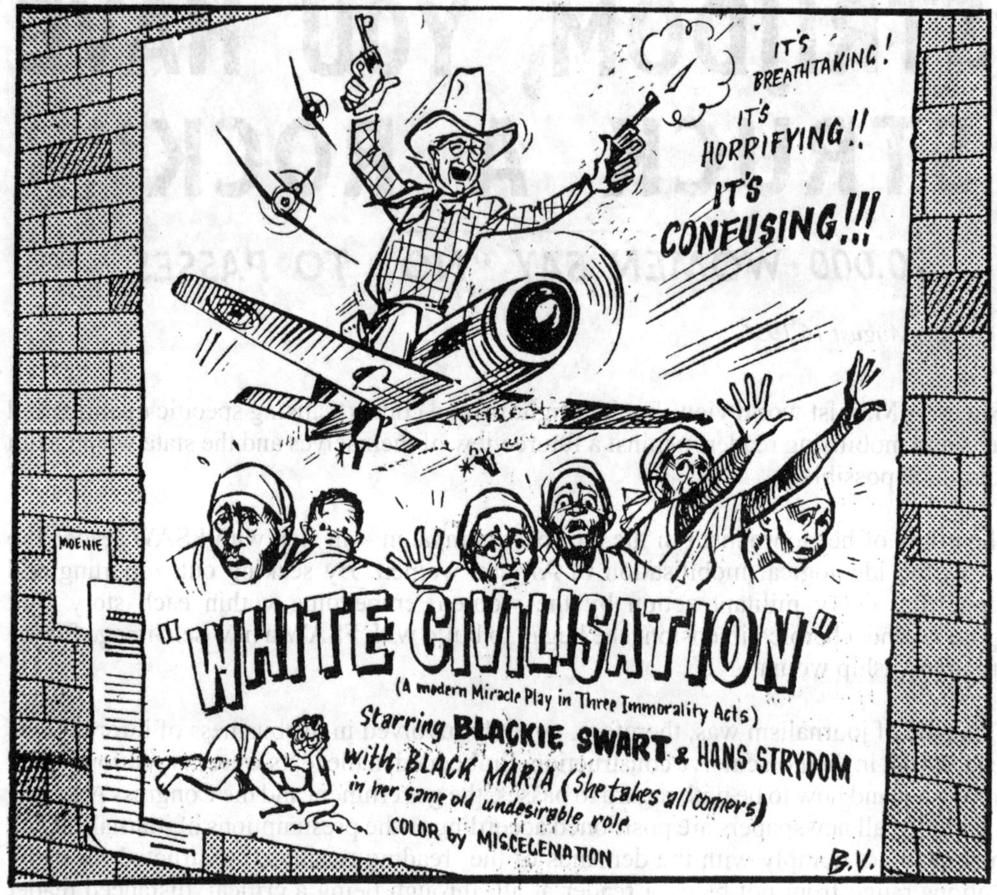

New Age, *November 14 1957.*

In one of the biggest headlines ever used on their front page, *New Age* told its readers: 'Jo'burg women say 'no' to passes.' Ruth and Tennyson Makiwane, who covered the march, gave graphic descriptions of the arrests and the snowballing demonstrations. Goals were 'overflowing with the women and their children', and in The Fort there was 'no space left for a rat.'[39] In rowdy demonstrations 'reminiscent of the Defiance Campaign and the bus boycott', African men 'handed over (their) pants to the women' who were beaten and herded into vans singing 'a new song with the words: "The enemy of the African is the pass."'[40] The paper also reported that the pass laws had 'claimed their first woman sacrifice' – Martha Qoba who was trampled to death in a pass queue. *The Star* pictured the women on its front page, but its report clearly reflected the preoccupation of most of its perceived readers: 500 women arrested in reference book protest – no nannies today.[41] The following day its leader page article consoled readers with a story headlined: No servants? Why, it's easy to do without them![42]

Following the 1955 march on the Union Buildings, Ruth tracked the anti-pass campaign tirelessly. In one week she investigated and wrote about the position of African women in Welkom, Stilfontein, Krugersdorp, Roodepoort, Boksburg, Springs, Germiston, Brakpan and Johannesburg.[43] In November 1955 some 600 people attended an anti-pass meeting in Bloemfontein, described by *New Age* as the largest such meeting ever held there. Then in early 1956 Ruth found out that the government was to begin issuing reference books to women in Winburg in the Free State and she began a media campaign to block the move.[44] She also discovered the route of the pass teams and made it public, forewarning women in other Free State towns.[45] *Die Transvaler* responded to the exposé with irritation, and complained of 'screaming headlines in which gall is spewed against the issue of reference books to women which are appearing in periodicals and newspapers distributed among Natives.'[46]

A week later the national secretary of the ANCWL, Mary Ranta, warned that 'if Africans in the Free State could oppose the pass system 40 years ago, they can easily do so today!'[47] At first the pass team met with no resistance, and by March 22 had issued 1 429 reference books. Then the newly elected National President of the ANCWL, Lilian Ngoyi, slipped into in the district and held a meeting with Winburg women.[48] Spurred by the presence of their national leader, the women decided that the only response to the newly-issued passes was to burn them. The next day they collected a pile of reference books, marched to the magistrate's office and publicly torched the lot.[49]

*Police address women outside the Johannesburg Pass Office. Eight hundred women were arrested in Johannesburg in two days. (*Rand Daily Mail, *n.d.)*

The burning of passes in Winburg had deep significance for African women and produced a grass-fire effect on the women's campaign. A huge wave of protests swept the country. In the first seven months of 1956 alone, the FSAW estimated that about 50 000 women took part in 38 demonstrations against the pass laws in 30 different centres. These protests fed into the second historic march of 20 000 women on the Union buildings on August 9 and carried on unabated through 1957 and 1958.[50] Throughout these demonstrations a new self image was being built by the women – they had seen African men 'disappear' in pass raids and families destroyed by imprisonment for failure to have passes in order, and they were not going to have it happen to them. The mood of the time was captured in a Zulu freedom song first sung on the steps of the Union Buildings: *Strijdom uthitta abafazi, uthinti imbokotho* (Strijdom, you've tampered with the women, you've knocked against a rock).

From the moment passes burned in Winburg, the incineration of the documents became a symbolic retrieval of self esteem. Passes represented state control and excommunication from the cities. The women responded by invasions of city centres and 'cleansing rituals' around the 'open alter where passes are burnt.'[51] This perspective was reinforced by the state's response to pass burning – outrage and mass arrests.

In the area of Zeerust in the Western Transvaal, rural anti-pass demonstrations led to exceptional police brutality, a state of emergency and the deposition of Chief Abraham Moiloa.[52] Police action in the area was exposed by Ruth in a series of searing articles which led to a complete ban of press access to the area.[53] *Fighting Talk* carried an intriguing report about an 'unknown man' who appeared beside the road in the wake of the mobile pass column in the area and lit a large bonfire. Women passing him asked him why he had lit the fire as the day was warm. He replied:

> I do not incite you to burn your Reference Books. I am a man of peace. I do not snatch away your books or threaten you. I sit quietly by my fire and I say only this: If you have rubbish to burn, if you envy the women of the other villages who have freed themselves of the passes – well, the fire is here and it will save you trouble.[54]

Buy this time the pass had become the most powerful symbol of opposition to the Nationalist government. A woman from Zeerust told Ruth: 'We have been murdered because of passes. Machine guns have been used against the people. I have seen people being shot. Men have been handcuffed hands and feet. I have escaped from hell at Zeerust. But there are still those in this hell who stand firm against passes.'[55]

In Natal, two years later, women took action against dipping tanks, beer halls and passes in a series of demonstrations which were to turn violent and see hundreds in court for incitement and illegal gatherings.[56] During these uprisings a rural woman in Cato Manor was to provide an answer to *Drum's* letter-writer who had suggested in 1954 that women were harmlessly inferior and should put on their bonnets: 'They forced us to take off our headdoeks (to be photographed for passes). It was against our custom but we had to do it ... The light got to our brains. We woke up and saw the light. And the women have been demonstrating ever since.'[57] In the end, African women were to lose the battle against passes. After the pass-burnings and shootings at Sharpeville and Langa, the pass laws were suspended. But in February 1963, with the state emboldened and the ANC banned, they were made compulsory. However, the anti-pass campaigns of the 1950s had a radicalising effect on women's perceptions of themselves and their place in society. In the nine years since the launch of FSAW in 1954, the Federation and the radical press had helped women to move, whether consciously or not, beyond the traditional boundaries that had formerly circumscribed their lives.

Notes

1 Although the actual gatherings at Langa and Sharpeville were called by the PAC, which had been organising in these areas, little preparatory work and challenges to the state around passes had been done by that organisation, which merely jumped in ahead of the ANC's already-announced anti-pass campaign.

2 See Wells, 1991.

3 Posel: *Construction of apartheid...* 1987 and Lazar: *Verwoerd vs the 'Visionaries'...* 1987.

4 Quoted in Sachs 1973, p162.

5 Lazar: *Verwoerd* ...op cit, p10.

6 Ibid, p9.

7 *Volkshandel*, June 1948. Quoted in O'Meara, 1983, p175.

8 Adam Ashforth has argued that the 'Native Question' should be seen 'as a central aspect of state formation in 20th century South Africa. It was an intellectual construct in which the relationship between land, labour and legitimation were understood and articulated by the ruling orders of the state'. And one of the principal forms in which it was 'solved (and re-solved)' was that of the commission of inquiry. See Ashforth: 'Reconstructing the native question in the area of apartheid,' Unpublished Oxford University seminar paper, 1987, p1.

9 Tomlinson 105;34, quoted in Ashforth, ibid.

10 Ashforth, Ibid, p18.

11 Report of the Commission for the Development of Bantu Areas, Parliament, May 14 1956. In *Verwoerd Speaks*, 1966, P103.

12 Ibid, p103.

13 See Ashforth, op cit, p37.

14 Moll: 'Growth without development: The South African economy in the 1950s.' Unpublished seminar paper, Oxford, 1987.

15 Government Notice No.2495 of October 31, 1952.

16 Federated Chamber of Industries Memorandum on 'Industrial Native Labour in Urban Areas, 1955, paragraph (A)(4). Quoted in Posal: 'Doing business with the pass laws...' Unpublished Oxford University seminar, 1987, p9.

17 Work Colonies Act of 1949.

18 Old Age Pensions Act 22 of 1928.

19 Natives (Abolition of Passes & Co–ordiantion of Documents) Act of 1952.

20 Ibid. Section 36(a).

21 The Black Sash, June/July 1959, p16.

22 Walker, 1982, p143.

23 *Drum*, May 1954. In Walker, ibid, p149.

24 Walker, 1982, p91 and *Drum*, February 1954, p11.

25 Joseph, 1966, p68.

26 Walker, op cit, p158.

27 *Advance* 29.4.54.

28 *Fighting Talk*, May 1954, p8.

29 Joseph, op cit, p85.

30 Report by FSAW on the anti–pass campaign. FSAW document CI 6 p6.

31 Joseph, op cit, p71.

32 *New Age* 3.11.55.

33 Fowler, 1991, p232.

34 Ibid, p82

35 Ibid, p54.

36 Ibid, p93.

37 Of course no text is merely absorbed passively by a reader. And consequently every reading involves some reconstitution of the text. See Kress, 1989, p42.

38 Walker, op cit. p216 and *New Age*, October 30, 1958.

39 *New Age* Ibid.

40 Ibid.

41 *The Star*, October 21, 1958.

42 *The Star*, October 22, 1958.

43 *New Age*, May 10, 1956.

44 *New Age*, January 6, 12, March 22, April 5, 1956.

45 *New Age*, March 22, 1956.

46 *Die Transvaler*, January 7, 1956.

47 *New Age*, January 12, 1956.

48 Walker, op cit, p192.

49 *New Age*, *Drum* and Walker, op cit.

50 A FSAW fact sheet listing women's demonstrations during those two years ran to seven closely-typed pages. See 'Resistance of women to Passes during 1957', FSAW C1 5, and 'Resistance of women to Passes during 1958', FSAW C1 6. FSAW collection, Witwatersrand University.

51 *New Age*, August 8, 1957.

52 He was replaced by Lucas Mangope, who was to become president of the Bantustan of Bophuthatswana.

53 *New Age*, June 20, 1957.

54 *Fighting Talk*, November, 1960.

55 *New Age*, January 29, 1959.

56 See *New Age*, from 13.8.59.

57 In J Yawitch: 'Natal 1959 – the women's protests'. Paper presented at the Conference on the History of Opposition in South Africa, University of the Witwatersrand, January 1978.

7

The economy of poverty

The economic facts, the poverty of a people that reckons its income in pennies, sparked off the boycott, and those who argue the economic basis for this protest could not be on firmer ground
– Ruth First

Removals from Sophiatown, in Johannesburg's Western Areas

Alexandra was an anomaly in white South Africa. A teeming African slum in the heart of the northern suburbs of Johannesburg, it became a prime candidate for removal. But for complex reasons – it fell just beyond the municipal boundary of the city – it remained intact. However, there was to be a cost, and whereas Sophiatown came to epitomise the best of Johannesburg ghetto culture, Alexandra was to became the symbol of anger which was to manifest as both grassroots organisation and crime. Its people were to show Ruth the worst, and the most heroic, aspects of African urban life.

At the heart of township life in South Africa lay a terrible poverty: too many people with too few resources and with employers, backed by the government, intent on keeping wages to the barest minimum and facilities as cheap as possible. This was never reflected in reviews of the South African economy by government statisticians, banks and economic indicators. Focusing, as they did, on broad profits and narrow privilege, they spoke of a 'reality' which seemed oddly out of step with conditions on the streets. In 1956 a leading firm of United States underwriters declared the Union's industrial growth to be 'an outstanding feature of the country's economy.'[1] In 1957 the Standard Bank told investors that 'new record levels of production were achieved in mining, farming, power and transport, and manufacturing. National income for the year 1956/57 reached a new peak.'[2] In its annual survey it reported the third successive record in gold production, with income up from the previous year to £212-million. This trend, it said, could be traced in all other mining apart from tin and manganese. In 1957 the motor trade enjoyed a 'brisk year', tyre production was a record, furniture sales were 'keen', clothing production was 'well maintained' and good progress was recorded in the production of paints, sweets, chocolates, paper packaging, gummed tapes, tags and labels, perfumes and toilet requisites.[3] Adjusting for population increase, the bank calculated that the real net income per head of population in 1957 rose by 3.4% over the previous year.

The Nationalist government was equally enthusiastic. According to the Minister of Economic Affairs, AJ van Rijn, by the mid-1950s retail sales had jumped 16% over 1947 levels, the income from maize had gone up 200%, the wool clip was up 600% over pre-war levels and the gross national product had increased 130% since 1946.[4] The Minister said this 'unprecedented expansion' had brought 'increased prosperity and much higher living standards to the people'. Just who these people were could be gleaned from an article written by the chairman of the Industrial Development Corporation, Dr H van Eck:

> We, who are a little older and experienced the difficult times when one quarter of our White population was in danger of becoming poor whites, can never relax our vigilance.... Our South African people ... by their own efforts, lifted themselves out of the depths of economic stagnation and the hopeless prospects of 30 years ago to a state of relative well-being.[5]

Ruth's Marxist perspective, however, led her to measure progress by a different set of indices. She saw the relationship between the wealth of the whites and the poverty of Africans, and the way in which apartheid cemented in place the class divisions of the emerging capitalist state. Her journalistic exploration of township poverty began during a freezing July in 1951. That month the Johannesburg City Council voted to virtually double rents in all its locations and townships. The daily press reported that the council's manager of non-European affairs, L Venables, immediately 'retired' due to ill health, but Ruth found he had resigned in protest over the rent increase.[6] She discovered that the increase had emanated from the council's Finance Committee 'presided over by the tight-fisted Mr GB Gordon' which had insisted that the Native Revenue account be reduced drastically. Ruth swung into action on the front page of the *Guardian* with an incisiveness with which she was to rake the City Council, her previous employer, for the next 12 years.

The Finance Committee's squeeze, she said, placed the burden 'on the shoulders of the poorest, instead of the wealthiest ratepayer in Africa's wealthiest city'. She ended the article with a warning which proved prophetic and was to signal a major focus of her investigative journalism:

> Placing new burdens on the Africans – the city's poorest, hardest hit by the soaring cost of living, at the lowest end of the cost of living allowance scale, the most fleeced by profiteers and black-marketeers in every shortage, carrying the heaviest burden of transport fares, because they are pushed into the furthest locations – can only cause trouble. Has the City Council forgotten the tragic aftermath of the increase in Western Areas tram fares?[7]

Two weeks later, informed by her investigations into links between farm labour and capitalist accumulation, Ruth began looking at the underpinnings of the South African economy. Under a front page lead: 'South Africa drifting towards economic crisis,' she used a go-slow by railway artisans as a point of departure to show how State inefficiency in the transport networks, together with bad labour relations, were leading to massive shortages of coal, maize, sugar and cement. The result, she said, would be more unemployment and more urban problems.[8] The following month she took a fine-grained look at these problems. 'The average African family on the Reef', she wrote, 'is struggling to meet an essential budget of £17 4s.4d. with an income of only £12 6s.6d. The basic wages of most African workers have remained unchanged for the last six years, and are wholly inadequate to maintain healthy existence.'[9] She found that between 1944 and 1951 food prices had risen by 48% and this was having 'a disastrous effect on the expenditure of Africans' who had to spend 87% of their meagre wages on this item alone. These wages did not meet even the minimum requirements for subsistence, health and decency, 'not to speak of emergency requirements such as doctors fees and medicines, the replenishment of furniture, crockery and other utensils, blankets or other bedding, or the claims of civilised life, such as church dues and children's school books.'[10] This situation, she said, would lead to growing conflict among ordinary workers around transport services and would accelerate urban crime. On the former point she was most emphatic. 'All transport between locations and the city should be cheap and adequate. If not it should be subsidised. Africans should not be forced to pay the penalty for the Europeans' insistence that they must live far from European residential areas.'[11] Early in 1952 the economic squeeze on township residents took an ugly turn. In Newclair a Basotho gang known as the Russians went on the rampage, killing nine residents and injuring at least a hundred. Investigating the affair, Ruth found that – contrary to accusations by the police, the *Sunday Times* and *Die Transvaler* that the attack was 'communist inspired' – the Russians had been extorting money from residents:

> Their tactics were to round up peaceful citizens in the dead of night or early morning and compel heads of families to pay £1. (Then) so bold did they become that their womenfolk went from door to door in daytime, demanding 5s. from every women they met, threatening with violence those who resisted… .In a little over a day the Russians collected £200 in this fashion.[12]

When residents resisted, the Russians attacked with heavy sticks, pieces of iron, battle axes and other sharp instruments.

The following week, under a headline 'Life a hell in Newclare,' Ruth asked: 'Why is the government doing so little about the situation? Why are the police not cooperating with the (Newclair) Civic Guard? Why don't they remove the Russian menace and restore law and order to Newclare? Where will all this end?'[13] Ruth's Marxist perspective was clearly able to discern the economic underpinnings of township problems. But, as a result of the conceptions of struggle which emerged from the 1953 Discussion Clubs, she was to focus her writing elsewhere for nearly five years.

Conceptions of struggle

On the one hand, the Nationalist government was at pains to show that apartheid assisted capitalists. On the other, it went to extraordinary lengths to argue that the political effects of apartheid were in no way connected with capitalist development or even with apartheid. Out of this split vision was to develop the agitator theory – the 'natives' were contented unless stirred up by 'outside agents', generally communists.

These views were almost unanimously supported by the mainstream press and its sponsors because it allowed business as usual under apartheid and assisted those who had to explain racist policies to a skeptical world. This perspective was even adopted by many liberals who benefited from apartheid but did not want to consider themselves to be part of the problem. Perry Anderson has argued that 'the bourgeoisie always seek to separate politics from economics, because it understands very well that if it succeeds in keeping the working class within a corporative framework, no serious danger can threatened its hegemony.'[14] In South Africa, this separation was maintained by growing repression throughout the 1950s and a widely-accepted official discourse which made economic growth a white achievement and African poverty and conditions the product of black backwardness. The result was highly successful, and the economy produced figures which satisfied investors.[15] TC Moll has aptly characterised the 1950s as a decade of 'growth without development.'[16] White incomes, skills levels and social welfare rose along with growing profitability in mining and manufacturing and massive white nepotism in the civil service. But for Africans 'the decade was one of increasing economic inequality and worsening rural poverty, and various quality of life aspects of black experience clearly suffered – decreased political choice and freedom, fewer economic and residential rights, and greater state control over all areas of social life'.[17] The Communist Party of South

Africa (and later the SACP) was well placed ideologically to understand the economic underpinnings of deteriorating African social conditions. Involvement in strike action during the 1940s as well as grassroots organisation in Brakpan and other urban areas had sensitised members to popular political will in the townships. But the dissolution of the Party had created an organisational hiatus, and in the talks which led to the re-formation of the Party a distinct shift in emphasis occurred.

One of the key issues in the 1953 Discussion Clubs was about appropriate forms of struggle and, importantly, which class should lead this struggle. *Viewpoints and Perspectives*, the published debates of the Johannesburg Discussion Club, reflected a tension over this issue which had roots in the conflict at the Second Congress of the Communist International between Lenin and Roy over the form of struggle against imperialism. Roy allowed for no collaboration with the bourgeois nationalist movement in this struggle, whereas Lenin argued that because of the extreme numerical, economic and ideological weakness of the working class in the colonies, the leadership would remain in nationalist hands in the first stage of transformation. Debates in South Africa which led to the theory of 'colonialism of a special type' returned to these earlier positions and two views emerged over whether precedence should be given to political or economic forms of struggle and over which class should take the lead.[18]

The argument polarised around two personalities, Party ideologue Michael Harmel and trade unionist Danie du Plessis.[19] The Harmel line – which was to predominate – emphasised the political strengthening of the national movement, and was underpinned by the notion of the South African state as fascist. Harmel had an 'inveterate hatred of fascism', and because of the Nationalist Party's support for the Nazis he argued that from 1948 the state began to be transformed along these lines.[20] With the banning of the Communist Party, according to Rowley Arenstein, 'many expected the arrival of the prison camp', and Harmel argued that 'this was the beginnings of the terroristic rule by monopoly capitalism.'[21] Ben Turok remembered that the slogan of fascism arose because of the 'terrible attack' on the Party:

> It was a wrong slogan, theoretically, but it was a slogan that represented our struggle to survive, and to build something under conditions of extreme repression.... We were trying to survive and an element in this was a terrible need to mobilise the African masses. Under these conditions our understanding was that you could not mobilise and organise the African masses on the basis of a class appeal.[22]

Du Plessis' position, on the other hand, was that the struggle for freedom should be uninterrupted and permanent in character. In his assessment, the ANC was essentially

THE BUS BOYCOTT

RUTH FIRST

Editor of "Fighting Talk"

Now undergoing Preparatory Examination on a charge of High Treason.

a bourgeois movement, and he stressed the need for economic class struggle and the organisation of trade unions. The emergence of a national bourgeois state could not be envisaged, for it could not solve the national problems of the emancipated groups within the framework of the soon-to-collapse capitalist system. Workers had to gain control and leadership of the movement which, according to du Plessis, they were capable of doing in the 1950s. He argued that

> The weakness of the national liberatory movement up to the present time has been its failure to bring the economic (or class) issues before the people as a major part of its campaign. The building of a strong proletarian force is a prerequisite for the national struggle.... The need for a movement where everyone participates in an organised manner was not fully appreciated by the leaders.[23]

Those who agreed with du Plessis did not see their tendency as alternative to Party positions, but argued for a shift of emphasis in the form of struggle.

The outcome of the debates was a triumph for Harmel's position and was to have strategic implications for SACP activists, and the internal colonialism debate, as we have seen, became the dominant view of those members in the Congress Movement influenced by Party activists. It was generally held that 'the emphasis had to be placed on the building of the national movement as this was the cutting edge of the fight for democracy in South Africa.'[24] There is no indication that Ruth, who was involved in the debates, disagreed with Harmel's reasoning, but their outcome was to have a marked effect on her journalism. Her agreement of the centrality of political struggle and the building of the national movement can be seen from the energy she expended in establishing the Congress of Democrats and the Congress of the People. Following the Discussion Club meetings, the number of articles she wrote on the cost of living, township poverty and even on trade union issues virtually disappeared, to be replaced by stories about politics and repression.[25] But this was to change dramatically early in 1957.

We will not ride!

In January 1957 the Public Utility Transport Corporation (PUTCO) decided to raise its bus fares to 5d. – an increase of 1d. 'Like a single shot fired', people in the affected townships on the Reef refused to board the buses and voted to walk.[26] Ruth reported their action movingly, convinced she was witnessing a new and significant level of grassroots struggle:

> The streets were strangely quiet. First the great lumbering green buses came ... empty. (Then) over the rise that obscures Alexandra Township from the main road came the eruption of workers in the dawn hours when mists and brazier fires mingle indistinguishably together. End to end the road was filled with shadowy, hurrying figures. Then the forms thinned out as the younger men with the firmest, sprightly step drew away from the older people, the women, the lame.
>
> Later...the same crowds turned their backs on the city and again took to the roads. Down the hill the footsloggers found it easier ... the spindly-legged youngsters trotted now and then to

> keep up, the progress of the weary women was slower still, here a large Monday washing bundle carried on the head, there a paraffin tin, or a baby tied securely to the back. In pelting rain, running the gauntlet of police patrols, the boycotters walked on.[27]

Alexandra had a history of struggle over bus fares. In 1939 bus companies operating in the township had proposed a 1d. rise in fares. A committee of residents was formed and it fought the increase for eight months and won, the increase being disallowed by the Road Transportation Board.[28] Then in 1944 independent bus owners increased the fares without consultation. For six weeks the people of Alexandra walked instead, and in the seventh week the bus companies caved in. They were taken over by PUTCO which reverted the fares to 4d.

So by 1957 the township had a history of successful struggle. But Ruth was to point out that the 1957 boycott was different:

> The United Party Government in 1944 was still to some extent sensitive to public opinion, to public pressures. The Government of Mr Strijdom is intransigent, intractable, unyielding. And nine years under this Government has changed African opinion too. It is not only more united, but also more demanding, more angry, increasingly suspicious because of promises never fulfilled, of undertakings that were never realised.[29]

Employers and the Johannesburg City Council were keen to settle the affair. Before the boycott, PUTCO was transporting 45 000 Africans workers a day. From January 7 this number was practically zero, with streams of tired and often late and hungry workers flowing in to the city from the townships of Alexandra, Sophiatown, Lady Selborne, Eastwood and Mooiplaas. Sympathy boycotts soon broke out in the Soweto townships of Moroka, Jabavu and Dube, as well as in Randfontein, Brakpan Port Elizabeth, East London, Bloemfontein and Worcester.[30]

The government, however, took a hard line. The Minister of Transport, Ben Schoeman, announced that the boycott must be broken. It was, he said, 'a political movement, launched by the African National Congress to test its strength and to find out how much support and discipline it could exact from the Bantu through intimidation.'[31] He appealed to 'all the thousands of law-abiding Natives who are not in favour of the boycott to repudiate their leaders.'[32]

The police took this as a signal to victimise boycotters as well as those who assisted them by offering lifts. Drivers were ordered to produce their licenses, passengers had their papers checked, African taxi drivers were harassed for minor traffic oversights, a ban was placed on the operation of taxis outside the municipal area and about 100 Africans were arrested for crossing an intersection on foot against a traffic light at 5.30 am when there were no cars in sight Police raids were conducted in Alexandra and nearly 15 000 people were arrested or subpoenaed on minor offenses.[33]

These tactics initially created anger in the white community. In an article reviewing the boycott, Ruth noted that calls were made to increase the PUTCO subsidy or to increase the Native Services Levy through which employers would subsidise the bus company. The City Council, under pressure from employers, offered to contribute to a subsidy scheme, the boycott committees announced their willingness to negotiate and, in the first few weeks, white public sympathies were clearly with the walkers. But the Government stood in the way of a settlement. In February it moved an amendment to the Native Labour Regulations Act which would ban all meetings of Africans who had not obtained the Minister's permission, and PUTCO threatened to permanently withdraw its services from Alexandra. As the boycott continued, the mainstream press began to reflect a 'break-the-boycott' perspective.[34] A month after the 'long walk' began, the *Rand Daily Mail* spread a seven-column headline across its front page asking employers to 'warn their workers' against 'The Four Men of Alexandra' – those who had 'branded themselves as unworthy leaders of their people. It called on the people not to be misled by these agitators.[35]

Behind the *Mail's* call was the perception that there was a factor in the Alexandra boycott which had not been present in other demonstrations – the boycott was not being led by the ANC or any other recognisable political body. This was not a demonstration co-ordinated from above, but a popular surge of anger from below. African leaders, many caught up in the Treason Trial, became bystanders to a new kind of politics. And Ruth, reporting on the issue almost daily, had a close-up view of the chemical processes taking place in the streets of Alexandra.

The issue of the 1d. fare increase was first taken up the Alexandra Standholders and the hastily-created Vigilance Committee formed to confront PUTCO. The bus company's intransigence led to the formation of the Alexandra People's Transport Action Committee, which helped to establish similar committees in Sophiatown, Lady Selborne, Eastwood and other affected areas.[36] Despite the ad hoc nature of these organisations, attempts by the State, its police, PUTCO and the press to bully and threaten the boycotters simply strengthened their resolve and spread the action wider and wider. Beerhalls began to be boycotted.[37] The City Council, the Native Affairs Department and Chambers of Commerce held secret talks with African 'moderates' in an attempt to reach a solution. But they were simply ignored by the walkers. Following these attempts, Ruth reported that 'the boycott could not be more solid.... One man said: "If it has to be, this can be a boycott without an end."'[38] The ANC fared no better, and in a leaflet issued by the Alexandra People's Transport Committee it was labelled a group of 'purely loud-mouthed self advertisers':

> The ANC leaders are from time to time the main anti-boycott spokesmen. A struggle properly conducted – a struggle in which the interests of the people are placed FIRST – above the individual leader – above self-importance – above organisations – such a struggle will always expose quislings in our midst. We must take note. A man in the police uniform is easy to spot, but a man dressed in strong talk and weak actions – has to be DISCOVERED through his actions. This is the case with the ANC....[39]

Ruth realised the people had found a method of struggle which could not easily be stamped out by law. 'It might come to that', she wrote. 'But there is not yet a law on the Union statute book imposing penalties on Africans for walking to work and home again by way of protest against a bus company.'[40] In her assessment of the government's role in the boycott, she was also to re-think the strategies which had been hammered out in the Discussion Clubs four years earlier:

> The Government denunciation of the boycott as 'political' was one of the sticks it hoped to use to beat the boycott, to ruin all chances of settlement, to frighten employers ... and White South Africa as a whole. The bus boycott did, undoubtedly, develop into a political campaign. (But) the economic facts, the poverty of a people that reckons its income in pennies, sparked

> off the boycott, and those who argue the economic basis for this protest could not be on firmer ground. But those who would separate the economic background from the political, who would see the African protesting only against a penny rise in fares ... erect distinctions which must be blown over in the first gusts of any African protest or campaign.[41]

African workers, she said, were no longer bewildered, mute, raw tribal creatures. The boycott had shown that they were industrialised, politically aware, articulate and purposeful. Their organisations were mature and resourceful. It had shown them that 'active campaigning for basic human and economic demands' held the key to their success. In this she was echoed by the Director of the Institute of Race Relations:

> The African people have ... shown that amazing ability to communicate and organise without an organisation, which has been apparent on other occasions in the past. The 1944 bus boycott, the mineworkers strike, the shantytown movement, the Port Elizabeth strike – each of these has shown this quite amazing ability. It is significant.[42]

Popular entry of the boycotters into politics around economic issues clearly alerted Ruth to what she regarded as a new concept of struggle. It was to effect her political perspective, and was to shape her understanding of popular resistance in the years which followed. The boycott formally ended in April 1957. By this time each Alexandra worker would have walked about 2 000 miles. But the walkers had won, and the fares were restored to 4d. This was hailed by the General Secretary of the ANC, Oliver Tambo, as the beginning of a new phase of struggle.[43] The newly-formed Congress of Trade Unions (SACTU) immediately launched an economic campaign to secure £1-a-day for all workers which, ultimately, did not succeed in its goals but which placed economic demands squarely on the political agenda of the Congress Alliance.

JO'BURG'S "SLAVE MARKET"

Arrested Men "Persuaded" To Take Farm Work

(From RUTH FIRST)

JOHANNESBURG.

DR. JANSEN, Minister of Native Affairs, talks about setting up labour bureaux. Africans call them slave markets.

A new phrase has been coined by Africans this year. A man arrested for a pass offence who is sent to work on a farm will tell you: "I was sold to a farmer at the jail", or the court.

Reading Ruth's articles from this point, it is clear that the bus boycott shifted the focus of her journalism. She returned to the urban themes she had laid down in the early 1950s, and began campaigning for better housing, improved conditions and a living wage. Between the Alexandra boycott and the state of emergency in 1960 her journalism increasingly reflected the rhythms of the streets of Johannesburg. But Alexandra remained a key focus, and here she traced the growth of gangs, poverty and alcoholism. She also drew the links between poverty and official neglect, crime and police inaction:

> Each year the picture gets uglier: new batches of school leavers strike out to find their first jobs, many get them, only to have them snatched from their grasps at the pass offices.
>
> So the township turns in on itself. Life must go on. A man must eat, dress, do something in his working hours. Some are caught in the daily manhunt in the township for farm labour. Some take another road. The crime wave in Alexandra Township ... is one of the by-products of this throttled community. There are small-time gangs, the pick-pockets, the bag-snatchers, the thieves who waylay people at night and strip them of their clothes. There are youngsters who pounce on the ... bus queues, rush a victim from the queue, surround him and empty his pockets.[44]

But when the authorities threatened to 'clean up' Alexandra, Ruth – in her usual interrogative style – demanded to know exactly what this meant:

> Native Affairs Department 'clean-ups' are suspect and the people live in fear of them. In the Western Areas slum clearance meant the abolition of freehold, the death of a long-established township, the forcible removal of an entire community. In Evaton the clean-up meant the vicious imposition of influx control. Will it be the same in Alexandra?[45]

Her solution was more (and more involved) policing. By 1958 she had dubbed Alexandra 'Hells Kitchen', a township with 63 000 people and only 105 policemen. It was, she said, full of 'trigger-happy cowboys' firing shots at random: 'Let's face facts. Can 105 policemen of whom 86 are Africans rid Alexandra Township of this unruly element... gangsters? Or control crime? Definitely NOT.'[46] In Evaton, where the 'Russians' ruled, she accused the police of colluding with the gangsters:

> Why have no prosecutions followed the attacks on Evaton homes, the looting and stealing and the assaults? No serious attempt has been made to disarm the 'Russians'.... Police policy seems to be to let the trouble run on. Their attitude seems to imply that they believe the (bus) boycotters are the 'agitators' behind the trouble.... Could that be a reason why the police have their hands in their pockets in Evaton where some prompt action by them could bring and end to armed attacks?[47]

In 1959 Ruth's worst fears about government intentions were realised when it announced that Sophiatown, which had gradually been dismantled by the State since 1955, would finally be completely demolished. She added her voice to demands to halt the demolitions, to set up an emergency housing scheme for stranded families and an end to police raids. But the demolition continued, and with anger and disgust she documented the human suffering this caused. 'Old people, children, even new-born babies sleep each night in the open, while daily demolitions go on in Sophiatown and even more families are turned out of their homes .... What will happen' she asked, ' when the rainy season starts next month?'[48]

Then in March 1960 a state of emergency was declared and Ruth was forced to flee to Swaziland. Shortly after her return, she was prevented from attending any political gatherings in terms of a banning order, and this was later extended to cover all social gatherings. By entering a township she risked prosecution. Her days as an investigative journalist in South Africa were coming to an end.

Notes

1 *Digest of South African Affairs*, March 1956.

2 Union of South Africa National Income and Production Indices (1946-1957). Standard Bank. 1957.

3 Ibid.

4 *Digest of South African Affairs*, June 1957.

5 Ibid.

6 She reported that Venables' health was excellent. *The Guardian,* July 5, 1951.

7 Ibid.

8 *The Guardian*, July 19, 1951.

9 Ibid, August 30, 1951.

10 Ibid.

11 Ibid.

12 *The Guardian*, March 13, 1952.

13 Ibid, March 20, 1952.

14 Perry Anderson in The Antinomies of Antonio Gramsci, in *New Left Review*, No.100, November 1976/ January 1977, p171.

15 Between 1947 and 1962 the total real output of the economy grew at just over four percent a year.

16 C Moll: 'Growth without development: The SA economy in the 1950s.' Seminar delivered at the ICSS, Oxford University, 1987.

17 Ibid.

18 See Chapter 3.

19 Du Plessis was a militant Afrikaner whose father had been through the 1922 mine strike. As a result of his father's experiences du Plessis always publicly referred to Smuts as 'the butcher'.

20 See, for example, *The rise of the South African Reich* by Bunting. Corroborated in an interview with Rowley Arenstein, 1988.

21 Arenstein quoted in Lambert, 1988 p79.

22 Turok in Lambert, ibid, p79.

23 *V&P*, Vol.1, No.3, February 1954.

24 Lambert, op cit, p75.

25 The exception is her work on farm labour conditions, which continued throughout the 1950s.

26 The quote is from Ruth First: The Bus Boycott, in *Africa South*, Vol.1, No.4, September 1957, p56.

27 Ibid, p55.

28 Ibid, p59.

29 Ibid, p60.

30 Survey of Race Relations, 1956-57, p131.

31 Hansard 1 cols. 131/2 1957.

32 Ibid.

33 Survey of Race Relations, op cit. p132.

34 First, op cit, p62.

35 *New Age*, February 28, 1957.

36 Survey of Race Relations, op cit, p130.

37 *New Age*, January 31, 1957.

38 *New Age*, February 7, 1957.

39 Karis & Gerhart, Vol.3, Doc.22, 1977, p395.

40 *Africa South*, op cit, p63.

41 *Africa South*, Ibid, p64.

42 Survey of Race Relations, op cit, p138.

43 *New Age*, April 25 1957. Michael Harmel, however, complained at the ANC's failure to give it positive leadership to the boycott. *New Age*, April 4 1957.

44 Ibid, June 12, 1957.

45 Ibid, June 27, 1957.

46 Ibid, February 20, 1958.

47 Ibid, August 9, 1957.

48 Ibid, September 24, 1959.

A battle won

South Africa, as Mr Strijdom says, is not a police state! But, as the monkey said to the keeper, that depends on which side of the bars you are – Ruth First

© Mayibuye

Ruth with Albertina Sisulu at a mass meeting.

The challenge of the Congress Alliance and its press was clearly not going to be ignored by the state. In the sense that to oppose something is often to confirm it, they were both creatures of each others making. And while communist discussion clubs were hammering out a new policy on non-racial co-operation in the wake of the Defiance Campaign, the National Party began consolidating its power for the next assault on integration. When the new government was voted into power in 1948 it found itself in a politically weak position. It had won with a small majority of seats but only 39.4% of the votes. During its first term of office it had passed several key apartheid laws but remained cautions in their implementation. However, in 1953, the National Party was returned with an increased majority and it took this as a mandate to tackle the race question with a vengeance.

During the 1953 session of Parliament it passed laws which gave control of African education to the Department of Native Affairs, prevented the Indian dependents of South African residents from joining their husbands, reserved public amenities (including 200 miles of Cape beaches) for whites, outlawed strikes by African workers, prescribed severe penalties for breaking the law as a political protest and provided for rule by decree in an emergency. From this date the pace of social restructuring accelerated, measures enacted earlier were implemented with greater alacrity and the Security Police moved to smash the Congress Alliance.

From the perspective of the political police, the situation in the country since the Defiance Campaign must have seemed ominous. The campaign, even though it had failed in its final objectives, had made the African National Congress enormously popular. And within eight months of the formation of the 'communistically inclined' South African Peace Council, no fewer than five left-wing organisations had sprung up.[1] Then, in 1955, the Congress Alliance had set up an 'army' of Freedom Volunteers to assist in the election of a 'People's Parliament' and the creation of a Bill of Rights.[2] In considering the rise of the extra-parliamentary opposition, the defenders of apartheid inevitably turned their thoughts to treason.

In broad Nationalist Party terms treason was simple to define; it was committed by those who did not support their views. For the editor of *Inspan* it was even closer to home. 'Every time an Afrikaner supports a stranger rather than a fellow-Afrikaner', he wrote, 'he commits treason.[3] In law, the definition was equally vague: 'High treason is committed by those who with a hostile intention disturb, impair or endanger the independence or safety of the state, or attempt or actively prepare to do so.'[4]

It was, however, going to prove difficult to catch the Congress Movement in a treason trap. Early warnings of the state's attempt to do so took place during the planning stages of the Freedom Charter. As a result of a court interdict, police were expelled from a SACOD meeting about the Congress of the People at the Trades Hall in Johannesburg during July 1954. In reply to the interdict which expelled them, Major Spengler of the Security Police said it was the duty of the police to 'know what was going on at the meeting in order to protect internal security'. The police were, he claimed, 'investigating a case of high treason.'[5] In September 1955 hundreds of homes and offices were raided by police searching for 'evidence of an alleged design to overthrow the Government by force.'[6] A few months later, when police confiscated forms from activists campaigning for a million signatures in support of the Freedom Charter, they claimed they were investigating a charge of suspected treason.[7] But for three years talk of treason had gone on and nothing beyond the irritating police raids had happened. By the time the Minister of Justice, 'Blackie' Swart, announced in Parliament that 200 people would soon be arrested and prosecuted for treason the question of treason was beginning to be forgotten. The dawn raids in December 1956, therefore, shocked Congress activists. *New Age* editor Lionel Forman, one of the accused, was to document the moment dramatically:

> At dawn one morning in 1956, twenty days before Christmas, police knuckles and police batons hammered at the doors of one hundred and forty homes all over the Union of South Africa; the doors of luxury flats and the tin entrances of hessian shanty pondokkies, the oak of a parson's manse and the stable openings of farm labourers; doors in comfortable white suburbs, in grim African locations, in Indian ghettos, in cities, in villages and on farms far out on the veld.
>
> One hundred and forty families were wakened that morning – Africans, Indians, Europeans, Coloureds, doctors and labourers, teachers and students, a university principal, a tribal chief. ... Those who asked were shown warrants of arrest. The crime charged in every single case: HIGH TREASON – HOOGVERAAD.[8]

Houses were searched and people were bundled into police vans and military aircraft on route to The Fort in Johannesburg. Bail was refused, visitors were denied access to the arrested and *Die Transvaler* regaled readers with an account of the old penalty for treason – the tearing of a man's limbs apart by four horses, or burning at the stake.[9] Eleven days after the first arrests, Ruth First and Joe Slovo were detained. Joe had been briefed by the defence to appear at the preparatory examination. He had visited Public Prosecutor van Niekerk soon after the arrests to see if there were any outstanding matters to attend to before the family left for a holiday in Cape Town. 'Sure,' said van Niekerk. 'Go ahead and take your holiday. Have a good rest'. At 4.30 the next morning the police banged on their door with a warrant for their arrest.[10] According to *Drum* editor Anthony Sampson

> the whole spectacular manner of the operation – the arrests at dawn, the military planes arriving secretly at a military airport, the barred police vans rushing the prisoners straight to the jail, and the reiteration of the sinister phrase 'allegations of high treason' – all this, coming in the wake of the Suez crisis abroad, suggested that a most dangerous plot had been uncovered in the nick of time.[11]

Forman was to observe that 'in his younger days, (Prime Minister) Swart had worked as an *extra* in Hollywood and now he combined the ideas of Hitler with the technique of Hollywood to produce a spectacular, dramatic, stupendous, staggering plot.'[12]

While the white population remained divided in its reactions to the arrests, the African people were galvanised by the state's action. The breadth of the arrests – which included members of the most respectable professions and several moderate and cautious leaders – ensured that the prisoners would be regarded as genuine representatives of the people. By assembling leaders of all the Congresses in one place and keeping them there day after day in confinement, the Government was not only trying the opposition, it was creating it. People from a broad spread of political tendencies had been suddenly locked together in the embrace of the law and pressed into a single force. *New Age* (which was owned by the only company listed as one of the accused) printed the names of those detained under the headline: *Roll of honour*.

There are good reasons, in a book about radical journalism, to focus on the Treason Trial: it was to be an assault on the radical press and its journalists. The centrality in the trial of the language in oppositional newspapers, reports, and speeches was not without good reason. Language is not merely a reflection of social practices, it is not merely about politics, it *is* politics. Ideological struggle in the 1950s took place preeminently in words and definitions. This struggle could be thought of as not only *in* language in the obvious sense that is contained in reports and speeches, but also *over* language. This was because language itself was a stake in the social struggle as well as a site of social struggle. In the legal battle which was to follow, Ruth's journalism, together with everything she believed in, was to go on trial for treason.

A battle of ideas

The Preparatory Examination began in a converted drill hall in Johannesburg in December 1956 as a huge crowd of Congress supporters gathered outside. The gist of the Crown charge, on 53 typed pages, was that treason took place at meetings held all over the Union at which the accused

> advocated, instigated and preached a Marxist-Leninist account of society and the state, a Marxist-Leninist interpretation of history and contemporary politics, and called for the establishment of a people's democratic state based on the principles of the system in the Soviet Union, the People's Democracies of Eastern Europe and in China.[13]

The Crown, however, declined to define what exactly constituted the charge of treason. In rebutting the charge, Vernon Berrange for the defence said the accused openly admitted supporting the ideals expressed in the Freedom Charter, and would 'endeavour to show that what is on trial here are not just 156 individuals but the ideas which they and thousands of others in our land have openly espoused and expressed.[14] We will endeavour to show', he said, 'that these prosecutions, and the manner of their presentation, are for the purpose of testing the political breezes in order to ascertain how far the originators thereof can go in their endeavours to stifle free speech, criticism of the Government and ... democracy.'[15]

Berrange said the Security Police had set out to deliberately create a fantastic atmosphere of treason around everything that the accused had worked for. They had done this by attempting to intimidate the public with their attendance at open public meetings, by conducting mass raids and countrywide searches, and by flourishing sten guns, fixed bayonets and truncheons. The trial, he said, was instituted in an attempt to silence and outlaw the ideas held by the accused and the thousands they represented:

> A battle of ideas (has therefore) been started in our country; a battle in which on the one side ... are poised those ideas which seek equal opportunities for, and freedom of thought and expression by all persons of all races and creeds and, on the other side, those which deny all but a few the riches of life, both material and spiritual, which the accused aver should be common to all.[16]

From the opening speech of the defence, it was clear that it was more than the accused who were on trial. 'The accused had decided without hesitation', wrote Forman, 'that they were going to go on the attack. Their aim was not only to prove that they were not traitors to their country. They wanted to prove who the real traitors were.'[17]

The Treason Trial, which was to last four years, was therefore, in Berrange's words, 'no ordinary trial'. Year after year the accused and their defence team were to engage the state in a battle over the definition of only three words: communism, treason and violence. And in each exchange in the battle over language both sides were to find themselves in the dock. The trial records include printed books and pamphlets, magazines and newspapers, mimeographed reports, bulletins and circulars, typewritten and handwritten documents and a miscellaneous assortment of flyers, memoranda, official and personal letters. These were found, during more than a thousand searches and raids in offices and homes and at meetings, on open tables, in bookshelves, in desks and briefcases and in the possession of individuals.[18]

At one level, the trial was a battle of the ideologies of the Congresses and the State, but at another level it was also a war between state spies and the journalists of the Left. The early proceedings left Ruth in no doubt that her journalism was on trial. For the first six weeks of the preparatory examination, the prosecution did nothing but hand in thousands of documents seized in the many raids, most of which were articles, pamphlets, newspapers, magazines and books, many of which were from Ruth's pen. Indeed, in charging both the publishing company of *New Age* and many of its staff, the state was sending a clear signal to left-wing journalists.

The process of handing in exhibits was maddeningly slow, fuelling fears among the accused that the purpose of the trial was to keep them in the dock forever.[19] When, for example, a two-year series of *Fighting Talk* was dealt with, instead of having the whole collection identified as a single exhibit, the prosecutor handed them in one by one doggedly maintaining the pace of an ox:

> Is that *Fighting Talk* dated January 1954?
> It is, your Worship.
> Do you hand that in?
> I do, your worship.
> Across the court walked the orderly to the magistrate. Across the court walked the prosecutor to collect another *Fighting Talk*. Across the court he walked and handed it to the witness.
> Now is that *Fighting Talk* dated February 1954?
> It is, your Worship....[20]

The purpose of this chapter is not to document the long and complicated trial.[21] It is, rather, to analyse the Crown's changing position on communism, treason and violence in order to understand the ideas which formed the dialectical opposite of Ruth's journalism and against which she would do battle for her entire life.

© Ely Weinberg

Torching the red devil

The Broederbond, which masterminded Afrikaner strategy, and the Communist Party shared a dislike for imperialism and, at different times, they both saw nationalism as the engine of political change.[22] In the 1950s they were both also secret organisations. Perhaps for these reasons – because the two organisations utilised similar tactics for opposing goals, and because in Calvinist thinking the Devil is not that which is furthest from you but that which is closest – the Broederbond took it upon itself to excommunicate the Party and to torch it out of every crevasse of society.

Up until the 1950s the struggle between the Communist Party and Afrikaner nationalists had a practical foundation – both were competing for the heart of the Afrikaner working class. For the Afrikaner intelligentsia in the Depression years it was clear that Afrikaners were disadvantaged, poor, disunited and generally perceived to be 'burning in hellfire'. The only route to self-respect and power lay in uniting all stray Afrikaners into a national *volkseenheid*.[23] The Communist Party, particularly through the mine, garment and railway unions, was seen as a threat to this process. Nico Diederichs, who was later to become State President, wrote in 1937 that 'there are forces at work in the bosom of the People which seek to unite our workers with the proletariat of other lands ... the headquarters of this movement is in Moscow.... If the worker is drawn away from our nation, then we might as well write Ichabod on the door of our temple.'[24]

Increasingly, Deiderichs began to speak and write against communism and was ably assisted by Piet Meyer, who was later to become chairman of the South African Broadcasting Corporation. For Meyer the two most serious threats to *volkseenheid* were the conciliatory party politics of the United Party, particularly on racial affairs, and the divisive effects of 'communist-inspired' class conflict.[25] He proposed that the Federation of Afrikaner Cultural Organisations (FAK), of which he was a leader, together with the Afrikaans churches, become involved in organising Afrikaner workers into 'Christian National' labour unions in order to reintegrate them into the organic unity of the volk. To this end, the National Council of Trustees was formed and it backed successful struggles for control of white railway and mine workers. Meyer also became leader of the Labour Front started by the militarist organisation Ossewa Brandwag which, according to OB leader Hans van Rensburg, was intended to 'cement urban and platteland Afrikaners, through the OB, into an effective bastion against communism and other insidious foes.'[26]

The struggle for Afrikaner workers found its martyrs when Afrikaans garment workers at a Germiston factory discovered that coloured women were being employed and called a strike. The Clothing Workers Union under Solly Sachs refused to consider the strike and dismissed the two white workers who had led the challenge. The Ossewa Brandwag and Dutch Reformed ministers rallied behind the two women and the affair became a national issue. On the insistence of the National Party it was debated for several days in Parliament.[27] The Dutch churches called protest meetings and the Broederbond established the White Workers' Protection Society 'to fight the Communist evil within the trade unions.'[28] The issue, which had been largely manufactured, was clearly seen by the Broederbond as an issue which could unite the volk on the behalf of the Afrikaner 'wife and mother' in opposition to communist racial equality. The issue was kept alive within the Dutch churches and in 1946 a large congress was called by them at which all Christians were called on to fight communists 'with all permissible means.'[29]

From the 1930s, therefore, fear of a 'red threat' provided a basic exigency in attempts to unite Afrikaners. And since communism advocated racial equality and was envisaged as the inevitable concomitant of British imperialist liberal capitalism, this home-grown anti-communism combined both anti-British and anti-black sentiments. Each ideological strand within Afrikanerdom was able to employ its own logic and discourse in defining communism as a major threat. For the Dutch churches, communism represented 'atheistic materialism', an 'idolatrous attempt to transcend the separate spheres of authority laid down in the ordinances of creation.'[30] For Afrikaner politicians and intellectuals the communist disregard for racial differences was a thrust at the very heart of their ethnic existence.[31] In uniting the volk around the 1948 election, the National Party linked the anti-communist discourses in Afrikanerdom with the 'black threat' and was thereby able to identify its major parliamentary opponents – particularly the government of General Smuts – with the communist threat. The unity of these two ideas was to emerge in the Report of the Commission on the Colour Problem of the Herenigte Nationale Party (Sauer Report) in 1948 which was to be the foundation of the new government's racial policies. The brief of the commission was 'to develop on the basis of apartheid a comprehensive policy for the National Party with regard to the colour problem in general....' According to the commission, there were two schools of thought on the policy of racial equality:

> The one school, communist-orientated, denies the fundamental nature of existing differences between white and non-white and therefore deliberately and openly drives towards the establishment of one mixed people in South Africa where colour apartheid and colour dividing

> lines are summarily and totally eradicated. The other school of thought is not exactly in favour of miscegenation nor does it openly advocate social equality but refuses to take active steps against miscegenation and advocates equal rights and opportunity for all developed persons, irrespective of race or colour.[32]

According to the commission, it was 'crystal clear that both schools of thought are heading for eventual equality' and must 'inevitably lead to the undermining and eventual annihilation of the white race as an independent and governing volk.'[33] It therefore recommended the elimination of racial mixing, the development of 'Native Fatherlands', the formation of labour bureaux to prevent 'wastage', the implementation of 'Bantu education', the repatriation of 'as many Indians as possible' and an attack on communism.

Most of these ideas were implemented after 1948, but the elimination of communism was to be first on the list. Early in 1949 the Minister of Justice, CR Swart, told Parliament that

> shortly after assuming office, the Government took steps to institute an exhaustive enquiry into the extent to which Communist activities had penetrated the Union… .Evidence already available showed that Communist activities had already poisoned the national life in many respects in an alarming way and had given rise to a condition of danger in the country.[34]

A few months later *Die Vaderland* found 'proof of a Soviet Plan against us' and said Swart was likely to take 'exceptionally drastic action' at the next Cabinet meeting.[35] By November of that year newspapers were reporting 'strong indications that the government will shortly outlaw the Communist Party of South Africa and its Press.'[36] The Suppression of Communism Bill was introduced at the end of the Parliamentary session of 1950 and rushed through its readings. The scope of the Bill was so wide that Opposition MPs claimed it would change the nature of the State. 'This is not the Suppression of Communism Act, said Labour MP Leo Lovell. 'This is a Bill for the suppression of the rule of law and a Bill for the destruction of one of the main pillars of democracy ... this is a Bill for the corruption of justice.'[37] LC Gay of South Peninsula warned that 'when this Bill becomes law we will be ruled by something very different from the principles of freedom and justice.'[38] A central problem in the parliamentary sessions was to be the definition of communism itself, a debate which was to re-emerge at length in the Treason Trial. Lovell complained that

> the crime called 'communism' remains undefined. It can mean anything. The hon. Minister can give it any meaning he likes.... No one can question his interpretation. The courts are banished. The Minister reminds me of Humpty Dumpty in Alice in Wonderland and I quote: 'When I use a word', Humpty Dumpty said in a scornful tone, 'it means just what I choose it to mean – neither more nor less.'[39]

JG Strauss, United Party MP for Germiston, pointed out that according to the Bill 'a Communist is a person who professes to be a Communist (but) the Minister decides whether a man has professed or not to be a Communist. And if he is deemed to have professed he cannot have recourse to the courts.'[40] Nationalist MPs responded by digging in behind the tabled definition and attempting to demonize communism and the Communist Party. The Minister of Justice, CR Swart, claimed to have information that a secret military branch within the Johannesburg Communist Party was preparing to poison water supplies and food and to take over power stations on a particular day. He told Parliament that 'people are taught to be in such a position that they can murder people whom they want to get rid of on that day.'[41] According to Nico Diederichs

> every Communist Party organisation has imposed on it the task of working consistently to bring nearer the moment when by means of violence, by revolt and by revolution it will cause its own country to collapse and thus make it the prey of another. ... Everything is permissible for that purpose of the world revolution, even high treason, theft and murder.[42]

'Communism', said Swart, 'is an undermining, devilish evangelism'. Indeed it was the 'religion of revolt ... devilish work in the sphere of internationalism' and part of the 'sinister, eerie, silent process' of Cold War.

The effect of the passing of the Suppression of Communism Act was to excommunicate former members of the Party. Communists were excluded from further meaningful discourse and projected by the state as being depraved, traitorous, alien, and even insane. Legally they were condemned to ideological non-existence. People on the 'list' of communists set up under the Act were not to be listened to, they were the target of vilification and their utterances were to be treated only as symptoms of a slavish adherence to Moscow's depravity. In terms of a later amendment to the Act, a person deemed to be a communist and who was not a South African citizen by birth or descent, could be deported. In terms of the law, listed communists had less rights than a pickpocket. They could be questioned, searched without a warrant and were guilty unless they could prove themselves innocent. If caught 'furthering the aims' of communism they could be jailed for up to 10 years.

In terms of the Act communism was described as

> the doctrine of Marxian socialism as expounded by Lenin or Trotsky, the..Comintern or ... the Cominform or any related form of that doctrine expounded or advocated in the Union for the promotion of the fundamental principles of that doctrine and includes, in particular, any doctrine
>
> - which aims at the establishment of a despotic system of government based on the dictatorship of the proletariat ... or
> - which aims at bringing about any political, industrial, social or economic change within the Union by promotion of disturbance or disorder, by unlawful acts or omissions ... or
> - which aims at bringing about any political, industrial, social or economic change within the Union in accordance with the directions or under the guidance of or in co-operation with any foreign government or any foreign or international institution (which aims to promote dictatorship of the proletariat), or
> - which aims at the encouragement of feelings of hostility between the European and non-European races of the Union the consequences of which are calculated to further the achievement of any object (in (a) or (b) above).

A communist, in short, was simply someone who professed to be one or who was deemed to be one by the state for advocating 'any of the objects' of communism.

The practical effect of the Suppression of Communism Act's vague, value-laden definition was to make it possible for the Minister of Justice to declare almost any political activist to be a communist. But the ideological implications went further. Communism is generally defined in relation to an economic arrangement where property and other means of producing livelihood are held in common, or where ownership is confined to the means of consumption and is excluded from the means of production and exchange. The Act was to define it, rather, as a doctrine (the held beliefs) of Marx, Lenin, Trotsky and (by way of the Comintern) of Stalin. These 'beliefs' were contained in hundreds of books, commentaries, articles and documents in many languages and throughout many countries, as well as in the public pronouncements of the largest country on earth. By a process of hyponymy – where the meaning of one word is included in the meaning of many others – the Act connected these 'beliefs' with dictatorship, disorder, lawlessness and the encouragement of racial hostility in South Africa. The phrase 'promotion of ...' gave no guidance on what physical, verbal or mental act would constitute a breach of law. The authoritative word 'means' in the Act's expression 'communism means ...' hid a subjective, ideologically-laden discourse which demanded of anyone deemed communist a defence they were virtually unable to give.

An Act of Parliament is essentially a speech act, a written statement which performs an action ('I deem you to be a communist ...'). Acts are written in a particular parliamentary language which appears to be value-free, seeming to be pronouncements of fact and direction. However, they disguise the messy, self-serving Party processes of their initial drafting and rely on the formal dignity of Parliament to perform the task of ideological legitimation.

The effect of the Act was to colonise legal discourse and to restructure the subject position of political opposition in South Africa. It could be seen, in words of French anthropologist Pierre Bourdieu, as an attempt to bring about the 'recognition of legitimacy through misrecognition of abritariness.'[43]

The immediate consequences of the Suppression of Communism Act was to provoke the dissolution of the Communist Party and the establishment of a list of communists. The practical implications of the definition of communism, however, was to await the Treason Trial where it was to face its test of fire.

In search of a communist conspiracy

The prosecution for the Treason Trial was led by Oswald Pirow QC, who was brought out of retirement for the occasion. He was not an unbiased public servant. He had been a Minister of Defence in the Smuts government and was well-known for his Nazi sympathies. After meeting Hitler in 1938 he had described him as 'the greatest man of his age, perhaps the greatest of the last 1 000 years.'[44] A member of the far-right New Order movement, he was on record as having said that 'if every Jew could vanish from the earth, the world as a whole would be a better place'. During the war he had published a pamphlet claiming that 'no influence which might create the possibility, even in the remotest future, of any form of equality between European and non-European will be tolerated.'[45] And if 'non-Europeans 'intruded among Europeans this was an occasion 'when a blow of the fist is a sign of vitality and not a lack of refinement ... throw them out on their necks.'[46] An ardent supporter of an Afrikaner republic, he had claimed in 1945 that the 'new order' would abolish all other parties (but his own). 'We can dispute the actual form of the republic, but he who wants to strike a compromise over its nature commits treason.'[47]

Pirow and his Crown team were to accuse the Congress Movement of advocating treason, communism, and violence. However, on the matter of communism, they were to find their task complicated by the description of communism as a 'doctrine' in the 1950 Act. To prove that the 156 accused adhered to a doctrine, it would be necessary to spell out that doctrine and then prove that each of the accused adhered to it. To do this the Crown required an expert in 'Marxian socialism as expounded by Lenin, Trotsky, the Comintern and the Cominform'. They produced what *New Age* was to describe as a 'star witness': Professor Andrew Murray, a former Rhodes scholar and a lecturer in political philosophy at the University of Cape Town. Murray had spent many years arguing that Communism in South Africa was a dangerous liberal philosophy based on pluralism and that in South Africa racial groups should have separate social existences and separate education.[48] He was, he claimed, an expert on communist doctrine.

Murray found himself in the unfortunate position of having to give substance to the statutory definition of communism. Both in the preparatory examination and, later, in the trial itself, he ploughed his way through expositions of communist doctrines and lengthy extracts from communist classics. For weeks the court echoed to definitions, theories and quotations. The Professor's evidence covered a wide field. According to Helen Joseph, 'we found ourselves traveling from Africa to China, from the USA to North Korea.'[49]

His definition of communism was that it was 'a doctrine which criticises the western system – the capitalist system – and bases its criticism on the philosophy of dialectical materialism.'[50] He did not describe what he meant by dialectical materialism, and gave as the rest of his definition a list of standard communist objections to capitalism. On this definition Murray devised four tests in his 'analysis' of documents and reports:

1. Does it preach direct communism by quotations from the communist masters?
2. Does it do so by paraphrasing the masters?
3. Non deviation. That is, does it support Soviet policy internationally?
4. Aesopism. Is the superficial meaning intended to mean more?[51]

Having established his criteria, Murray then produced a list of 33 'communist dicta', phrases against which the confiscated documents could be measured for communist influence. These 'dicta' included 'the teaching that parliament as at present constituted should be abolished; a dual authority should be established; that the courts serve the interests of the ruling class and that ownership of property means political power. A tedious process then ensued in which Murray was asked to pass judgment on hundreds of documents which constituted the Crown evidence. Helen Joseph remembered it as

> a strange sight to see this man of letters passing his comments on a steady stream of books and journals, some four hundred altogether, pulled from the bookshelves of one hundred and fifty people during four years of police raids. It became monotonous, mechanical, almost

> hypnotic. (He would open the book) and pass judgment on it with a terse 'Straight from the shoulder of Communism' or 'Contains Communist matter' or 'Communist propaganda.'[52]

Long quotations from *New Age* and *Fighting Talk*, many of them written by Ruth, were read into the court records and declared to be communistically inspired and treasonable.

In December 1957 the prosecutor outlined the indictment against the accused. He said they had committed treason between October 1952 and December 1956 by secretly plotting a violent revolution which would overthrow the state and replace it with a communist state. They intended to do this by

- calling the Congress of the People which adopted the Freedom Charter which outlined a communist state
- inciting people to break the law and to use violence to oppose the government
- campaigning against the Western Areas removals, Bantu Education and the pass laws and
- advocating the views of Marx and Lenin.

The prosecutor also outlined two 'alternative' charges under the Suppression of Communism Act which would come into force if the Crown failed to prove the crime of treason. These were that the accused advocated, advised or encouraged communism, and that they did things in order to achieve one of the objects of communism. The Crown held the view that although each individual article or speech was insufficient grounds for prosecution, taken as a whole they constituted furtherance of the aims of communism. On the first alternative charge, the Crown had argued that the word 'advocate' in the Act did not require an audience. 'If I write a communist speech down on paper I am advocating, even if no one ever hears the speech', said Prosecutor Hoexter. 'That doesn't make sense,' said Sidney Kentridge for the defence. 'The normal usage of the word must be looked to. If I prepare my argument for a trial on the day before, in my chambers, can I be said to be advocating my client's case? No. I begin advocating when I stand up to argue in court.'[53] When the Judges appeared to agree with the defence, Mr Hoexter suggested that 'any failings in the indictment could be cured by cutting out the bad parts.'[54] The following exchange then ensued:

> Kentridge: My learned friend suggests surgical treatment, but the alternative charges are beyond surgery.
> Justice Bekker: They still seem to show some movement.
> Mr Kentridge: Then your lordships should be merciful and put them out of their misery.[55]

The judges did just that, throwing out first one, then the other alternative charge and ordering the prosecutors to revise the main treason charge to show more clearly how each of the accused was personally involved in conspiracy.

In the end, therefore, Murray's labours were to come unstuck. His undoing was the result of the definition of communism in the 1950 Act. By dutifully building his evidence around the need to see the hidden Red hand everywhere, he ended up convincing the judges that he was unable to find it anywhere. Under withering cross-questioning he was forced by attorneys for the defence to concede that nationalist movements in Africa were grievance-based and not products of the hidden hand of Moscow. He was reminded by the defence that in the preparatory examination he was shown an unidentified statement and had pronounced it communistically-inspired without realising that he had written it himself. Through Murray, the Crown had attempted to link the Congress Alliance to communism and thereby to violence, arguing that communism (and the Freedom Charter) envisaged a state so different from that which existed in South Africa that to advocate communism was tantamount to advocating the violent overthrow of the state. In this it had failed, as had its star witness. In their final judgment all three judges were to agree that the Crown had not proved that the ANC, as the primary organisation of the Congress Alliance, was communist or that the Charter pictured a communist State or that the accused could be proved to have broken the law with respect to the two alternative charges.

Treason, violence and murder

After charges under the Suppression of Communism Act had been dropped, the Crown was left with the charge that those in the dock had conspired to commit acts of treason. 'If the Crown fails to prove conspiracy', said Pirow in a statement which surprised both the Judges and the defence, 'then all the accused go free.'[56] In the argument which followed,

Advance, *December 11 1952.*

the judges appeared to side with the defence in its view that in order for the accused to have acted treasonably, they would have to have been planning violence. It was therefore necessary for the Prosecution to provide particulars showing that the accused had indeed planned to act violently. The Prosecution's response was to suddenly withdraw the indictment:

> After ten minutes whilst Mr Trengrove (for the Prosecution) was in the middle of a sentence, Mr Pirow suddenly jerked his gown pulling him down into his seat and then jumped up and announced the withdrawal of the indictment. Looks of complete amazement came over the faces of the judges and the Crown.[57]

But the Prosecution insisted on proceeding with the trial and Pirow told the court he would immediately re-indict the accused.[58] Shortly afterwards, the Minister of Justice said 'this trial will be proceeded with, no matter how many millions of pounds it costs.... What does it matter how long it takes?[59]

The essence of the crime of high treason, said prosecutor Pirow, was 'hostile intent'. This intent, he said, was evident in the demands of the accused for full political equality. They knew that to achieve the demands of the Freedom Charter would 'necessarily involve the overthrow of the state by violence.'[60] The accused, he said, were 'inspired by communist fanaticism, Bantu nationalism and racial hatred in various degrees.'[61] To prove 'intent', the Prosecution said it would look at the circumstances in which words were uttered or written, as well as the intention of the person uttering or writing them. This would involve assessing whether the accused, particularly writers of speeches, articles and the Charter itself, were possessed of a 'treasonable intention', a 'wicked heart' and an 'evil mind'. If the Crown proved that there was a 'treasonable mind', said Pirow, any action done in such a mind, however innocent in nature, could still be an overt act of treason: 'The act itself is only evidence of the state of mind ... any manifestation of a hostile state of mind renders a person guilty of high treason.'[62]

'Treasonable intent', said Pirow, could partly be determined by 'gauging the probable reaction of the people who formed, for example, the bulk of the audience at meetings'. He said the Crown had evidence that 'the country's non-European population is likely to respond more quickly, more irresponsibly, and more violently to illegal agitation than would the case with a group whose general standard of civilisation is higher.'[63]

The Crown's dilemma, following the collapse of the first indictment, was that it could no longer link communist intent (which, for the Crown, equalled violence) with the charge of treason, but it was required to prove that violence was intended in order to ensure a charge of treason. Its solution was to declare calls for political equality to be treasonable because, it claimed, the only route to equality in South Africa was by way of violence. But, because in countless meetings and articles the Congress Movement had called for non-violent methods of struggle, the Crown alleged that the accused had an unwritten agreement to provoke 'violence by retaliation' from the police.

> We propose to demonstrate that this policy of non-violence is double-talk and a ruse, so that when the fat is in the fire, (the ANC) could stand back and say 'our policy is non-violence'... Non-violence is just a slogan. It is misleading to have a slogan of non-violence when your methods are unconstitutional. This policy of non-violence is unlawful(sic.).[64]

Violence, said the Crown, 'ran through the case in an unbroken thread.' And the form of this violence 'was not to be limited to minor street-corner skirmishes or beerhall brawls'. The speeches and writings of the accused 'bristle with references to the spilling of blood.'[65] When the defence demanded evidence of planned violence the prosecutor simply replied that 17 of the accused had pledged themselves to achieve the demands of the Freedom Charter, which implied the violent overthrow of the state 'within five years from 1955.' The Prosecution later alleged that the Congress's Freedom Volunteers, were a semi-military force under oath to carry our orders, even if these were illegal. Conspiracy, said the Crown, was no longer held to be between individuals but between the organisations of the Congress movement. These organisations conspired to set up an illegal extra-parliamentary opposition which intended to overthrow the state.

So the actual trial – which only began in August 1959, two and a half years after the accused had been arrested – was to become a bitter contest between those who advocated a non-racial democracy and those who advocated racial separation. The alteration in the state's focus from charges of furthering the aims of communism to charges of treasonable intent had much to do with the development of the trial itself. But the shift was also influenced by changes in the state's conceptualisation of apartheid. By the time the actual Treason Trial began in 1959, the consistently successful attempts by the Alliance and its press to dig out and make visible the effects of apartheid was held to be treasonable.[66] The three main ways in which the Alliance was seen to have done this was through meetings, media and the Freedom Charter. The entire trial was, in fact, an attempt to re-interpret Congress Alliance discourse and actions in these areas in terms of National Party ideology.

The ANC, said the Crown, supported *New Age*, *Advance*, *Liberation* and *Fighting Talk* without qualification.'[67] Reports in these journals, it said, would be used 'to prove that the policy of the Congress Movement is one of violence' and that the newspapers were involved in 'the incitement of violent policies.'[68] And if reporting was done with a 'wicked heart', with intent to incite an audience, it constituted treason.

It is clear that the Prosecution had ample proof that this Press was hostile to apartheid and had supported an oppositional culture during the 1950s. The Crown, however, seemed unclear on how to proceed against the left Press beyond claiming that it was communistically inclined and, through its opposition to apartheid, had incited violence. The battle over words was therefore focused on the one document which crystalised the beliefs and demands of the entire Congress Alliance and its Press: the Freedom Charter.

In the second indictment, the Prosecution said it would prove the existence of treasonable conspiracy by 'an irresistible inference' from the history of the world-wide communist movement and the history of extra-parliamentary opposition in South Africa. Pirow admitted that the Prosecution's case was 'intricate' and included 'voluminous particulars ... all kinds of evidence of spoken and written words, attendance at meetings, possession of documents and so on....'[69] But by 1959 the number of documents submitted as evidence had been reduced from nearly 10 000 to 5 000. With these, said Pirow, the Prosecution would attempt to prove a connection between 'world communism at least since 1949 ... the extra-parliamentary movement since 1952 ... the ANC, the World Peace Council, opposition to the foreign policies of Western European countries and the United States ... and the entire range of tactics of protest, including agitation over minor grievances.'[70] The 'unifying element' in this was the Liberatory Movement, and the key document was the Freedom Charter. If the Charter could be found to be treasonable, then all Congress media which supported it or reflected its sentiments would also be deemed treasonable.

Much of the Crown case, therefore, rested on the Charter and, at the close of the preparatory inquiry, Pirow had treated it as the cornerstone of the Prosecution's case. In the second indictment, Pirow said the Charter was 'a revolutionary document' which made demands involving 'the complete smashing of the entire state apparatus in its present form.'[71] The indictment specified five demands to support this claim – mainly those concerned with public ownership and re-division of land.

So late in 1959 Professor Murray was called back to assess the Charter. In Murray's estimation there were 'no parts of (the Freedom Charter) which could not be interpreted into the Communist doctrine.'[72] As each phrase of the Charter was read out Murray proclaimed, as he had done during the Preparatory Examination: 'Communist doctrine', or 'the word people has two meanings ... one of them Communistic', or 'this falls within Communist policy'. However, on questioning Murray, Advocate Maisels for the defence got him to admit that the Charter could be seen as a detailed statement of human rights. It therefore referred to the removal of grievances:

> Mr Maisels: It is not necessary therefore to look for Communism. The state of grievance is a natural reaction to a position in which the Non-Europeans find themselves in this country. You may agree with me, is it not? – Yes.
> Mr Maisels: It is not unnatural to expect these grievances from the Non-Europeans? – Yes.
> Mr Maisels: The stress is laid on liberty, fraternity and equality?
> Prof. Murray: It is on democracy.
> Mr Maisels: That is not far removed from liberty, fraternity and equality? – Yes.
> Mr Maisels: The emphasis is on franchise rights and civil liberties? – Yes.
> Mr Maisels: More sections are on that than anything else? – Yes.
> Mr Maisels: What I am suggesting is that in this document one hasn't got to look for Communism or non-Communism but one has to understand the position of the Non-Europeans.

In the discussion which followed, Murray conceded that the word 'revolution' did not necessarily mean violence.

> Mr Kentridge: In other words, professor, if you look at the Freedom Charter of the ANC as it stands, on its face value, there is nothing in Communist theory which says that it can only be attained as far as it goes.
> Prof Murray: Not as far as the document goes.

With this admission the Crown's case against the Charter, and with it the case against the 'grievance' reporting of the left Press, had collapsed and from this point the Charter was downgraded as evidence by the Crown.

The issue of violence

The final line of attack by the Prosecution was against the provocation of violence by way of public speeches. And in this they had what they considered to be a water-tight case. Nine days before the treason arrests a police detective hiding in a cupboard at a meeting had recorded on tape a speech made by the Transvaal chief of the ANC's Freedom Volunteers, Robert Resha. Resha, a *New Age* sports reporter, had told the audience 'when you are disciplined and you are told by the organisation not to be violent, you must not be violent. If you are a true volunteer and you are called upon to be violent, you must be absolutely violent, you must murder! murder! murder! That is all.'[73]

Until this point the court had heard seemingly endless reports of speeches made by the accused and taken down in long-hand and short-hand by Special Branch detectives. Many of these were incoherent and the defence spent months demolishing the credibility of the 'long-hand writers'. The taped speech, however, demanded a different approach, and was the single most damaging piece of evidence produced against the accused. The defence had only one option open to it: to attempt to separate Resha's 'language of the beerhalls' from Congress policy.

The Crown, in its turn, threw in every piece of evidence it could muster to support its charge of violence. It drew together the evidence of long-hand and short-hand writers on meetings and speeches against passes, Bantu Education, women's rights and the Congress of the People. 'We say', said Mr Trengrove for the Crown, 'that although the Congress Movement told the people not to be violent, although this was a general approach, there were instances in which the ANC preached violence at meetings and in their writings, they preached violence in order to test the preparedness of the people for violence.'[74] And the Prosecution produced its evidence. At a meeting at the Trades Hall in Johannesburg in 1954, Elias Moretsele had said: 'We are a non-violent army for liberation'. He was bluffing the people, claimed the Prosecution. 'What he is telling the people is that we are non-violent, but if violence comes it will come from the Government.'[75]

At another meeting Gert Sibande of Bethal had said: 'In the same way that the Afrikaner took this country without violence, we will take away the Government with bare hands. We know the secret, they don't know'. This, said the Crown, did not mean the Congress Alliance was going to negotiate for a future South Africa.[76]

Accused Ahmed Kathrada had talked about police spies at a meeting. He had asked: 'What will we do with people like these?' The crowd had roared back: 'We will kill them'. This speech, said the Prosecution, 'was not inconsistent with the speech of 'murder! murder!' by accused Resha.' The Freedom Volunteers, said Prosecutor Trengrove, preached non-violence and had not committed violence during the period of the indictment. But they were standing in the wings 'to lead the masses into violence' when the time arrived.

The Prosecution again linked this alleged violence with the Communist Party, and police witnesses spent much of February 1960 testifying on Party meetings, despite a defence argument that this was irrelevant to the charges and would require a second trial on the policy of the Communist Party.

The defence opened its case in March and called to the stand, among others, the deputy president-general of the ANC, Dr Wilson Conco, its president, Chief Albert Luthuli, ANC executive member Nelson Mandela and Resha. Mandela denied that the Congress view of freedom was a direct threat to Europeans: 'We are not anti-white; we are against white supremacy', he told the court. 'And in struggling against white supremacy we have the support of some sections of the European population.'[77] Conco said the speech made by Resha was outside the policy of the ANC. Resha, who was reprimanded for refusing to address the Prosecution as 'their Lordships', agreed with Conco, but said he had talked this way because a number of things were 'working on his mind.'[78] Among these were 'the Western Areas removals ... the intensified permit raids in Sophiatown during which men had been killed running away from the raids, women fleeing from raids on their homes giving birth in the streets of Newclare and the veld near Sophiatown.'[79]

The Prosecution claimed that the ANC new 'full well that in the situation you were creating in Western Areas it would only need a spark to start off a conflagration. Resha denied this:

> Mr Resha: We knew the Government wanted to start a conflagration because it wants to rob the people of their rights and threatens them with force. The Government sent 2 000 armed police into Sophiatown.
> Adv. Trengrove: You regarded it as a victory?
> Mr Resha: Yes. Because 2 000 police went away without shooting one person![80]

The most impressive claim that the ANC was a non-violent organisation, however, had come from Luthuli. With his slow, erect walk, his large square head with its gray hair and deep, dark lines, his huge laugh and his courteous way of talking in simple, Biblical terms, he summed up everything that was meant by African dignity. He appeared, noted *Drum* editor Anthony Sampson, 'the perfect, docile Christian chief that missionaries delight to describe in their memoirs ... the kind of African of whom Afrikaner officials said: "that's the kind of Native we like to have, not those half-baked kaffirs in the towns."'[81] His high moral position confounded the upholders of apartheid. He had once said that he did not hold Whites responsible for racism as individuals: 'I don't hate the white man. You see this position of domination has placed him in a position of moral weakness. We must sympathise with him: why should we hate the poor blighter?'[82] When he was elected as President of the ANC in 1952 he asked: 'Who will deny that thirty years of my life have been spent knocking in vain, patiently, moderately and modestly at a closed, barred door. What have been the fruits of moderation?' [83]

Shortly after Luthuli took the stand the Government declared a State of Emergency following the shooting at Sharpeville. He was imprisoned and assaulted by a warder. Shortly afterwards he became ill and his testimony was restricted to two hours a day. Despite his bearing and his obvious illness, the sage old chief was savagely attacked by the Prosecution in a way which shocked the accused. Helen Joseph remembers:

> I think that if I had been Trengrove, the Prosecutor, I would have carried with me to my dying day the memory of the look on Luthuli's face. So Christ may have looked, when He stood before His accusers. It was a look of agonized disbelief that his word could be so doubted. I think that in all his life, no one had ever before accused Albert Luthuli of dishonesty. He turned to look at the judges in sheer disbelief, in appeal. Their faces were stony as he protested that this was an attack on his integrity.[84]

Nonetheless, he clearly impressed the judges. He said that non-violence was the basic policy of the ANC and as far as the struggle in South Africa was concerned, he thought that violence would be national suicide. He said the ANC stood for an undivided South Africa which would be multi-racial. The call to share the land among those who worked it as written in the African Claims document and the Freedom Charter was not necessarily a socialist demand, he said. 'To us, it is a painful thing and all along the ANC has taken a strong stand in claiming our rights to land. Being dispossessed of land is almost to be dispossessed of life itself.'[85] The ANC was an omnibus organisation and its members might hold different political views, he said. People within the ANC might advocate violence on occasion. But the position of the ANC remained non-violent and 'I have had no suggestion to change that policy, not a whisper.'[86]

In November 1960 the Crown began its final argument. It alleged that all 156 of the accused were engaged in a plot against the state and if they had been left unchecked it would have led to death, a bloodbath and disaster[87] It reiterated that 'you can only achieve what the Freedom Charter wants if you overthrow the system. You can only achieve this over the dead bodies of Europeans.'[88] The ANC, said Trengrove for the Prosecution, must be judged by what it says. 'If you embark upon a programme which has certain probable consequences then in law you intend those consequences.'[89]

The Crown divided the accused into two camps: 'those who have knowledge of the violent doctrine of Communism and those who have no knowledge'. Heading the list of those who 'knew' was Robert Resha, who 'conspired to propagate Marxist-Leninist doctrine and knew that violent revolution was a principle inherent in Communism.'[90] The Crown also revised its list of co-conspirators, and Ruth First, together with Lutuli, Oliver Tambo and ZK Matthews, were included in a special list of 26 people deemed the 'real co-conspirators'.

On March 6 the defence opened its final argument. It rejected the charge of treason and denied that Resha's speech reflected ANC policy. For the Prosecution, African grievances had been exploited by agitators. For the defence, African grievances were to be expected in the circumstances of South Africa, and it was realistic to accept the fact that moderate and responsible African leaders saw in the Freedom Charter a vision of the future. Where the prosecution stressed the power of the accused to start a conflagration, the defence stressed the belief of the accused in the possibility of peaceful change in response to non-violent pressure. In short, the defence denied that the ANC was a conspiracy motivated by hostile intent. It denied the prosecution's contention that no middle ground existed between the ballot box and treason. Maisels posed to the judges some major legal questions: What are the essential ingredients of treason in peacetime? Can there be constructive treason? In other words, can one commit treason (as the Crown alleged) if one performs a non-violent act whose probable consequence is the use of violence by the state?[91] On March 29 1961 the judges announced that there was no necessity for the defence to continue with its argument. Justice Rumpff said the incitement to violence was the cornerstone of the case, but the prosecution had failed to prove that the ANC had acquired or adopted a policy to overthrow the State by violence. Nor had it proved 'a case of contingent retaliation' in which the ANC planned to provoke the State into committing violence and thus provoke retaliation from the masses. The Crown had also failed to prove that the ANC was a communist organisation, or that the Freedom Charter pictured a communist state.[92] The drama of the final judgment was captured by Helen Joseph:

> The Judge President begins to read the judgment. It takes forty long minutes. 'Silence in court!' Six times a day we have heard it, rising to our feet as the judges come in or go out. On this last day, when Judge Rumpff himself tells us to stand, we hear it again. 'Silence in...' the Sergeant at the back of the court begins to shout when he sees us getting to our feet for the last time. But his voice dies away. I am not sure what to do with my hands, so I put them behind my back. Judge Rumpff is speaking now, in a low voice, but very clearly, leaning forward a little, 'You are found not guilty and discharged and you may go'. The court is hushed.... We stand motionless, stunned. Then I see that Council is smiling and I know I am not dreaming.[93]

Through this victory the radical press had successfully defended the space it had created in order to support the Congress Alliance. But its triumph was not to last.

Pretoria's judgment

There is a supreme irony about the conclusion to the Treason Trial. The shock at the widely publicized shooting of unarmed, fleeing people at Sharpeville and Langa confronted the South African government with a crisis of unprecedented magnitude. Attempts by Prime Minister Verwoerd and his Cabinet to make light of the incident proved futile as waves of reaction mounted in South Africa and abroad.[94] The Johannesburg Stock Exchange, that sensitive barometer of investor confidence, witnessed massive, panicky selling as £600-million was slashed from the value of shares in the following six months and £50-million in foreign investment flowed out of the country.[95] The American State Department openly condemned the shootings and the United Nations Security Council discussed the incident[96] Huge rallies and a work stayaway were called in South Africa and the pass laws were temporarily suspended on March 26. Two days later the government declared a State of Emergency – effectively martial law.[97] In widespread political raids several thousand people were arrested (including most of the trial accused) and the ANC and Pan Africanist Congress were banned.

So the conclusions of Justice Rumpff in reaching a verdict of 'not guilty' were clearly out of step with the way in which the state now viewed the objective conditions of the time. The 12 months between Sharpeville and the treason judgment represented a critical change in the tactics of both the state and the Congress Alliance. In a sense, the logic of the trial was derived from the early years of Nationalist rule. The trial, it was hoped, would restrict the movements of the accused, intimidate others who might be similarly accused, and demonstrate at home and abroad, to a world immersed in the Cold War, that it was fighting communism by way of a highly-respected judicial system. The Government would be vindicated if it won. And if it lost it could blame defeat on the law's inadequacy and extol the meticulous standards of the judiciary. On the final decision it could base either further prosecutions (of the co-conspirators and others) or the need for tougher new legislation.

However, the trial had unintended consequences. It boosted the prestige of the ANC, further cemented the alliance between nationalists and communists, and vindicated the stance of the Congress Alliance and the Freedom Charter. The trial was of little value to the Government in its appeal to the white electorate, who were simply confused by the endless wrangling and who received little clarification from the mainstream Press. The trial also failed to promote acceptance abroad, where an interest in de-colonisation in Africa had overtaken fears of Soviet intervention. Foreign reports on the trial mainly impugned the Government's motives and sympathised with the tribulations of the accused. However, none of these consequences serve to explain the state crackdown on the Congress Movement. The crisis, for the Government, needs to be understood on another level.

The trial had failed to install apartheid as 'common sense', and served simply to highlight the differences between Nationalist doctrine and non-racialism. Attempts to excommunicate the ideas embodied in the Freedom Charter by due legal process proved to be unsuccessful, and by the late 1950s this failure appeared to have opened a breach in the power matrix which thousands of bus-boycotters and pass-burners seemed to symbolise.

The trial has been cited as an example of the excessively legalistic approach of both the Congress Alliance and the Government.[98] However, this misses an essential point. At root, the trial was, as Berrange had indicated, a battle of ideas. It was to become a testing-ground for the racist discourse of the newly-elected Nationalist government and an attempt to ghettoise and excommunicate the ideas of the Alliance. In this it failed, and the banning of the ANC was inevitable in that the failure of the trial – even before it had ended – to stigmatise ideas of liberation was a serious danger to the state's ideological dominance. As accusations of communism, treason and violence lost their power, the protective shielding of the state's discourse began to crumble. The state, therefore, dispensed with the legal ritual.

Notes

1 These were the SA Peace Council, SACOD, SACPO, SA Indian Youth Congress and the SA Federation of Women. These organisations were all cited in the 1956 Treason Trial as being contributing organisations to acts of treason.

2 The Freedom Charter has come to be seen as the key focus of the Congress of the People. When the campaign was conceived, however, it was merely seen as a necessary addition to the convening of a People's Parliament at Kliptown. ZK Matthews' original idea had been to run a multi-racial, extra-parliamentary national election.

3 *Inspan* 8,1, October 1948, quoted in John Lazar 1987.

4 FG Gardiner & CWH Lansdown: *South African Criminal Law and Procedure* (Cape Town 1957).

5 Len Lee-Warden, unpublished autobiography, p88.

6 *Counter Attack*, October 1955.

7 Ibid, November 1955.

8 Forman & Sachs, 1957, p11.

9 Sampson, 1958, p7.

10 Forman & Sachs, 1957, p43.

11 Ibid, p7.

12 Ibid, p184

13 *New Age*, 27.12.56.

14 Foreman & Sachs, op cit, p66.

15 Ibid.

16 Ibid, p69.

17 Forman & Sachs, op cit, p57.

18 The thousands of documents provide the researcher with an extraordinary record of the political assumptions of the main protagonists.

19 The trial structure was complex and can be broken into a number of phases: Phase 1: Preparatory examination – 156 accused (December 1956 – January 1958). Phase 2: First indictment argued – 92 accused, 152 alleged co-conspirators (August to October 1958). Phase 3: Second indictment argued – 30 accused, 129 alleged co-conspirators (January to June 1959). Phase 4: The trial begins. Arraignment and evidence (August 1959 – March 1960). Phase 5: Trial during the State of Emergency (March to July 1960). Phase 6: defence back to normal. Evidence concluded (August to October 1960). Phase 7: Closing arguments and judgment (November 1960 – March 1961). Ruth was discharged after the Preparatory

Examination but remained an alleged 'main co-conspirator' throughout the trial and therefore continued to face a charge of high treason.

20 Forman & Sachs, op cit. p70.

21 For a description of the trial see, particularly, *The Treason Cage* by Anthony Sampson, *If This be Treason* by Helen Joseph, *The South African Treason Trial* by Lionel Forman and Solly Sachs, and *The Treason Trial in South Africa* by Thomas Karis.

22 The Broederbond was a secret Afrikaner cultural organisation dedicated to Afrikaner power and the unity of the volk. It had links into the highest echelons of Afrikaner power. See *The Super Afrikaners* by Ivor Wilkins and Hans Strydom (1978) and *Volkskapitalisme* by Dan O'Meara (1983).

23 Volk is a cultural term which implies more than merely 'people' or 'nation'. *Eenheid* means unity.

24 *Die Oosterlig*, 8.11.47.

25 *Die Republikien*, May 1 & 8, 1936. See also T Dunbar Moodie: *The rise of Afrikanerdom* (1975).

26 *Wapenskou*, September 1944. Quoted in Dunbar Moodie, op cit.

27 *Die Vaderland* 4.3.44. and *Volkstem* 22.3.44.

28 The executive committee included Hendrik Verwoerd, Nico Diedrichs, Ben Schoeman, Jan de Klerk and Albert Hertzog.

29 Dunbar Moodie, op cit, p255.

30 *Kerkbode*, 29.9.43 and Dunbar Moodie, op cit, p251.

31 See Eric Louw's National Party pamphlet: *Die Kommunistiese Gevaar* (n.d).

32 Saur Report, private translation.

33 Ibid.

34 *Daily Dispatch* 17.2.49.

35 *The Guardian* 11.7.49.

36 *Natal Mercury* 7.11.49.

37 Leo Lovell, Benoni, in *Hansard*, 1950 at 9551. Lovell was a Labour Party MP. He was later to become Minister of Finance in Swaziland.

38 LC Gay, South Peninsula, in *Hansard*, 1950 at 9577.

39 Lovel, op cit.

40 *Hansard*, op cit at 9510.

41 Ibid, June 17, 1950.

42 Ibid, Ibid at 8961.

43 Fowler, 1991, p91.

44 *New Age*, 11.7.57.

45 Ibid.

46 Ibid.

47 Ibid.

48 *New Age*, 30.5.57.

49 Joseph, 1963, p33.

50 *New Age*, 30.5.57.

51 Ibid.

52 Joseph, op cit, p33.

53 *New Age*, 28.8.58.
54 Ibid.
55 Ibid.
56 Karis, op cit, p13.
57 *New Age*, 16.10.58.
58 A further indictment against 61 other trialists was quashed.
59 Karis, op cit, p15.
60 Ibid.
61 Ibid, p19.
62 Ibid.
63 Second Indictment, Treason Trial microfilm.
64 *New Age*, 17.11.60.
65 *New Age*, 13.8.59.
66 The state considered *New Age* to be largely responsible for resistence to the issue of womens' passes.
67 *New Age*, 1.12.60.
68 Ibid, 24.9.59 & 8.10.59.
69 Karis, 1965.
70 Ibid, p18.
71 Ibid.
72 *New Age*, 12.11.59.
73 Ibid, 4.2.60.
74 Ibid, 1.12.60.
75 Ibid.
76 Ibid.
77 *New Age*, 8.9.60.
78 Ibid.
79 Ibid.
80 Ibid.
81 Sampson, 1958, p185/9.
82 Ibid, p189.
83 Ibid.
84 Joseph, 1963, p90.
85 *New Age*, 31.3.60.
86 Ibid.
87 *New Age*, 10.11.60.
88 Ibid, 17.11.60.
89 Ibid.
90 Ibid, 16.2.61.
91 Karis, op cit, p22.
92 *New Age*, 30.3.61.

93 Joseph, op cit, p141.

94 Karis & Gerhart, 1977, p337.

95 *New Age*, September 8, 1960.

96 Karis, op cit, p336.

97 A week later a deranged farmer, David Pratt, shot Dr Verwoerd while he was addressing a crowd in Johannesburg. The bullet passed through the Prime Minister's face but missed his brain.

98 Turok interview; Sampson, op cit.; Karis, op cit.

9

Towards new horizons

White South West Africa digs its trenches for survival, as its Algerian and Congolese counterparts did so many corpses ago – Ruth First

The sands of Namibia

Political activists, ever watchful of their enemy, had sensed that a crack-down was coming in 1960. In Cape Town after the shooting the PAC took virtual control of the African townships of Langa and Nyanga and black anger was to culminate in a march to the city centre by 30 000 demonstrators.[1] Elsewhere in the country an upsurge of protest began to assume national dimensions. On Thursday March 24 Chief Lutuli called for a Day of Mourning and a worker stay-at-home the following Monday. The night before the stay-at-home, which was 90% successful in Johannesburg, Durban and Port Elizabeth, Lutuli publicly burned his pass. Sharpeville was a turning point in the history of African anger, and both the government and the Left sensed it. By the time Verwoerd declared the State of Emergency on March 30, Congress leaders had established a network to warn each other about a possible raid. Rica Hodgson remembers being phoned by Nelson Mandela. 'He gave me a message which was gobbledygook ... so I immediately wrote it out. When Jack (Hodgson) came back I gave him the message and he said: 'Oh my God, that means arrests ... I must go out and warn people.'[2]

The debate among Congress leaders was whether to go into hiding or to stay visible. Joe Slovo had commitments and was not prepared to 'disappear'. He was to spend the Emergency in jail. Ruth dyed her hair red, packed the children in the car and made a midnight dash for the Swaziland border. She and the girls were joined by many others in hiding, and the four Slovos moved into an apartment block in Mbabane with another family.[3] Eight days later the ANC and the PAC were banned.

According to Robyn Slovo, who was eight years old at the time, Swaziland was 'tense but fun ... though none of us really knew what was going on. It was at times also very fearful – a huge amount of insecurity ... But my most outstanding memory was Ruth's red hair![4] Before the Emergency was over, Ruth left the girls in the care of the other couple in the flat and was smuggled back to Johannesburg by Jack Hodgson. She was put up in a house of an architect near Zoo Lake who, Rica Hodgson remembers, 'was a very attractive man, bearded, with an incredible home and this very earthy wife who made wonderful vegetarian foods and salads.'[5] But they became ill at ease with the arrangement and activist Wolfie Kodesh found her a room with 'an artist couple along a road adjoining Louis Botha Avenue' where she stayed until the end of the Emergency.[6]

Ruth's return was probably connected with discussions about the public launch of the SA Communist Party, of which she was a key member. When the Emergency was declared, Moses Kotane, Michael Harmel and Ben Turok had gone underground in Johannesburg. And there they remained, a Party secretariat of three, throughout the five months of the Emergency, moving at least 10 times and only going outdoors at night.[7] Some way into the Emergency a meeting of six or seven people was called around the question of the emergence of the Party. Harmel had been one of the two dissenting voices on the dissolution of the Party in 1950 and he had always been opposed to a secret Party. He now argued that, historically, no Party could stay silent if it wanted to influence events. Acording to Turok, Harmel argued that

> You can't influence events simply by working in another frame. You have to say something as a communist, you have to talk about socialism and Marxism, and you can't do that in the liberation movement. If you did it there you would destroy the liberation movement. You had to speak in your own right. And you couldn't say after the revolution: 'Hey, by the way, we're also here and we want power...'[8]

After a 'fairly tense meeting' it was decided that the Party would emerge by way of a leaflet, which was drafted, run off in substantial numbers and distributed 'one dark night'. The public launch of the Party caused a considerable stir in the Press, coming as it did in the middle of the Emergency. According to Turok, even some members of the movement were shocked, 'but they came to accept it pretty quickly'.

So when the Emergency was finally lifted on August 31 the Congress Movement found itself on a completely different playing field. The Treason Trial trundled towards its now almost irrelevant conclusion. But the defence team found itself being rapidly overtaken by events – a visible Communist Party and a state which had dispensed with the courts in its attack on the Congress Alliance.

When Ruth re-surfaced in Johannesburg she found herself in a changed country. *New Age* began printing again and *Fighting Talk* needed attention. Joe was released and the family started to pick up the pieces scattered so suddenly six months before. But the mood around them had changed. Being politically Left was considerably more dangerous.

Ruth was back at her desk at *New Age* in time for the first post-emergency edition. But it was soon clear that the scope for investigative journalism had been massively curtailed. She found reporting to be increasingly difficult, and was living what she was to term 'a more and more schizophrenic existence.'[9] She was a key member of the SACP underground, had just emerged from a marathon treason trial and was confronting an increasingly aggressive government. She found she was being cut off from those areas where a political journalist most needed to go. She measured the situation with eyes sharpened by six months in hiding:

> Only in South Africa does government policy march steadily backwards into the past, offering tear gas instead of conciliation, entrenching itself in power with guns instead of votes, denying Africans the last shreds of their parliamentary representation and promoting despotic chiefs as their rulers instead, encouraging balkanization with dreams of small, separate Bantustans.[10]

But this situation did not block her writing: it simply heightened her need to know more. Although the repression pushed her back from weekly journalism, her knowledge of migrant labour, together with her interest in the campaigns of her old friend Michael Scott, was to launch her into deeper and more reflective forms of investigative reporting. In 1960 she turned her attentions towards the mandated territory of South West Africa, and in so doing she was to reach out to an audience beyond the barbed-wire borders of her increasingly isolated country.

The Reverend Michael Scott was a left-wing journalist's dream. He had an unerring nose for injustice and was as fearless as he was tenacious in his attempts to expose it. Exceptionally good looking and intelligent, he was a man with absolutely no personal ambition and one so self-effacing that it was difficult to persuade him to use the word 'I' if it could be avoided.[11] He constantly made news, but had no wish to be news. However, he welcomed press cooperation in giving publicity to the matters he had at heart, and he believed in the power of the Press for making known the truth and for digging out secrecy and dark dealings. To their loss, the commercial Press often portrayed him as a crank, but Ruth tracked his course across the face of South African history with alert attention.

His links with Ruth went back for more than a decade. When Scott arrived in South Africa from Britain in the 1940s, he was appointed chaplain of an orphanage for coloured children. In an action which was to become characteristic, he spurned the orphanage house and moved into a small rondavel in the orphanage grounds which was on the edge of Sophiatown. From here he launched himself into the life of the township, returning to pour over government Blue Books to find the causes of poverty and segregation. He would appear at Ismael Meer's flat while Ruth was a student and discuss and argue about South African politics over cups of coffee. His tall figure, in a shabby cassock, sometimes black, sometimes white, with thick boots muddied in the long walk through the streets of Sophiatown, brief-case bulging with papers, pockets often as not bulging with sweets, was known and greeted everywhere.[12]

In 1946 he had become involved in the Passive Resistance campaign against the so-called Ghetto Act, and together with Indian resisters he was battered by white thugs as they stood, not defending themselves, in the streets of Durban – and spent three months in jail sewing mailbags and cleaning latrines on an incitement charge. Soon after his release, he moved into a hessian shelter in the Johannesburg squatter camp of Tobruk in order to draw attention to slum conditions, and in 1947 he and Ruth began exposing labour conditions on the Bethal farms.

Then Scott received a letter which was to catapult him from public nuisance in the eyes of the state to being considered a major threat to state security. The letter was a request from Frederick Maharero, Paramount Chief of the Hereros in exile in Bechuanaland, that Scott come to see him. The old chief asked the priest to assist his people in their appeal for the return of their lands in South West Africa. Scott then journeyed to the mandated territory to meet 'this little tribe which was to become for him the prototype of all the oppressed of the earth' and on whose case the credibility of the United Nations was to teeter.[13] Together with Maharero, a petition to the United Nations was drawn up and Scott was appointed the official representative of the Hereros to deliver it in New York.

On his return from South West Africa, Scott gave a copy of the petition to Ruth who led *The Guardian* with it in October 1947. Her summary of its contents neatly set out the parameters of the wrangle which was to land her in Windhoek 14 years later gathering material for her first book:

> Arrogant, and doing his best to be cock-sure, Minister Lawrence, the leader of the Union's delegation at the United Nations, asserts that the people of South West Africa earnestly desire incorporation into the Union.
>
> And yet, in their own words, the Herero, Ovambo and Nama people of South West Africa are totally against incorporation of their territory. They believe that the Union's administration of the mandate has proved disastrous for the native peoples of South West Africa.[14]

Scott was not allowed to present the petition to the UN General Assembly, and the South African government did all in its power to discredit him. But his astonishing clarity of vision, communicated to those he lobbied at Lake Pleasant, transmuted his plea for a forgotten desert tribe into a one-man mission for the wretched of the earth – and captured the imagination of the New York Press. However, his vision left him with no illusions about the power of the United Nations to change things. Snowbound in New York, he reflected over the days proceedings:

> I have spent a good deal of time thinking about the enormous number of words that have been uttered during these debates on the problems of South Africa and of Hereros who for me have become symbolical of all the landless and dispossessed people of the world. Words signifying all the passions and emotions, hopes and fears of humanity, words like snow crystals of all shapes and sizes, and I could wish they had as much power as the delicate fluttering flakes whose accumulated mass have seemingly brought civilization to a standstill.[15]

Gandhian to the core, Scott believed that patience, petitioning and justice would in the end prevail, and that others would follow to take up the fight. In 1961, amid rising political tensions over rumours of a threatened United Nations 'invasion' of South West Africa and a pending court case at the International Court of Justice over the validity of South Africa's mandate to rule the territory, Ruth did just that. Anticipating police bans and taking 'as devious route as possible', she slipped into Windhoek and checked into a hotel. Her secrecy afforded her a small breathing space:

> I had four clear days unhampered by political police scrutiny in which to attempt a meeting with the African South West. Then suddenly the Special Branch ... woke up with a jerk. There was an outsider in town, talking to Africans, asking questions, taking notes, riding around in the conspicuous salmon-pink American car of the Herero Councillors, asking for government reports in the Archives.[16]

This time there was no midnight thump on the door, which by now she fully expected. A police state in action, she was to record, is not noisy or dramatic, it can also be relaxed, even slovenly. The detectives who arrived on surveillance duty wore shorts and rugby socks, worked in pairs and padded along six paces behind her, smiling sheepishly when she caught their eye. But the scrutiny never faltered. 'The trail to the dry-cleaner and the shoemaker, the skulking next to the telephone booth, both ends of the road and every exit of the hotel patrolled, detectives following me to the airport, watching me at breakfast, interviewing people I had seen – "What does she want from you?"'[17]

The Archives suddenly denied her access to documents written after 1946. But Africans were bursting to talk. Interviews were conducted on street corners, in motor cars, under a tree, in crowded shops; though some were cancelled following police intimidation. But times had changed from the weeks Michael Scott had camped in the bush near Windhoek airport, waiting for permission to consult with the Hereros. South West Africa, Ruth observed, 'is no longer the obsession of a lone, whimsical priest. In 16 years it has grown to be a major international issue, more central to the survival of the world body than ever Michael Scott or the Hereros dreamed.[18]

Government retribution for the visit came four days after her return from Windhoek. The thump on the door brought with it a banning order which restricted her to Johannesburg and made it illegal for her to prepare or compile material for publication or to communicate with other banned people.[19] The banning order crippled her journalism:

> I could take part in no further exposés of forced labour like my work on Bethal; from entering African townships, so that I could no longer personally establish the contacts of African men and women who alerted our office first of all when some new vicious scheme of the police and administration came to light; from attending meetings, so that others had to take the notes and the photographs; from writing anything for publication, so that I had to sit at my desk with a legal opinion that sub-editing someone else's copy might just slip past the ban. Working in the midst of these ministerial bans and under continuous raids and scrutiny of the Special Branch was like going to work in a mine field. ...[20]

But with regard to her work on South West Africa, Ruth simply ignored the ban and began to assemble her material. The leap into longer narrative required for a book was not an easy one for her. The quality, volume and effortless flow of her later books concealed a nagging anxiety she had about her abilities as a writer. Only her closest friends saw the struggle. Ronald Segal was one:

> Many remarkable journalists cannot make the leap from the article to the book. They are at home in the sentence and the paragraph, but they lose their way in the larger landscape. Ruth was all too aware of this. Some people, and I know there were some, who saw her self-assurance amounting to arrogance, never knew the turmoil of nervousness of suspected inadequacies that she brought to the writing of her books. It was a turmoil that I found difficult to understand.[21]

There were also political pressures. Ruth and Joe were now part of an underground structure which was laying the foundation for Umkonto we Sizwe and for clandestine radio broadcasts which were to mark the beginning of Radio Freedom. And all the time they were being watched by the Special Branch, their post opened and their telephones tapped. Slowly at first, then with increasing confidence, Ruth began to write her first book.[22] The narrative was built around three themes, racism, labour and the League of Nations mandate – and held together (rather uneasily) by the theory of internal colonialism – 'two South West Africas locked in conflict'. The whites constituted 'a monolithic political force (for the exceptions are too few to affect the pattern), heavily armed because South Africa is heavily armed, (who) monopolize government and its various benefits.'[23] The many African groupings were the last of the tribal warriors:

> heroic figures on horseback in an age of mechanized warfare. Skirmishing for grazing land, they were outflanked by the armed powers of Western Europe, busy maneuvering for concessions, treaties and strategic spheres of influence. Missionaries who traded bemused them; traders who advertised not only their wares but also the accompanying benefits of Christian civilization, despoiled them. Tragically divided among themselves by different origins and history, languages and customs, before the days of a unifying African nationalism ... they did not see the common fate preparing to overtake them.[24]

But Ruth's Marxist eye cut through the politics of the territory to the labour needs of South Africa. South West Africa, she wrote, 'is on the lips of the politicians, in the hands of the farmers, and in the pockets of the great mining and finance corporations.'[25] While the political system was a 'stern and parsimonious boarding school', she said, labour recruitment was a national institution. The territory was one vast labour camp:

> Men – and boys – at station sidings with labels tied around their necks: Thomas Abnael, looking about 15 years old, and marked 'UNDER AGE' on the contract form he clutched; Shikingo Isaak, who had herded karakul sheep from before sunrise till after sunset for 12 months at a wage of 25s a month and for the next six months at 35s, warned that if he lost a sheep he would have to pay for it: all are products of the huge labour recruiting organization that covers South West Africa.[26]

And if the incentives to work were not strong enough, men were simply 'jailed into labour'. Inside the 'Police Zone' to the south, the contract system did not apply, but here the Herero, Nama and Berg-Damara were enclosed in an iron framework of laws, regulations, ordinances, proclamations and official instructions:

> Men are 'handcuffed' by slips of paper. They must have permits to seek work, permits to be in the area for any purpose other than to seek work, service contracts to prove that they are working, passes to prove that they are schoolboys and too young to carry passes, certificates of registration authorizing residence in the area, permits to travel, tax receipts, exemptions from night curfew. Passes and permits constitute their license to live....[27]

League of Nations trust territories, she concluded, were areas where colonial powers could not be trusted to govern. She documented Michael Scott's lonely campaign, his attempts to turn a tedious legal wrangle into a crusade to save a people, and the angry mutter of Africa which had broken through the crust of the United Nations. She noted the tactics of Eric Louw, South Africa's representative at the UN: 'Sulky, truculent, the wrongdoer acting the wronged, (he) had perfected jack-in-the-box blackmail diplomacy: first he would talk in debate, then he would stage a walk-out, and then return, only to leave again with another protest against "interference."'[28]

The reasons for this truculence were clear: 'A crack in Nationalist control over South West Africa (will) inevitably spread across the border into the Republic itself.'[29] Documenting the origins of the South West African People's Organisation (SWAPO) and the National Union (SWANU) she asked: How much time has white rule left in Africa? 'If the UN cannot make South West Africa a land fit for Hereros to live in, the Hereros and others will seek other ways'. Sixteen years of the UN's inability to budge South Africa on the mandate challenged the whole authority of the world body. The danger of the dislocation that UN intervention would cause, she wrote with political prescience, is not as serious as the inevitably bloody consequences of non-intervention in the future. 'This is the hour of battle. There is still time to stop it. Must blood flow before the world body will act?'[30]

Ruth's manuscript was smuggled out of South Africa and published by Penguin in 1963. The risk of publication was high and Ruth's decision to go ahead with it was an act of considerable bravery. She had clearly broken her banning order and was now publicly airing the dirty laundry of a government already ill-disposed towards her. Unable to stop publication of the book, the state took its revenge on the author. On January 16 1963 Ruth received two five-year banning orders. The one confined her to the magisterial district of Johannesburg and prevented her from entering any township or factory or communicating with any other banned person. The other banned her from any political or social gatherings 'at which the persons present also have social intercourse with one another.'[31] She was in virtual quarantine. When the book appeared on news stands in South Africa it was banned. Any person possessing it was liable to a fine of R2 000 or five years in jail.

However, the book received high accolades from reviewers and boosted Ruth's self-confidence. Basil Davidson, writing in the *New Statesman*, placed *South West Africa* in a 'rare and admirable category':

> Every now and then there comes a book of political reporting that hits a new mark. Thereafter the tired old lies and evasions can never be the same again: they live on but they also wither, laid bare to the root.... Well-read and well written, cautious in judgment yet consistently pointful, personally modest but carrying the stamp of toil and thought, preferring irony to exhortation and satire to solemnity, it's devastating picture of the German, British and Boer connection with a lost and silent land appears to be as complete as it is equivocal.[32]

Malcolm Rutherford of *The Spectator* called the book 'journalism of the highest kind' and R Smirnova of *Soviet Women* noted with approval her application of the internal colonialism theory to the territory.[33] But an unsigned scrap of paper from a friend, preserved in Ruth's personal files, must have given her the sort of support she needed as the state's net closed around her:

> How great a thrill I got when I saw your book on display in a London bookseller's window in Piccadilly: how warm I felt when I went in to buy a copy.... I've always thought you're thunderingly clever, lovely brain, so I'm not insulting you when I say that the book is even better than I anticipated. And it has come out 'better' because ... the work is rich with you. It was only you and no-one else who wrote the hundreds of pieces of gently etched irony. You're very good at that – distilling your own hate and disgust and heartbreak in a neat, brief ironical statement.... All that writing and you with a thousand other preoccupations of family and other affairs.[34]

Notes

1 Lodge 1983, p219.

2 Interview with Rica Hodgson, 1988.

3 Interview with Robyn Slovo, 1992.

4 Ibid.

5 Hodgson, op cit.

6 Kodesh, private correspondence.

7 Turok interviewed by David Everatt, 1988.

8 Ibid.

9 *117 Days*, p116.

10 First, 1963, p232.

11 Troup, 1950, p122.

12 I have relied on Freda Troup's sensitive book on Scott for many of these details.

13 Troup, Ibid, p142.

14 *The Guardian*, 2.10.47.

15 Troup, op cit, p166.

16 First, 1963, p13.

17 Ibid, p13.

18 Ibid, p17.

19 Shula Marks: Ruth First: a tribute. In *Journal of South African Studies*, Vol. 10, No.1, October 1983.

20 *117 Days*, op cit, p118.

21 Segal: Memorial speech at her funeral, Maputo, September 8 1982.

22 Twenty years later one of South Africa's finest historians, Shula Marks, could still insist that 'in a field which has been notoriously neglected by scholars (*South West Africa*) remains one of the best and most readable books'. Marks: JSAS, op cit.

23 First, op cit, p56.

24 Ibid, p82.

25 Ibid, p151. An appendix supporting this assertion was to be the beginning of a later book, *The South African Connexion*, on Western investment in apartheid.

26 Ibid, p129.

27 Ibid, p129.

28 Ibid, p193.

29 Ibid, p20.

30 Ibid, p241.

31 Banning orders addressed to Heloise Ruth Slovo, Ruth First Trust Collection.

32 *New Statesman*, June 21, 1963.

33 *The Spectator*, September 6, 1963, and *Soviet Women*, No.3, 1964.

34 Letter in Ruth First Collection, London.

10

A battle lost

Can this be history? Have we who live today left our mark on the future? To answer these questions, historians looking back from a future time will one day give the answers – Ruth First

*Protesters calling for Mandela's release and the imminent Sabotage Bill, (*New Age*, August 23 1962)*

In the dock at the Rivonia trial, Nelson Mandela said that after the Emergency African people had been faced with two choices – to submit or fight. Submission was clearly out of the question, and the birth of Umkonto we Sizwe was the result of a decision to take the other road. In forming Umkonto, Congress leaders took the only route they saw open to them. And in the repressive atmosphere at the time it is difficult to see what other course of action they could have chosen. But on July 11 1963, when a baker's van drove slowly into the grounds of Lilliesleaf Farm in Rivonia, its presence was to utterly alter the struggle against apartheid. As police burst from the van, others came round the back of the farm house and most of the leaders of Umkonto were under arrest. Also captured was voluminous evidence of plans for sabotage and revolution. By this time nearly 200 acts of sabotage had been committed.

By pure chance Ruth was not at Rivonia when the raid took place. She had been party to the decision to purchase the farm and other properties with funds from outside the country and was involved with the development of the underground movement which used the Rivonia house as its base.[1] According to Joe Slovo she knew 'almost everything'.[2] Joe, on the High Command of Umkonto, was also a constant visitor to the farm but was not there on the day of the raid. He had been sent out of the country with JB Marks on a mission two months earlier.

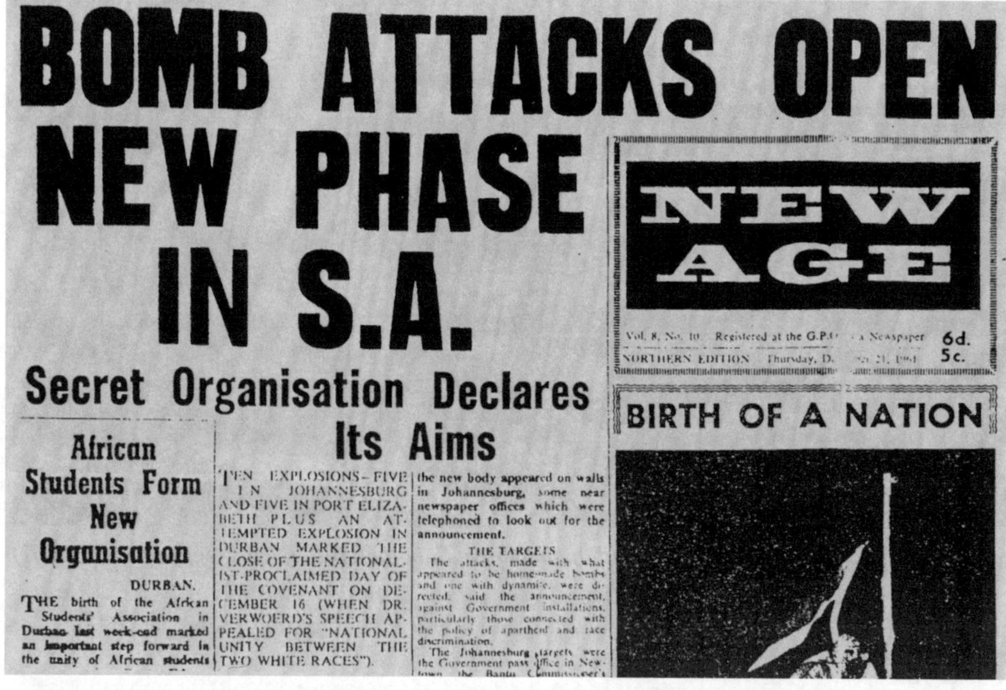

BOMB ATTACKS OPEN NEW PHASE IN S.A.

NEW AGE

Vol. 8, No. 10 Registered at the G.P.O. as a Newspaper 6d. 5c.
NORTHERN EDITION Thursday, D... 21, 1961

BIRTH OF A NATION

Secret Organisation Declares Its Aims

TEN EXPLOSIONS – FIVE IN JOHANNESBURG AND FIVE IN PORT ELIZABETH PLUS AN ATTEMPTED EXPLOSION IN DURBAN MARKED THE CLOSE OF THE NATIONALIST-PROCLAIMED DAY OF THE COVENANT ON DECEMBER 16 (WHEN DR. VERWOERD'S SPEECH APPEALED FOR "NATIONAL UNITY BETWEEN THE TWO WHITE RACES").

the new body appeared on walls in Johannesburg, some near newspaper offices which were telephoned to look out for the announcement.

THE TARGETS

The attacks, made with what appeared to be home-made bombs and one with dynamite, were directed, said the announcement, against Government installations, particularly those connected with the policy of apartheid and race discrimination.

The Johannesburg targets were the Government pass office in Newtown, the Bantu Commissioner's

African Students Form New Organisation

DURBAN.

THE birth of the African Students' Association in Durban last week-end marked an important step forward in the unity of African students

Umkonto we Sizwe opened its sabotage campaign with explosions across South Africa. (New Age, *December 21 1964)*

The Rivonia and other 'communist' trials that followed, which have been well documented elsewhere, were to decapitate the Congress movement so thoroughly that it was to be several decades before the state would again feel itself evenly remotely challenged by the liberation movement. The thoroughness with which the Special Branch was able to do decimate the movement, and the failure of armed resistance to detonate mass action, begs the question about the strategy and tactics of the Congress leaders of the post-Emergency period. [3]

The leadership in 1961, many banned and isolated, some in exile and others in jail, were faced with the almost impossible task of raising the majority of a nation from passive protest to open revolt. Time was short, the moment of transformation was considered to have arrived, and armed rebellion was seen as a way to 'bring the government to its senses' and to ignite a revolution. Within the Left after the Emergency a curious triumphalism prevailed. Despite the obvious willingness by the state to shoot down protesters and to imprison thousands of people opposed to its rule, Congress leaders read these as signs of a desperate administration on the brink of collapse and began to plan accordingly. Ruth was to write that the Nationalist leaders were 'frightened men in their shrivelled little hearts'.[4] When *New Age* reappeared the week after the restrictions were lifted, it carried the optimistic headline: 'Freedom is within our grasp.' The Emergency had ended, it said, but the real crisis of White Supremacy had only just begun:

> The oppressed peoples of South Africa are on the march, and not all the savagery of the Verwoerd government can prevent their ultimate victory. The Emergency proved one thing to all our peoples – THAT LIBERATION IS NEAR. There is no longer any question of whether freedom will come. It is only a question of when and how. [5]

But had freedom really been within their grasp? Their efforts produced no cracks in the ruling bloc. Their methods of popular organisation – exhortation and the promise of magical solutions – were appropriate to a different phase of resistance. And in the end, Congress leadership committed a cardinal political sin: they believed their own propaganda. The sabotage campaign, a triumph of spirit, was a failure of ideas. As a propagandist and journalist supporting the Congress movement, Ruth was central to the formulation and dissemination of these ideas. The failure symbolized by the Rivonia raid was to be her failure too.

The turn to violence

The view in *New Age* that freedom was within sight reflected a conviction within the Central Committee of the Party and elsewhere that South Africa was faced with a revolutionary situation. The flight of capital, coupled with white political hysteria and black anger were seen to be indicators of a government in trouble. Increasingly, the solution was seen to be in the detonation of mass action through armed opposition by groups of trained saboteurs. The idea of sabotage was not a new one in South Africa. It had been discussed during the Defiance Campaign in 1952 and was an ever-present issue among young African activists.[6] But in 1959 it was taken up by the intellectual Left. In an article in *Africa South* which (considering the non-violent stance of the treason trialists) was politically daring, editor Ronald Segal argued that change and revolution had become inseparable.

In a country in which 'revolt walks always in the shadow of massacre', he said, a clear analysis of the 'rapidly decomposing' government was necessary in order to understand the strategy of resistance:

> It can go on like this ... for a few years more. And then it can go on no longer.... It is temptingly easy to think of revolution in sudden terms, a storming and a surrender, lightening in the streets. But revolution is slow and persistent, a wearing away of resistance to the point of snap. Revolution is now.[7]

The article sparked off a heated debate in the journal. Julius Lewin argued that 'the present state of the Union was likely to go on 'almost indefinitely' and that revolution was out of the question.[8] Party theorist Michael Harmel disagreed:

> The Afro-Asian revolution is proving even more rapid and dynamic than the European-American; there can be few people today, outside Southern Africa, Alabama and Notting Hill who think that democracy and self-government are *slegs vir blankes* (for whites only).[9]

This revolution need not involve violence, he said, but 'we cannot tell what exact form the changes will take, how exactly or when they will come'.

From about this time, the leaderships of the Communist Party, the ANC, the PAC, Trotskyists and some liberals began to create an ideological climate in both their publications and their private meetings which included ideas of armed retaliation. In an article anticipating the Sharpeville crisis, old Party stalwart Eddy Roux warned in March 1959 that the spores of revolution had long been scattered and had germinated:

> The final swing over to non-acceptance may be sudden and dramatic and may be triggered off by some event, great or even trivial, which we at present cannot foresee.... Under such circumstances a government might attempt to rule by permanent martial law, but the strain of this would prove intolerable and inevitably concessions would have to be made, as in Kenya.[10]

These discussions were amplified by a sense that African independence was rolling towards the borders of South Africa. In December 1959 *New Age* reported that during the following year no less than eight African states would be freed from the colonial yoke.[11] And early in 1960 the British Prime Minister, Harold Macmillan, in a speech before Parliament in Cape Town, goaded the Nationalist Party by criticizing apartheid and proclaiming that 'winds of change' were sweeping through Africa.[12]

RIVONIA ACCUSED GET LIFE

Judge says it was treason

Vorster Murders "SPARK"

SPARK

WE SAY

GOODBYE

BUT WE'LL BE BACK

Farewell issue, March 28 1963.

In December 1960 the SACP held a national conference which instructed the Central Committee, of which Ruth was a member, to formulate a plan of action. The programme, which the conference adopted, called for 'economic sabotage as a first stage to guerrilla warfare.'[13] The Party's position was based on the view that the state was in retreat. Every display of state force simply confirmed the Party's view that the government was grasping at straws in an effort to reassert the control it had lost through a breakdown of the usual channels of coercion. Events which seemed to confirm this view was the panic buying of guns by whites, the enlargement of the police force, the temporary suspension of the pass

FREEDOM IS WITHIN OUR GRASP

Govt. Received Terrific Setback From Emergency

NEW AGE

Vol 6, No. 26. Registered at the G.P.O. as a Newspaper

NORTHERN EDITION . Thursday, September 8, 1960 6d.

From Our Political Correspondent

THE Emergency has ended—but the real crisis of White Supremacy has only just begun. The oppressed peoples of South Africa are on the march, and not all the savagery of the Verwoerd Government can prevent their ultimate victory.

The Emergency itself proved one thing to all our peoples—THAT LIBERATION IS NEAR.

There is no longer any question of whether freedom will come. It is only a question of when and how.

B.A.D. Minister de Wet Nel thundered at Bothaville last week: "I wish to make it very clear that the Bantu will never get political rights except in his own territory."

He predicted further that if South Africa did not become a republic and a multi-racial state developed, South Africa would return to the same state of barbarism as existed before the Voortrekkers.

De Wet Nel is whistling [illegible] to keep his spirits up. IN THE EYES OF THE MAJORITY OF THE PEOPLE OF SOUTH AFRICA, THE EMERGENCY ITSELF WAS A PIECE OF NATIONALIST BARBARISM, A CRIME FOR WHICH THEY WILL STILL HAVE TO PAY DEARLY.

Let us just remind ourselves of what the Emergency was all about.

How It Started

It started with peaceful, non-violent demonstrations by the African people against the pass laws. At Langa and Sharpeville these demonstrations were drowned in blood. Unarmed men, women and children were shot down by police bullets.

It was the wave of anger set off by these shootings in South Africa and the rest of the world that forced the Government to take refuge in a state of Emergency.

The people themselves showed no violence to the State. Their three-week stay-at-home in Cape Town was entirely peaceful. The great march of the 30,000 on Caledon Square police station was provoked by police brutality in the townships.

But the march itself was entirely peaceful. Those tens of thousands of people marched through the streets of Cape Town, assembled and dispersed without a single incident.

Violence did occur during those March events, but almost invariably it followed police interference with the people, not vice versa.

There was no rebellion or plot from the side of the people. Not all the interrogations of detainees in prison has produced the slightest shred of evidence to this effect.

Vicious Reprisals

Yet the Government resorted to the most vicious reprisals. In the first wave of arrests on March 30, most of the active political leaders of the people were thrown into prison. There was no warrant for their arrest, no charge was preferred, no bail or court appearance allowed.

For most people there was merely the 2 a.m. knock on the door, and they were dragged away from their families to spend months rotting in detention.

One week later there was the second wave of arrests—of named Communists, to lend colour to the Government allegation that a Communist plot was brewing. Many of those arrested in this second wave had been inactive politically for 15 years or more—nevertheless, their presence was required by the Special Branch dictators who ruled our country during those five months, so they were dragged willy-nilly from their homes and cast into prison despite all their protests.

(Continued on page 7)

5 Months Jail Could Not Get Them Down

Home they go at last, after 5 months in jail. Treason trialists Duma Nokwe and Nelson Mandela, held till the very end of the emergency.

Pondos Rebel Against Bantu Authorities

DURBAN.

PONDOLAND is a troubled area, an area of tension and unrest.

Noted for their cheerfulness and hospitality, the Pondos have changed almost overnight to a grim and determined people—determined to oppose their Chief, Manzolwandle Botha Sigcau, and his councillors who have accepted Bantu Authorities; determined never to accept Bantu Authorities at any price.

The history of the struggle against Bantu Authorities dates back to the latter part of 1957, when the Pondo people were first officially notified about the Act.

Meetings were held all over Pondoland by the Chief Magistrate and by Botha Sigcau. They attempted to persuade the Pondos to accept Bantu Authorities, but on each occasion the people rejected them.

In 1958, however, Botha Sigcau in conjunction with the Native Affairs Department organised a feast to which all the people were invited. They did not know that they were being called to give the impression that the Pondos had accepted what they had in fact rejected. The Minister of Native Affairs, Mr. De Wet Nel, announced at this "Indaba" that the Government had decided to implement Bantu Authorities in their area.

Events moved swiftly immediately following this announcement. Numerous tribesmen, interviewed by New Age, stated that bribery and corruption became the order of the day. Previously when tribesmen were entitled to land allotment, their allotment was pointed out to them by their Induna. Now Bantu Authorities often demanded varying sums between £10 and £18, they alleged.

Old age pensioners who because of their illiteracy could not produce birth certificates were charged a fee to be "introduced" to the Native Commissioner.

Whereas previously, groups of tribesmen were in charge of allocating grass for the purpose of roof thatching, now the people were asked to make their requests to the Chief in their area who demanded money before allowing tribesmen to cut grass for this purpose.

In some areas Chiefs have seized plantations which belong to the people and claimed them as their own.

Contrary to all Pondo custom and law, the Chief has granted himself a farm without consulting the people.

In the past tribesmen were issued with summonses personally if they were required to appear before their Chief on any charge. Since the introduction of Bantu Authorities, however, there are many cases where, the husband being away working in the city, the summons is served on the wife, the case heard against the husband in his absence and the cattle of the absent husband removed as a fine by the chief.

These are only a few of the many grievances of the people. There are very many more, far too

(Continued on page 6)

Important Notice To Subscribers

1. All subscriptions current at the time our paper was banned will be adjusted to ensure that all subscribers receive full value for their subscriptions.
2. Subscribers are requested to inform us immediately should they fail to receive their copies in good time.

After the state of emergency was lifted, New Age *predicted the government's demise. It was to stay in power for another 34 years. (*New Age, *September 4 1960)* laws and the economic crisis which the Sharpeville massacre had precipitated. There was also a strong sense that Pretoria would find few friendly governments to turn to for help in crushing the Congress Alliance.

Six months after the SACP conference, underground activists formed Umkonto we Sizwe, which geared its activity to the sabotage of economic and symbolic targets. Its formation was prompted, Mandela was later to claim in court, by a need to channel the rising anger of the masses away from random acts of terrorism. Also, by the early 1960s, official assaults on opponents of the state had steeped the whole society in an atmosphere of violence, blurring easy ideological distinctions.[14] Pressure was also coming from the formation of other sabotage groups – the National Committee of Liberation under Monty and Myrtle Berman (which was later to give birth to the African Resistance Movement), the Trotskyist Yi Chi Chan Club (later known as the National Liberation Front) under Neville Alexander, and POQO, the guerrilla wing of the PAC.[15] In his work on the period, Douglas Tilton has suggested that (given the prevailing mood within the black community, the fluidity of political affiliations after the banning of the ANC and PAC, and the emergence of other organisations better placed to capitalize on the growing spirit of militancy) ANC and SACP leaders faced no lack of evidence to fuel their fears that the traditional leadership of the Congresses might be undermined.[16] Even Chief Lutuli accepted the arguments behind Umkonto's formation and acquiesced to a decision to permit ANC members to become involved in its activities.[17] Ruth warned that if the government suppressed every peaceful protest with violence, 'then the time will come when they will be met with violence and terror. Such is the law of history.'[18] The signal for armed resistance, however, was to be the failure of the Republic Day strike. In October 1961 the Berman group planted the first bombs of the sabotage campaign. A new phase of struggle had begun. Its inception was to be grounded, not on strategic considerations, but upon a mythology. The nature of this mythology was based on several assumptions.

Help from beyond

An important leg of the armed resistance campaign was the belief that African de-colonisation was unstoppable. This growing mood of black independence was reinforced by articles in *New Age* about Mandela's clandestine six-month trip to the capitals of Africa. Vicariously, through the newspaper, readers met black leaders and traveled the lands of their spiritual ancestry.

During 1962 and 1963, there seemed to be an almost a magical belief in the inevitability of African independence, and this was nowhere more apparent in the writings of the Party's chief theorist, Michael Harmel, in the *African Communist*. Harmel was central to strategic planning in the Party and his ideas would reflect the thinking of most within the Party leadership at the time. For Harmel the winds of change seemed to blow with mechanical precision:

> The national liberation is sweeping on uninterruptedly to its completion with ever-increasing pace. Yesterday Nigeria, today Tanganyika, tomorrow Kenya.... It is difficult to keep pace with the speed and sweep of the transformation.[19]

A similar movement was happening in Latin America, he said, where (inspired by 'the glorious example of Cuba') her millions of poverty-stricken, oppressed people 'are being drawn into militant and determined struggle to break the chains of Yankee imperialism and its local agents, to win land and freedom'.

Connected to the idea of a rolling revolution from the north was the assumption that the Soviet Union would be an ever-present midwife to colonial transformation. Harmel noted that in South and Central America during the previous century a similar de-colonial movement had occurred but this had fallen prey to United States imperialism because it had been led by bourgeois nationalists. The current African and Asian revolutions, however, were taking place in the era inaugurated by the October Socialist Revolution whose main content was 'the transition, on a world scale, from capitalism to socialism'. The Soviet Union and other socialist countries, he said, were a formidable barrier against the plans of the imperialists to start new wars, either internationally or wars of colonial conquest. The 'fantastic progress and development of the socialist countries' together with the ideas of Communism and Marxism-Leninism had 'tremendous attractive force'. To an ever increasing degree, it was 'not the bourgeois nationalists but the working class and peasantry, led by Communist parties, which were providing the leadership and setting the pace in the national liberation revolution.'[20] Harmel was less than precise, however, about the exact nature of this support in the transformation process. While Moscow was able to provide some ideological and financial support to the Congress movement, the nature of the Cold War prevented anything more substantial.

Ruth was to be a key player in the generation of hope around African independence. As a political journalist she was both central to creating the climate of political euphoria after the Emergency and for planning a strategy in the light of those conditions which were seen to warrant it. This process was taking place in *New Age, Africa South* and other left-wing publications, but it was nowhere more apparent than in *Fighting Talk*. The journal had ceased publication during the Emergency and, when it resumed in August 1960, its focus was squarely on Africa. Although local articles filtered into the following editions, the new focus remained, and readers were treated to ideas and events which located South Africa in the broader canvas of revolution and transformation of the continent.[21] In June 1961, the month Mandela and other leaders met to plan sabotage, Ruth widened the debate to a retrospective on 'the presence of history'. In her introduction she promised to devote the journal to 'events and incidents (which) do not, in the main, appear in any of the standard history text-books.'[22] Mixing the historical work of local writers such as Joe Matthews, Lionel Forman, Norman Levy, Moses Kotane, Rusty Bernstein and Ben Turok with articles from around Africa, Ruth began to assemble the ideological building blocks of a new political strategy for the Left. *Fighting Talk*, she said, looks backward 'because history is a process of looking backward'. But its purpose was not to dramatise the past, it was rather 'to illuminate the present ... as a tribute to the men and women of all races (who are) bringing a new life and a new nation to birth before our eyes':

> Looking back along the long and trying road we have come, we are inspired with the knowledge that we are near the top of the hill, and within sight of freedom in our lifetime. We live in the presence of history.[23]

From that June edition to the journal's closure a year later *Fighting Talk* was to combine retrospective assessments with an attempt to link local struggles to the inevitability of African revolution. Ruth's writing and editing at this stage is a remarkable exercise in 'insider' journalism – she was now not merely reporting the passage of history but was

Pylons near Durban dynamited by Umkonto we Sizwe.

helping to make it. She commissioned articles tactically, and her editorial intention seems to have been to bring her readers to conclusions supportive of the secret decisions being arrived at by Congress leaders.

In a long and clearly-written article in the June edition of *Fighting Talk*, Joe Matthews traced the history of the ANC and the impact of Sharpeville on its activities. Norman Levy explored the influence of the Defiance Campaign on Congress unity and Lionel Forman looked at the lessons of armed insurrection learned in the 1922 strike:

> The strikers had only a few hundred rifles, but 1914-18 had made them no strangers to war and two soldiers were killed for each of the 39 strikers who lost their lives.... As a result of the strike the Smuts Government fell.[24]

Fatima Meer, assessing the Gandian tactics of passive resistance, concluded that:

> The Indians will not march again as Indians, not as long as hope exists for a South Africa march towards an integrated democracy, but, like all democrats, they will be found readily available for any onslaught on racialism.[25]

The November 1961 edition was a 'special issue on the independent states of Africa'. In it Rusty Bernstein, who by then was on the High Command of Umkonto, wrote an article on Albert Lutuli, casting the Nobel Peace Prize winner as the final broker between peace and violence. But he concluded with a warning:

> We are moving into new times. The old days of legal ANC organisation and campaigns have gone; the prospects of peaceful mass pressure exerting its will on the government have

© Mayibuye

The aftermath of the Sharpeville massacre

> been whittled down by the growing weight of military preparations which the government assembles against it. The menace of violence hangs heavy in the air.[26]

In February 1962 the journal focussed on 'the road to uhuru'. Writing about Tanganyika, 'Africa's newest state ... and the continent's most southern independent government,' Ruth said in an editorial:

> The African revolution has converged closer and closer on the last White-Supremacy states in the south.... Has Tanganyika's independence any meaning for South Africa? Conditions in the two countries differ vastly; yet an independence revolution in any one country in Africa has meaning for all.[27]

A few months later *Fighting Talk* focused on 'the front lines of the battle to free Africa', bringing readers news of liberation struggles in Algeria, Angola and Kenya. In the following edition Ruth wrote that the striving of the people for freedom was 'like an elemental force that cannot be thwarted' and through their superior numbers and 'the sympathy and support of Africa and the whole world' they would win their freedom[28] The final edition, in July 1962, celebrated Freedom Day on June 26 with another retrospective and a 'salute to free Algeria'.

The popular uprising

Another assumption made by the Johannesburg leadership of Umkonto, and perhaps the most problematic one, was that the masses in South Africa were in a revolutionary mood and that the Congress Alliance had the ability to lead them into open revolt. In 1962 Michael Harmel saw mass support for an anti-colonialist struggle as being almost an iron law of social development. Imperialists were not giving up their colonies in Africa, he said, they were being kicked out by the struggles of the colonial peoples themselves:

> They are being forced out by the triumphant march of world history, by the inexorable laws of social development.[29]

The following year a statement of the Central Committee of the Party, written in a style which suggests that it was penned by Harmel, developed this theme further. The great mass of people, it said, were determined to win their freedom, whatever the cost. However heavily armed, a minority could not prevail over the great majority of the people when this majority was organised, determined and clear in purpose. Every new act of tyranny would call forth revolutionary protest and mass resistance:

> The people will organise and fight back on every front – against pass laws, Bantustans and group areas, against starvation wages, against mass evictions, against police state terrorism. They will take bold local initiative against grievances: merging every local and partial struggle into a mighty river of people's insurrection that will sweep away minority *baaskap* and win people's rule in a free South Africa.[30]

If the government resisted, warned the statement, the sabotage would develop into a full-scale civil war, beginning with guerrilla operations and culminating in 'an armed insurrection of the whole oppressed people throughout the country'. It is difficult to sort our exhortation from analysis here, but in the light of Umkonto's actions one is forced to assume that the sabotage campaign was based on these type of assumptions. Even after the Rivonia raid, Harmel was still claiming that:

> The Nationalist juggernaut, top heavy with its crushing weight of military might, is crumbling and rotting at the base.... The steeled freedom-fighters of our country, whatever the cost in blood and sacrifice, will sent the rotten regime crashing to its foundations.[31]

Tom Karis and Gail Gerhart have written in their substantial documentation of the period that, looking back, it is difficult to appreciate the extent to which African leaders and other radical opponents of the government felt that the trend of events was in their favour.[32] It is also difficult to appreciate the reasons for this feeling.

Soon after the Emergency ended the International African Ministers' Federation called for the convening of an 'all-in' conference of apartheid opponents in order to plan the assault on state power and a continuation committee was elected to organise the conference for March 1961. The highlight of the March conference was the dramatic appearance of Nelson Mandela, whose bans had lapsed eleven days earlier. He was elected secretary of a National Action Council which was given the task of organising a country-wide stay-at-home to coincide with the proclamation of the Republic on May 31.

If the strike was a referendum on popular readiness for revolt, it was a poor basis for belief in the ability of a sabotage campaign to detonate revolution. Yet the failure of the strike was given as the reason for Umkonto's inception.

Shortly before the stay-at-home, new legislation was passed providing for detention without trial or bail for 12 days and in the run-up to the strike 10 000 Africans were arrested.[33]

© Mayibuye

Residents of Sharpeville township, Vereeniging, return to pick up the dead.

Military and civilian forces were brought to a state of readiness, police loudspeakers and pamphlets attacked African leaders and helicopters with searchlights flew low over townships looking for gatherings. Saracen armoured cars patrolled the streets.

The strike was partially successful on the first day, particularly in Port Elizabeth. But on the second day Mandela conceded the failure of the stay-at-home and called it off, describing it as 'not the national success I had hoped for.'[34] But he told foreign journalists that the massive state mobilisation had been 'a striking testimony to our own strength and a measure of the weakness of the government'[35] And in his speech from the Rivonia dock he was to date the decision to employ violence to the outcome of the 1961 strike. 'If peaceful protests like these are to be put down by the mobilisation of the army and the police,' he said, 'then the people might be forced to use other methods of struggle.[36]

If the strike proved that the ANC could no longer sustain protest activities, later events were to show that it was also a poor vehicle for covert activity. During the 1950s, emphasis in the ANC had been on meetings rather than on organisation building, and this was to leave the Congress extremely vulnerable to state repression. The implementation of a closed, hierarchical structure like the M-Plan on a traditionally open movement had been an onerous task for local branches even under the best conditions.[37] After the banning of the ANC, these difficulties were multiplied, and only Port Elizabeth ever successfully got the plan working reliably.[38]

The ANC was patently not an insurgent organisation and had dissociated itself publicly and in court from anything that could be construed as insurgency. Its members were often ill-disciplined (if its annual reports are anything to go by) and its branches not only acted on their own but also seldom informed higher bodies of their activities.[39] Its treasury was often empty and its only national link was often the weekly reports of *New Age*. In addition, the ANCs strong commitment to non-violence had been the backbone of the movement's policy for so long, and revered leaders like Lutuli and ZK Matthews were known to avidly support this line. Many Congress members also backed non-violence out of moral or religious convictions. That there was black anger over Sharpeville, Langa, Pondoland and township conditions was undeniable, but to assume that this represented large numbers of people who could be brought over to armed revolution was questionable. The ANC was, in the early 1960s, hardly an organisation capable of igniting an armed insurrection.

Banning worsened these problems. Its members were among the most independent-minded of people, volatile and talkative. Security was therefore a constant problem and police spies easily penetrated the cell structures. Bruno Mtolo, an Umkonto member who was to turn state witness in the Rivonia trial, was to cite the appalling lack of security precautions as one of his reasons for turning against Umkonto.[40] Joe Slovo was later to concede that important mistakes were made, particularly around security, organisational structure and the neglect of 'mass work.'[41]

Because of the conditions of the time, the decision to form Umkonto was also made by a relatively small group of leaders in the Johannesburg area. With the benefit of hindsight, some activists have portrayed the decision as elitist and unilateral. A former Umkonto technician is quoted by Douglas Tilton as saying:

> When it came to Umkonto, we were actually tricked into the notion of armed struggle. It was taken by relatively few people at the top. It was totally undemocratic, make no mistake about it ... I didn't think it was possible ... but there were all those gods in Jo'burg ... they had their names in books and things like that. And they must have had some sort of secret that we didn't have. They didn't have any secrets. All they had was a lot of grandiose views, and quite juvenile ones at that.[42]

Tom Lodge agrees there is little evidence to suggest that the underground work of the ANC occupied much of the attention of the Congress/SACP leadership. 'Little was done to co-ordinate the activity of Umkonto cells and ANC branches so the latter could play a significant support role.[43] Former Umkonto member Ben Turok was even more bluntly critical:

> The sabotage campaign failed on the main count – it did not raise the level of action of the masses themselves. Although it seems that the masses supported and even welcomed the resort to force, they could find no way of joining in.... They were left on the threshold, frustrated bystanders of a battle being waged in their name.[44]

Perhaps the greatest tactical error of Umkonto's leadership, however, was to read popular inclinations to revolt in very localised and specific conditions as a signal that mass insurrection was possible without too much attention being given to organisational agitation. The womens' pass campaign, the potato boycott, squatter resistance, fights against Bantu Education, bus boycotts and rural uprisings seemed to provide a compelling argument that the people had revolution in their hearts and that the state was in crisis. Howard Barrel has argued that although Umkonto strategists paid lip-service to mobilisation through political means, in practice they downplayed this in favour of mobilisation through militarism:

THIS IS THE POLICE STATE

Sabotage Bill Aims To Stamp Out All Opposition

New Age, *May 17 1962.*

The idea took root .. .that political and military struggles could somehow be separated from each other and conducted in parallel. This was to remain MK's greatest problem in the years to come.[45]

The guerrilla orthodoxy

Another factor in calculations about the possibility of revolution was the sense that the peasantry could be relied on to support an insurrection. Practical evidence of this was available from the uprisings, within a short space of time, in Witzieshoek, Marico, Zeerust, Sekhukhuneland, Zululand and Pondoland. This intersected with strategic thinking in the early 1960s which was centered largely upon a rurally-based guerrilla war – what Colin Bundy has called the 'guerrilla orthodoxy.'[46] At the time, considerable store was being set by the Cuban experience and the victory of the guerrillas in the Sierra Maestra, as well as guerrilla successes in Algeria and Vietnam. Operation Mayibuye, the strategic document central to the Rivonia trial, envisaged external training of a core group of guerrillas who would then return in secret, recruit local platoons, set up rural base areas and then engage the state's forces.[47] There was also a theoretical link between Colonialism of a Special Type (CST) and guerrilla struggle. The theory, which specified South African society as a colonial one, naturally directed the search for models towards anti-colonial struggles. It also directed attention towards '*focismo*', the Guevarist notion that pockets of armed struggle would detonate broader, mass involvement.[48]

The local possibilities for this form of struggle were worked out during the early 1960s by *New Age* journalist Govan Mbeki and assisted by Ruth. Mbeki was an intellectual activist and was well-versed in writings about peasant militancy elsewhere in the world. But he was also a man of the soil with deep roots in rural Transkei. Peasants, he was to write, had 'always been consistent in thinking along military lines.'[49] He was to recall a meeting of peasants during the Defiance Campaign when an aged man voiced his criticism of the passivity of the campaign:

> With typically down-to-earth peasant logic he argued that Africans had lost the Wars of Dispossession because the weapons they had used did not match those of the Boers and British. According to him, unless that imbalance was corrected there was no point in embarking on a defiance of unjust laws. Any talk of non-violence in conducting such a campaign was merely to tickle the Boers.[50]

The book he was writing on the peasantry was being put together in fits and starts on rough tables in the kitchens of several African homes in Port Elizabeth townships:

> Its progress was frequently interrupted by police raids, when the sheets of paper had to be hurriedly secreted, or moved away from where their writer lived and worked, for his safe-keeping.[51]

A first draft of the book, later to be called *The peasant's revolt*, was almost complete in 1962 when Mbeki was arrested and held in prison for five months on a charge of making explosives. But the work continued – on rolls of toilet paper smuggled out of the cell. A typist was found who, Ruth wrote, 'pored over the faint pencil writing on thin paper, by candlelight and in the privacy of her township room.'[52] After his acquittal, Mbeki continued the work, some of it from his hiding place at Lilliesleaf Farm after he was drafted by the ANC National Executive to direct Congress campaigns from underground.

Clarion Price Now 3d.

The Clarion

NORTHERN THURSDAY, AUGUST 7th, 1952 PRICE 3d.

GOVERNMENT PREPARING FOR GRAND CONSPIRACY TRIAL

MANY IRREGULARITIES IN C.I.D. "FISHING" RAIDS

JOHANNESBURG.

IN the biggest police raids ever conducted on political organisations, squads of detectives of the Special (Political) branch of the C.I.D. last week swooped on the offices and homes of men and women connected with the Defiance of Unjust Laws campaign in all main centres of the Union.

Dozens of bundles of papers were examined and carried away. Many people were subjected to a personal search, and the police in some centres did not scruple to act illegally and search people and organisations for whom they had no warrant.

THE AIM APPEARS TO BE TO FIND EVIDENCE FOR A GREAT CONSPIRACY TRIAL. FOR THE GOVERNMENT IS DESPERATELY ANXIOUS TO CUT OFF THE HEAD OF THE EVER-GROWING DEFIANCE CAMPAIGN.

Supported by a guard of uniformed police, detectives broke into the office of the Transvaal Indian Congress during last week's raid. A panel in the door was smashed open to the jeers and barracking of a crowd of Africans and Indians who witnessed the scene.

It will be remembered the Smuts Government's great sedition trial against the leaders of the Communist Party, launched after the African mineworkers' strike of 1946, failed miserably when the prosecution was unable even to frame an indictment.

ALSO FAILED

Recent efforts by the Government to drag all possible Non-European leaders into a big trial, and then to put them out of the way in prison for long enough to cripple the defiance movement, have also failed.

S.A.I.C. secretary Y. Cachalia and African leader N. Mandela were arrested with the June 26 batch of resisters who defied the curfew regulations and for a month the police tried to work up a serious charge under the Riotous Assemblies' Act. In the end all were brought to court on the curfew charge and after the batch leader had been acquitted on a technicality all, including Cachalia and Mandela, were released.

An Evaton case against Mr. Cachalia and five others has also fizzled out.

Yet despite the warning of all these blunders, the police have once again been ordered to scratch around among the private and official papers of Non-European leaders, and to dig up at all cost some evidence that could be used to convict them of treason, sedition, Communism, incitement to public violence or what have you.

The raid included not only the large centres such as Johannesburg, Pretoria, Cape Town, Durban, East London and Port Elizabeth, but also such places as Vryburg, Dundee, Kimberley, Mafeking, Ladysmith, Worcester, Pietermaritzburg, Hermanus, Thaba 'Nchu and Middledrift.

IRREGULARITIES

The raiding squads let little stand in their way. Although no search warrant mentioned "Spark", the youth newspaper which shares an office with the Transvaal Indian Congress, its records were scrutinised and a number removed to police headquarters.

Congress members in the vicinity of the offices during the raid had their persons searched; personal letters were confiscated and one man even had his personal cheque book taken from him.

Finding the home of an African congressman in Jabavu [illegible]ted, as no one was home, detectives obtained a key from the office of the location superintendent, and carried out their search.

Raiding the flat of the president of the Transvaal Indian Youth Congress, Mr. A. Kathrada, who was not present when they arrived, the detectives searched the pockets of a young Chinese student, who lodges in the flat but is a member of none of the organisations raided. When these detectives found the doors and drawers in the room of another student lodger in the same flat locked, they used their own keys to open up, and searched through all his clothes and possessions. "It is our country: we can do what we like", was the retort of the detective during this raid.

CLARION OFFICE RAIDED

DURBAN.

Many irregularities were committed by members of the C.I.D. when they raided Durban offices and homes last week.

The C.I.D. carried out raids on the offices of the Natal Indian Congress and the African National Congress and raided the homes and places of work of officials of both the organisations.

(*Continued on page 4*)

The Clarion Must Change Its Name

Dear Readers,

The Department of the Interior has informed us that it is unable to register our newspaper because another paper called the Clarion, although no longer in publication, is already registered with the Department.

The Department has invited us to submit another name, and we propose to announce this new name in our next issue. Readers who wish to send in suggestions must do so by telegram before noon on Monday, August 11. Our Address is,

6 BARRACK ST.,
CAPE TOWN.

DEFIANCE STARTS IN CAPE TOWN

Ten Break Railway Apartheid

CAPE TOWN.

THE first Cape Town batch of resisters in the defiance of unjust laws campaign went into action on Sunday afternoon, when, under the leadership of Mr. Thomas Esitang, a group of 10 Africans defied railway apartheid by entering a "Europeans only" waiting room.

Wearing their A.N.C. armbands, the resisters marched in formation through the station and, entering the waiting room, sat on the benches there. In a matter of minutes, railway police ordered them out. When they refused to go, the police ordered the Europeans who were in the waiting room to go out and closed the doors.

A minute later they escorted the resisters out of the waiting room to the charge office. Witnessing the incident, people on the station gave the "Afrika" salute, and the "Afrika" cry.

When the resisters appeared in court on Monday, the prosecutor told the magistrate: "This is part of the passive resistance movement".

The hearing was adjourned till August 15. No application was made for bail. Going down to the police cells, the resisters gave the "Afrika" salute.

Port Elizabeth's biggest batch of resisters went into action on Friday, when 179 resisters defied railway apartheid.

In East London, over 700 resisters are in jail for defying unjust laws.

The police took action against the spectators who came to court when the batch of 302 resisters came up for trial last week. The police arrested 133 African men and women for "loitering" or shouting in a public street. They were subsequently fined £1 or 10 days hard labour.

In Worcester, 8 railway apartheid defiers, 6 men and 2 women, were each fined £5 or 20 days last week. None of the fines were paid.

The cases of the other Worcester railway apartheid defiers will be heard tomorrow (Friday August 8).

The Clarion, *August 7 1952.*

At this point Ruth was called on to help. Mbeki asked her to reconcile the two versions and edit the final form into a book. He and Ruth began the slow process of assembling chapters and, because the second version had been written completely from memory, checking references. Both she and Mbeki had been banned from compiling any material for publication:

> We had more time to work on the Bantustan book, but it all had to be written under cover, both to secure the manuscript and to guard ourselves against arrest, prosecution and imprisonment for writing in defiance of the government ban.[53]

They were also unable to meet openly to discuss the book, because both were banned from communicating with other banned people. The terrible tension of this time is impossible to recapture. Under the probing eyes and ears of the state they were planning an insurrection, and were writing the history of that which underpinned it on pain of imprisonment. But with one chapter left to finish, Mbeki was arrested in a raid on the Rivonia house and he was not to emerge from a prison cell again for nearly three decades.[54] Ideas within the book had a powerful effect on Congress leadership. In the final chapter he was to write before being detained, Mbeki argued that the solidity and endurance of peasant struggles gave them a long-range superiority over urban ones:

> The struggles of the peasants start from smaller beginnings (than urban ones), build up to a crescendo over a much longer time, are capable of pinning down large government forces, and are maintained at comparatively lower cost.[55]

A rural revolt which took place in Pondoland, particularly, succeeded by example, he said, in 'accomplishing what discussion had failed to do in a generation', convince the leadership of the importance of the peasants in the reserves to the national struggle:

> The leaders realised at last that a struggle based on the Reserves had a much greater capacity to absorb the shocks of government repression and was therefore capable of being sustained for a much longer time than a struggle based on the urban locations.[56]

Writing in *New Age*, and later in *The peasant's revolt*, Mbeki was to communicate two indelible images – the heroic daring of the Mountain Committee which planned the uprising and the spontaneous combustibility of the peasantry:

> The march through Bizana, when an old man carrying a black flag at half-mast led a procession of 5 000 peasants without any experience of mass forms of pressure, must be one of the greatest feats of organisational ability that the liberation movement and the oppressed people of this country have so far accomplished.[57]

These ideas, developed and worked on by two members of the Party's Central Committee, one of whom was on the High Command of Umkonto, were to have a considerable impact on strategic planning within Umkonto. It was classic guerrilla thinking. But, Colin Bundy was later to ask, was South Africa classic guerrilla territory?

> Was it not industrialising too rapidly to make sense of a rural strategy; was not its peasantry too shrunken or marginalised to provide the social base for guerrilla forces... [58]?

Writing in *New Age* towards the end of 1961, Mbeki commented that 'Bantu Authorities marked the end of the road in the people's endurance of Nationalist oppression in the reserves. Signs are not lacking that the workers in the cities have also reached the end of their tether.'[59] Assumptions such as these were developed further by other members of the Congress movement and, taken together, these ideas built a conviction among the Umkonto leadership that the moment was right to launch their final assault on apartheid. They were to be proved devastatingly wrong.

The crumbling white state

Within the Party, therefore, political propagandists were failing to understand the implications of their own propaganda. They also seemed to have overlooked their own theory of internal colonialism. As early as 1959, Joe Matthews had pointed out that in the typical colonial situation, members of the foreign imperialist nation did not settle in large numbers in the colony. Much of the actual administration of the country, with its coercive machinery in the army, the police and the courts, was manned by the indigenous people:

> Naturally as the clamour for independence grows louder, the imperialist power finds a vast section of the machinery of rule in its colony becoming increasingly unreliable.[60]

In South Africa, on the other hand, the foreigners had settled in large numbers and had made the country their home. Because of this, he said, it was possible to establish a complete monopoly of government, including all the machinery of coercion, in the hands of the settlers. 'This appears to place the South African ruling class in an unassailable position as long as the Whites are united.'[61]

From the vantage point of 1970, Ruth was to rake those 'typical colonial situations', almost bitterly, with her pen. In her book *Barrel of a gun* – written in an attempt to understand the failure of African independence upon which her group had invested so much hope – she was to write:

> In the phase of de-colonisation, power was transferred, through virtually unchanged institutions of government, to largely hand-picked heirs. These heirs are the new ruling groups of Africa.... Spoilt children of yesterday's colonialism and of today's governments, they organise the loot of whatever national resources exist.[62]

At the time, however, Matthews' warning seems to have gone unheeded. Umkonto strategy was not derived so much from an accurate reappraisal of the strength and indivisibility of white South Africa as it successfully contained the African challenge, but rather from an illusion of that group's vulnerability.[63] In their attempts to generate a climate of rebellion, Congress leaders seem not to have seriously contemplated the willingness of the settler minority to murder, maim, torture and literally drench the soil of Africa in blood to retain their hold on the South. Lodge comments that having talked of fascism for a decade and more, the Congress movements were nevertheless caught by surprise when the police behaved like fascists.[64]

Far from dividing the white group, Umkonto sabotage acted to cement the otherwise divided elements of white society, demonise dissenters and force agreement on legislation which obliterated the rule of law. Legislation passed between 1960 and 1964 was among the most oppressive in the world. The government, virtually unopposed, gave itself the right to ban organisations, indemnify policemen for the Sharpeville killings, detain without bail or trial indefinitely for the purposes of interrogation, hang people found guilty of sabotage and jail people who refused to give evidence in court. Commenting on the Sabotage Act, an ANC statement said that 'every claim to human dignity, every objection to injustice and every form of protest, however peaceful, is a crime punishable by death.'[65]

The hoped-for Western disapproval of the Pretoria government was also short-lived. As some forms of capital moved out after Sharpeville, other forms replaced it as the West showed its willingness to trade with apartheid. By 1962 the British-backed Imperial Chemical Industries had contributed technical know-how and £10-million to the building of new armaments factories in South Africa.[66] Pretoria was also receiving from Britain imports of military aircraft, warships and armoured cars. The United States indicated that it was prepared to supply military transporter aircraft and France furnished Mirage jet fighters. Belgium granted Verwoerd license rights to manufacture F.N. assault rifles and West Germany offered 63 troop carriers. In 1963 the French armament firm, La Carbone, began setting up a factory in South Africa to make missile equipment.[67]

This was not the sort of support the Soviet Union could possibly supply to Umkonto, and in the end brute force was to carry the day. In late 1960 Prime Minister Verwoerd had declared that the government would be 'as unyielding as walls of granite' in dealing with its attacks on apartheid.[68] In 1961, Brian Bunting had countered this, writing that 'never since the Nationalist Government came to power have conditions been more propitious for an all-out assault on the citadel of apartheid.[69] They were worlds apart. Less than two years later Rivonia was raided and dreams of assault collided with Verwoerd's granite wall.

Time of tension

By the time of the Rivonia raid, the strain on Ruth of clandestine living must have been considerable. The Congress leadership were well known to the Security Police and were being harassed day and night. Ruth had been under a banning order since her return from South West Africa but she retained her high-profile job on *New Age*. Her writing skills were also constantly being called on in the drafting of propaganda pamphlets and articles. In addition she was attending cell meetings of the Party and was involved in moves to broaden the ANCs M-plan. According to Walter Sisulu she was, during that period:

> One of the most dynamic personalities in the movement.... She was moving in the circles of the ANC, the Indian Congress, the trade unions and as editor of *New Age* in Johannesburg she was central to nearly every thing.[70]

But many of her activities were necessarily secret – even to her family. As her daughter, Robyn, remembers: 'None of us (children) ever knew what was going on. It was at times very fearful – a huge amount of insecurity. It was considered better not to tell the children anything.'[71] The mood of the time was powerfully captured in a book about the period by a close friend of Ruth's, Hilda Bernstein:

> It is as though our ability to acknowledge what is happening to a whole nation is like the possession of a fundamental truth that others refuse to recognise. We feel like Mrs Moor in *A passage to India*, who has visited the caves and holds the knowledge of truth and evil. The truth is clear; it is heard all the time in the terrible, sad boom of the caves, echoing inside our ears, reverberating within the hard-boned skull, full of foreboding. The reverberations, if you succumb to them, can bring madness and death.[72]

In the 1960s, the old fraternity of the Left began to thin out as its members left the country, went underground or were sent to jail. In white Johannesburg, the SACOD activists became increasingly isolated, shunned by their neighbours who were scared of the constant police attention, leading double lives of ultra-respectability and clandestine night meetings. 'Everything in South Africa is like a mirror with two sides', wrote Bernstein. 'One side reflects what you know best; the other is a dark pool into which you must peer constantly to realise the strange and changing scenes it reflects'.

By early 1963 *Fighting Talk* had finally gone beyond the boundaries of state tolerance. In the penultimate edition Ruth wrote what amounted to a farewell editorial in the face of the 'Censorship and Sabotage Bills'. *Fighting Talk*, she said, 'has always been ... the voice of the fighters with weapons or with words.'[73] The journal was 'under sentence of death', and after 20 years of unbroken publication it faced 'the severest test' of its history. 'Our editor, our contributors and staff', she wrote, 'face punishment imprisonment and fines – for almost every word they dare to write.' Her scorn, however, was reserved for 'the Press magnates, united in the 'Press baron's association' – the Newspaper Press Union':

> The proprietors of the English dailies have ... fastened the gag upon themselves in exchange for their own immunity and censorship. They have traded their freedom to write as they please and as they think for the right to be excluded from the Censorship Bill; they have retired from the battle before it is half fought, and in doing so they have thrown all other publications to the Nazi wolves and many more. This in not surrender; it is treachery. [74]

For 20 years *Fighting Talk* had tried to live up to its name and it did not intend to 'change our colours now, nor haul them from the masthead':

> We will carry on the fight for as long as we are able. And if, in the future, they bring such force against us that we can no longer continue, then we shall go down. But at least we will go down as we have lived, fighting.[75]

There came a time, Ruth said, when talk was not enough – deeds and action were needed. But an element of doubt had crept in. Using 'we' in the broadest sense, she wrote:

> We will try to match our actions ... to our talk over these many years. We are confident that this way lies victory for our ideas. ... Perhaps not now. Perhaps not for some time to come. But in the end it must be so. ... In the end of ends, it is not the government of this country which will crush the people; but the people who will crush the government.[76]

But the life of Congress publications inside South Africa was clearly over. SACOD was banned in September 1962 and two months later *New Age* was proscribed. Then in

After the shooting at Sharpeville, corpses littered the ground, two in the foreground, others near the ambulances in the background.

MASS SLAUGHTER BY POLICE

Bloody Reprisals Against Anti-Pass Demonstrators

Vol. 6, No. 23. Registered at the G.P.O. as a Newspaper 6d.
NORTHERN EDITION Thursday, March 24, 1960

News and Pictures By
Joe Gqabi

JOHANNESBURG.

THE FIRST DAY OF THE PAN AFRICANIST CAMPAIGN AGAINST PASSES BROUGHT FRIGHTFUL REPRISALS FROM THE POLICE IN THE AREAS WHERE THE PEOPLE CAME OUT EN MASSE IN ANSWER TO THE CALL TO STAY HOME FROM WORK AND HAND IN THEIR PASSES AT THE POLICE STATION.

At Sharpeville Township and at Langa a total of 70 were killed and several hundreds wounded.

Sharpeville Township (Vereeniging) saw one of the ugliest bloodbaths ever. At one stage we counted 34 bodies (including those of at least eight women) lying about the ground in front of the Sharpeville police station as though on a battleground.

They seemed all dead, many with bullet head wounds. Some of the injured were shot in the back, some had more than one bullet wound.

Vereeniging Hospital was deluged with ambulance loads of wounded who had to be treated on the lawns outside the hospital, so many were there crowding the casualty room and wards.

The police firing was without any warning, some told New Age. Saracens were on the scene and some said the firing had been from them, though we have not confirmed this and the police denied it.

This murderous shooting was done from behind a wire fence into the centre of the crowds standing about the police station.

THE POLICE SAID, AS JUSTIFICATION, THAT THEY WERE BEING STONED AND FIRED UPON, BUT ON THEIR OWN ADMISSION ONLY THREE POLICE WERE INJURED ON MONDAY.

A police official pointed to scratched paintwork as evidence of stoning. Their attitude seemed to be: "Demonstrate or throw stones at even our Saracens and we will teach you a lesson."

PITIFUL SCENES

There were tragically pitiful scenes after the shooting. Women wailed and sobbed over the dead

(Continued on page 4)

LANGA'S NIGHT OF TERROR

From Fred Carneson and
Alex La Guma

CAPE TOWN.

AT least five people were killed and an unknown number injured during a night of clashes between the people and the police at Langa last Monday.

The trouble started when police arrived at a peaceful mass meeting called by the Pan Africanists at the New Flats at 6 p.m. The people were unarmed, as they had been specially asked not to bring any weapons. About 6,000 people were present at the meeting.

As all meetings had been banned under the Riotous Assemblies Act, the police tried to break up the meeting. Members of the crowd told New Age they heard no order to disperse, and they deny emphatically police reports that firing first came from the crowd.

ATTACK LAUNCHED

The police launched an attack with batons and shortly afterwards started firing on the crowd.

As darkness fell, the incensed people hit back. Police were stoned and buildings were set on fire. The labour bureau, administrative offices, library, market hall and schools were gutted.

Saracens and armoured cars were operating in the township throughout the night, and bursts of firing were heard. Army units were called in to help the police.

On Tuesday morning a tense atmosphere persisted in the township. The police were going from door to door ordering the people to work and beating those who refused. There were reports of people being lined up and herded to the station like cattle.

We ourselves saw a man whose face was streaming with blood after being beaten by a policeman.

Sporadic bursts of shooting continued to take place.

Soldiers in the township made no secret of the fact that they were ready to "shoot kaffirs." We heard a number of disgusting remarks from them.

One soldier said to us as we went

(Continued on page 4)

ANC STATEMENT ON AFRICANIST CAMPAIGN

JOHANNESBURG.

An ANC statement issued on Monday night expressed severe shock at brutal police violence which serves only to incense and inflame the people. "Could not methods be used to disperse crowds without killing and maiming people", asks the statement.

The authorities are keen to use any excuse to shoot fear into the hearts of the people, concludes the ANC.

The ANC says its national anti-pass campaign is aimed to prepare the people for a powerful, united national action which alone can destroy the pass law system which is at the root of oppression. This cannot be done by ill-defined forms of action, less still by action in isolated areas.

While the ANC cannot oppose any people's spontaneous demonstrations, it is convinced that ill-organised, ill-defined action can cause harm and reduce the struggle's effectiveness. The ANC feels it cannot call on or encourage people to participate in the ill defined PAC campaign.

The injured crowded on the lawn in front of the Vereeniging hospital.

New Age *reports the Sharpeville massacre. (March 24 1960)*

March 1963, in terms of the 'gagging clause' of the new Sabotage Act, both *Spark* and *Fighting Talk* were forced to cease publication when all their writers, including Ruth, were prevented from writing for any publication whatsoever.

Joe was overseas and was clearly unable to return to the country. And Ruth was out of work. In an attempt to train for a new profession which did not fall foul of her banning order she enrolled for a course on librarianship at the University of the Witwatersrand and took some temporary work with Jack Leviton, an attorney. A letter about her to the university from Julius Lewin may have reflected her feeling of vulnerability at the time. 'She hoped', he said, 'to qualify and to get an appointment enabling her to support her three young children.'[77] But she knew time was running out. Her phone conversations were being bugged, her mail was being tampered with and she was being followed: 'About a fortnight after the Rivonia arrests I'd seen two policemen in a car watching me ... something was happening.'[78] On Friday August 9 1963 Ruth was working in the main university library. She's been followed the day before but didn't think the Special Branch would come to the university:

> When I came out of the main building there were these two blokes standing, and though I'd never seen them they looked like what we took to be caricatures of Special Branch men. They're very tall, very gangly, very badly fitting suits with baggy trousers and big feet. They didn't say an awful lot:
> We are from the police.
> Yes, I know.
> Come with us please. Colonel Klindt wants to see you.
> Am I under arrest?
> Yes.
> What law?
> Ninety days....[79]

They led her straight to her Citroen, which seemed to unnerve her: 'I hadn't seen them following me in the morning and there are hundreds of cars parked there in rows ... this is where you get that creepy feeling that they've got mechanical contrivances that you can't see'. A house search followed, during which the police turned up an 'illegal' copy of *Fighting Talk* which had been banned for possession. Finally, at about six in the afternoon they reached the police station.

> The largest of my escorts carried my suitcase into the 'Europeans Only' entrance. As he reached the charge office doorway he looked upwards. 'Bye-bye, blue sky,' he said, and chuckled at his joke.[80]

Notes

1 Interview with Walter Sisulu, Sept.1992.

2 Interview with Joe Slovo, 1992.

3 See particularly Karis & Gerhart, Vol.3 (1977), Lodge (1983), Bernstein (1967), Feit (1971), Mtolo (1966), Mbeki (1992), Benson (1966), Bunting (1975), Mitchison (1973).

4 *Fighting Talk* June 1962, p2.

5 *New Age*, September 8, 1960.

6 Mbeki: *The struggle for liberation*, 1992, p88.

7 *Africa South* Vol.4 No.1, Oct/Dec 1959, p5.

8 Ibid, Vol.3. No.2 Jan/March 1959, p12

9 Ibid, p13.

10 *Africa South*, Vol.3, No.2, Jan/March 1959, p19.

11 *New Age* December 24, 1959.

12 Karis & Gerhart, Vol. 3, p330.

13 Tilton: *The road to sabotage*, p18.

14 Ibid, p16.

15 Interview with Walter Susulu, September 1992.

16 Tilton, op cit, p23.

17 Ibid, p28.

18 *Fighting Talk* June 1961, p3.

19 *African Communist* (AC) 8, January 1962, p13.

20 Quotations from *African Communist* 8, January 1962, pp13-15.

21 Local articles were often prudently not signed, or authors were given names like 'R Hamble' or 'Economist'.

22 *Fighting Talk* June 1961, p2.

23 Ibid, p3.

24 Ibid, p13.

25 Ibid, p7.

26 *Fighting Talk* November 1961.

27 Ibid, February 1962, p2.

28 Ibid, June 1962, p3.

29 Ibid, p15.

30 The revolutionary way out. In *African Communist*, Vol.2. No.3 Apr/June 1963. p18.

31 South Africa is at war. In *African Communist* Vol.2 No.4 July/Sept 1963 p22.

32 Karis, & Gerhart, Vol.3. p359.

33 Ibid. p363.

34 FIbid, p364.

35 Benson, 1966, p236.

36 Karis & Gerhart, op cit, p364.

37 The M-Plan, devised by Mandela in the mid-1950s but never properly implemented, was a system of closed, secret cells linking ordinary members through area and regional cells to a High Command.

38 See Tilton, op cit, p15.

39 Feit, 1971, p97.

40 See Mtolo, 1966. Umkonto was set up separately from the ANC. But by 1963 ANC and Umkonto cells were virtually indistinguishable from each other.

41 Lodge, op cit, p239.

42 Tilton, op cit, p27. The informant is not named but is probably Rowley Arenstein.

43 Lodge 1983, p237.

44 Ibid, p239 and Bundy: Alliance, exile and armed struggle, the SACP from 1961 to 1991. In *The History of the SACP*, University of Cape Town, 1991, p56.

45 Barrel: *MK:The ANC's armed struggle*, quoted in Bundy, op cit, p57.

46 Bundy, op cit, p56.

47 Ibid.

48 Ibid. Strategy and tactics, the policy document of the ANC's Morogoro conference in 1969, endorsed guerrilla war but distanced itself from '*facismo'*.

49 Mbeki: *The struggle for liberation*, 1992, p88.

50 Ibid, p88.

51 Ruth's preface to *Peasants' revolt*, 1964, p9.

52 Ibid.

53 Ibid, p11.

54 The manuscript of the book was later smuggled out of the country, and the final chapter was written by Ruth in London in late 1964. Her excellent editing skills were to produce two more similar partnerships: Mandela's *No easy walk to freedom* which Ruth researched and edited, and *Not Yet Uhuru*, which she worked on with Oginda Odinga and for which she was deported from Kenya.

55 Mbeki, 1973, p131.

56 Ibid, p130.

57 Ibid, p133.

58 Bundy, op cit, p56.

59 *New Age* December 7, 1961.

60 Revolution: Further reflections. In *Africa South* Vol.3 No.4 July/Sept 1959, p15.

61 Ibid.

62 First, 1970 p11 & 28.

63 See Lodge, op cit, p225.

64 Lodge op cit, p239.

65 FANC statement from Dar es Salaam, quoted in Kotane, 1975, p271.

66 Harmel in *African Communist* Vol.2 No.4 1963, p14.

67 Ibid.

68 Karis & Gerhart, op cit, p360.

69 *Africa South* Vol.5 No.4 Jul/Sept 1961, p66.

70 Sisulu, Ibid.

71 Interview with Robyn Slovo, August 1992.

72 Bernstein, 1967, pxxi.

73 *Fighting Talk* June 1962, p4.

74 Ibid, p5.

75 Ibid.

76 Ibid.

77 Letter from J Lewin to Prof ID Macrone dated August 20 1963 relating to her need to study during detention. Wits University archives.

78 Tape transcription of interview with Jack Gold of the BBC, n.d.

79 Ibid and First, 1965, p11.

80 First, 1965, p13.

11

The Struggle for Silence

In prison you see only the moves of the enemy.
Prison is the hardest place to fight a battle – Ruth First

Ruth, acting in the BBC film, Ninety Days, *about her detention.*
*(*Radio Times, *June 16 1966)*

There was a supreme irony about Ruth's detention. As a journalist, her job had been to obtain information and disseminate it to others. When she was detained she knew, on her own admission, 'a helluva lot, really an awful lot' about the underground movement.[1] She desperately needed to find out what her interrogators knew about Rivonia – the security leak had been eating at the leadership – and to do this she resolved to use her time in detention and her skills as a journalist. But she had to do this without giving her captors any information at all, for to talk would be a betrayal of her comrades. In her book *117 Days* she was to capture this dilemma:

> What did they know? Had someone talked? Would their questions give me any clue? How could I parry the interrogation sessions and find out what I wanted to know, without giving them the impression that I was resolutely determined to tell them nothing? I had to find a way not to answer questions, but without saying explicitly to my interrogators, 'I won't tell you anything.'[2]

This problem was to lead her, after months of solitary confinement amounting to torture, into waters so deep they would threaten her very existence. In prison three things which had made her a good journalist – her political convictions, her confidence in soliciting information and her human vulnerability – were to conspire against her. Her captors were no longer the bumbling policemen of the 1950s. They were both perceptive and cruel. 'We're not holding you', they told her. 'You're holding yourself. You have the key to your release. Answer our questions, tell us all we want to know, and you will turn the key in the door. Make a statement and in no time you will be back with your children.'[3]

Ruth's first two months of detention, punctuated by routine questions from the Security Branch, did not dent her resolve to give away absolutely nothing. Her impression was that the police were leaving her to 'stew' and she decided to make the best of it by being as difficult as possible:

> I'm fighting fit ... I was a lot of bother to them. I really had the whip hand all the way through ... right through the first two months in Marshall Square (police cells). I was a lot of trouble. You know, agitating away in the cells for hot water and making moans and complaints, and really I was very buoyant.[4]

But her interrogators began to pile on the pressure and, in the isolation, fears began to intrude. 'She thinks she's clever' said one. 'She's just trying to probe ... what were you doing at Rivonia?' And then: 'You're an obstinate woman, Mrs Slovo. But remember this. Everyone cracks sooner or later. It's our job to find the cracking point. We'll find yours.'[5] Shortly after this interrogation session she discovered two bits of information which 'froze my limbs'. One was that someone who was at a highly confidential meeting which Ruth had attended was talking to the police, and the other was that the police were investigating both her father and her mother. This prospect unnerved her. 'How would she live in the grime and filth of a cell', she worried. 'The children had lost Joe in June, me at the beginning of August ... my father might well be in hiding. I had left the children with heartache but I had the comfort of my mother as a substitute. If she was taken, they would be abandoned.'[6]

Her parents and her children were being pulled into the line of fire. Shortly afterwards Ruth's brother, Ronnie, was detained. She began to worry, sleep eluded her and she found difficulty disentangling her fears from her facts. 'Hardest of all, I would struggle not to think about the children.... I needed all my concentration to handle my own situation ... but of course I could not stop thinking about them.'[7] On the children's first visit, Shaun was tearful and on subsequent occasions contact always took place with a prison official in the room and were always strained.[8] The tension was having an effect on the family as the knock-on effect of white fear around the Rivonia leadership collided with the Slovo children. At school and in their neighbourhood the girls were being treated like social outcasts. 'There was this vacuum around us', Robyn remembered. 'We just stopped fitting in at that point. We were very public. It was like walking into an environment in which everybody was talking about you or looking or pointing.'[9] Other children gave the Slovo girls a wide berth and the strain of social isolation began to build up at school. In frustration Robyn punched her hand through a school window, for which she was shown no understanding and was punished by having to stand out in the back yard. Gillian, who was in another classroom, remembered hearing the sound of breaking glass and said she knew it was Robyn, who was at that stage being extremely disruptive. 'I was very angry', Robyn later remembered. 'I spent a lot of time standing in the courtyard. People knew, the school knew, but nobody ever discussed it with me. Nobody ever said was I okay or how was Ruth or had I seen my mother lately.'[10]

After two months Ruth was moved to Pretoria Central Prison, clean, sterile and cold. 'Pretoria shone of bright polished steel', she was to write. 'And I grew increasingly subdued. My imprisonment was an abandonment in protracted time.... I felt alien and excluded.... I was bereft of human contact and exchange. No echoes reached me. I was suspended in limbo, unknowing, unreached'. In the Bible, her only reading matter, she memorised a passage which resonated with her predicament:

> A fool's mouth is his destruction
> And his lips the snare of his soul.[11]

The deathly stillness of Pretoria was eating away at her nerves and she was having problems with an ulcer. She began craving conversation, 'even with a detective'. Seven days before the end of the first spell of 90 days she found she was talking to herself, trying not to build up hopes of release. Then a bombshell dropped. During a visit from her family, her mother whispered to her: 'B-'s talking ... something has gone terribly wrong'. 'B' was probably Bruno Mtolo, the Natal member of the High Command who was often at Rivonia. There was little he did not know about Umkonto. 'If B was talking', wrote Ruth, 'that put an end to my prospects of release' and introduced a critical change to her position. 'I felt as though I had been poised on a high diving board above a stretch of water, when someone had suddenly pushed me. And in the hurtle downwards the water below had dried up.'[12] As she struggled to control her panic, she was told that she was to be released. But as she walked down the street looking for a telephone she was re-arrested for another period of 90 days. Back in her cell again, she was overcome by a wave of self-pity. 'If only I could have stood outside myself; if only I had not believed that I would always have the strength to do whatever I wanted and that emotional shock was something separate from and

*Ruth, with Gillian (left) and Robyn, stepping into the aircraft which would take them to a new life. (*Sunday Times *March 15 1964)*

*Ruth with her daughter, Robyn, shortly before leaving South Africa. (*The Star, *n.d.)*

Letter bomb kills ANC VIP Ruth First

Argus 18/8/82

MAPUTO. — Ruth First, a prominent member of the African nationalist movement and a well-known researcher, was killed here yesterday by a letter bomb.

She was the wife of ANC and South African Communist Party leader Joe Slovo, who narrowly escaped a South African raid on ANC bases in Maputo 18 months ago.

She was director of research at the Centre for African Studies at the Eduardo Mondlane University in Maputo.

At about 4.30 pm local time while she was in her office at the centre, she opened a letter which exploded, killing her instantly.

BLAME

Three other people in the office were slightly injured. They are Aquino de Braganca, director of the centre, Bridget O'Laughlin, a professor at the centre, and Paulo Jordan, a South African sociologist who was at the centre for a conference which ended last week.

In a statement last night, the Mozambican government blamed the "South African secret service" for the bomb.

Mr Jordan had attended last week's Unesco-sponsored conference on

Ruth First

or attempted murder of leading members and representatives of the African National Congress of South Africa in Zimbabwe, Swaziland, Lesotho, Zambia and England," said the agency.

DETAINEE

It said a spokesman for Mozambican security commented: "The attack is similar in nature to others carried out in the region and which were proved to be the work of the South African secret services."

To many she was the intellectual power behind the South African liberation movement — to others Ruth First was just a notorious communist, just Joe Slovo's wife.

But the attractive dark-haired woman was respected internationally as a writer of rare perception.

Professor First, 59, was arrested for high treason, together with more than 100 other South Africans, in December 1956 though the charge against her was dropped in 1958 after the withdrawal of the faulty indictment.

In 1962, while Transvaal editor of New Age, which was subsequently banned and also of the banned magazine Spark, she was restricted under the Suppression of Communism Act to the magisterial area of Johannesburg for five years.

In 1963 she was arrested by security police in the main hall of the Wits University library. Six policemen then searched her Roosevelt Park home for two and a half hours.

She was later detained, without being brought to trial, for 117 days. After serving 90 days she was released. Once outside the then Marshall Square police station she was re-arrested.

PERMISSION

Report of Ruth's murder in The Argus, *August 1982.*

subordinate to my reason.... I was lonely, I was anxious, I longed for human company.'[13] She had been floating in suspense for 90 days, hovering in indeterminate doom, and she felt she had to force a counter-move from the Security Branch. She had to provoke events to move. When SB detective Nel next asked if she would make a statement she said she would. But at The Greys, the Security Branch headquarters, she received a shock. This was not to be a question and answer session. No questions were to be asked – she would talk and they would write. 'Start at the beginning', they said. 'Omit nothing'.

Ruth tried desperately to tell the story of her life and political involvement without giving the detectives anything she thought they did not know, but in her emotional condition this was an impossible mental task. She had decided from the outset to play out a small measure of rope, but she suddenly realised she was winding it fast around herself. Her journalistic skills had deserted her:

> There was no time to wriggle, to fabricate, to gauge reaction, to probe, to find out anything for myself. I was breaking down my own resistance. It was madness for me to think I could protect myself in a session like this, in any session with them. I had no idea what they knew, what contradictory information they had wrenched from someone else. They were giving nothing away; they were already becoming too experienced for that.[14]

One of her interrogators, Swanepoel, raged at her: 'I know you Communists by now.... And I've learned that they have to be put up against a wall and squeezed, pushed and squeezed, into a corner. Then they change, and talk'. This bombardment at the end of a gruelling session 'split my bamboozlement wide open and it dropped from my head like a broken husk.'[15] Shortly after this session, Ruth was granted a visit from her mother. Given the circumstances, Tilly said what was probably the last thing Ruth needed to hear: 'We're depending on you'.

She felt beaten. She was wide open to blackmail and she felt the blackmailer was herself. Having made a statement she was now fighting to salvage her self respect. Her greatest fear was that her willingness to make a statement would be communicated to her comrades. 'I was in a state of collapse not for fear of what would happen to me physically ... but for the gnawing ugly fear that they could destroy me among the people whose understanding and succour I most needed, and that once they had done that I would have nothing left to live for.'[16] She had not signed the statement, but it hung over her like doom. 'I had never been afflicted by a fatalism quite so deep', she wrote in *117 Days*. She was persecuted by a sense of dishonour and the feeling that it would be impossible to explain such an act to her friends:

> Joe had always told me that my weakness was my extreme susceptibility to acceptance and fear of rejection and criticism: were these the qualities that propelled me to make a statement? Or was it again my arrogance, my conceit ... that I was different and could try my own way? My air of confidence had always been useful in keeping others from knowing how easily assailed and self-consciously vulnerable I was; it had worked many a time, but it could do nothing for me now.[17]

She concluded that there was only one way out, 'the truest indication that I had not let the Security Branch have it all their own way'. Because of her insomnia her doctor had left some sleeping pills with her. After writing a note to Joe apologizing for her cowardice, she swallowed the lot.

The dose, however, had not been sufficient to kill her. When she came around she was in a state of shock, and her cries and weeping echoed through the police station. When she asked her doctor, who was summoned, whether she was heading for a crack-up he told her: 'You've already had one'.

Her recovery was gradual but the act of taking the pills shocked away any further intention of doing so. However, her world had turned inside out – detention had become a security and the outside world a place of uncertainty. Had she betrayed her comrades by making a statement or hadn't she? She was in no emotional state to know. She resolved to 'kill the part of me that yearned for other lives, and resign myself to continued imprisonment as the price for the life I had chosen myself.[18] When one of her interrogators, Colonel Viktor, continued to pursue her, she welcomed his conversations but gave him little in return. When Viktor came with her release orders Ruth refused to believe him. But this time it was genuine. 'We left Marshal Square eventually and by the time I got home it was lunch time, though Viktor had brought his release order early that morning. When they left me at my own house at last I was convinced that it was not the end, that they would come again.'[19] When she arrived home Tilly and the girls were horrified at her condition. Robyn's memory of the moment was one of massive disappointment. In her perception, Ruth had come out in time for her tenth birthday, which was the day before. But 'she looked absolutely terrible. I was horrified at the state of her and the fact that she seemed to have lost power and was ... insubstantial.'[20] Ruth was unable to cope with demanding social contact and the girls were sent on holiday to Port Alfred with Hilda Bernstein. She began the slow recovery with the help of close friends like the playwrite Barney Simon and Moira Forajz. According to Barney: 'She was so vulnerable, one just kept her company'.

Ruth, determined to get herself together, immediately applied to write supplementary examinations in librarianship. And there were still political duties. When Joe appealed to her from London to get herself and the children to England, she admonished him: 'I don't want to be indecently hasty for reasons you will understand. Rushing ahead oblivious to a local consideration will be sad and misunderstood.'[21] These 'local considerations' were the tottering underground, and Joe commented that 'I still blush at the fact that it was she, who had just been through so much, who had to remind me.'[22]

But her time in South Africa had clearly run out. The decision to leave was greeted with delight by the girls, who couldn't wait to leave the city which seemed to have turned against them. Robyn remembers being 'absolutely delighted. ... I just wanted to get out of here as quickly as possible. I felt like I didn't have any friends, which I didn't.' As a small, but in white terms a cynical, gesture her classmates gave her a black Zulu doll as a farewell present. 'I smashed it on the way home'. But for Ruth the leaving was harder. On the day of departure she penned a brief note to Sadie Forman:

> My dear Sadie,
> Have to say goodbye. Wretched! But must make the best of it. Will try to. Love to you and all.

By then Ruth had regained her strength, and with her passion for lists and organisation the departure happened quickly. At Jan Smuts Airport, on March 14 1964, she stepped off of South African soil for the last time.

REFUGEE FATHER FLEES TO DAR

MR. Julius First, well-known Johannesburg furniture manufacturer and father of two 90-day detainees — Mrs. Ruth Slovo and Mr. Ronnie First, arrived in Dar es Salaam from Mbeya by air yesterday afternoon. Four other South African refugees were in the same plane. They are Mrs. E. Anderson, Mr. A. Kasrils, Mr. M Molefe and Mr. A. Bennie.

Meanwhile, Dr. Kenneth Abrahams, the coloured physician who was returned to Bechuanaland by the South African Government early last month after claiming he was kidnapped by South African police, was reported from Francistown to be on his way by air to Mbeya.

MR. FIRST

When Mr. First spoke to the *Tanganyika Standard* yesterday he said he was puzzled as to why the South African police wanted him and why a warrant for his arrest had been issued.

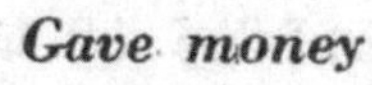

Gave money

Recently the Security Branch of the South African police issued a photograph of Mr. First with an appeal to any member of the public who saw him to telephone the police.

The 68-year-old semi-retired businessman said that he was not listed as a Communist, did not belong to any political party and had not been issued with a detention order. He had, at one

(Continued in Page 3 Col. 4)

Ronnie, his son, had never had anything at all to do with politics. There was absolutely no reason for his arrest.

Mr. First said that the detainees under the 90-day detention law suffered greatly from mental cruelty and this could not be dissociated from the physical, although the South African authorities had said that no detainees were physically punished. Detainees were kept in solitary confinement

New route

The report from Francistown on Dr. Abraham said that he and his wife, Ottilie, left there by lorry last Sunday with 24 other South African refugees.

Mr. Bally, of Tim-Air Charters was ferrying the group three at a time through a new "escape corridor" where Bechuanaland adjoins Northern Rhodesia over a distance of a few hundred yards.

- TANGANYIKA STANDARD

DAR ES SALAAM 17-10-1963

Tanganyika Standard, *Dar es Salaam, October 17, 1963.*

SUNDAY TIMES, JOHANNESBURG, MARCH 15, 1964 5

Ruth Slovo and her children quit S. Africa for good

By MARGARET SMITH

MRS. RUTH SLOVO, former treason trialist and 90-day detainee, left Jan Smuts Airport, Johannesburg, for Europe last night on an exit permit. This means she will not be allowed to return to South Africa.

Mrs. Slovo was arrested in August last year and held for 117 days in solitary confinement at Marshall Square, Johannesburg, and in Pretoria Central Jail.

She left last night with her two younger daughters, Gillian, 12, and Robyn, 10. The third daughter, Shawn, aged 14, left South Africa earlier this week by ship.

A number of Security Branch policemen were present at the airport when she left.

Friends said the family was going to London to join Mr. Joe Slovo, the Johannesburg advocate who escaped from South Africa in June last year. They said that Mrs. Slovo had not wanted to leave South Africa permanently. But her application for a passport, was refused and an exit permit was granted a few days ago.

"The various bans and restrictions imposed on Mrs. Slovo made it impossible for her to continue living in South Africa," a friend said yesterday.

Ruth Slovo, a journalist and author, was forbidden to write and barred from entering premises connected with printing or publishing or to assist in any way with the dissemination of news. Nothing she said could be quoted and she could not write for overseas publications.

Mrs. Slovo was formerly Johannesburg editor of New Age and later, when this newspaper was banned, of Spark. The prohibition of its entire staff from having anything to do with newspapers forced its closure.

When she could no longer work as a journalist, Mrs. Slovo started a post-graduate course in librarianship. It was while she was working at the library of the University of the Witwatersrand in August last year that she was arrested and detained under the 90-day law.

At the end of 90 days, she was taken from her cell and told that she was free.

Rearrested

Ruth Slovo then walked out of Marshall Square police station on to the pavement outside. She was looking in her handbag for a tickey to make a telephone call to her children when she was rearrested.

While she was under detention, a warrant was issued for the arrest of her father, 70-year-old Mr. Julius First—described by the police as "South Africa's most wanted political figure." Despite watches at the borders, Mr. First escaped and is now overseas.

Ruth First's brother, Ronnie, was also arrested under the 90-day law and held in solitary confinement for three weeks. At the end of this time police told him they did not believe that he was involved in suspicious political activities.

MRS. RUTH SLOVO, former 90-day detainee, left South Africa last night on an exit permit.

Sunday Times, *March 15 1964.*

Notes

1 Interview with Jack Gold of the BBC, Ruth First Collection, ICS, London. She told Gould that she took out a paragraph in her book, *117 Days*, in which she listed her involvement because she thought it would 'give something away'. She also knew beforehand about the closely-guarded plans concerning the escape from prison of Harold Wolpe, Arthur Goldreich, Jassat Moolla and Mosie Moolla.

2 First, 1965 p14.

3 Ibid, p83.

4 Gould, op cit.

5 First, 1965 p54.

6 Ibid, 1965 p55.

7 Ibid. p57.

8 Many years later, when her daughter Robyn asked her why, during the visits, she hadn't said: 'I miss you', she replied that she couldn't allow herself to, because if she had verbalized 'one small piece of being frightened or missing her family or feeling scared that she would never see us again she would have been engulfed by it'. Interview with Robyn Slovo, 1992.

9 Ibid.

10 Ibid.

11 First 1965 op cit, p65.

12 Ibid,. p107 and notes on writing *117 Days* (First Collection).

13 Notes ibid, p113.

14 *117 Days* ibid, p122.

15 Ibid, 1965 p123.

16 Ibid, p128.

17 Ibid, p130.

18 Ibid, p138.

19 Ibid, p143.

20 Robyn, op cit.

21 Joe Slovo's introduction to the 1988 edition of *117 Days*, p6.

22 Ibid.

12

Postscript

A farewell published by an ad hoc memorial committee, University of Cape Town, 1982.

After arriving in London, Ruth was burdened by two defeats – of the liberation movement and of what she perceived as her own in detention. She set about dealing with these in the way she knew best – writing. Her first exploration in this direction was the hardest; to write about herself. She was urged to do this by Joe, by Ronald Segal who was now an editor at Penguin Books, and by other friends who saw her need to heal the scars of detention. So in a remarkably short time, secluded mostly in the flat of her friend Cecil Williams, she sketched out and wrote *117 Days*. The task was especially hard for Ruth, private person that she was. Well able to write about others, her tentativeness about her own abilities as a writer of more than journalism assailed her. In a later edition of the book, Joe was to write that 'she was moved to go ahead in the hope that the narrative would help focus world attention on the plight of the growing number of victims of the regime's physical and mental torture-machine.'[1] But the book also had another function. Looking back to a year before, she wrote: 'I had been reeling towards a precipice and I had stopped myself at the edge. I had not tbeen too late to beat them back. I had undermined my own resistance, yet I had not after all succumbed. In the depth of my agony I had won.'[2]

Later, in an interview with Jack Gould of the BBC in preparation for a film about *117 Days* in which Ruth acted herself, she told Gould: 'I can see now, guilt was irrational'. The scars had begun to heal.

Her second assault on the problems of defeat was to produce a book very different from *117 Days* but as powerful. After finishing her work on detention and guiding into print Govan Mbeki's *The Peasants' Revolt* and Nelson Mandela's *No Easy Walk*, Ruth began to look at the failure of independence struggles in Africa. Between 1964 and 1968 she traveled the new African states studying military coups. The resulting book, *The Barrel of a Gun*, was essentially about the seizure of power by arms. This was not to be a book about South Africa, but for her comrades in that struggle it was both a lesson and a warning. It was also clearly a continuation of the focus on Africa she had begun in *Fighting Talk* after the Sharpeville Emergency.

In it she analyzed the claim of mass parties to mobilize the people for socialism – and found them wanting. Coups were the result of the 'failure of politics'. She wrote: 'There has been eloquent, inexhaustible talk about politics, side by side with the gaping poverty of political thought.... Mostly it is about politicking, rarely about politics. Politicians are men who compete with one another for power, not men who use power to confront their country's problems.'[3] But her work on the failure of African independence was not to make her cynical, nor to blunt her efforts to win freedom for South Africa. Political theorist Ralph Milliband was to write of her work:

> She was the least 'utopian' of revolutionaries; but she was not in the least 'disillusioned'; she never gave the slightest hint of doubt about the justice of her cause or about the urgent need to strive for its advancement. She deplored the shortcomings, stupidities and crimes of her own side. But this never dimmed her sense that there was a struggle to be fought against the monstrous tyranny that is South Africa ... . Beyond all disappointments and setbacks, it was (the) sense of the reality of oppression which moved her.[4]

By the time *The Barrel of a Gun* was published, Ruth had established her reputation as a skilled writer of books: the days of weekly journalism were behind her. More books followed: *South West Africa: Travesty of Trust* (with Ronald Segal), *Libya: The elusive revolution* and a co-edited book, *The South African Connection: Western investment in apartheid.* Her final works, for which she received international acclaim, were the beautifully-crafted biography of Olive Schreiner which she wrote with Anne Scott and *The Mozambican Miner: A study in the export of labour.*

In Britain, she taught first at Durham University, then in 1977 she took up a key post as Professor and Research Director of The Centre for African Studies at the Eduardo Mondlane University in Mozambique. After organising a successful UNESCO conference at the Centre in August 1982, she was in her office with colleague Pallo Jordan opening mail when a letter bomb exploded in her hands. Pallo was injured but the blast killed Ruth instantly. 'They' had come again.

In a police bar in Pretoria two years later, Captain Dirk Coetzee, commander of a Death Squad, told *Rapport* reporter Jaques Pauw that after the killing, superspy Craig Williamson had told Coetzee: 'We got First'. The plan had been hatched at the police-owned farm Daisy, next to Vlakplaas, the base of Section C1 counter insurgency force. The unit assigned to do the job was Section A of the Security Police under Brigadier Piet Goosen, the man who had interrogated black consciousness leader Steve Biko. On this farm, Goosen and his colleagues manufactured the bomb and placed it in an envelope, stolen five years previously from the offices of the United Nations High Commission for Refugees in Swaziland, and posted it.[5]

After the bomb exploded, Coetzee said he remembered it was a joyous occasion for the police. 'The men drank beer and brandy and coke and patted each other on the back. All agreed they had dealt the enemy a terriffic blow.'[6] Shortly afterwards *The Star*, quoting an 'anonymous' Western diplomatic source (which turned out to be Williamson), wrote that Joe Slovo had killed Ruth to solve a marriage problem. Joe sued for defamation and was awarded £125 000 by a British court, but *The Star's* lawyers claimed they were not required to accept British jurisdiction and refused to pay.

In a memorial service for Ruth, Ronald Segal recalled the brilliance and honesty of her writing:

> She had the crucial qualities of a good author. She had the sweep and the closeness of vision to see all the necessary pieces that make up the design of the whole. She never succumbed to the temptation, so strong when there is so much space to fill, of using words for how they sound rather than for what they mean. She had that rare ability to recreate – in a short phrase or two – a face, a gesture, a smell, a mood. She might write, though not often, an untidy sentence. She never wrote a lazy or a phony one.[7]

The bomb, he said, was the apartheid government's final act of censorship.

Notes

1 First, 1965, p5.

2 Ibid, p138.

3 First, 1970, p9.

4 Milliband, quoted in G Williams: *Ruth First: A tribute*. Ruth First Collection.

5 This information is from Jacques Pauw and made public at the Ruth First Colloquium in Cape Town in 1992 and reprinted as The future beyond darkness in *Democracy in Action* Vol.6, No.6, October 1992.

6 Ibid.

7 Segal: Memorial speech, op cit.

Bibliography

A

African National Congress: Unity in Action: A photographic history of the ANC, South Africa, 1912-1982(ANC, London, 1982).

Ali, T: *The Stalinist legacy*. (Pelican, Harmondsworth, 1984).

B

Barthes, R: *Image Music Text*. (Fontana Press, London, 1987 ed.).

Barthes, R: *Mythologies*. (Plaldin, London, 1973).

Benson, M: *A far cry: The making of a South African* (Penguin, London, 1989).

Benson, M: *The African patriots: The story of the African National Congress of South Africa* (Faber, London, 1963).

Benson, M: *The struggle for a birthright* (IDAF, London, 1985).

Berger, J: *The success and failure of Picasso* (Penguin, Harmonsdworth, 1965).

Bernstein, H: *The world that was ours*. (Heinemann, London, 1967).

Bernstein, J: 'Media active: the politics of progressive media production and State control in South Africa, the case of *The Guardian*, 1937-52.' Honours thesis, UCT 1988.

Bloom, H: *Episode*. (Collins, London, 1956).

Bohmer, EW: Left-*radical movements in South Africa and Namibia, 1900-81* (SA Library, Cape Town, 1986).

Boyd-Barrett, O: *The International news agencies* (Constable, London, 1980).

Bozzoli, B: *Women of Phokeng: Consciousness, life strategy and migrancy in South Africa, 1900 – 1983* (Heinemann, Portsmouth, 1991).

Brokensha, M and R Knowles: *The fourth of July raids*. (Simondium, Cape Town, 1965).

Bundy, C: *The history of the South African Communist Party* (UCT Extra-Mural Studies 1991).

Bunting B: *Moses Kotane, South African revolutionary*. (Inkululeko Publications, London, 1975).

Bunting, B: *The rise of the South African reich* (IDAF, London, 1986 ed.).

Burns, C: A *historical study of the Friends of the Soviet Union and South African Peace Council* (Honours thesis, University of the Witwatersrand, 1987).

C

Carlson, J: *No neutral ground* (Thomas Cromwell, New York, 1973).

Chapman, M: *The* Drum *decade*.(University of Natal Press, Pietermaritzburg, 1989).

Claudin, F: *The communist movement: From Comintern to Cominform* (Part 1&2). (Monthly Review Press, New York, 1975 ed.).

Clingman, SR: *The novels of Nadine Gordimer*. (Ravan Press, Johannesburg, 1986).

Cohe, S & J Young: *The manufacture of news: Deviance, social problems & the mass media* (Constable, London, 1973).

Cope, RK: Comrade *Bill: The life and times of WH Andrews, workers' leader*. (Stewart Publishers, Cape Town, 1943).

Cranfield, GA: *The press and society: From Caxton to Northcliffe* (Longman, London, 1978).

Crwys-Williams, J: *South African despatches: Two centuries of the best in South African journalism* (Ashanti, Johannesburg, 1989).

D

Davenport, TRH: *South Africa: A modern history* (London, Macmillan, 1977).

Davies, R: *Capital, state and white labour in South Africa, 1900-1960: an historical materialist analysis of class formation and class relations* (Harvester, Brighton, 1973).

De Kiewiet, CW: *The history of South Africa* (Oxford University Press, London, ed. 1942).

Dubb, A: 'Jewish South Africans: A sociological view of the Johannesburg community.' (ISER Occasional Paper 21, Rhodes University, Grahamstown 1977).

Dunstan, J: *Alexandra, I love you: A record of seventy years* (Future marketing, Johannesburg, 1983).

E

Ellis, S & T Sechaba: *Comrades against apartheid: The ANC and the SACP in exile* (James Curry, London, 1992).

Everatt, D: *Politics of nonracialism: White opposition to apartheid, 1945-1960*, PhD thesis, Oxford, 1990.

F

Fairclough, N: *Language and power* (Longman, Harlow, 1989).

Feit, E: *African opposition in South Africa, the failure of passive resistance* (Hoover Institution, Stanford, 1967).

Feit, E: *Urban revolt in South Africa 1960-1964* (Northwestern University Press 1971).

First, R & A Scott: *Olive Schreiner*. (Andre Deutsch, London, 1980).

First, R: *117 Days* (Bloomsbury, London, 1988 ed.).

First, R: *South West Africa* (Penguin, Harmondsworth, 1963).

First, R: *The barrel of a gun* (Allen Lane/Penguin, London 1970).

First, R: *Black gold: The Mozambican Miner, proletarian and peasant* (Harvester Press, Sussex, 1983).

First, R: *Libya, the elusive revolution* (Afrikana Publishing, New York ,1974).

Fiske, J: *Introduction to communication studies* (Methuen, London, 1982).

Forman, S & A Odendaal: *A trumpet from the housetops* (David Philip, Cape Town, 1992).

Fowler, R: *Language in the news: Discourse and ideology in the press* (Routledge, London, 1991).

Frederikse, J: *The unbreakable thread: non-racialism in South Africa* (Indiana University Press, Bloomington, 1990.

G

Gilomee, H & L Schlemmer: *Up against the fences: Poverty, Passes and privilege in South Africa* (David Philip, Cape Town, 1985).

H

Halliday, M: *Language as social semiotic*. (Edward Arnold, London, 1978).

Hansard (various).

Hartley, J: *Understanding news*. (Methuen, London, 1982).

Hachten W, and Giffard, C: *Total Onslaught: The South African Press under attack*. (University of Wisconsin Press Wisconsin, 1984).

Harris, R (ed).: *The Political economy of Africa* (Massachusetts, 1975).

Harrison, S: *Poor Men's Guardians*. (Camelot Press, London, 1974).

Harrison, WH: *Memoires of a socialist in South Africa*. (Cape Town, 1948).

Herrman, L: *A history of the Jews in South Africa*. (SA Jewish Board of Deputies, Johannesburg, 1935).

Hirson, B: *Yours for the union: Class and community struggles in South Africa*. (Witwatersrand University Press, Johannesburg, 1989).

Hofmeyer, JH: *South Africa* (Ernest Benn, London, 1931).

Houghten, DH: *The Tomlinson report: A summary of the findings and recommendations in the Tomlinson Commission report* (SAIRR, Johannesburg, 1956).

J

Johns, S: *The history of the CPSA*. PhD thesis.

Johnstone, FA: Class*, race and gold: A study of class relations and racial discrimination in South Africa* (Rouledge, London, 1976).

Joseph, H: *Tomorrow's sun* (Hutchinson, London, 1966).

Joseph, H: *Side by side* (Zed, London, 1986).

Joseph, H: *If this be treason*. (Private MS).

K

Karis, T & GM Carter: *From protest to challenge: A documentary history of African politics in South Africa 1882 - 1964*, Volumes 1-4. (Hoover Institution Press, Stanford, 1977).

Klein M: *New directions in psycho-analysis* (Marsfield, London, 1955).

Klinghoffer, AJ: *Soviet perspectives on African socialism*. (Fairleigh Dickinson University Press, Rutherford, 1969).

Kress, G: *Linguistic process in sociocultural practice* (OUP, Oxford, 1989).

Krut, R: *Building a home and a community: Jews in Johannesburg 1866-1914* (Doctoral thesis, SOAS, London 1985).

L

la Hasse, P: *Brewers, beerhalls and boycotts: A history of liquor in South* Africa (Ravan, Johannesburg, 1988).

Lacey, M: *Working for Boroko: The origins of a coercive labour system in South Africa* (Ravan, Johannesburg, 1981).

Lenin, N: *Left-wing communism – an infantile disorder*. (CPGB, 1920).

Lerumo, A: *Fifty fighting years: The South African Communist Party 1921-1971*. (Inkululeko Publications, London, 1980ed.).

Leschinsky, J: *Rakishok Memorial Book* (Johannesburg 1952).

Letsoalo, E: *Land reform in South Africa*. (Skotaville, Johannesburg, 1987).

Lewsen, P: *Voices of protest: From segregation to apartheid 1938-1948*. (AD Donker, Craighall, 1988).

Lipton, M: *Capitalism & apartheid: South Africa 1910-1986*. (David Philip, Cape Town, 1985).

Lodge, T: *Black politics in South Africa since 1945*. (Ravan Press, Johannesburg, 1983).

Luckhardt, K & B Wall: *Organize or starve! The history of SACTU* (Lawrence & Wishart, London, 1980).

Luthuli, A: *Let my people* go (Fount, London, 1962).

M

Mandela, N: *No easy walk to freedom*. (Heinemann, London, 1987 ed.).

Marks, S & A Atmore: *Economy and society in pre-industrial South Africa* (Longman, Essex, 1980).

Marks, S & R Rathbone: *Industrialisation and social change in South Africa: African class formation, culture and consciousness, 1870-1930* (Longman, Essex, 1982).

Marquard, L: *The peoples and policies of South Africa* (OUP, London, 1952).

Mattelart, A & S Siegelaub: *Communication and class struggle: 1. Capitalism, Imperialism. 2. Liberation, Socialism*. (International General, New York, 1979).

Matthews, ZK: *Freedom for my people* (David Philip, Cape Town 1983).

Mbeki, G: *South Africa: the Peasants' Revolt* (Peter Smith, Gloucester, 1964).

Mbeki, G: *The prison writings of Govan Mbeki* (James Curry, London, 1991).

Mbeki, G: *The struggle for liberation in South Africa* (David Philip, Cape Town 1992).

Mitchison, N: *A life for Africa: The story of Bram Fischer* (Merlin Press, London, 1973).

Moodie, TD: *The rise of Afrikanerdom: Power, apartheid and the Afrikaner civil religion* (University of California Press, Berkeley, 1975).

Mtolo, B: *Umkonto we Sizwe: The road to the left*. (Drakensberg Press, Durban 1966).

Munger, ES: *Afrikander and African nationalism: South African parallels and parameters* (OUP, London, 1967).

N

Nattrass, N and E Ardington: *The political economy of South Africa.* (OUP, Cape Town, 1990).

O

Odendaal, A: *Vukani Bantu! The beginnings of black protest politics in South Africa,* (David Philip, Cape Town, 1984).

O'Meara, D: Volkskapilalisme*: Class, capital and ideology in the development of Afrikaner nationalism 1934-1948.* (Ravan Press, Johannesburg, 1983).

O'Sullivan, J Hartley, D Saunders & J Fiske: *Key Concepts in communication* (Methuen, London, 1983).

P

Pampallis, J: *Foundations of the new South Africa* (Maskew Miller Longman and Zed, Cape Town, 1991).

Paton, A: *Hofmeyer* (OUP, London 1964).

Pike, HR: *A history of communism in South Africa.* (Christian Mission International of South Africa, Germiston, 1985).

R

Rich, P: *White power and the liberal conscience: Racial segregation and South African liberalism 1921-60.* (Ravan Press, Johannesburg, 1984).

Roux, E: *Rebel Pity* (Published by the author).

Roux, E: *SP Bunting*. (Published by the author, 1944).

Roux, E: *Time longer than rope*. (Gollancz, London, 1948).

S

Sachs, A: *The jail diary of Albie Sachs* (David Philip, Cape Town, 1990).

Sachs, B: *The road to Sharpeville.* (The Dial Press, Johannesburg, 1961).

Sachs, B: *Mist of Memory* (Vallentine, London, 1973).

Sachs, B: *The Fordsberg-Mayfair Hebrew congregation, 1893-1964* (Eagle Press, Johannesburg, nd).

SACP: *South African communists speak.* (Inkululeko Publications, London, 1981).

SACP: *The red flag: A popular history of the South African Communist Party 1921-1990.*

Saron, G & L Hotz: *The Jews in South Africa, a history*. (OUP, Cape Town, 1955).

Schadeberg, J: *The fifties people in South Africa* (Bailey's African Photo Archives, Johannesburg, 1987).

Segal, R: *Political Africa* (Stevens, London 1961).

Segal, R: *Into exile* (Jonathan Cape, London, 1963).

Shain, M: *Jewry and Cape Society* (Historical Publication Society, Cape Town, 1983).

Shimoni, G: *Jews and Zionism: The South African experience, 1910-1967*. (OUP, Cape Town 1980).

Simons, Jack & Ray: *Class and colour in South Africa, 1850-1950*. (IDAF, London, 1983 ed.).

Slonim, S: *South West Africa and the United Nations: An international mandate dispute* (Johns Hopkins University Press, Baltimore, 1973).

Slovo, J: *Ties of blood*. (Headline, London, 1989).

Slovo, S: *A world apart* (Faber & Faber, London, 1988).

Small, C: *The Printed Word, An instrument of popularity*. (Aberdeen University Press, Aberdeen, 1982).

South African Communist Party: *A distant clap of thunder: 40th anniversary of the 1946 mine strike*. (SACP, 1986).

South West Africa cases, second phase (transcripts of debates 1966).

Stadler, A: *The political economy of modern South Africa*. (David Philip, Cape Town, 1987).

Stadler, A: *The political economy of modern South Africa*. (David Philip, Cape Town, 1987).

Strydom, H: *For Volk and Fuhrer: Robey Lebbrant & Operation Weissdorn*. (Jonathan Ball, Johannesburg, 1982).

Switzer, L & D: *The black press in South Africa and Lesotho*. (G K Hall, Boston, 1979).

T

Tambo, A: *Preparing for power: Oliver Tambo speaks* (Heinemann, London, nd).

Tomaselli, K & PE Louw: *The Press in South Africa, Broadcasting in South Africa and the alternative press in South Africa* (Anthropos, Bellville, 1991).

Trotski, l: *Stalin* (Hollis & Carter, London, 1947).

Troup, F: *In face of fear: Michael Scott's challenge to South Africa* (Faber & Faber, London 1950).

V

Vansina, J: *Oral tradition as history*. (James Currey, London, 1985).

W

Walker, C: *Women and resistence in South Africa*. (Onyx Press, London, 1982).

Walker, EA: *A history of Southern Africa* (Longmans, London, 1947).

Walshe, P: The *rise of African nationalism in South Africa, The African National Congress 1912-1952,* (University of California Press, Berkley 1971).

Weinberg, E: *Portrait of a people: A personal photographic record of the South African liberation struggle* (IDAF, London, 1981).

Wells, J: *We have done with pleading: The women's 1913 anti-pass campaign*. (Ravan Press, Johannesburg 1991).

Westmancoat, J: *Newspapers*. (British Library, London, 1985).

Williams, R: *Culture & Society, 1780-1950* (Pelican, Middlesex, 1958).

Williams, R: *Keywords* (Fontana, London, 1976).

Wilson, F: *Migrant labour in South Africa* (Spro-Cas, Johannesburg, 1972).

Wilson, F: *Labour in the South African gold mines 1911-1969* (CUP, Cambridge, 1972).

Wilson, M and LM Thompson (eds): *The Oxford history of South Africa* Vol 2 (Clarendon Press, Oxford, 1971).

Woollacott, J: *Messages and meanings*. (OUP, Oxford, 1977).

Significant articles, pamphlets, reports, speeches, seminar papers and interviews

Ad-Hoc Ruth First Memorial Committee, UCT: Ruth First 1925-1982 (n.d.).

Adams, J: On the development of nations in South African Marxism Today July 1959.

AK: Ruth First in The annual obituary (St James Press, London 1983).

Albertyn, C: The political trial and the construction of apartheid, 1956-64.ICS seminar, London University, 1988.

Andrews, Sir L: The unending struggle for the freedom of the press in Africa SouthVol.2 No.3 Apr-June 1958.

Anonymous: Diary from refuge in Africa SouthVol.5 No.1 Oct-Dec 1960.

Anti-Apartheid Movement: Political Prisoners (nd.)

Arking, L: Notes on Congress of the People, June 1954.

Ashforth, A: Reconstructing the 'Native Question' in the era of apartheid; official discourse, state ideology and the Tomlinson Commission.(Unpublished conference paper: South Africa in the 1950s. ICS, Oxford University, 1987).

Barclays Trade Review (March 1960).

Barrel, H: Shaun Slovo: Growing up as Ruth First's daughter in *Weekly Mail* 18.9.87.

Basner, HM: A nation of 10 000 000 – challenge to SA's native policy (nd.)

Berman, H (ed.): *Viewpoints & Perspectives* Vol. 1 & 2 (Johannesburg Discussion Club, September 1952 & March 1953).

Beyleveld, P: Where do we go from here? in *Liberation* No.32, August 1958.

Blumberg, M: Durban explodes, in *Africa South* Vol.4 No.6 Oct-Dec 1959.

Brittain, V: South Africa's creeping brand of intervention, in *The Guardian* 19.8.82.

Brown, A, M Burns, L Cocking, R Diski: A world apart: film study guide (Screen Guides 1988).

Brown, P: The Liberal Party (Seminar paper presented at the Liberal Party Workshop, Rhodes University, 1985).

Buchan, N: Heroes of our time, in *Apartheid News* July-August 1965.

Bunting, B: Apartheid, the road to poverty (*New Age* pamphlet, n.d.).

Bunting, B: On the murder of Ruth First in *Morning Star*, Tuesday August 4 1982.

Bunting, B: The story behind the Non-white press (*New Age* pamphlet, n.d.).

Bunting, B: Towards a climax, in *Africa South* Vol 5 No.4 July-Sept 1961.

Cachalia, DN: Interview with IC Meer (SAIRR Oral History Archive, Durban 23.9.82).

Chaskalson, M: The road to Sharpeville: The council and the townships in Vereeniging, 1950-60 (Unpublished conference paper: South Africa in the 1950s. ICS, Oxford University, 1987).

Clay, G and S Uys: The press: Strydom's last barrier, in *Africa South* Vol.2 No.1 Oct-Dec 1957.

Communist Party of South Africa: Communists in conference (report of 1943-4 conference).

Communist Party of South Africa: Democracy in action (March 1945).

Communist Party of South Africa: The Unlawful Organisations Bill destroys civil liberties (May 7 1950).
Communist Party of South Africa: Towards socialism (n.d.)
Communist Party of South Africa: Trial of the communist party after the 1946 strike (n.d.).
Communist Party of South Africa: Vorster's Nazi law can never destroy communism (1950).
Communist Party of South Africa: What next? (n.d.).
Congress Alliance: In defence of South Africa (n.d.).
Cousins, T: A short history of The World (photocopy).
Cross, D: The price of gold, in *Democrat Monthly,* April 1949.
D.A.L.: The Treason Trial and the Press, in *Fighting Talk*, February 1960.
Davidov, J: Ruth First: a front line journalist, in *The world as we see it* (Sofia, Bulgaria, n.d.).
Davidson, B: Brave Ruth's fight against hate in *Daily Mirror* July 8 1963.
Davidson, B: Partners and patriots, in *New Statesman* June 21 1963.
Dick, N: Wages: black, brown and white, in *Fighting Talk* September 1961.
Digest of South African Affairs: The Red termites at work (Vol.4 No.6 March 15 1957).
Digest of South African Affairs: Economic trends in S Africa 1945-56 and 1957-67 (Fact Paper 36 June 1957).
Digest of South African Affairs: South Africa's finances – a USA review (Fact Paper 8, March 1956)
Digest of South African Affairs: The Union's capital market (Fact Paper 2 August 1960).
Edwards, I: Recollections: the Communist Party and worker militancy in Durban, early 1940s (*SA Labour Bulletin* Vol.2 No.4, Feb/March 1986).
Evans, D: Gandar & Co: unconscious agents of apartheid, in *Anti-Apartheid News* September 1971.
Federation of South African Women: Strijdom ... you have struck a rock (n.d.).
First, R (ed): South Africans in the Soviet Union. (n.d.).
First, R: After Soweto: a response (to Mafeje) in *Review of African Political Economy*, January-April 1978.
First, R: Bethal case book, in *Africa South* Vol. 2 No. 3 April-June 1958.
First, R: Building the future, in *South Africans in the Soviet Union.*
First, R: Europe today, in *The Rhodes Outlook* Vol.1 No.1 March 12 1946.
First, R: Revolutionary propaganda at home and abroad, Discussion guide (ANC position paper 1969).
First, R: South Africa today, in *Africa speaks* by J Duffy & RA Manners (eds) (D von Nostrand, New Jersey 1961).
First, R: The bus boycott, in *Africa South* Vol.1 No.4 July-Sept 1957.
First, R: The constitutional fallacy, in *Liberation* No.6 November 1953.
First, R: The facts about forced labour in the Union of South Africa, in *New African*, Vol.9 No.2 Feb-Mar 1950.
First, R: The farm labour scandal(*New Age* Pamphlet, n.d.).
First, R: The gold of migrant labour, in *Africa South* Vol.5 No.3 Apr-June 1961.
First, R: The gold of migrant labour, in *Spearhead* May-June 1962.
First, R: Wage inequalities, in *Fighting Talk* March 1957.
First: R: From the Freedom Charter to armed struggle (Anti-Apartheid Movement conference paper, London 1986).
Flegg, E: Ruth First: renew our support for her struggle, in *Socialist Challenge* 27.8.82.
For peace and friendship (various, 1954-56. Newsletters of Friends of the Soviet Union).
Forman, L: Background to the national question (private document circulated within the SACP).
Forman, L: Nationalism and the class struggle, in *Freedom* Vol.1 Nos. 27/28, Dec 15 1949.

Forman, L: The development of nations in South Africa, in *Marxism Today* April 1959.
Frankel, G: White communist who wants to end apartheid with a gun, in *The Guardian* July 28 1985.
Gault, R: Reports claim Slovo responsible for wife's letter bomb death, in *The Star* July 14 1984.
Gell, C: The press and the boycott, in *Fighting Talk* May 1957.
Gold, J, with Ruth First: Tape transcription, (BBC, n.d.).
Gordimer, N: The prison-house of colonialism, in *Times Literary Supplement* August 15 1980.
Hamilton Russel, J: 90-day torture (Speech made to Black Sash meeting, Johannesburg 1964).
Hanlon, J: Why South Africa had to kill Ruth First, in *New Statesman* Aug 27 1982.
Harmel, M: Forms and methods of struggle in the national liberation revolution, in *African Communist* 8 Jan 1962.
Harmel, M: Revolutions are not normal, in *Africa South* Vol.3 No.2 Jan-March 1959.
Harmel, M: South Africa is at war, in *African Communist* Vol.2 No.4 July-Sept 1963.
Heilpern, J: Bye, bye blue sky, in *Nova* January 1967.
Hepple, A: Censorship and press control in South Africa (Johannesburg, 1960)
Hepple, A: Press under apartheid (IDAF, London 1974).
Hirson, B: Rural revolt in South Africa, 1937-51, in *The societies of Southern Africa in the 19th & 20th centuries* Vol.8 No.22 (ICS, London).
Hornsby, M: Pretoria protests innocence, in *The Times* Aug 19 1982.
Innes, D: Ruth First: banned, detained, exiled, murdered, in *Hecate* Vol 10 No.1 1984.
Irwin, G: The press and the strike, in *Fighting Talk* July 1961.
Johnson, J: Can the Congress of Democrats win mass support? in *Liberation* 13 Oct 1955.
Jones, D Ivon: Lenin's first newspaper, in *African Communist* No.42 3rd quarter 1970.
Karis, T: South African liberation: the communist factor (*Foreign Affairs*, Winter 1986-7 Vol.65 No.2).
Kitson, D: Is the SACP really communist? in *Work in Progress* 73 March-April 1991.
Kotane, M: South Africa's way forward (*Advance* study document, May 1954).
Kotane, M: The great crisis ahead (New *Age Pamphlet*, n.d.).
Lambert, R: Political unionism and working class hegemony: perspectives on the South African Congress of Trade Unions, 1955-65, in *Labour, Capital and Society* 18:2 Nov 1985.
Lardner-Burke, JD: Adolescent posturings on South West Africa, in *The Forum*, March 1958.
Lawrence, P: The spectre of the red funeral flags, in *Weekly Mail*, April 11-17 1986.
Lazar, J: The Afrikaner Nationalist Alliance and capitalism, 1948-61 (Unpublished conference paper: South Africa in the 1950s. ICS, Oxford University, 1987).
Lazar, J: Verwoerd vs the 'Visionaries': The South African Bureau of Racial Affairs and apartheid, 1948-61 (Unpublished conference paper: South Africa in the 1950s. ICS, Oxford University, 1987).
Lee-Warden, L: Unpublished autobiography.
Legassick M: South Africa: capital accumulation and violence (photocopy).
Legassick, M: Class and nationalism in South African protest: The South African Communist Party and the 'Native Republic', 1928-1934. (Paper at Syracuse University, New York, 1973).
Legassick, M: Legislation, ideology and economy in post-1948 South Africa, in *JSAS*, Vol.1 No.2, October 1974).
Legassick, M: The rise of modern South African liberalism: its assumptions and its social base (photocopy).
Legassick, M: Class & nationalism in South African protest: the SACP and the 'Native Republic', 1928-34 (Syracuse University, 1973).
Lewin, J: No revolution around the corner, in *Africa South* Vol.3 No.4 July-Sept 1959.
Lodge, T: Class conflict, communal struggle and patriotic unity: The Communist Party of South

Africa during the Second World War. (Paper presented on Oct.7 1985. African Studies Institute, University of the Witwatersrand).
Lodge: T: Class conflict, communal struggle and partiotic unity: the Communist Party of South Africa during the Second World War (African Studies seminar paper, University of the Witwatersrand, October 1985).
Lutuli, A: Freedom is the apex (SACOD pamphlet, n.d.).
Mafeje, A: Soweto and its aftermath, in *Review of African Political Economy*, January-April 1978.
Mandela, N: Our struggle needs many tactics, in *Liberation* 29, Feb 1958.
Mantzaris, E: The promise of the impossible revolution: The Cape Town Industrial Socialist League, 1918-1921. (In *Studies in the History of Cape Town* Vol 4, UCT 1981).
Marks, S: Ruth First: a tribute, in *JSAS* Vol.10 No.1 October 1983.
Matthews, J: Revolution: further reflections, in *Africa South* Vol. 3 No.4 July-Sept 1959.
Matthews, J: Uncompromising struggle for the Freedom Charter, in *Liberation* 38 October 1959.
Matthews, ZK: Political arrangements in a multi-racial society (paper delivered at the Multi-racial conference on South Africa, n.d.).
McGrath, J: On the formation of nations in South Africa, in *Marxism Today* August 1959.
Mkele, N: The emergent African middle class (South African Congress of Democrats, n.d.).
Moll, TC: Growth without development: The South African economy in the 1950s. (Unpublished conference paper: South Africa in the 1950s. ICS, Oxford University, 1987).
Motsoane, P: The partisan press, in *The New African* Feb 20 1963.
Munger, ES: Communist activity in South Africa (American Universities field staff report, Johannesburg, June 8 1958).
Municipal Public Relations Bureau (Johannesburg): *Seventy golden years*, 1886-1956.
Murray, AH: Red strategy and tactics (SABC radio talk, n.d.).
Nokwe, D: The great smear: communism and Congress in South Africa (*Africa South in exile* Vol.6 No.1, Oct/Dec 1961).
Ozinsky, M: 'For land and freedom': The Communist Party of South Africa and the strategy of United Fronts in the 1930s. (Long paper, Economic History Department, University of Cape Town, 1983).
Peace Councils of South Africa: South Africans for Peace (various).
Peace Councils of South Africa: The Peace Movement and the Congress of the People (n.d.).
People's Defence Committee: We stand with our leaders (minutes of meeting of PDC 9.12.56).
Pertinax: The state of our press, in *The Forum* August 1957.
Posel, D: Doing business with the pass laws: Influx control and the interests of manufacturing and commerce in South Africa in the 1950s. (Unpublished conference paper: South Africa in the 1950s. ICS, Oxford University, 1987).
Posel, D: Language, legitimation and control: the South African State after 1978, in *Social Dynamics* 10(1)1-16 1984.
Posel, D: The construction of apartheid, 1948-61 (Unpublished conference paper: South Africa in the 1950s. ICS, Oxford University, 1987).
Rake, A: The pattern of South Africa's emergency, in *Africa South* Vol.5 No.1 Oct-Dec 1960.
Report of the Commission on the colour problem of the Herenigde Nationale Party, 1948 (Saur Report).
Rhodes University Honours project: On trial for treason (1989).
Roberts, Y: When the children don't come first, in *Good Housekeeping* March 1988.
Rogaly, J: The bus boycott, in *The Forum* March 1957.
Rutherford, M: An intervention, in *New Statesman* Sept 6 1963.
SA Institute of Race Relations: A survey of race relations (all relevant volumes).

SA Institute of Race Relations: African poverty April 1947.
SA Institute of Race Relations: An analysis of the proposed increases in African taxation 21.7.58.
SA Institute of Race Relations: The Tomlinson Report: a summary (SAIRR, Johannesburg, 1956).
SA Society for Peace and Friendship with the Soviet Union: Malenkov, Kaganivich, Molotov: Why they had to go (n.d.).
SA Society for Peace and Friendship with the Soviet Union: The Stalin cult (n.d. probably 1956).
SA Special criminal court, Pretoria: Regina vs Farid Adams and others. (Ike Horowitch papers, ICS, London).
SAIRR Oral Archive: Interview with Ruth Eastwood & Ilsa Wilson (nee Fischer) (24.10.83).
Sapire, H: Political mobilisation in Brakpan in the 1950s. (Unpublished conference paper: South Africa in the 1950s. ICS, Oxford University, 1987).
Saul, J: Laying ghosts to rest: Ruth First and South Africa's war, in *This* magazine Vol.17 No.5, (Canada 1985).
Scott, A: Olive Schreiner, in *Spare Rib* 7.
Scott, M: The sacret trust of South West Africa, in *Africa South* Vol.5 No.1 Oct-Dec 1060.
Sechaba: Obituary: Comrade Ruth First (Oct 1982).
Segal, R: Ruth First memorial speech, Sept 8 1982 (In Ruth First Trust Collection, ICS).
Segal, R: Ruth First, in *Index on Censorship* 6/82.
Segal, R: The final stroke, in *Africa South* Vol.2 No.2 Jan-March 1958.
Segal, R: The revolution is now, in *Africa South* Vol 4 No.1 Oct-Dec 1959.
Simons, HJ: The origin and functions of the pass laws (A Sachs Papers, ICS, London).
Slovo, J: Ruth First: assassinated (n.d.).
Smirnova, R: The truth about South West Africa, in *Soviet Woman* No.3 1964.
South African Communist Party: The revolutionary way out, in *African Communist* Vol.2 No.3 Apr-June 1963.
South African Congress of Democrats: Censored news No.1, May 1962.
South African Congress of Democrats: Changing Africa. Statement adopted at the 7th Annual Conference of South African Congress of Democrats, April 1961.
South African Congress of Democrats: Counter Attack (various editions).
South African Congress of Democrats: Educating for ignorance (South African Congress of Democrats pamphlet, n.d.)
South African Congress of Democrats: In defence of the Congress Alliance (South African Congress of Democrats pamphlet, n.d.)
South African Congress of Democrats: Memorandum to the Pan African Congress, Accra, December 1958.
South African Congress of Democrats: One Congress (South African Congress of Democrats pamphlet, n.d.)
South African Congress of Democrats: Rule by sjambok (n.d.).
South African Congress of Democrats: SA Government prepared for war (South African Congress of Democrats pamphlet, n.d.).
South African Congress of Democrats: South African Congress of Democrats: The facts (n.d.)
South African Congress of Democrats: The saracen republic(nd.).
South African Congress of Democrats: The struggle to live (South African Congress of Democrats pamphlet, n.d.).
South African Congress of Democrats: Think it over (n.d.).
South African Congress of Democrats: We are many (n.d.).
South African Congress of Democrats: Chairman's reports (various).
South African Congress of Democrats: Conference reports (various).

South African Congress of Democrats: National Executive Committee reports (various).
Springbok Legion: Active Contact, letters, 1952.
Springbok Legion: The history & policy. (Springbok Legion pamphlet, n.d.).
Springbok Legion: D-Day for Democracy. (Springbok Legion pamphlet, n.d.).
Standard Bank Review: National income and production indices 1946-57.
Standard Bank Review: No.432, March 1955.
Stevens, A: The loneliness of the long distance revolutionary, in *The Guardian* October 30 1970.
Summers, DH: Native earnings, in *Commercial Opinion*, August 1958.
The Guardian, *New Age* etc: Various letters (Thornton collection, UCT).
The Guardian: Various press statements.
Tilton, D: The road to sabotage: The ANC and the formation of Umkonto we Sizwe (Unpublished conference paper: South Africa in the 1950s. ICS, Oxford University, 1987).
Treason Trial Defence Fund: Press summary (copies covering the trial from 1959).
Umkonto we Sizwe: The message of Rivonia. (n.d.).
United Nations Document: Fascist Terror in South Africa, in *African Communist* No.17 Apr-June 1964.
Uys, S: The white opposition in South Africa, in *Africa South* Vol.1 No.1 Oct-Dec 1956.
Weldrick, A: The Potato Boycott of 1959 (Rhodes Journalism Honours essay 1991).
Williams, G: Celebrating the Freedom Charter, in *Transformation* 6.
Williams, G: Review essay, in *Social Dynamics* 14(1)57-66 1988.
Williams, G: Ruth First: a preliminary bibliography (Unpublished paper, Oxford Jan 1983).
Williams, G: Ruth First: Alle radici dell 'apartheid Seminario sull,' *Africa Australe*, Roma, Oct 1984.
Windass, S: The spirit's unhealed wounds, in *Catholic Herald* 9.7.65.
Wolfers, M: Ruth First murdered in Maputo, in *SWAM* newsletter No.6 (Stop the War Against Angola and Mozambique, n.d.).
Wolpe, AM: Tribute to Ruth First, in *Feminist Review* Spring 1983.
Wolpe, H: Capitalism and cheap labour power in South Africa: From segregation to apartheid. In *Economy & Society*, Vol.1,4,1972.
Wolpe, H: Class, race and the occupational structure, in *The societies of Southern Africa in the 19th & 20th centuries* (ICS, Vol.2 1971).

Newspapers and periodicals

Advance
Africa South
Africa X-Ray
African Communist
African Drum
Africanist
Agenda
Analysis
ANC Bulletin
Bantu World
Burger
Cape Argus
Cape Times

Citizen
Clarion
Contact
Counter-Attack
Daily Despatch
Democrat
Discussion
Drum
For Peace and Friendship
Forum
Freedom
The Guardian
Inkululeko
Inkundla ya Bantu
Liberal Opinion
Liberation
Natal Mercury
Natal Witness
New African
New Age
Passive Resister
Race Relations Journal
Race Relations News
Rand Daily Mail
Reality
Sechaba
South African Labour Bulletin
Spark
The Star
The Sundaytimes
The Torch
Transformation
Transvaal Communist
Trek
Umhlanganisi
Umsebenzi
Viewpoints and Perspectives
Work in Progress
Worker's Herald
The World

Manuscript and documentary sources

University of Cape Town
Amy Thornton Papers
Donald Molteno Papers
Harry Lawrence Papers

Leo Marquard Papers
Margaret Ballinger Papers
Oscar Wollheim Papers
William Ballinger Papers

Rhodes University
Christopher Gell Papers
Fighting Talk microfilm
Rivonia Trial microifilm
South African Political Materials (CAMP) microfilm
Treason Trial Papers
ZK Matthews microfilm

University of the Witwatersrand
ANC Papers
AS Paton Papers
Cachalia Family Papers
Federation of SA Women Papers
Helen Joseph Papers
Margaret & William Ballinger Papers
PAC Papers
South African Congress of Democrats Papers
SACTU Papers
SAIRR: Auden House Collection
SAIRR: Political Collection
SP Bunting Papers
Springbok Legion Papers
Thompson Papers

University of London
Albert Lutuli Papers
Albie Sachs Papers
Ike Horvitch Papers
Marion Friedman Papers
Ruth First Trust Papers
South African Congress of Democrats collection
SAIRR: Political Party Collection
ZK Matthews Papers

Oxford University
Africa Bureau Papers
Fabian Colonial Bureau Papers

University of Moscow
SA Communist Party Papers

Private collections
Len Lee-Warden Papers
Don Pinnock Papers

Interviews

Arenstein, Rowley
Barenblatt, Yetta
Barsel, Esther
Benson, Mary
Berman, Myrtle
Bernstein, Hilda
Bernstein, Rusty
Beyleveld, Pieter
Bunting, Brian
Cachalia, Amina
Cachalia, Yusuf
Callinicos, Luli
Carneson, Fred
First, Tilly
Forman, Sadie
Gelb, Trudi
Hepner, Bill
Hepner, Miriam
Heymann, Anne
Heymann, Issie
Hirson, Baruch
Hjul, Peter
Hodgson, Rica

Index

D

E

F

G

H

Q

R

S

T

U

V

W

X

Y

Z